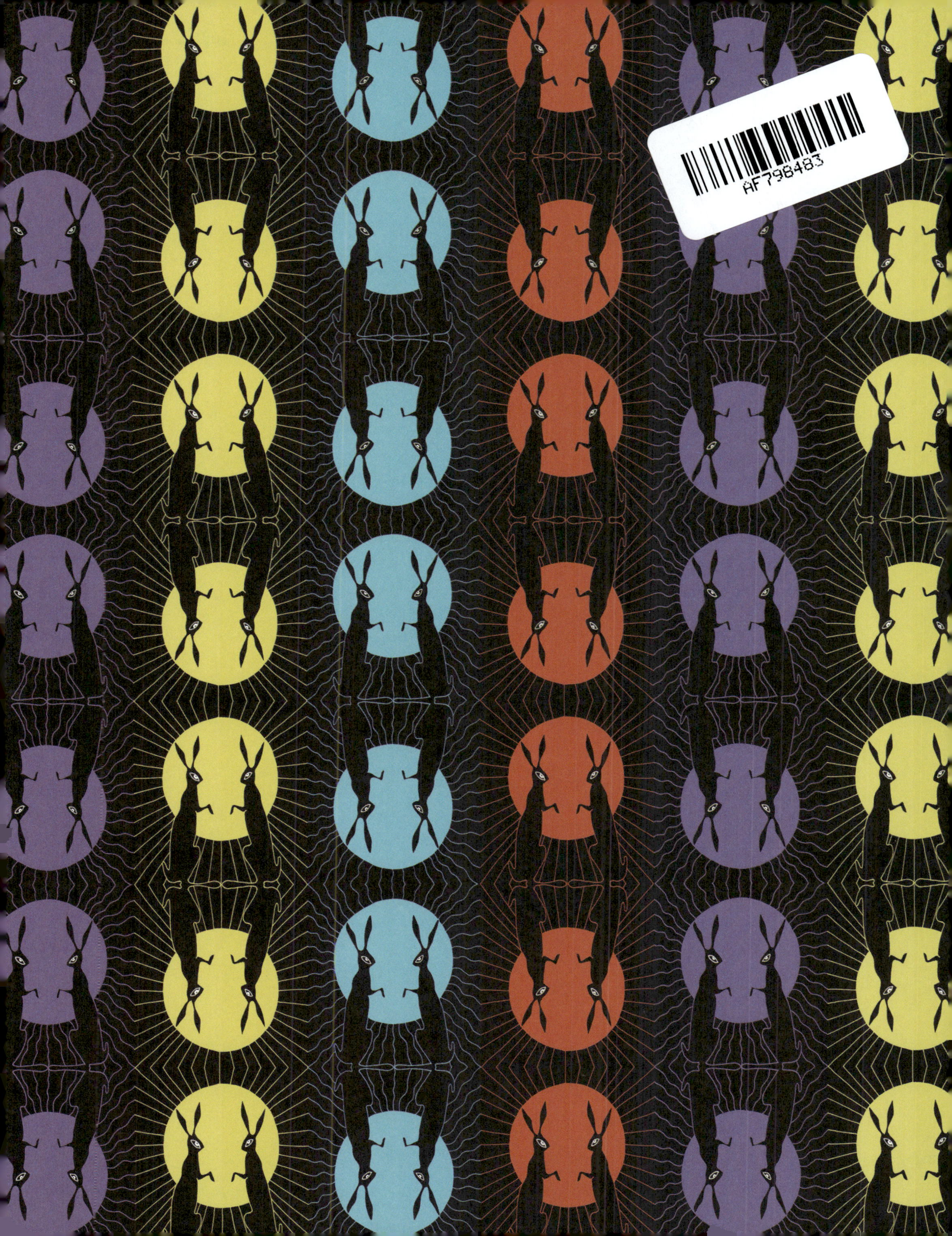

DAVID HARRISON

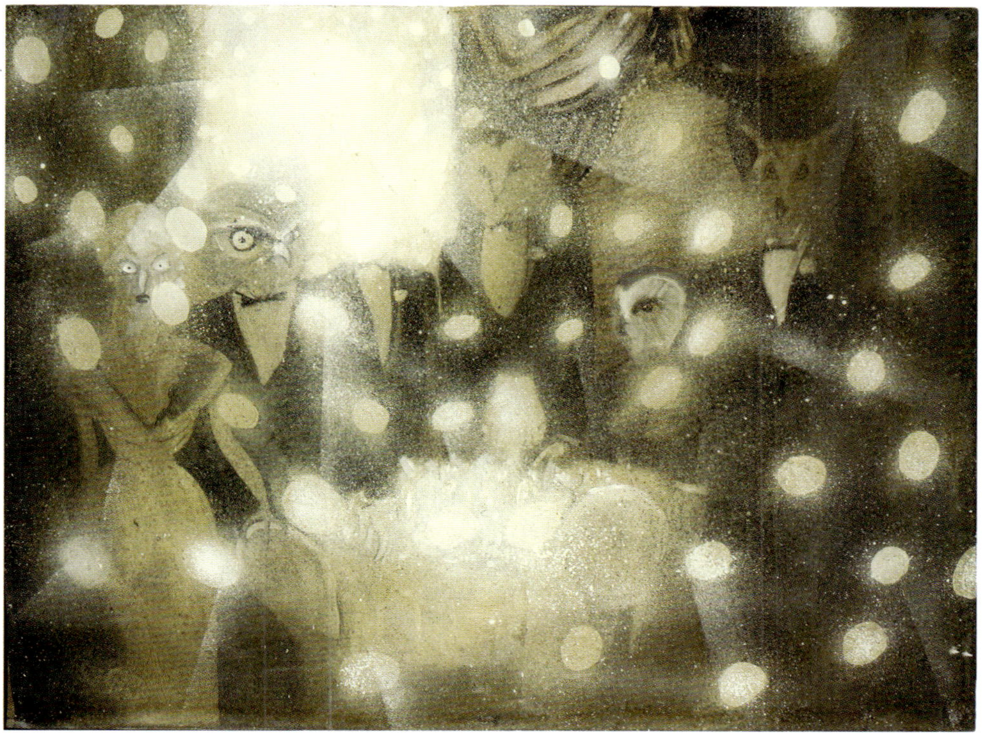

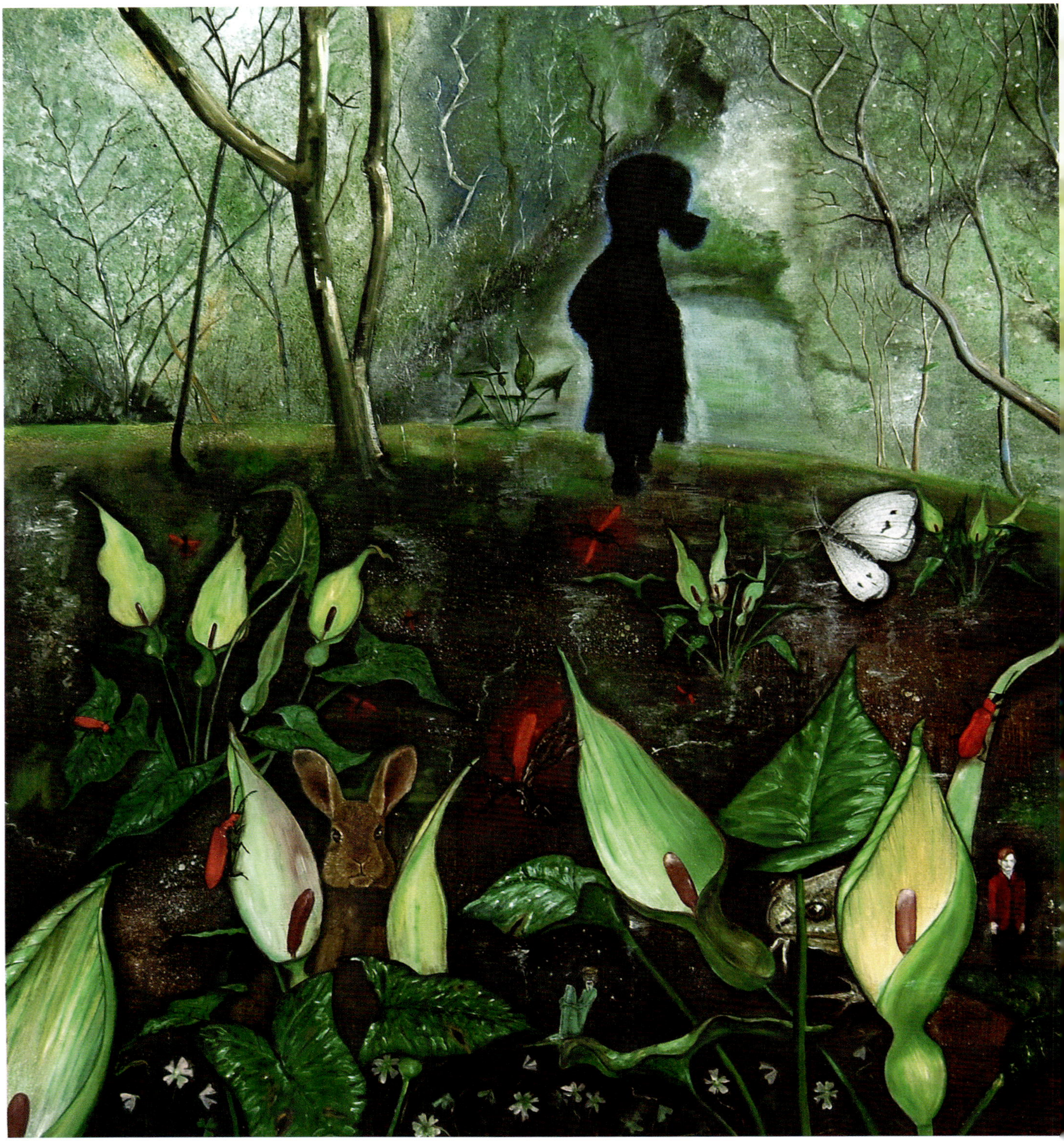

DAVID HARRISON

ALISTAIR ROBINSON
LUCINDA LAMBTON
PETER DOIG

PHILIP WILSON PUBLISHERS
LONDON

First published in 2009

Victoria Miro Gallery
16 Wharf Road
London N1 7RW
www.victoria-miro.com

Philip Wilson Publishers Ltd.
109 Drysdale Street, The Timber Yard, London, N1 6ND
www.philip-wilson.co.uk

Distributed throughout the world
(excluding North America) by:
I.B. Tauris & Co. Ltd.
6 Salem Road, London, W2 4BU

Distributed in North America by:
Palgrave Macmillan, a division of St Martin's Press
175 Fifth Avenue, New York, NY 10010

ISBN: 978-0-85667-671-0 (hardback)

Designed by Keith Pointing

Edited by Matthew Hartley and Dorothy Feaver

Printed in China by Everbest

Front cover: *Magic Moments* (detail), 2005
Half-title page: *Strange Meeting*, 2004, Oil and conté on paper, 30 x 42 cm
Frontispiece: *The Awakening*, 2008, Oil on wood, 110 x 100 cm
Back cover: *City Gent* (detail), 2005
Endpapers designed by David Harrison and Justin Phillips

CONTENTS

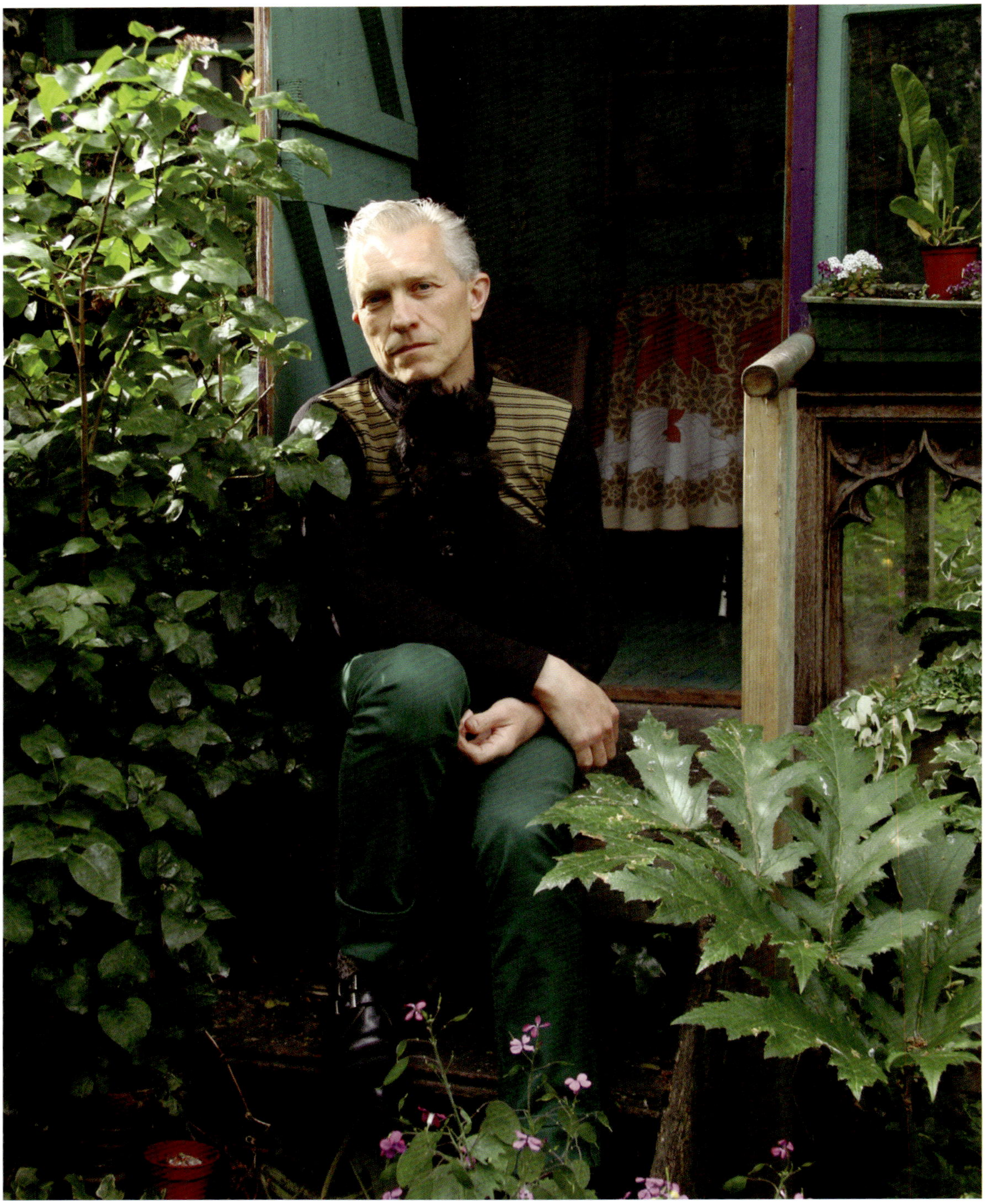

David and Harrison on the Hunting Lodge steps, May 2009

Foreword

David Harrison is my hero, a forever interesting and entertaining hero who, as well as being a spirited artist, has an instinctive and passionate knowledge of architecture, ornithology, botany, nature, music, poodles and downright tat, all coursed through with informative glee. Not so much a breath of fresh air, rather he is a gale howling daily with delight at the thousand sights and sounds that surround him, lacing everything through with uncommon niceness and hilarious originality. One of his friends once described him to me as 'pure gold dust'.

I shall never forget finding this rare bloom of a friend in the brutally barren surroundings where he then lived: a grim desert of a housing estate in Bow, slashed through with underpasses and overpasses. After plodding up a concrete stairwell, past floor after floor of stench-ridden gloom, suddenly, Abracadabra!, there was his domain: a white picket fence and a little latch gate, leading to a riot of flowers writhing around dolls, all spookily and picturesquely colonised with spiders. One step into his flat and you were immediately surrounded by giant jiving poodles rendered in deep plaster relief, and London's East End seemed a thousand miles away.

David delights as much in the cheapo charms of, say, Barbie's purple plastic handbag, as he does in the subtleties of a mediaeval wall painting. Everything catches his fancy, whether a visit to a Hawksmoor church, 'where your spirits are sent soaring', or finding a Dolly a Day for a Week, a pack of seven celluloid children with names such as Mandy Monday and Wendy Wednesday. Here, however, the cheapo reigned supreme with an exuberance that made you cheer out loud with delight!

To the wrath of animal rights protestors, David once dyed his pet poodle Hoover pink, and then purple with yellow and orange spots. When Hoover died, he built a shrine to his canine companion in the golden-walled dining room of the flat where they had lived together for ten years. Above a gilt-framed portrait of Hoover, his ashes, contained within a china poodle, were held aloft by a cherub, protected overall by the hand of Jane Mansfield – 'the patron saint of poodles' – gathering the canine soul into a polystyrene clouded heaven. A puce *Venus de Poodle* (1988) stood over a golden box of tissues 'for crying', and Hoover's diamante collar and lead lay in a china box.

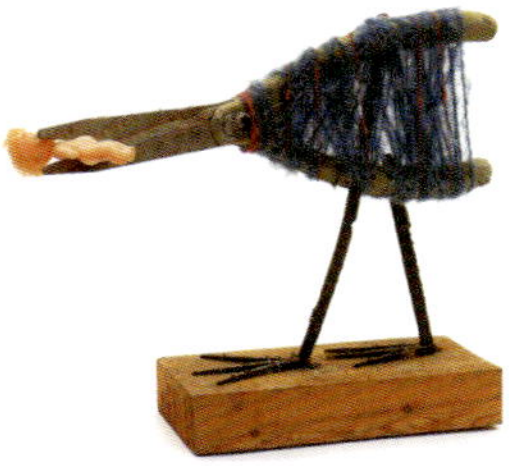

Bittern Eating Baby, 1996
Found objects, 46 x 46 x 20 cm

He creates and recreates his fantastical surroundings just as he does his sculpture and his paintings, using any old scraps picked up for a song or off the street. These he then gilds and glazes up to the nines and applies them to the work in hand. Thus, a windowsill might be piled high with plastic pearls, dolls and toy musical instruments, as well as broken bric-a-brac and architectural fragments, refashioned to produce a knocking-you-out-with-delight sensation. So it was that a rusty pair of shears and a plastic doll became *Bittern Eating Baby* (1996), inspired, said David, by a nature program on television where he saw a bird eating another bird's chick, 'which, after all, was someone's baby'.

Often the butt of mockery – most especially when Hoover was at his most colourful – David Harrison sails on regardless, always dressed to dazzle and to 'brighten things up'. At his graduation from St Martin's School of Art, when the students were asked to leave their exhibition spaces white, David secretly stayed on overnight, painting the walls surrounding his work electric pink and the floor scarlet, scattered with 'girlie' playing cards, which were then varnished over and sprinkled with glitter.

Daily creating silken purses from sows' ears, he has cleared mountains of rubbish from disused churchyards and has been endlessly thwarted in his attempts to make gardens out of derelict dumps. Walking along his local canal, he saw a dead swan floating in the water 'with a long flowing neck,' which seemed 'wonderfully tragic' to him. He delights in the memory of an enraged coot trying to make a nest out of an unsquashable crisp packet: 'you know how you can never successfully crush them into a pub ashtray'.

His latest triumph has been a magical one, quite magnificently so: a gothic 'Hunting Lodge'/dovecote in the back garden of the flat where he now lives. The Hunting Lodge is 'loosely based on Siena Cathedral', with black and white striped and shell-coated pinnacles, and with a wealth of gothic arches, great and small. Embellished with broken mirrors and

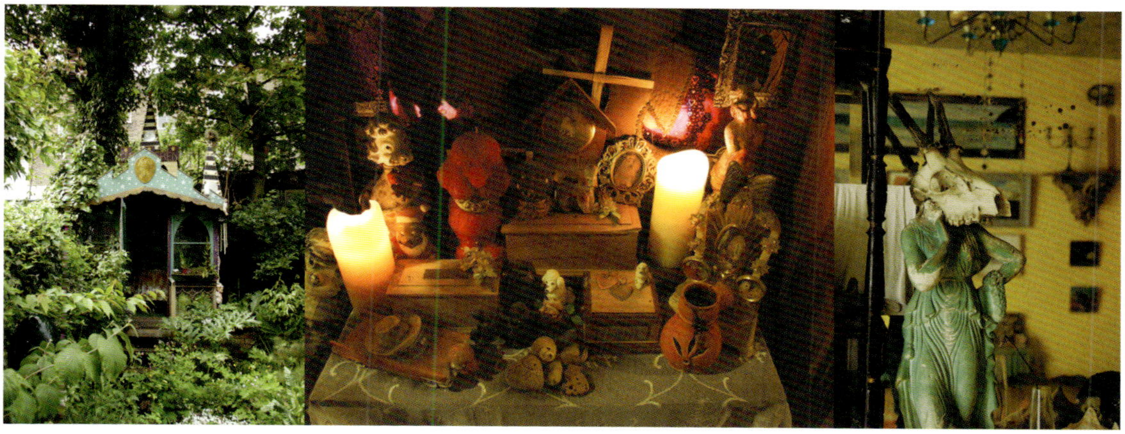

Photograph's of David's home, May 2009. Left to right: the Hunting Lodge and garden; David's poodle shrine; a view of David's sitting room.

writhing ivy, it soars some fifteen feet high. Beneath the words 'For My Fine Feathered Friends', pigeons perch on green crenellations painted with a great golden egg and surrounded by luminous stars. Inside, amid an abundance of swirling golden cherubim, hand-printed wallpaper and a huge gold Russian clock – painted with pastoral scenes and chiming on the hour – two whopping great Ionic columns loom overall. As if this were not enough enchantment for an Islington garden, this dazzling creation is now home to a lovingly looked after wild fox.

Every day, in every way, David Harrison cocks a cheerful snook at the art establishment, adding and taking away from his ever-changing works, giving fanciful flourishes to anything that he can lay his lands on. When you gasp and wonder at his ways, his answer is, as usual, tinged with magic: 'It is a 24-hour job…Why? Why does a bird fly?'

Lucinda Lambton

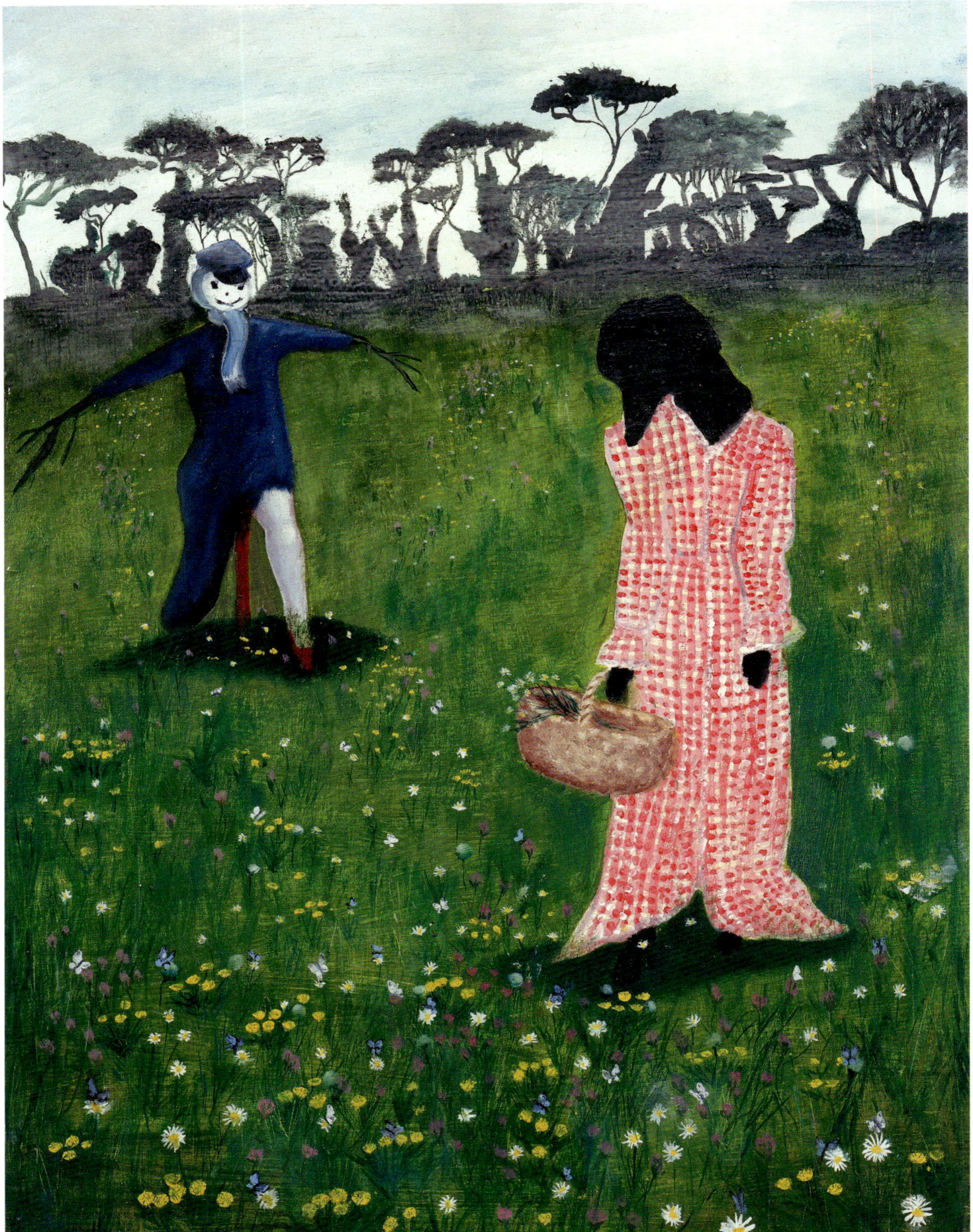

Chance Meeting, 2005
Oil on wood, 46 x 34 cm

Introduction

OVER THE COURSE of thirty years, David Harrison has created a body of work unique in contemporary British art. Throughout his career, Harrison's oeuvre has been characterized by wit, a playful love of contradiction and quiet erudition. Working across two and three dimensions, Harrison's paintings, sculptures and collages transform the natural and man-made worlds into mythical settings in which alarming, magical and incongruous narratives unfold. Yet it is for his representations and re-creations of the natural world that Harrison has become most celebrated. Nature in Harrison's work is a store of endless fecundity, though it is also very far removed from being safely harmonious and gentle, or consolatory. His natural world is also replete with an extraordinary symbolic density: every animal and plant species becomes an actor in a cast of mythical characters who populate an entire imagined universe. We should read Harrison's works as giving shape to an idiosyncratic personal mythology, akin to that of William Blake. However, it is also a mythology in which, paradoxically, every aspect of the natural world is used to speak about its 'other' – modernity.

Harrison's paintings, collages and sculptures yoke the natural with the supernatural, the symbolic with the personal, and the mythological with the contemporary. Moreover, his images transform the outmoded and unloved, the taboo and the talismanic into scenes that reimagine the state of the nation. Each of his works interweaves ideas from the history of art, from popular culture, from architectural history and from the myths associated with England's cities and landscape. In this way, each image is invariably built from collisions between incommensurable elements, and out of these, Harrison gives shape to a vision of the modern world that is novelistic in its scope. In recent years, Harrison's personal mythology has become increasingly complex, and has been nourished by wonderfully unlikely and ostensibly incompatible sources. Developing his personal iconography and highly distinctive style through the 1980s and 1990s, over the last decade the breadth of his achievement has secured recognition. In particular, Harrison's paintings have accrued an extraordinary symbolic density, which elicits alarm as well as delight. As Adrian Searle has described, Harrison's work has 'a strong (if sometimes off-putting) visionary intensity' fuelled by 'a genuine pantheistic mysticism and a ribald sense of humour'.[1]

The artist's imaginary world is a fully-formed one in which we move from urban to rural settings, and effortlessly between the mythical and the naturalistic. Although Harrison's imagined universe is one that is unified and in which each of the elements is interlinked in some way, it is not completely pointless to try to illuminate it by way of dividing it into areas of investigation or themes. With this in mind, the four sections here – which take their titles from some of Harrison's most representative works – investigate, for the most part, the artist's use of rural, urban and mythological imagery to show the ways in which he is able to create a potent affective charge, the sources of his iconography, and how the building blocks of his symbolic universe fit together.

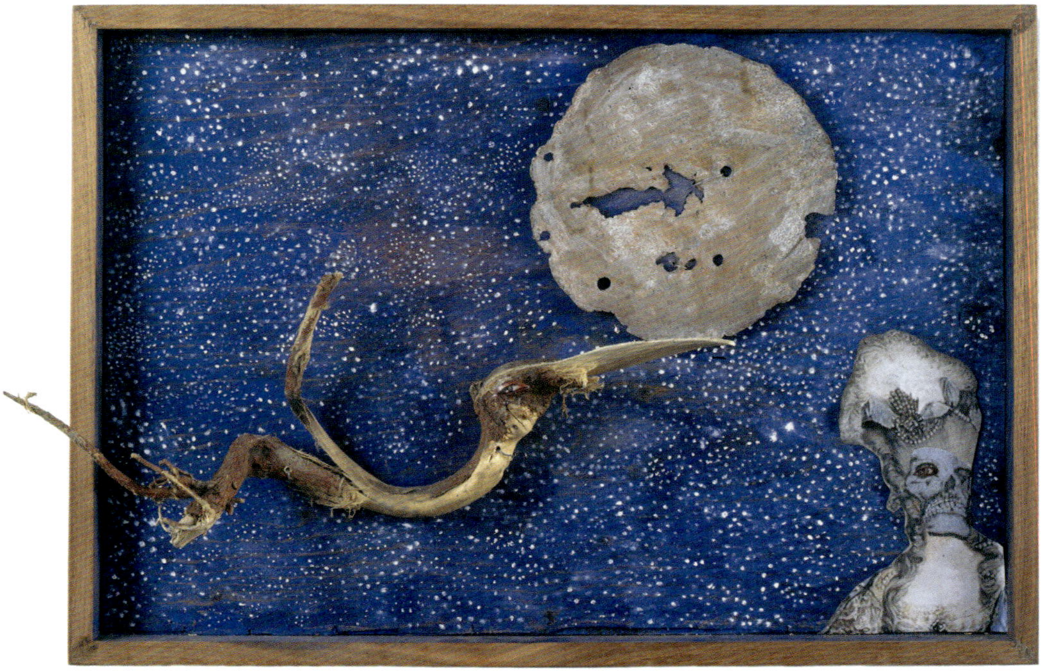

Moonbird, 2008
Oil and mixed media on wood, 40 x 57 x 14 cm

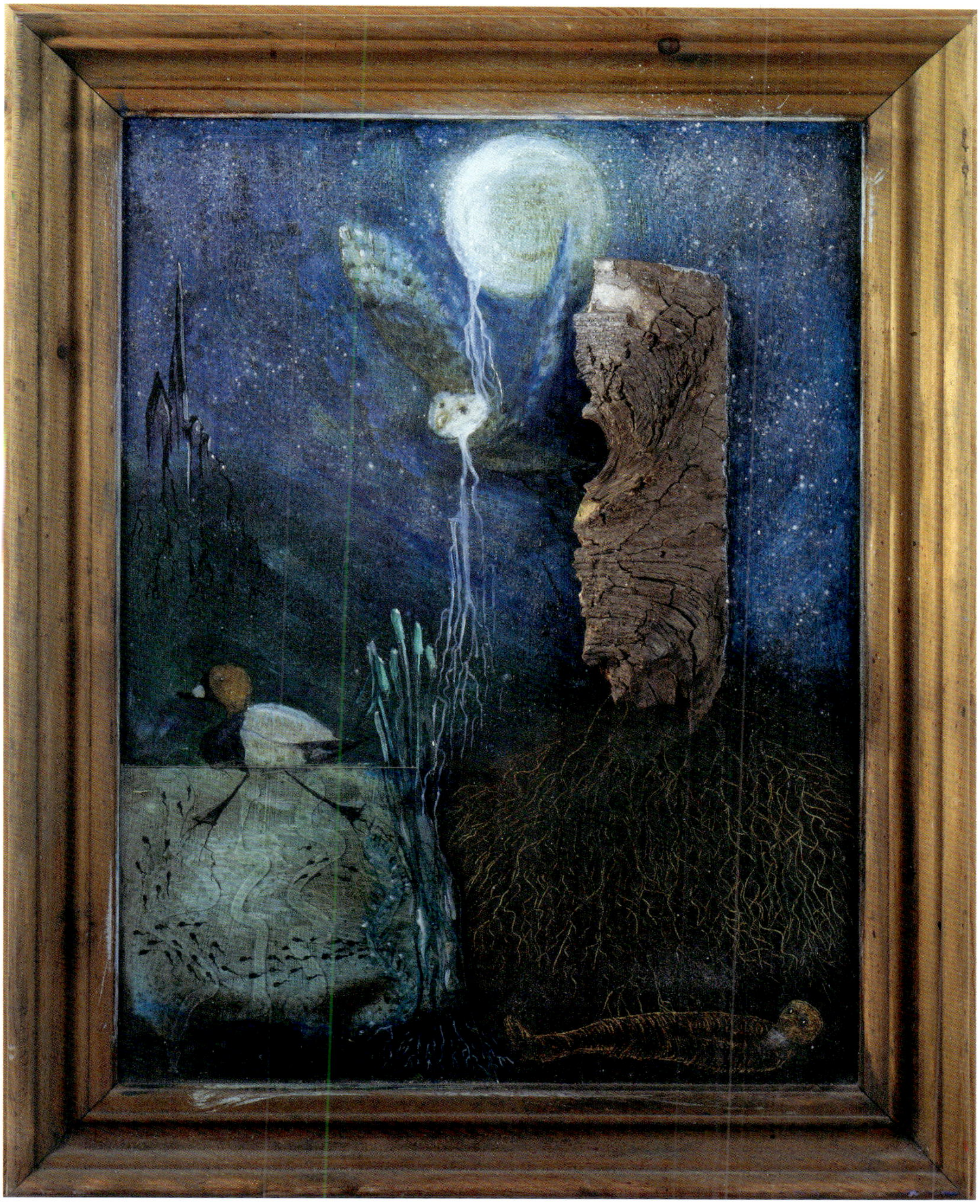

Cycles of the Moon, 2000
Found objects and oil on wood, 68.6 x 53.3 cm

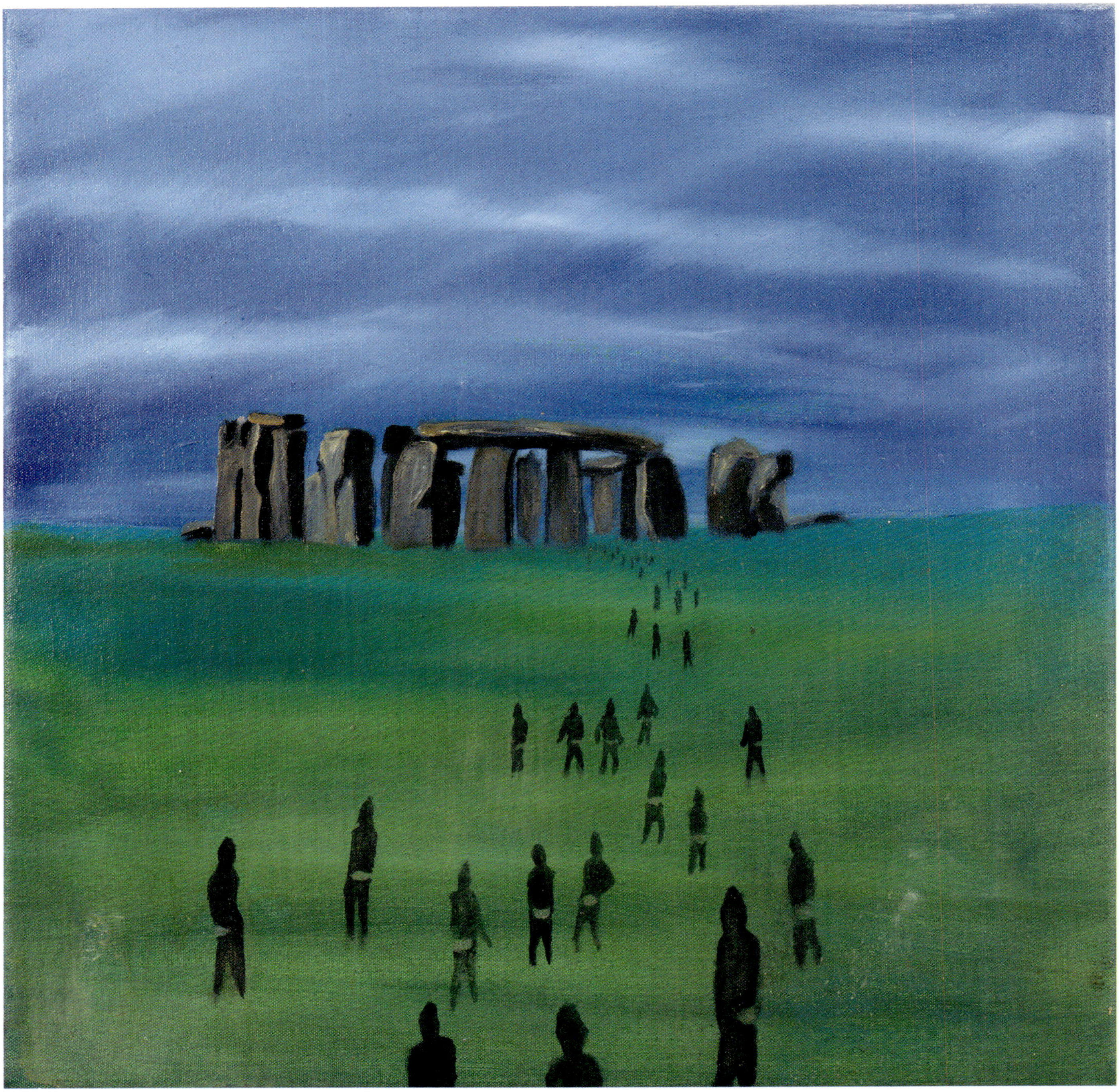

Green and Pleasant Land (Stonehenge the Ascent), 2006
Oil on canvas, 37 × 37 cm

Green and Pleasant Land

The condition of England, on which many pamphlets are now in the course of publication, and many thoughts unpublished are going on in every reflective head, is justly regarded as one of the most ominous, and withal one of the strangest, ever seen in this world.

Thomas Carlyle, *Past and Present*

THE QUESTION OF 'The condition of England', to use Thomas Carlyle's phrase, is central to Harrison's work. For him, this condition encompasses both the countryside and the city, and the overlaps between the two. Critics including Adrian Searle have noted that Harrison's iconography has grown out of the history of English art and literature, as well as his keenly observed sense of place.[1] To an extent, this is true, but we should be careful not to confuse the personal with the traditional. The artist's vision encompasses an unusually diverse range of references, which furnish his idiosyncratic mythology. His approach to the texture of English life almost invariably wrong-foots those with preconceived expectations about its character and requires us to make a series of imaginative leaps; his choice of subjects is often a means to reimagining things entirely. Accordingly, images of the natural world are means to throwing light on what 'modernity' both excludes and cultivates in excess; images from distant mythologies to discussing the gritty realities of urban life; and characters from the history of art to allowing him to talk about contemporary gay subculture.

From 2006 onwards, Harrison has created a monumental series of works whose titles begin with the prefix *Green and Pleasant Land*, explicitly evoking William Blake's mythical vision of the English countryside in his poem *Jerusalem*. Although the series is a landmark in his career, in essence, it expands his prior concerns onto a grander framework (throughout the 1990s, Harrison examined the 'state of the nation' across both urban and rural scenes). Whilst not confining himself to pastoral settings, the subject matter that Harrison has incorporated into *Green and Pleasant Land* includes iconic places associated with English heritage, like Stonehenge, as well as more archetypal scenes such as rolling lowland fields, remote rural cottages and handsome country houses. It is crucial to an understanding of Harrison's work that his use of titles such as *Green and Pleasant Land*, and the imagery outlined above are neither ironic or facetious, nor one-dimensionally nostalgic. We need to

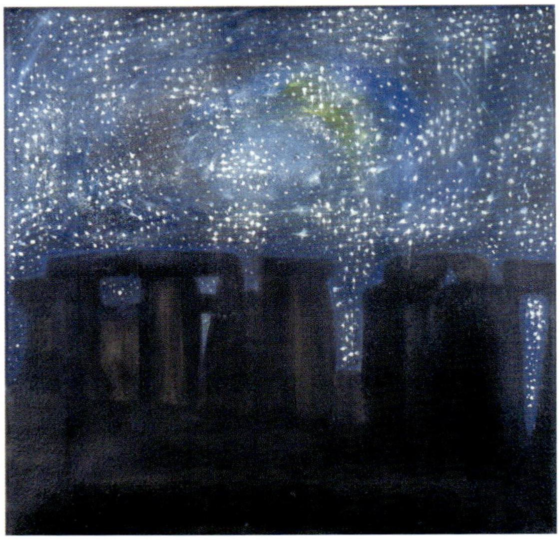

Twilight at Stonehenge, 2006
Oil on canvas, 37 x 37 cm

keep in mind Harrison's broader purpose, which he happily describes as being 'to remystify the natural world'.[2]

In Harrison's imaginary world, nature is a very long way indeed from the beatific, bucolic and reassuring visions of the English countryside habitually conjured by the mass media or associated with Georgian and Victorian landscape painting. What underpins all of his work is an almost pagan admiration for the fortitude and fecundity of nature. In Harrison's work, as in the natural world itself, every element, however small, is as important as any other. For many contemporary artists, however, any attempt to reconsider or reimagine the natural world is taboo. Firstly, in English art nature is often lazily assumed to be associated with conservative artistic positions, or with landscape painting *per se*. Secondly, the unspoken orthodoxy that the study of nature is simply incompatible with progressive art practice rests on the assumption that man and nature are distinct, and their domains separable. Harrison recognises that these assumptions are flawed. For him, much of our received wisdom about the relationship between the man-made and natural worlds is conservative in the extreme. Accordingly, he refuses to aestheticise nature for our ease of consumption: humans are merely one part of natural life, rather than on the outside of it

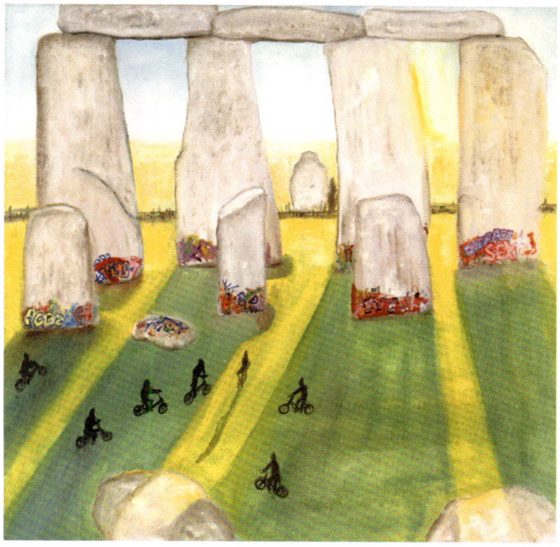

Green and Pleasant Land (Stonehenge), 2006
Oil on canvas, 37.5 x 37.5 cm

looking in. His work suggests that without this crucial recognition, we are doomed to an imaginative impoverishment in our understanding of works of art.

Whilst Harrison's conception of nature spans both the city and the countryside, much of his work is set in the latter. He is one of the few cosmopolitan and adventurous artists of note who has been able to create new and convincing visions of country life, that are neither baldly economic in focus, nor glibly consolatory. In fact, his representations of rural life offer no respite from the competition of the social world. Instead, they reverse the widespread assumption that the chief purpose of the countryside is to be a refuge or retreat from urban life, a secure place for rest and recuperation. In Harrison's fictional world, rural nature is instead a thrilling, intoxicating and even threatening presence. Vegetation and animals are portrayed by way of swirling patterns, extravagant forms and vortexlike compositions, in explicit contrast to the cool, magnificent geometries of the architecture he portrays. Such is the fullness and busyness of his portrayal of nature, in fact, that one might go so far as to say that Harrison's countryside echoes the mediaeval idea of nature abhorring a vacuum, famously signified by the phrase 'natura abhorret a vacuo' (translated by John Ruskin as 'nature abhors a vacuum').[3]

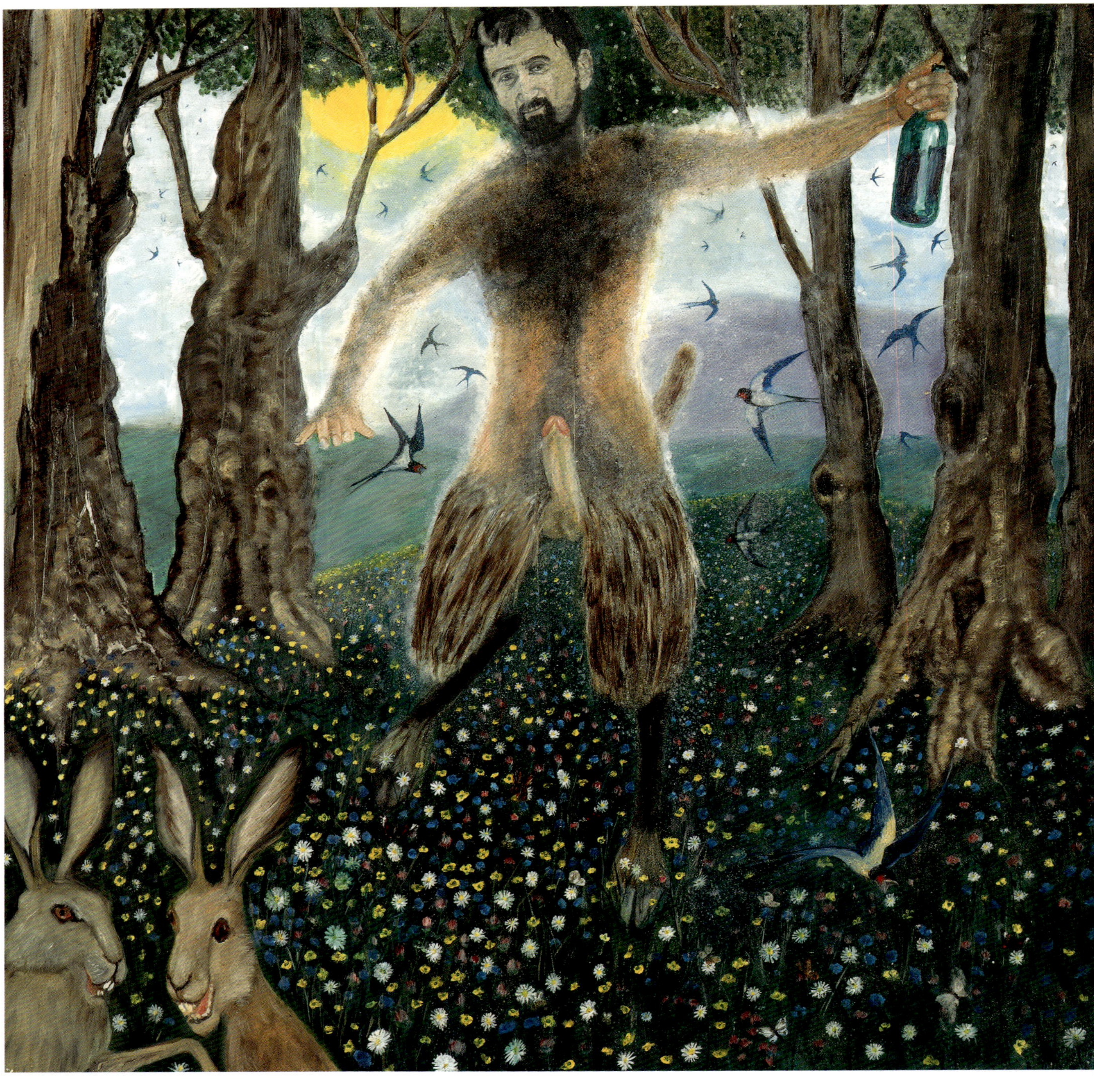

Pan Has Risen, 2007
Oil on wood, 60 x 60 cm

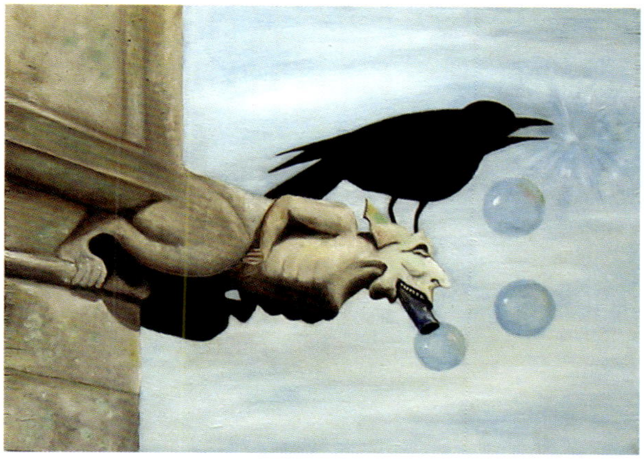

Ephemeral Nature, 2004
Oil on wood, 23 x 30 cm

Animals are a crucial part of Harrison's mature symbolism: they signify boundless vitality above all, but they also play numerous other roles. Often, they are presented as fighting to preserve their ecological niche in a contest between themselves and man, to carve out a space for themselves. In *Ephemeral Nature* (2004), a crow sits atop a gargoyle on a church roof, puncturing human illusions in the symbolic form of floating soap bubbles. Even in the sky, man competes for space with animals. Just as frequently, particular species are chosen for the wealth of associations they bring to a work. Harrison has developed a cast of creatures that are traditionally associated with malign behaviour or animistic pagan beliefs, and that occupy a violently transgressive space in which life flourishes, and even threatens. The principal characters, alongside humans, are hares, owls and cats – all of which were connected to witchcraft in premodern times, and have acted throughout the ages as symbols of vitality, virility and aggression.

Of these three species, hares in particular play a special role in Harrison's iconography. For him, they occupy a liminal position between the wild and the domesticated. They are untamed and seldom come into contact with man, but despite this, they are often closely associated with rabbits, the most sentimentalized of domesticated pets. Harrison sees that we humans know little about them: on the other hand, his works suggest that they know more about us than we realize. The hares in *Pan Has Risen* (2007) and *Hare and Chair* (2004) well illustrate Harrison's characterization of the animal. The works characteristically allude to several frames of reference. Firstly, they allude to the art of the past

– specifically, to images of hares by William Blake. Secondly, they allude to the cartoonlike representations of hares in popular fiction, especially those of the March Hare in the various illustrated editions of *Alice's Adventures in Wonderland*. And thirdly, they allude to witchcraft, since, of all species, hares were the most explicitly associated with witchcraft in late mediaeval Europe: witches were frequently imagined to be able to undergo a magical metamorphosis, transforming themselves into hares to evade capture by the authorities. Indeed, even today hares are dimly associated with madness, malignity and reverie: since at least the sixteenth century, the phrase 'mad as a March hare' has been used to describe irrational or hysterical behaviour. It seems clear, therefore, that both Harrison's idioms and subjects are intended to offer us chains of association that have dropped out of common currency or have been semiforgotten. Accordingly, the range of connotations they offer up can 'puncture' the viewers' consciousness and allow them to attach personal meanings onto them. As a result, Harrison's images only rarely offer up a monolithic reading or a single point of orientation. Instead, his references to classical and pagan myths, for instance, draw into play ideas that have a residual familiarity, but which are usually thought of as outmoded.

In *Hare and Chair*, Harrison joins one set of connotations – madness, malignity and reverie – to another that surround an even older imaginative convention – that of the mythical half-human, half-animal creature. This convention is one of the very oldest in Western art and fiction, running from Egypt's sphinxes and Greece's minotaurs to mediaeval mermaids. A half-human, half-hare creature, though, is one with few preexisting sets of associations; accordingly, we are forced to draw on our imaginative resources to interpret the picture. Like witches, Harrison's half-hare, half-human creatures appear to be in the process of metamorphosing between mortal and magical states of being. In *Hare and Chair*, Harrison's protagonist is set in an ordinary, but magically lit, environment, both familiar and yet unplaceable: a motorway siding. It is a nonplace, a setting instantly recognizable as a feature of the modern world, but which might be anywhere. Harrison extends the feeling of incongruity further, contrasting a design classic with the semirural, semiurban wilderness around it. The Eero Saarinen tulip chair is, by implication, as pointless for a hare as it is for a human. For him, it is a negative symbol of consumerism and petit-bourgeois materialism. So, whilst the scene is gloriously poetic, it has a sting in its tail.

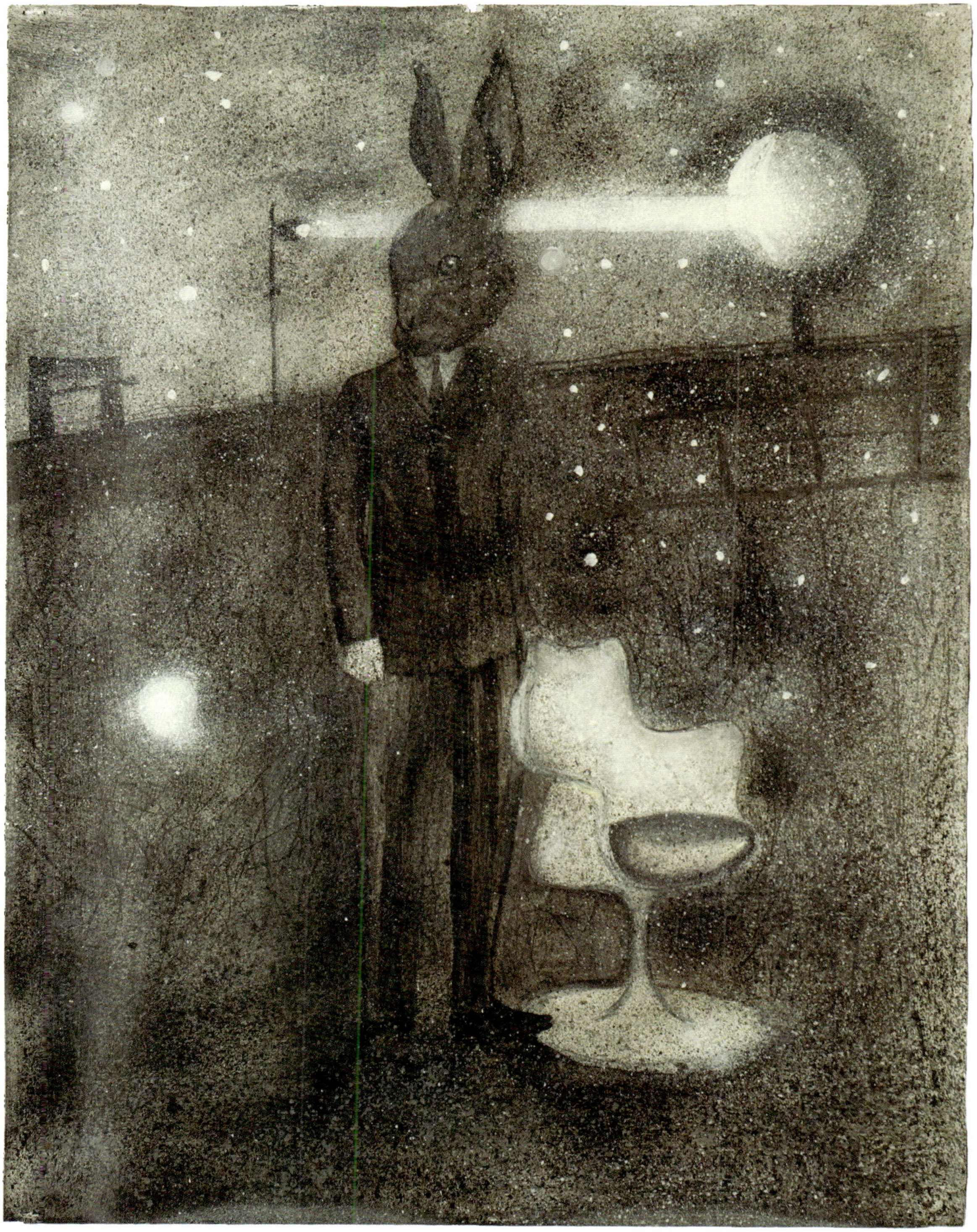

Hare and Chair, 2004
Oil and conté on paper, 42 x 30 cm

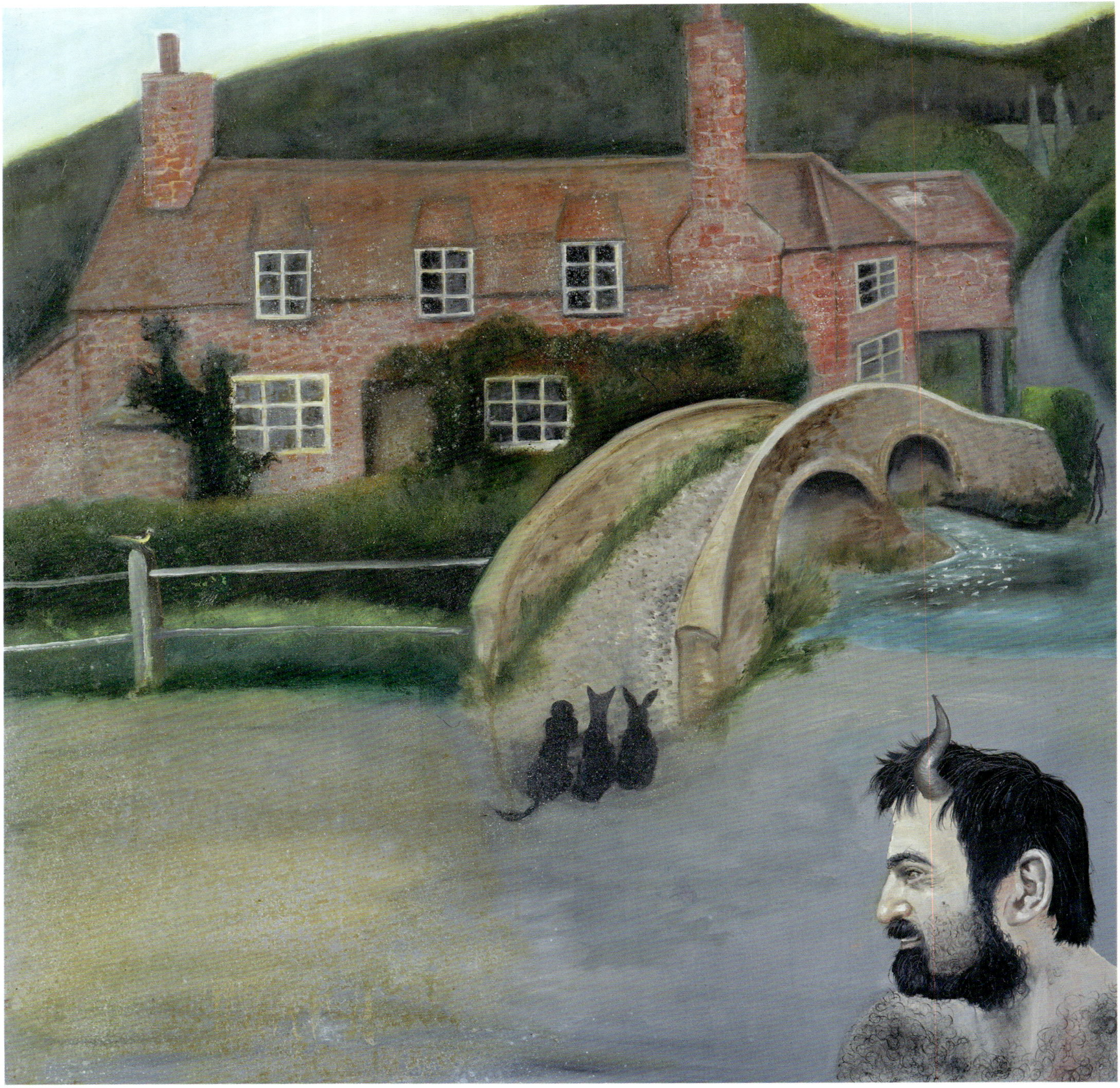

The Calling of Friends, 2007
Oil on wood, 60 × 60 cm

By contrast, the hares in *Pan Has Risen* are filled with joy, comedy and perhaps even sadness. They show us blood-red eyes, which are consistent with a naturalistic depiction, yet can be read symbolically. The hares' pin-prick pupils offer us no insight into their characters, but their raucous laughter suggests that they are all too human. The role that Harrison's animals play is to provide us with a point of entry into this strange and foreboding world. It is not too far-fetched to see them as narrators of this scene, in the manner of those in mediaeval mystery plays or Greek tragedies. They direct us towards the action depicted, behaving as intermediaries between the real space that we occupy, and the fictional universe behind the picture plane. The alarming proximity between us and them suggests that they stand exactly on the threshold between the actual and the imaginary, beckoning us into the latter but addressing us in the former.

Harrison has suggested that hares have a demonic, threatening presence – that they seem larger than life when encountered for real. The three animals – a rabbit, fox and poodle – in a related canvas, *The Calling of Friends* (2007), might well be seen as the unlikely equivalents of Francis Bacon's *Three Studies for Figures at the Base of a Crucifixion* (1944). Harrison, like Bacon, updates mythical tragedies to comment on what Bacon called 'The History of Europe in My Lifetime'.[4] The three animals in *The Calling of Friends* are schematically depicted so that we see only their silhouettes, which describe them standing to attention. Their forms provide a breach in the painting, blocking our imaginative pathway into it, as well as blocking the entrance to the bridge. Harrison has explicitly described them as symbols for 'the pathway to the underworld',[5] as guardians of the mysterious lower kingdom. This association becomes firmer when we consider the river that flows beneath the bridge and the number of figures that stand at its base: in classical mythology, souls of the dead first had to cross the river Styx before they could get to the underworld (though they were conveyed across this by the ferryman Charon, rather than a bridge), at which point they then had to pass Cerberus, the three-headed dog and guardian of the underworld's gates. On the other side of the bridge, a half-man, half-hare figure standing on its hind legs both threatens and beckons us. On Harrison's own interpretation, then, this picturesque Victorian village, an archetypal picture-postcard scene, is best viewed as the unlikely gateway to the underworld. Given this information, the painting seems to weave together the same kinds of menace and humour that Bacon wove together in his work, though with very different subject matter. Harrison's tactic is to wrong-foot his

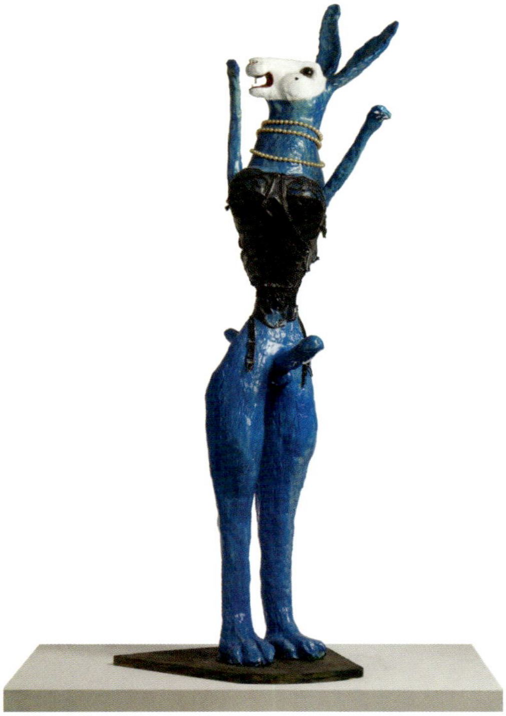

Blue Haremaphrodite, 2008
Mixed media, 144 x 44 x 41 cm

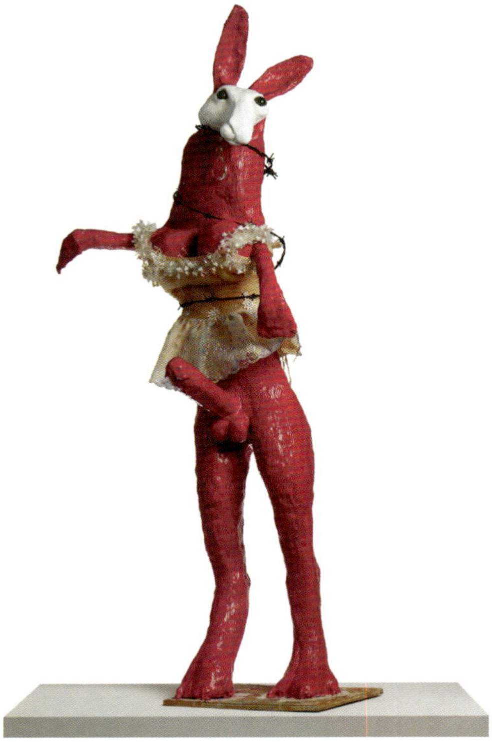

Pink Haremaphrodite, 2009
Mixed media, 146 x 54 x 52 cm

viewers, encouraging them to drop their guard and be seduced by the imagery on offer, before revealing that this too is one of the darker places on earth.

If *The Calling of Friends* conjures up a mysterious, yet pungently real, place, the artist's three-dimensional sculptures of hares seem to thrust fantastical creatures directly into our own space. Frequently, the artist manages to create magical objects that exert an alarming power over the viewer, through what should be entirely prosaic means. The overriding sensation is that these animals intrude on our own space. *Blue Haremaphrodite* (2008), aloft on hind legs, commands a majestic, yet comic presence. If Harrison's sculptures of human figures embody man's tragic and comic follies, his animals are always symbols of nature's infinite life-force. Seen on a human scale, the object is confrontational, yet joyous: the hare flaunts a proud erection, symbolizing his uncontrollable energy and fertility. Our sense of encountering an almost supernatural animal is reinforced rather than weakened by the artist's choice of materials. By using the most basic and disposable materials of our time, along with detritus, the artist creates objects that are like 'spectres glimpsed in a tarnished looking

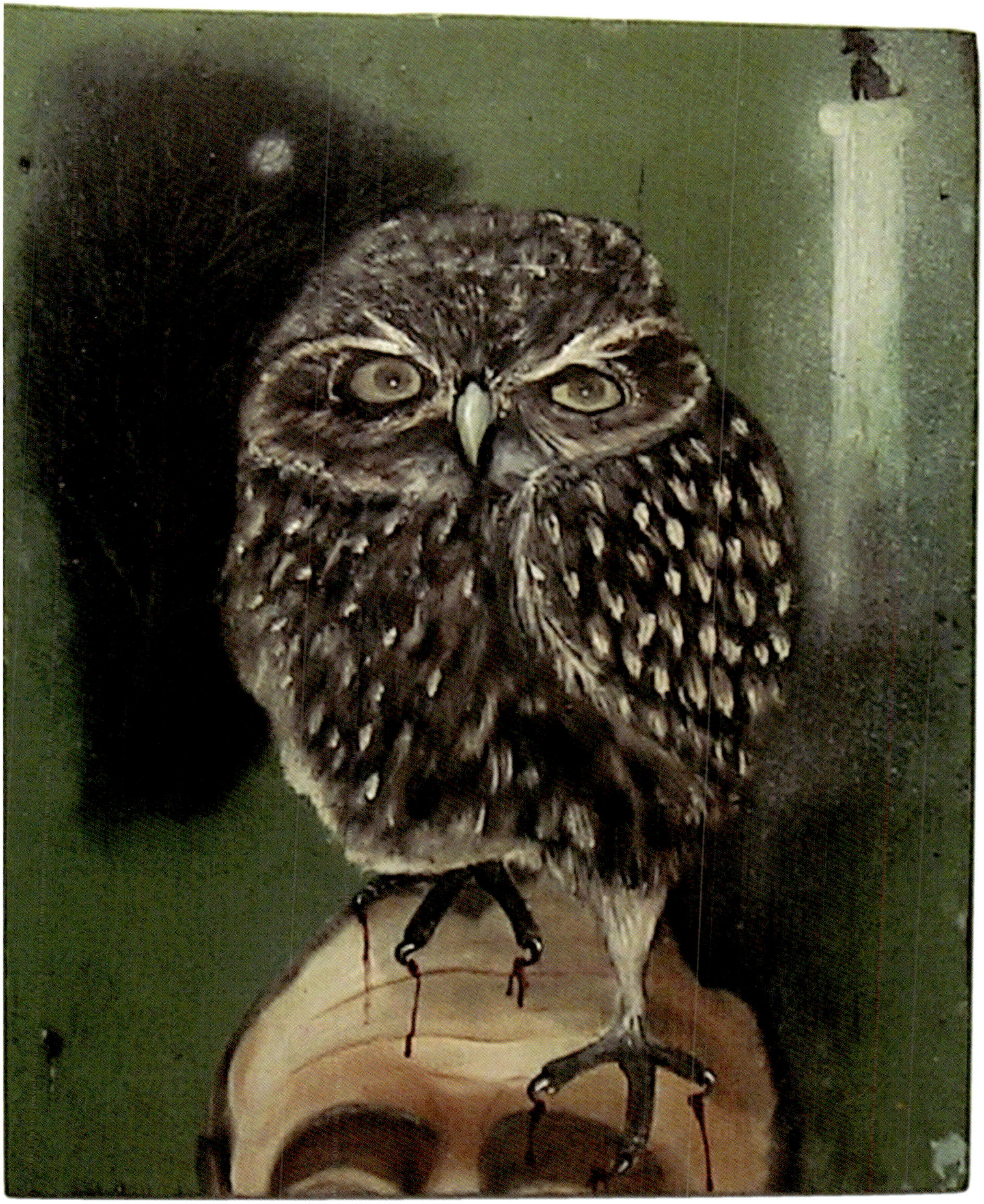

Headstrong Owl, 2003
Oil and collage on wood, 46 x 30 cm

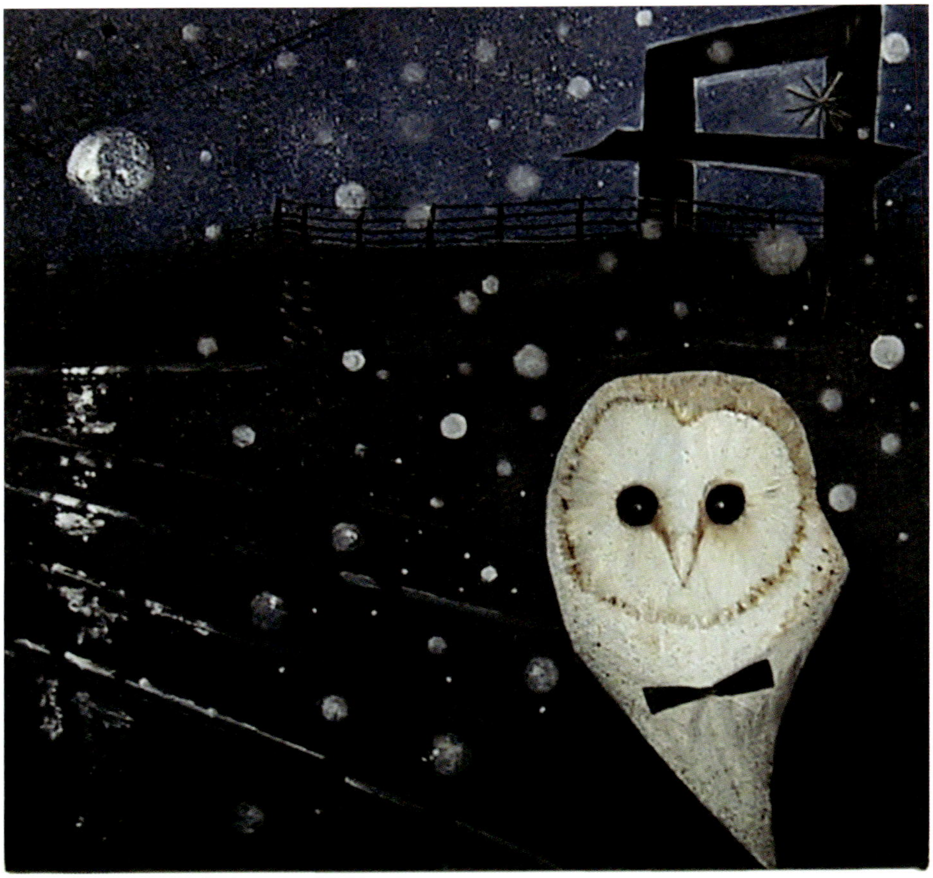

Blackpool Nightowl, 2003
Oil on wood, 35 x 34 cm

glass', as *The Village Voice* critic R.C. Baker has written.[6] Here, we encounter the animal as though through a looking glass darkly, or as if it were midnight: he is painted in an otherworldly, crepuscular midnight-blue.

Harrison's cast of owls, by contrast, are the principal creatures in his mythology that convey the mystery of the natural world. Owls are also one of the oldest symbols of magic and the black arts, and are traditionally associated with witchcraft. They also , however, serve another purpose, which is to provide Harrison with a formal and expressive challenge. As he has argued, of all species, owls are the most seemingly expressionless and inscrutable.[7] Accordingly, portraying them as distinct individuals with unique personalities and moods is a longstanding problem. This explains the fact that, rather than include owls in

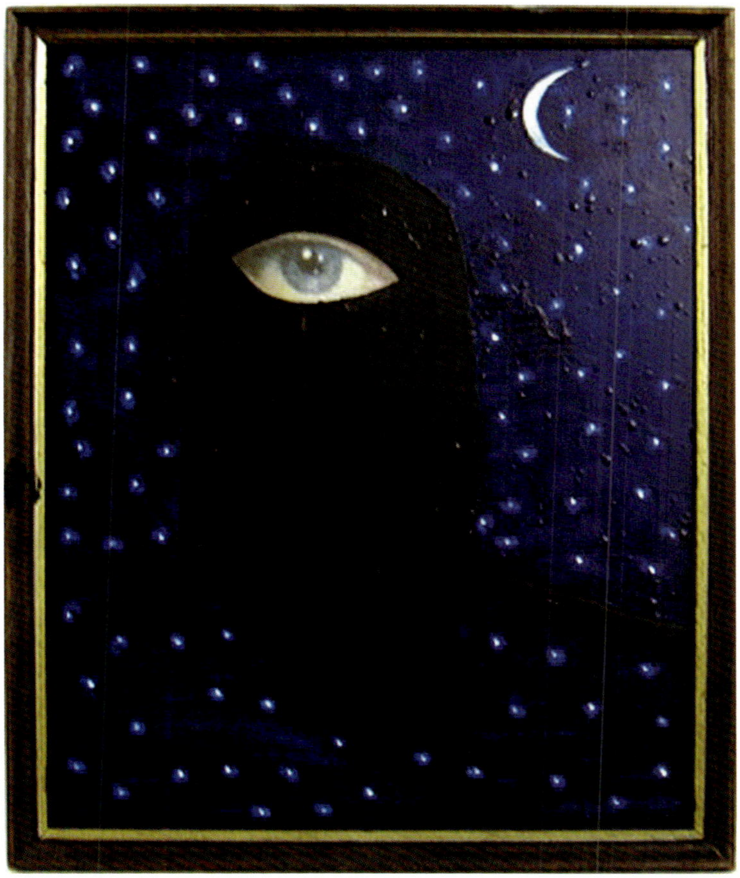

Cyclops Owl 2, 2005
Oil and collage on glass, 20 x 15 cm

broader compositions, Harrison frequently presents them as the subjects of portraits. *Blackpool Nightowl* (2003), and *Cyclops Owl 2* (2005), are iconic examples of paintings of this kind. *Blackpool Nightowl*, like *Hare and Chair*, depicts a character whose anachronistic costume distances him from us in time, whilst rendering him spatially all too close. Harrison, therefore establishes a disturbing push-pull of proximity and distance, a tension between proximity of space and distance in time. Cropped off at the waist, the Blackpool night owl is startlingly close to the picture plane, his attitude rudely confrontational. Harrison's tactic is to position his protagonist in a space beyond the foreground and on the fringes of our own: he seems to be pushing out through the imaginary 'window' that the picture offers, like the hares in *Pan Has Risen*. The effect is to create an unnerving and threatening proximity, which also borders on a conspiratorial intimacy. Should we trust a bird of prey at such close proximity? The bird's tuxedo suggests that we should: it endows him with a sense of authority, albeit one with a faintly absurd and archaic formality. Where does civilized life end and bestial life begin? Harrison's naturalistic yet abbreviated style of treatment underlines the question. His short, concentric brushmarks form a star-shaped halo around the owl's pupils. The halo draws us back to the owl's mesmerizing gaze, which has a confrontational, almost accusatory, undertow. The combination of his pose and his setting suggests that he is a messenger here to convey a message whose nature is implied only by the setting, a place between the city and the countryside. This is defined by an anonymous, seemingly purposeless, Modernist structure that scars the landscape. Though Harrison leaves open his rationale for the conjunction of these elements, one plausible reading is that the bird is akin to one of the mythical gods of vengeance, the furies, pointing to our folly in desecrating the landscape. The very inbetweenness of the location directs us to the beauty of the landscape and the lack of imagination we have demonstrated in adding to it.

In *Cyclops Owl 2*, the subject similarly returns our gaze with impudence, if not outright aggression. In the art historian Michael Fried's terms, the picture is at the extreme end of 'theatrical',[8] the subject seeming to thrust out into our own space rather than lead our gaze gently into an imagined depth. The human eye incorporated into *Cyclops Owl 2* plays the role the suit does in *Blackpool Nightowl*, tempering the bestial and aggressive with the human, the civilized and the polite. The inclusion of photographic elements in works such as *Cyclops Owl 2* stops us short: it convincingly confuses the realms of the real, the imagined and the symbolic. Harrison's magical world is rudely interrupted by the real one. The sculpture *Hand of Fate* (2005; overleaf) performs a similar feat in three dimensions. An owl armed with green false eyes gazes imperiously into the middle distance, his lids set into densely worked, thick glue with wood dust covering a doll's torso. Bereft of one wing, the owl has a monstrous human hand outstretched in place of the other, as if in warning of forthcoming terror. An emphasis upon magical transformation recalls predecessors such as Henry Fuseli, whom Harrison has explicitly quoted in other works. The art historian Linda Walsh has written that the essence of Romantic painting is the wish to 'express … inherently invisible phenomenon in a medium constituted by the visual'.[9] Many of Harrison's works function through a direct dialect between what is presented and what is at the very threshold of the visible, and indeed, like the Romantics, 'find endless new ways of seeing things and "see" things previously unseen.'[10]

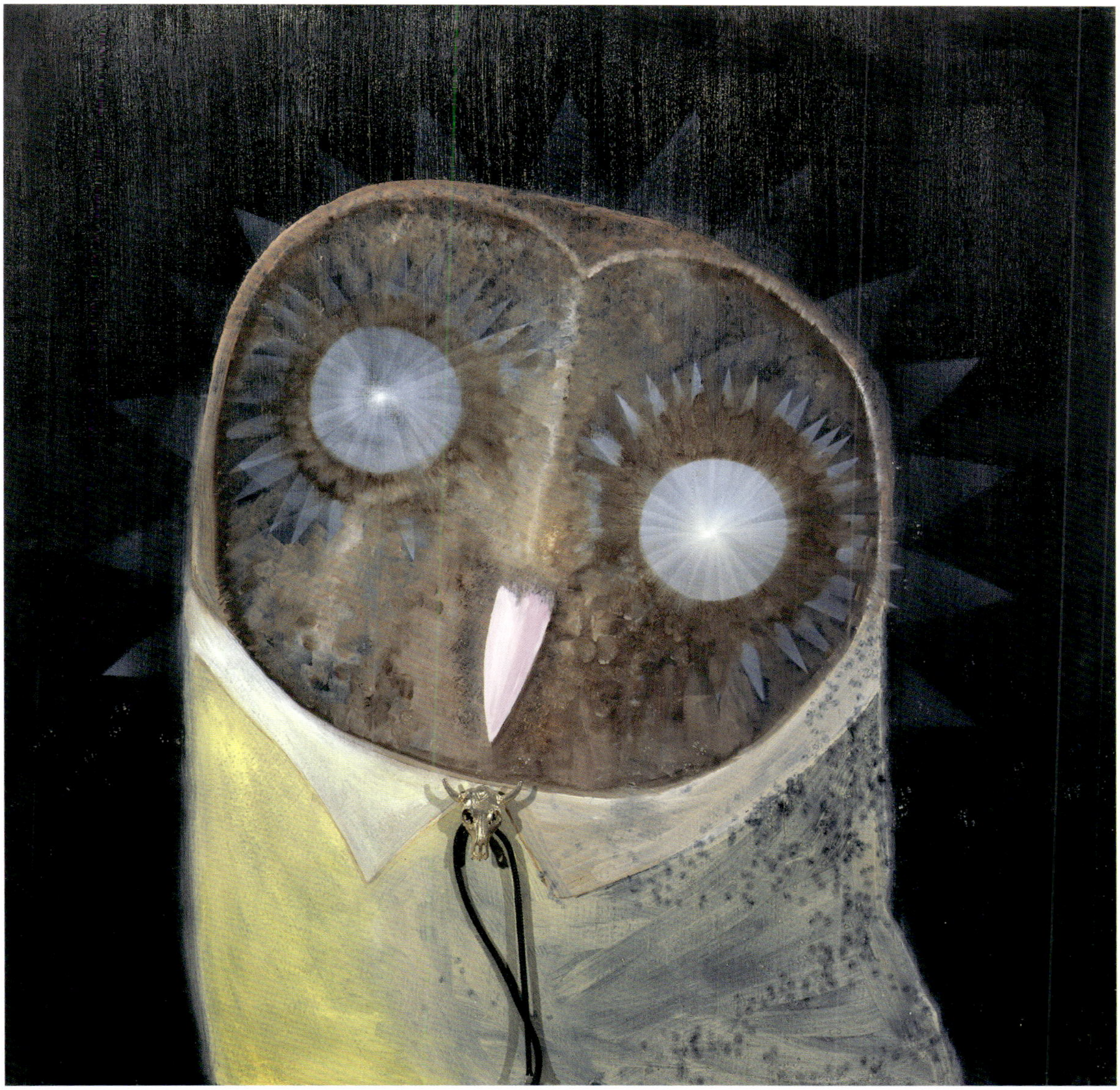

A Twist of Fate, 2007
Oil and collage on wood, 60 × 60 cm

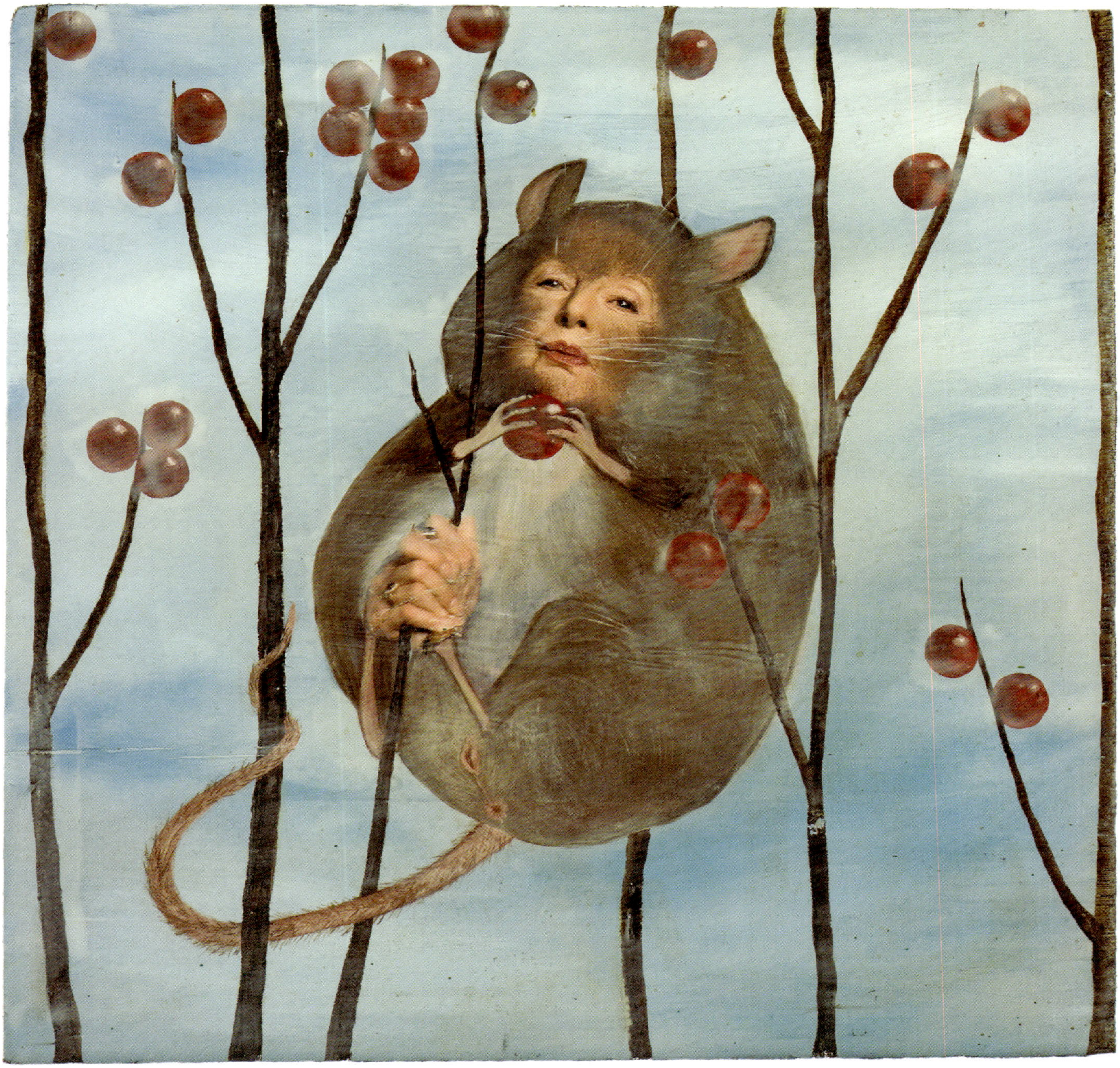

Margaret Mouse, 2005
Oil and collage on wood, 46 x 47 cm

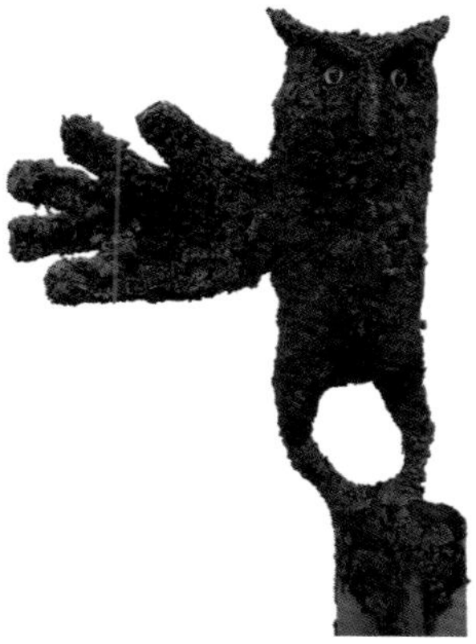

Hand of Fate, 2005
Found objects, glue and wood dust,
71 x 38 x 30 cm

As well as presenting the 'previously unseen', the artist has also re-presented existing images by incorporating them into painterly compositions. In works such as *Margaret Mouse* (2005), he has taken photographic elements – here of Margaret Thatcher's face and hands – and seamlessly interwoven them into a fictional whole. The two elements, real and fictional, sit on the same plane even whilst operating upon our imagination in different capacities. This painting presents the unlikely spectacle of Margaret Thatcher as a field mouse, chewing contentedly on blood-red berries. We might expect her to have been in the form of a predatory owl: figuring a divisive, towering personality in British public life as a helpless, rotund rodent has an amusing incongruity to it. In fact, the frame of reference used in the painting is entirely outside the iconography in existing Thatcher caricature. Throughout his career, Harrison has been ahead of the curve, one step ahead of the dominant critical tendencies, waiting for the art world to catch up. The political think-tank Progress recently argued that the current fashion in political self-presentation is to 'constantly engage in counter-intuitive positioning'.[11] This charming phrase is a perfect summation of every aspect of Harrison's thought and practice in this painting and elsewhere, where new metaphors and similes are used to enliven familiar subjects.

Indeed, every aspect of the national landscape in the series *Green and Pleasant Land* is presented in a counterintuitive light. *Green and Pleasant Land (The Ascent)* (2006) weaves

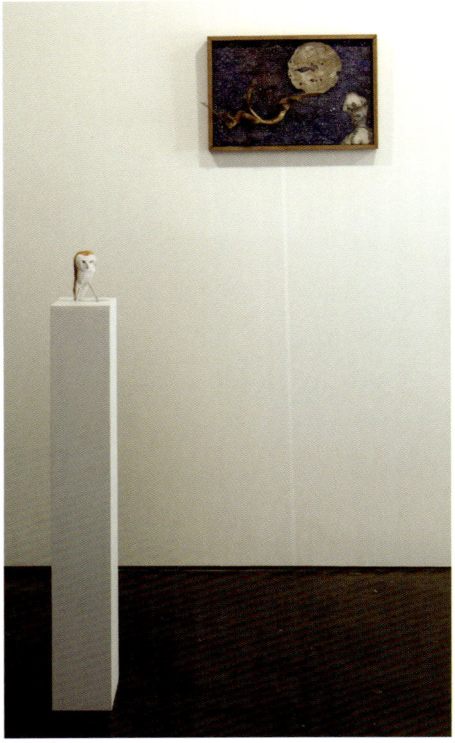

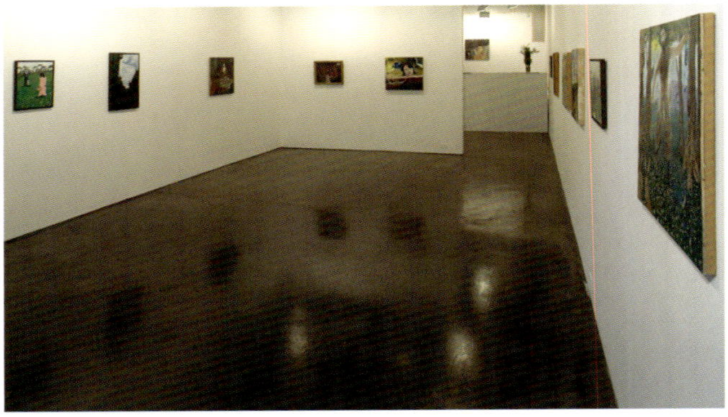

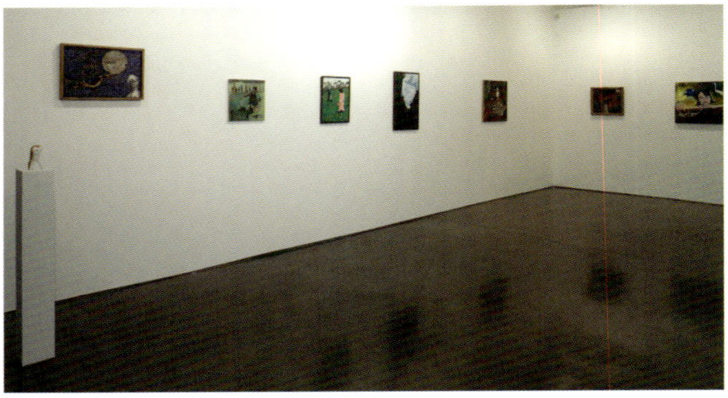

Installation view, Green and Pleasant Land, Daniel Reich Gallery, New York, 6 September–18 October 2008

together unexpected motifs into an erotic and comic scene. The composition is a cinematic celebration of England's more remote places. Harrison's tactic here is to set the city inside the country – to reverse the classical idea of *rus in urbe*, changing it to *urbs in rure*. Here, we encounter a group of 'hoodies' defiling a rural site. The contrast between the garish palette of their clothing and graffiti and the gentle play of ochres and umbers of the country is jarring. Moreover, the teenagers' ascent is towards what might be called a temple of ignorance, rather than knowledge. Their zombified nature is signified by their arbitrary arrangement, along with their lack of features. By contrast, despite being desecrated with graffiti tags, their vertical counterparts, the trees, stand tall and strong, with their height and life-spans many times our own. In spite of the malevolence of man, nature retains its fortitude. The simple symmetry of the trees' arrangement signifies their solidity and strength. Even whilst

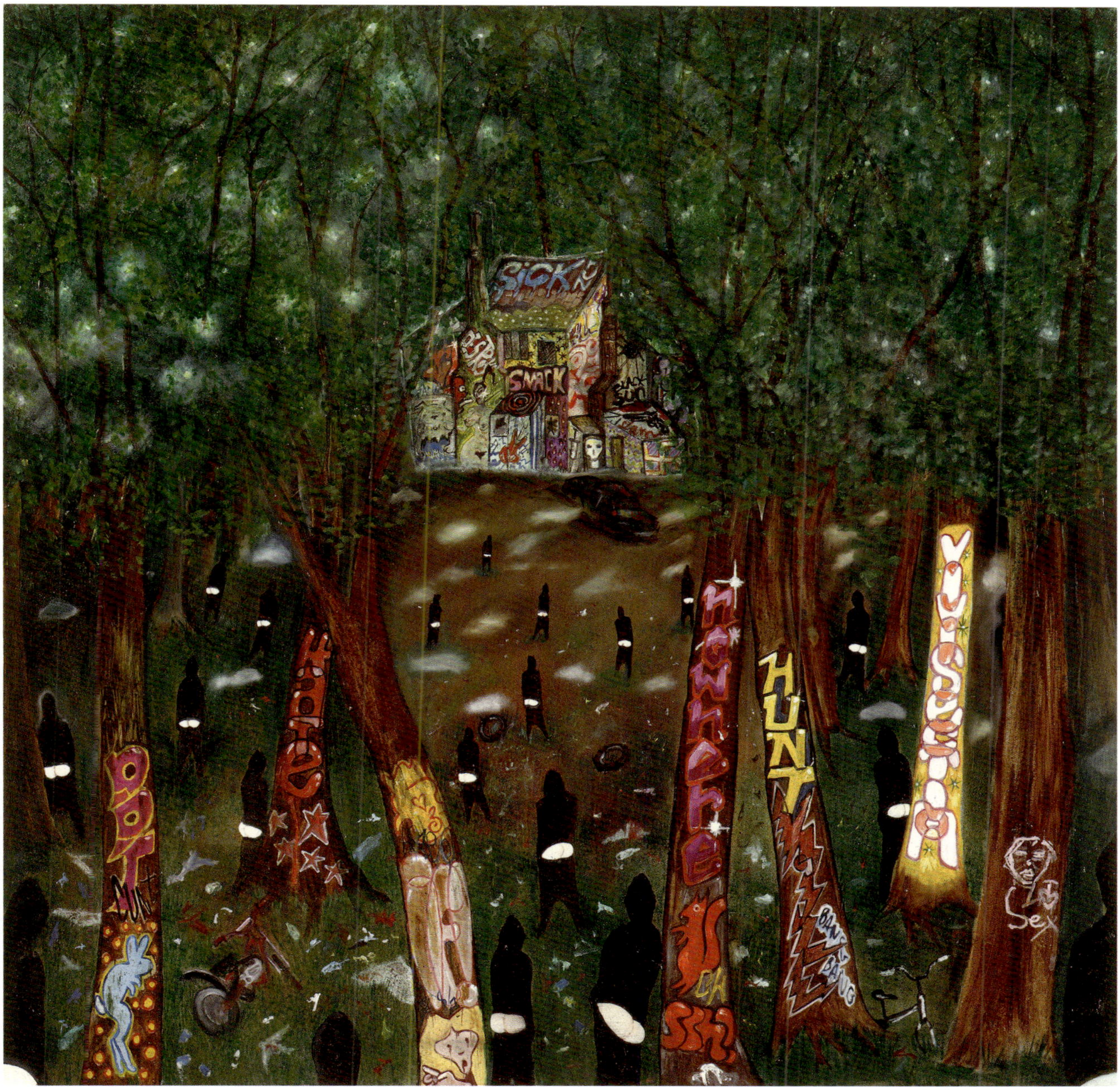

Green and Pleasant Land (The Ascent), 2006
Oil on canvas, 76.2 × 76.2 cm

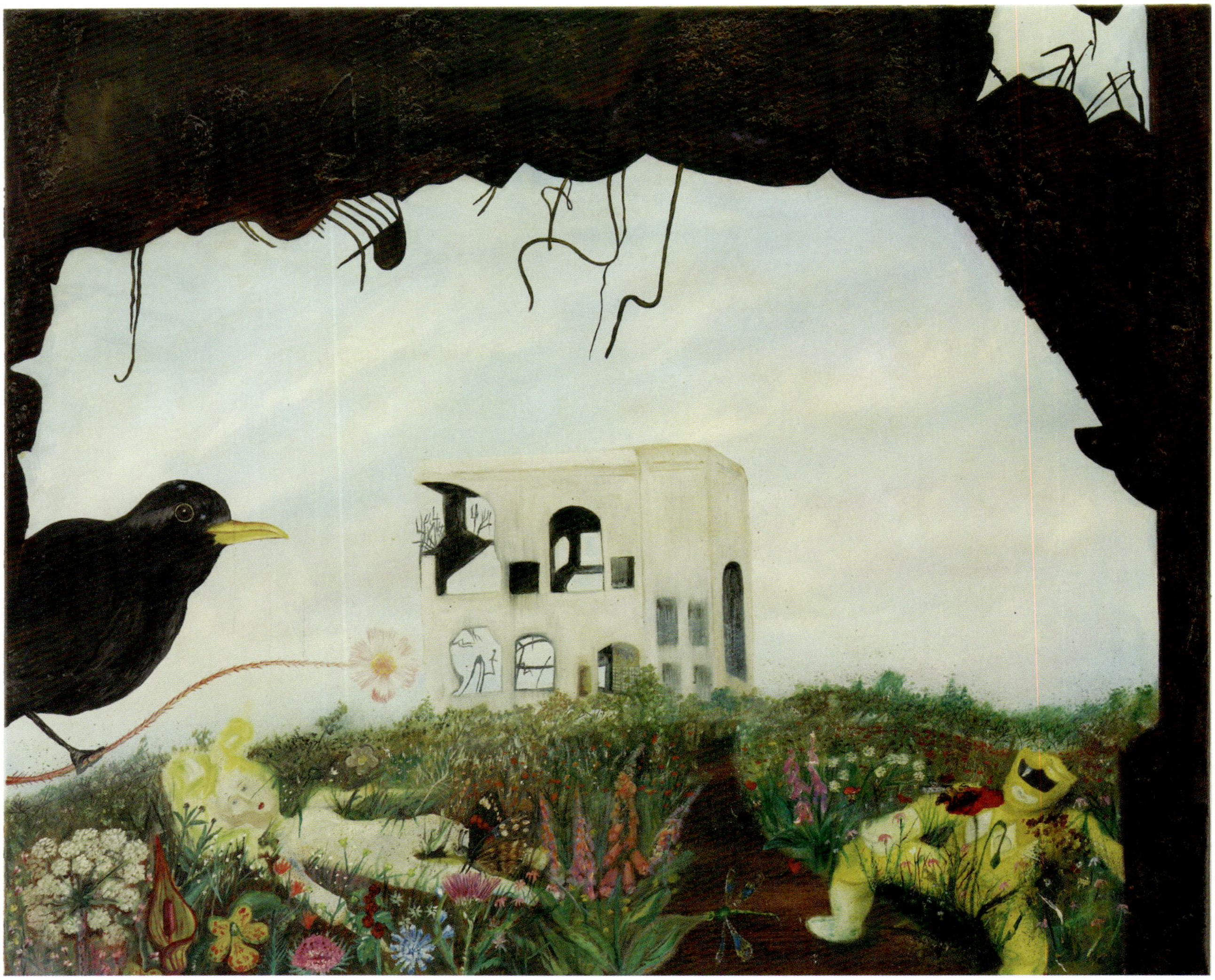

Lords and Ladies, 2000
Oil on canvas, 76 × 92 cm

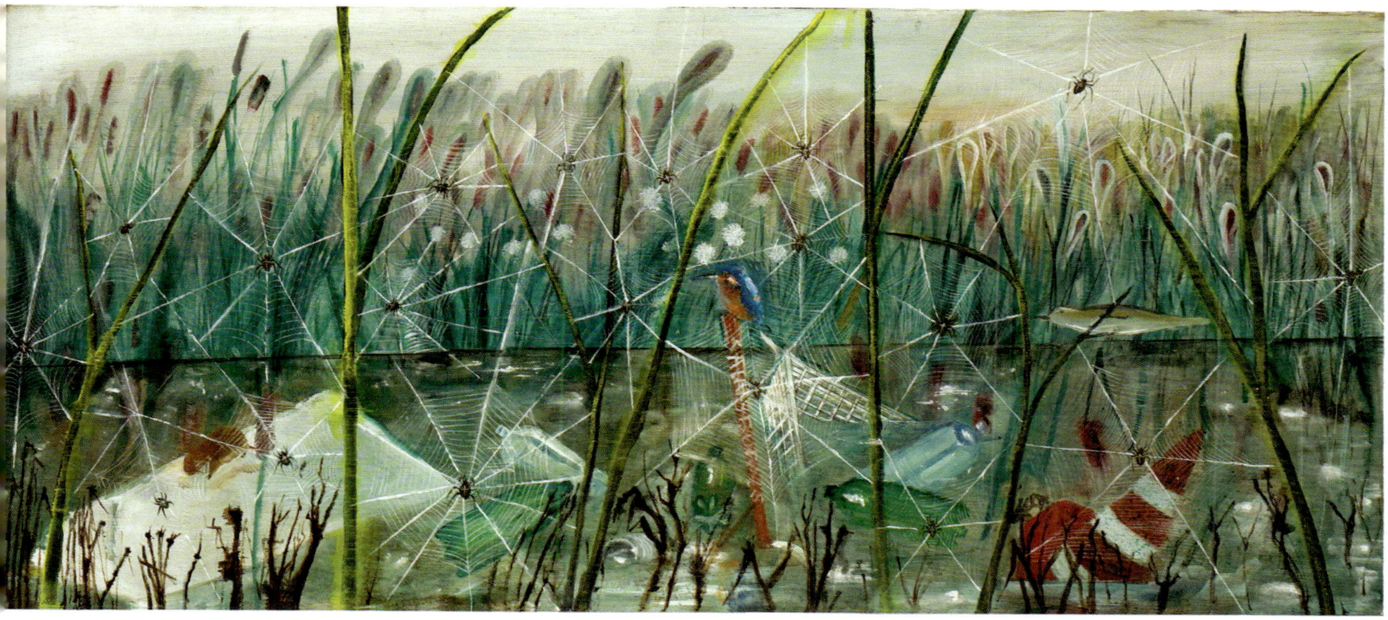

Green and Pleasant Land (Another English Country Stream), 2008
Oil on wood, 31.9 x 71.5 cm

daubed with graffiti, their foliage shimmers magnificently. It also sways, so that apertures allow through pools of moonlight onto the ground. Dappled with zones of brilliant, pure white light, we feel that the scene is animated by malevolent white sprites swirling through the air. The slow-witted hoodies, behaving with a pack mentality that even Harrison's animals lack, simultaneously perform a sign of base mockery that doubles as an erotic tease. What the scene does not reveal but presages, however, is the natural world reoccupying the land after we have despoiled it. Whilst *Green and Pleasant Land (The Ascent)* might initially be read as pessimistic, we should bear in mind Harrison's remark that 'whatever we make ugly, nature makes beautiful again'.[12] This painting bears testimony to the artist's belief that, even in the midst of destruction, new life will triumph.

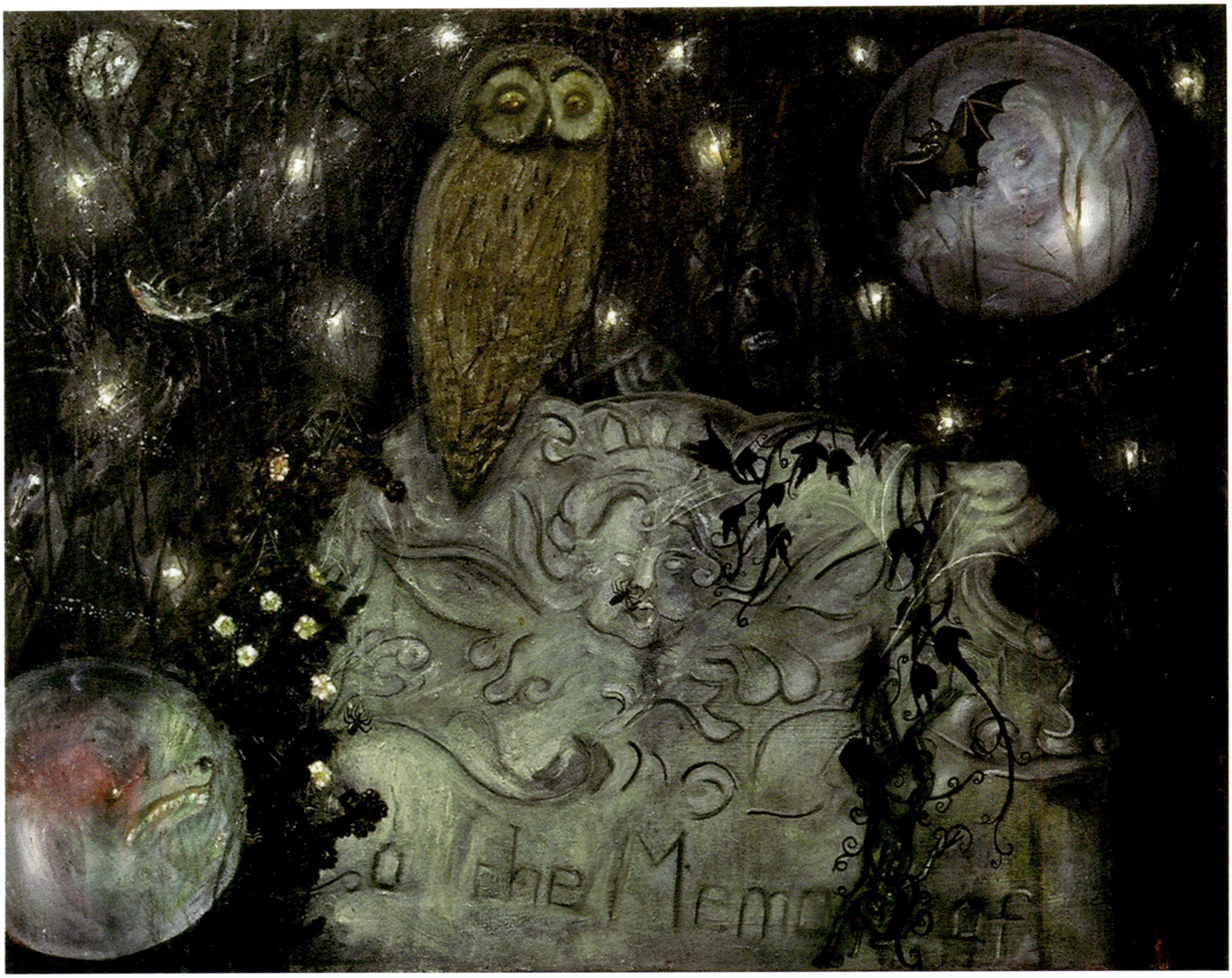

To the Memory of, 1999
Oil on canvas, 76 × 92 cm

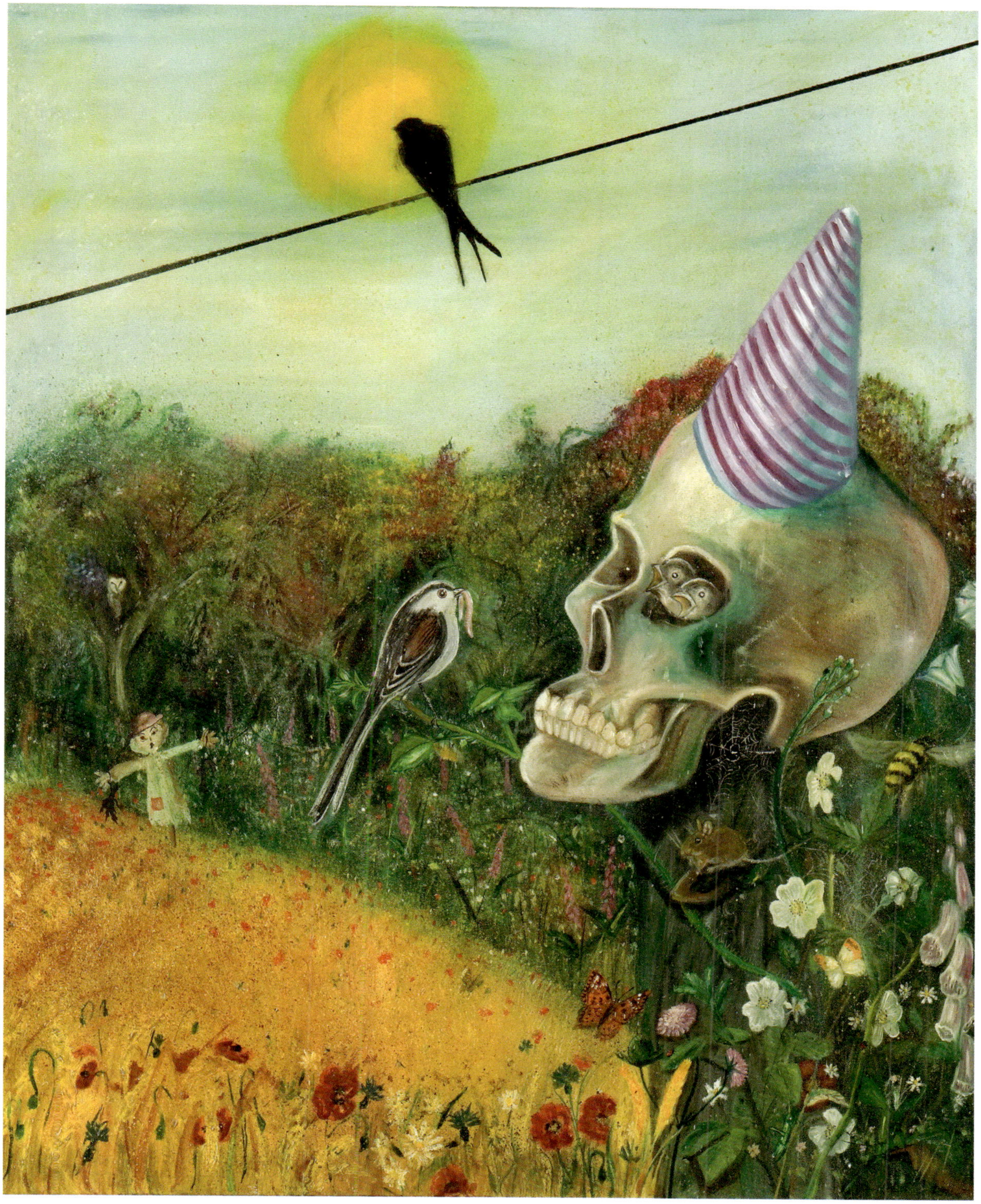

The Dead Laugh at the Living, 2000
Oil on canvas, 100 x 81 cm

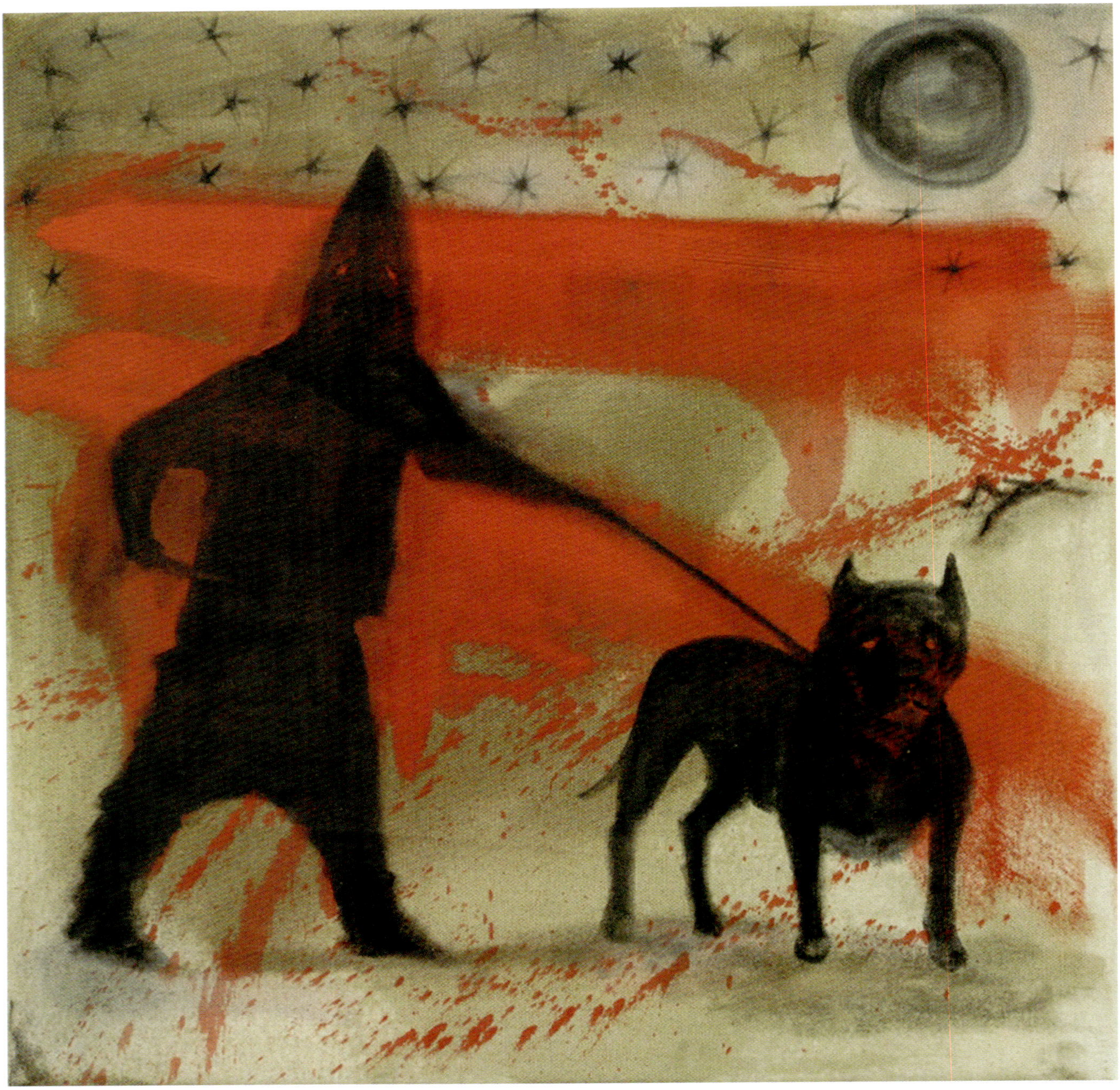

Black Stars, 2009
Oil on canvas, 37 × 37 cm

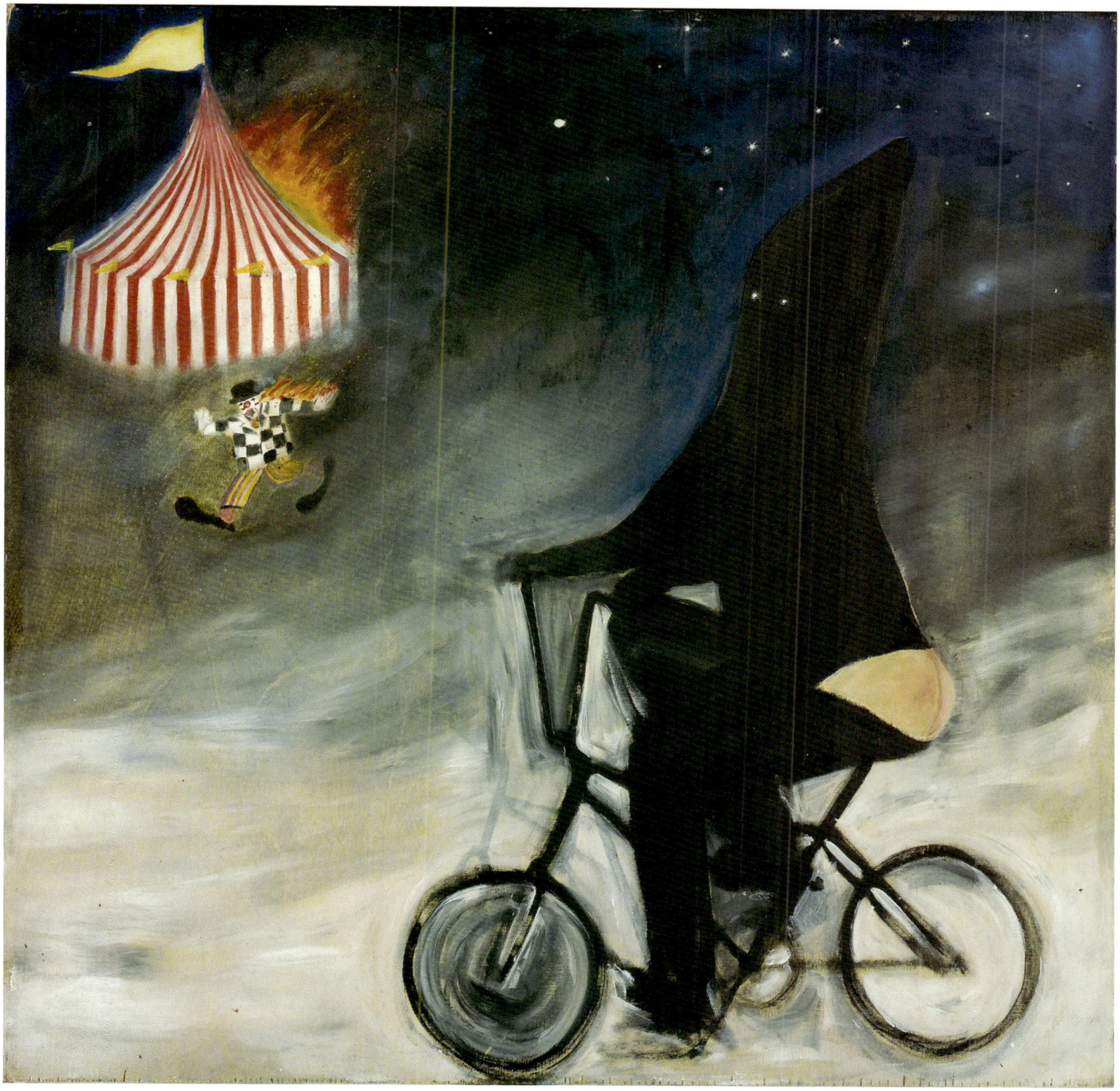

Stars in Their Eyes (Fun at the Circus), 2007
Oil on wood, 45.7 x 45.7 cm

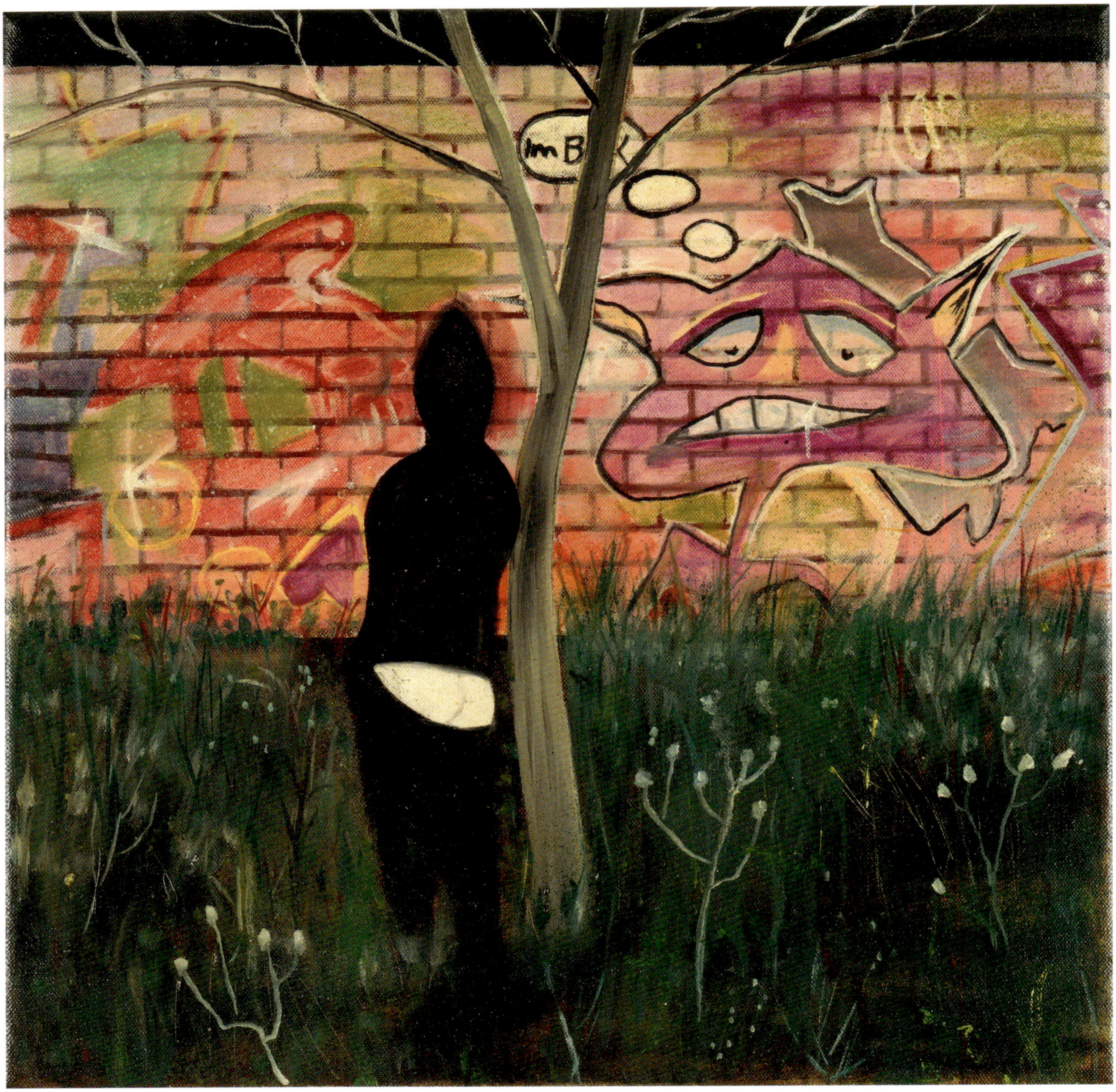

Green and Pleasant Land (The Wall), 2006
Oil on canvas, 37.5 x 37.5 cm

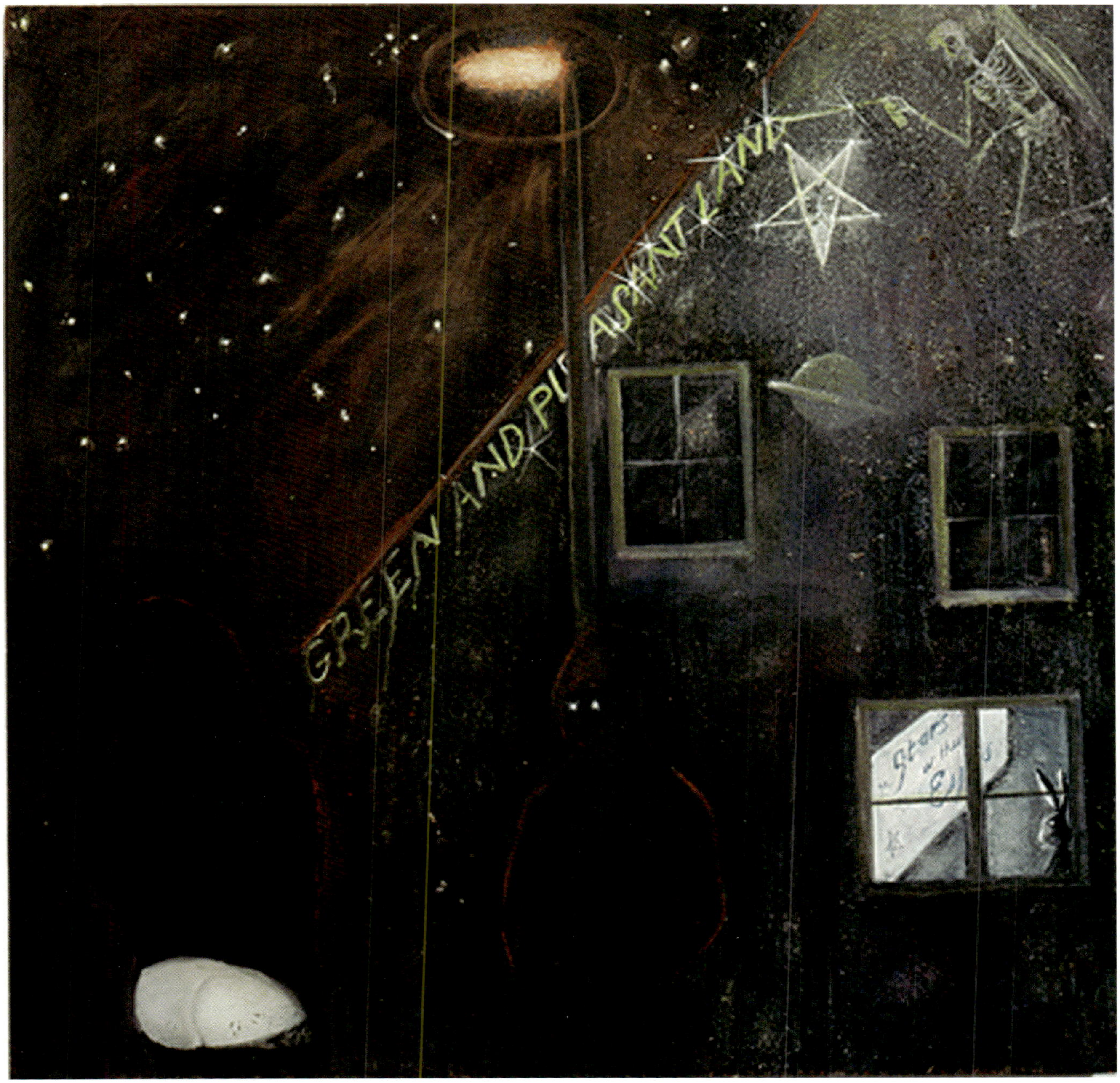

Stars in Their Eyes, 2007
Oil on wood, 60 × 60 cm

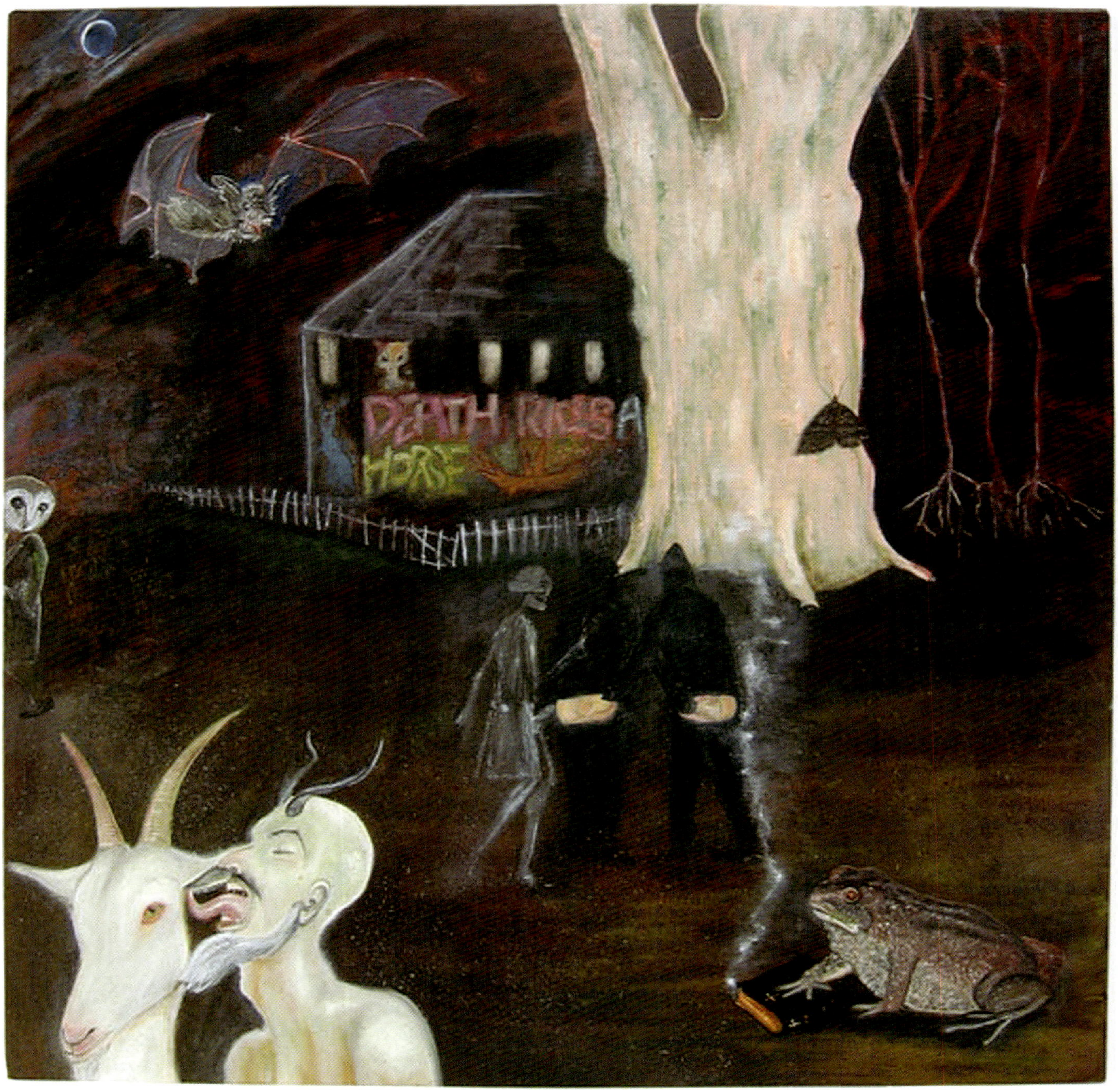

Death Rides a Horse, 2006
Oil on canvas, 71 x 71 cm

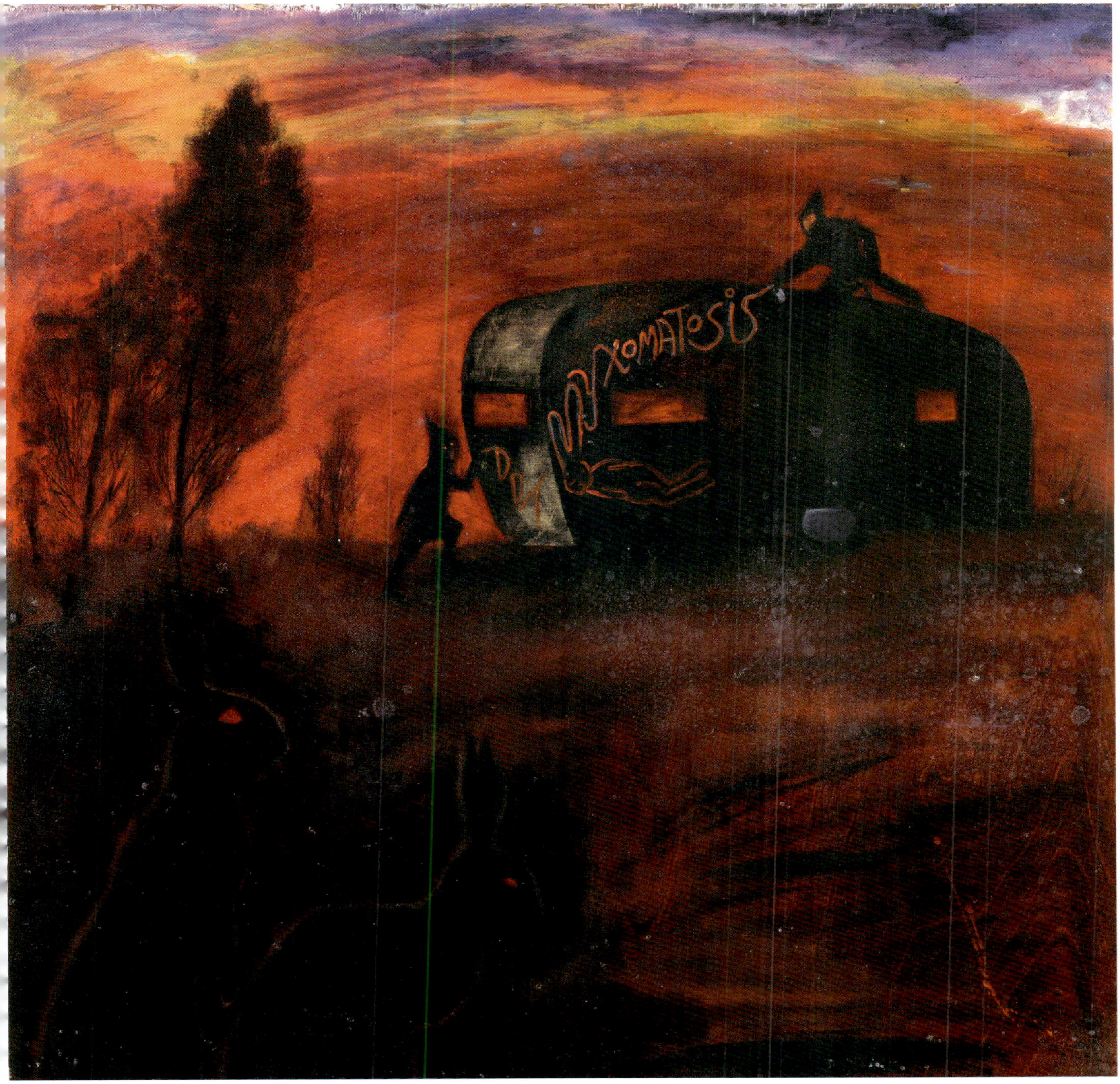

Green and Pleasant Land (Final Sunset), 2007
Oil on wood, 60 x 60 cm

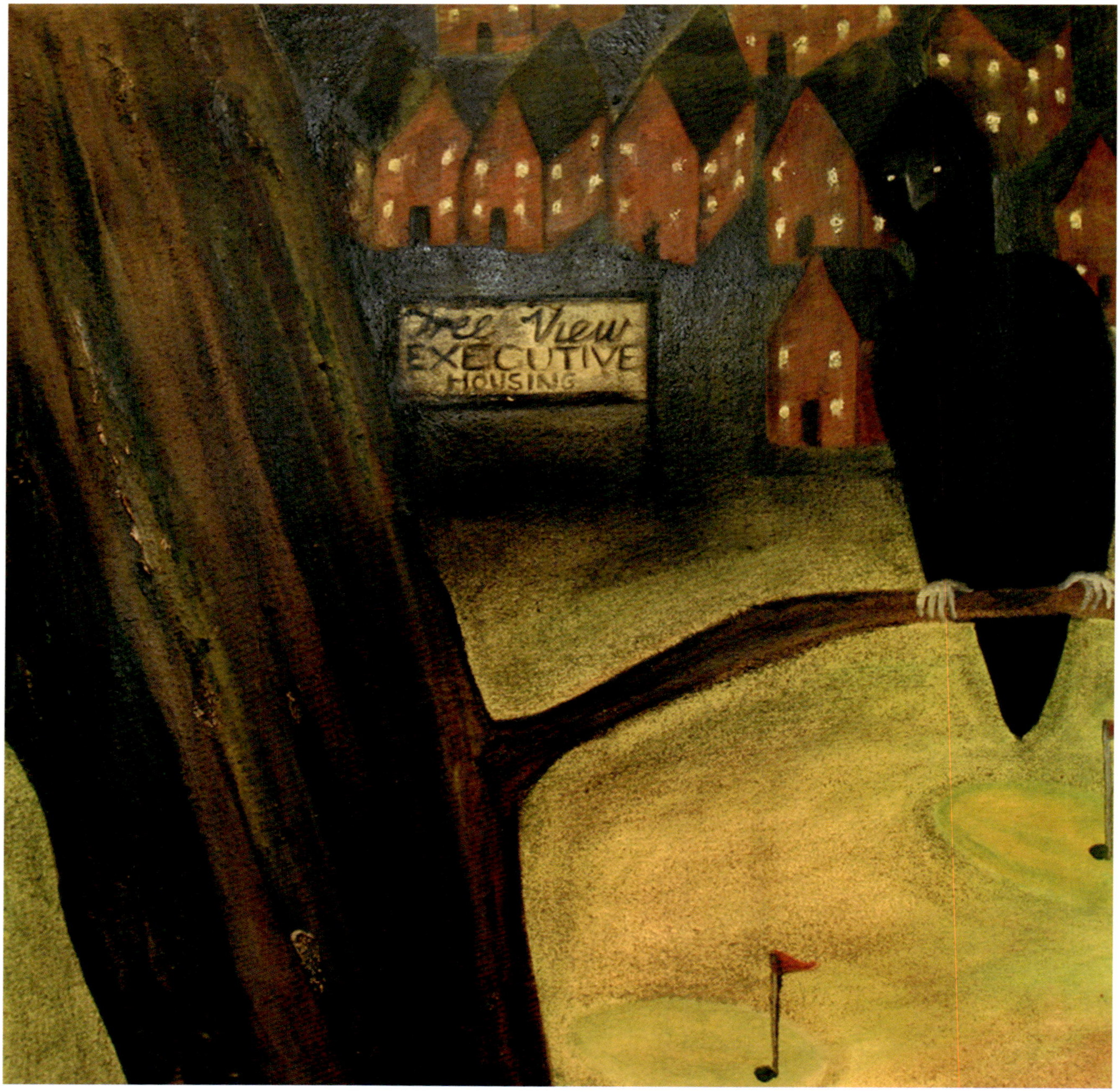

Green and Pleasant Land (Perched Hoodie), 2006
Oil on canvas, 37 x 37 cm

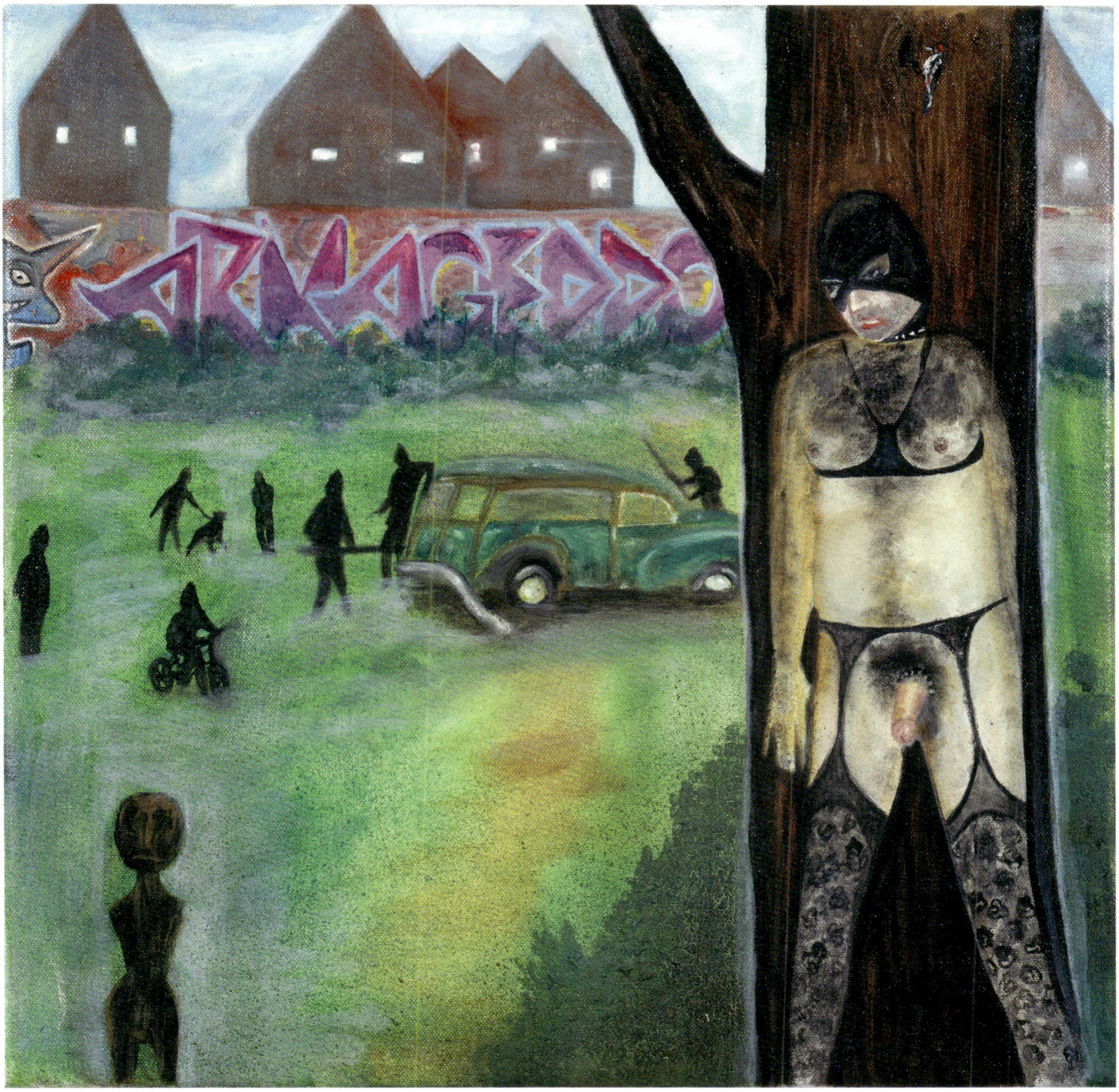

Green and Pleasant Land (Woodland Walk), 2006
Oil on canvas, 37 × 37 cm

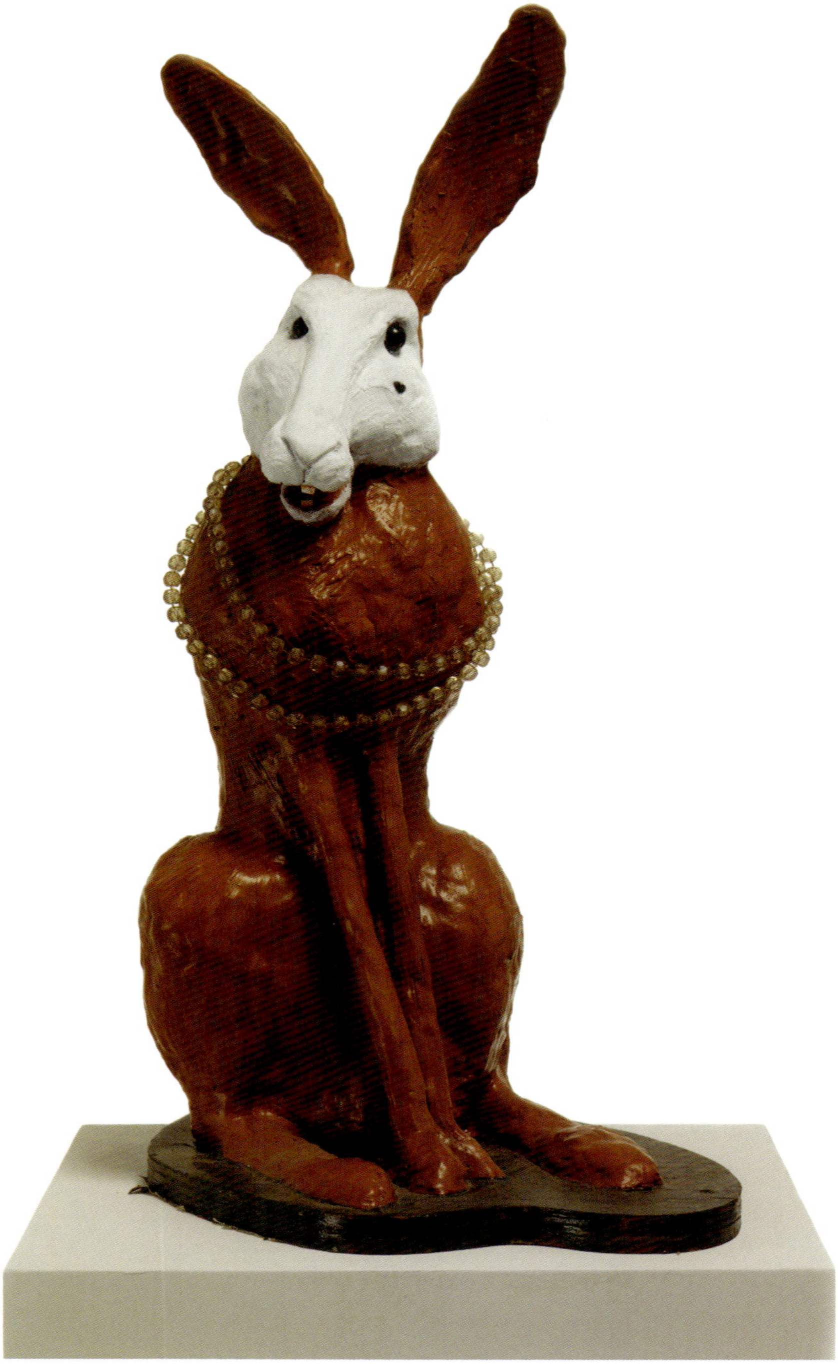

Hareditary, 2008
Mixed media, 66 × 43 × 26 cm

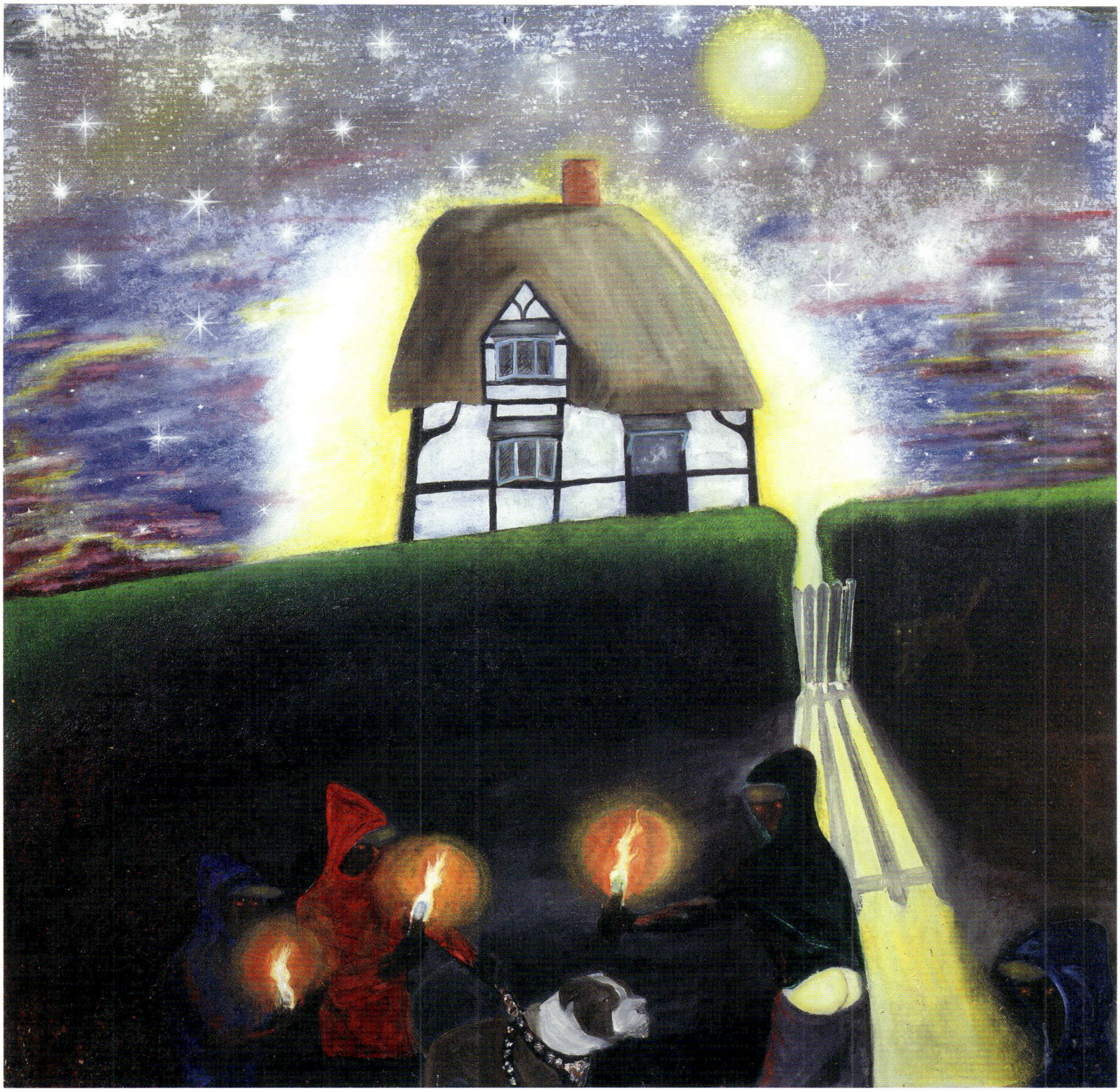

Green and Pleasart Land (Burn the Witch, She's Not Like Us), 2007
Oil on wood, 60 x 60 cm

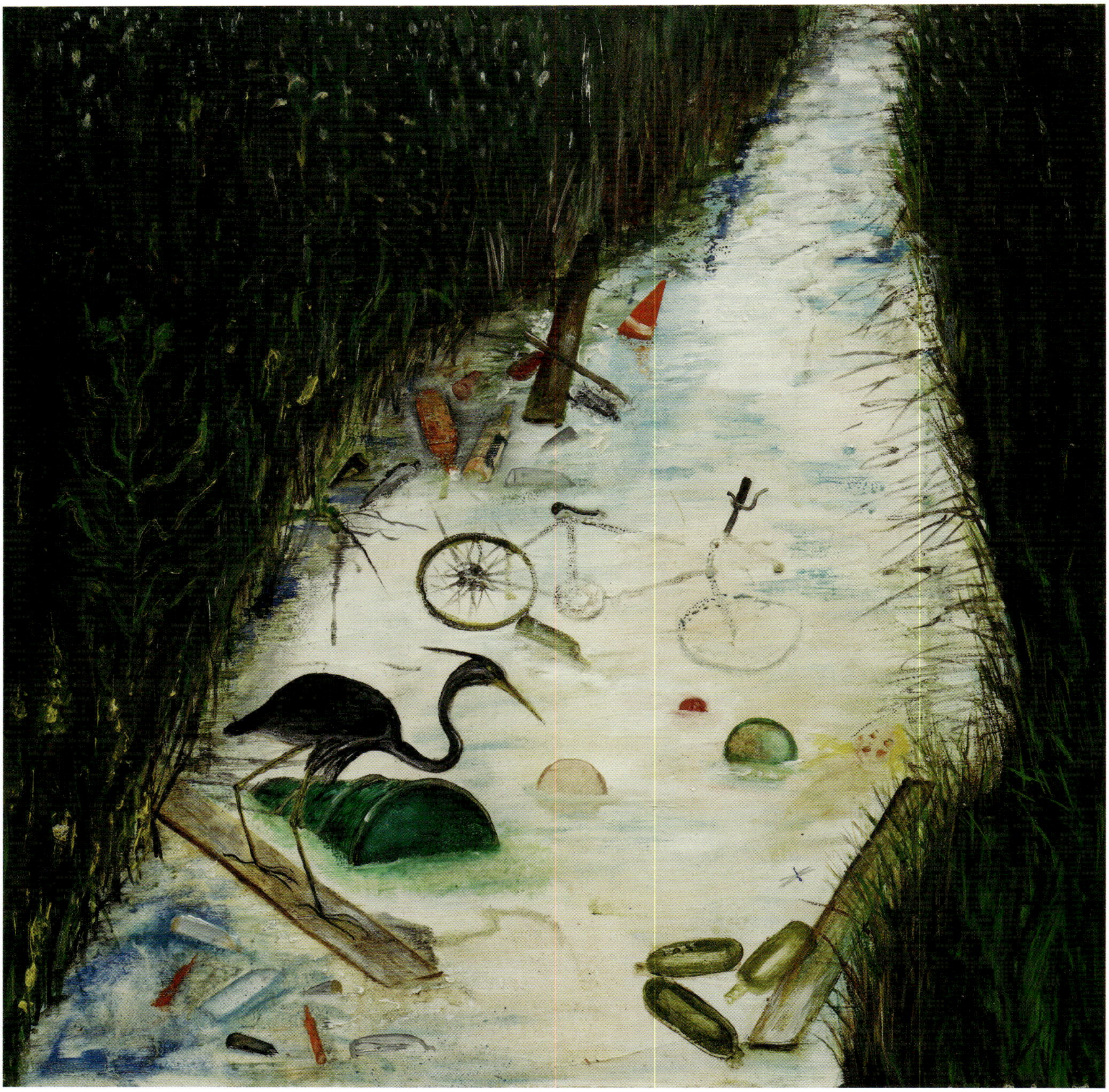

Green and Pleasant Land (An English Country Stream), 2008
Oil on wood, 55 x 55 cm

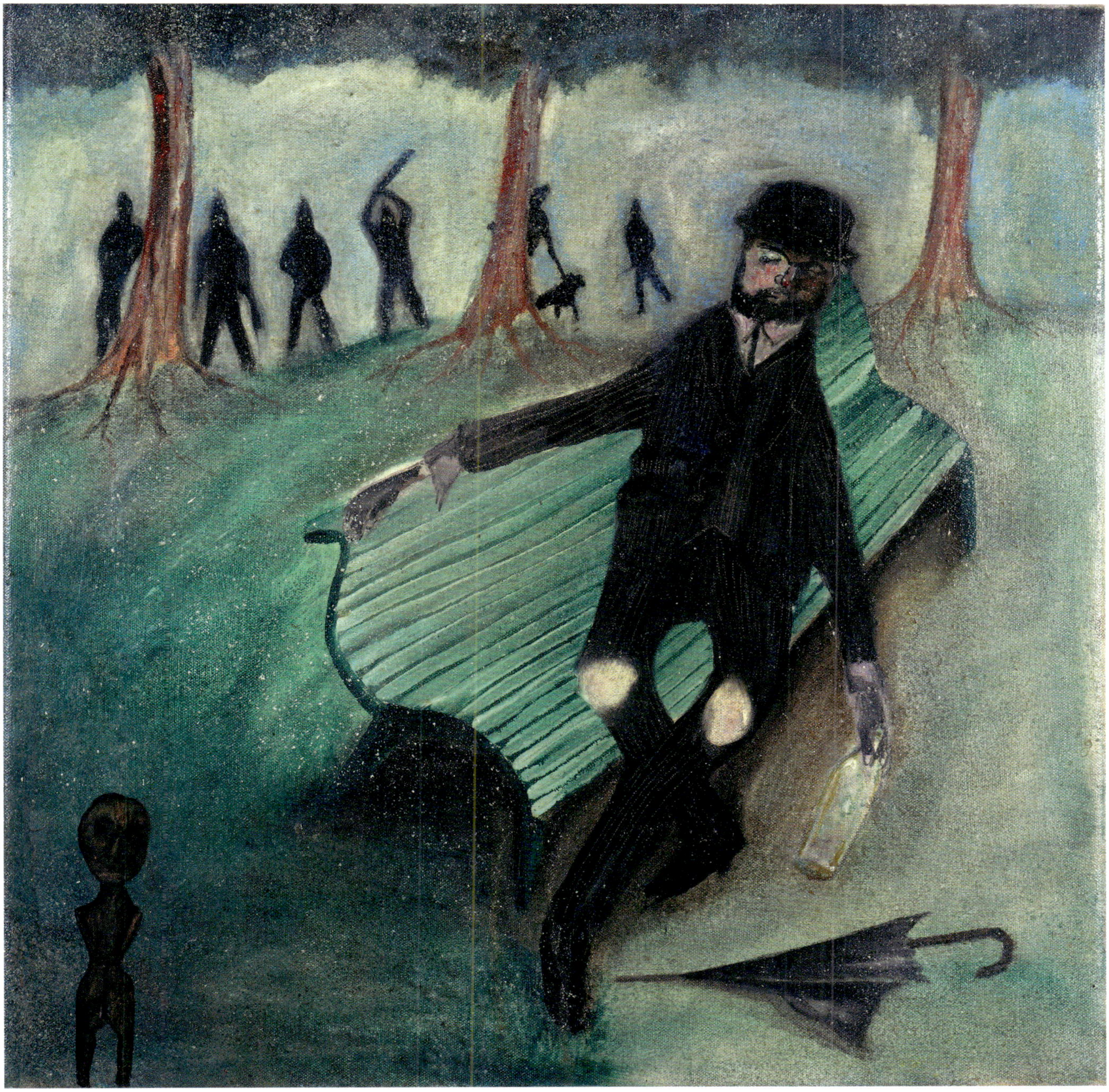

Green and Pleasant Land (In the Park), 2006
Oil on canvas, 37 x 37 cm

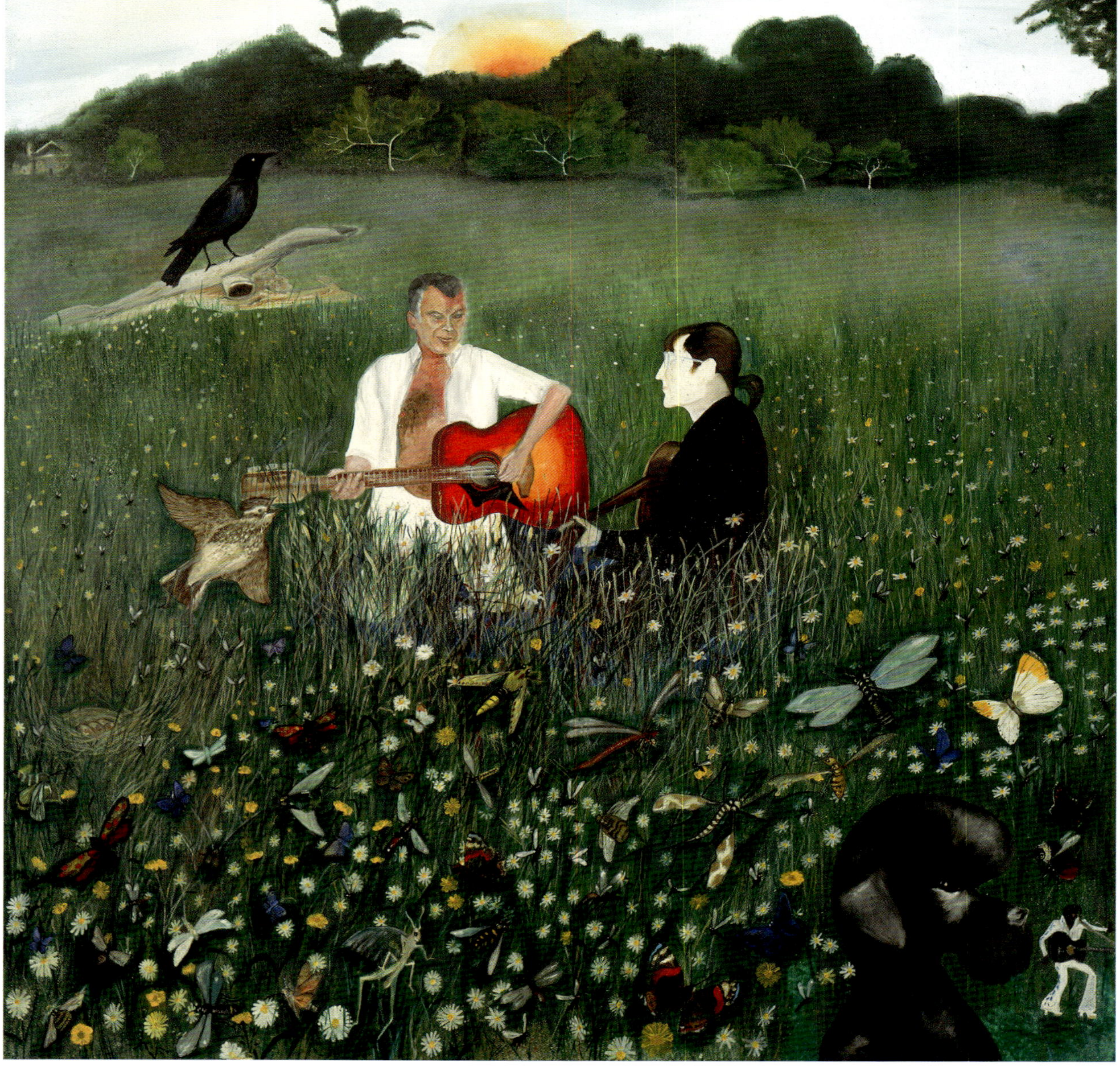

Serenade, 2006
Oil on canvas, 93 x 93 cm

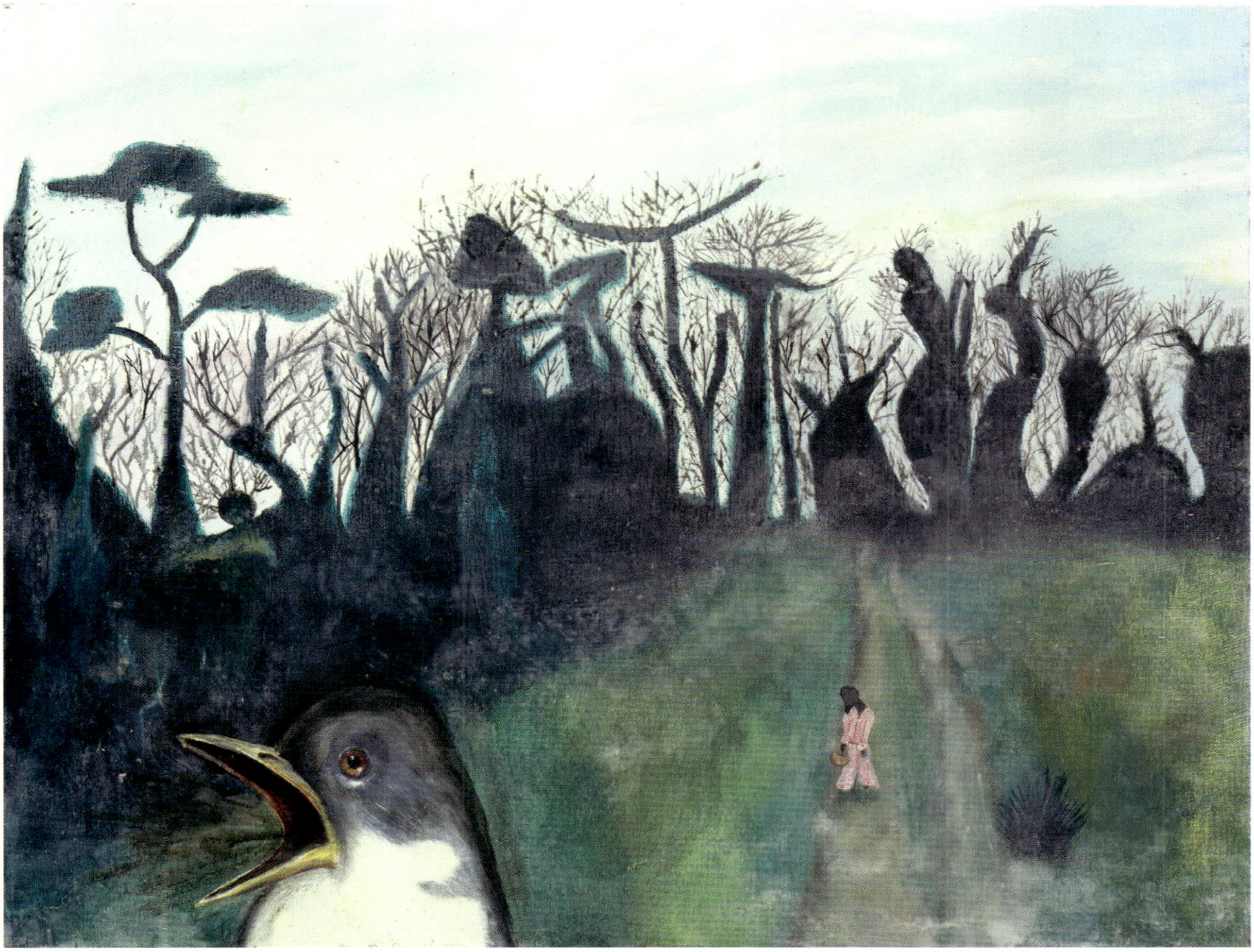

And Your Bird Can Sing, 2005
Oil on wood, 33 x 46 cm

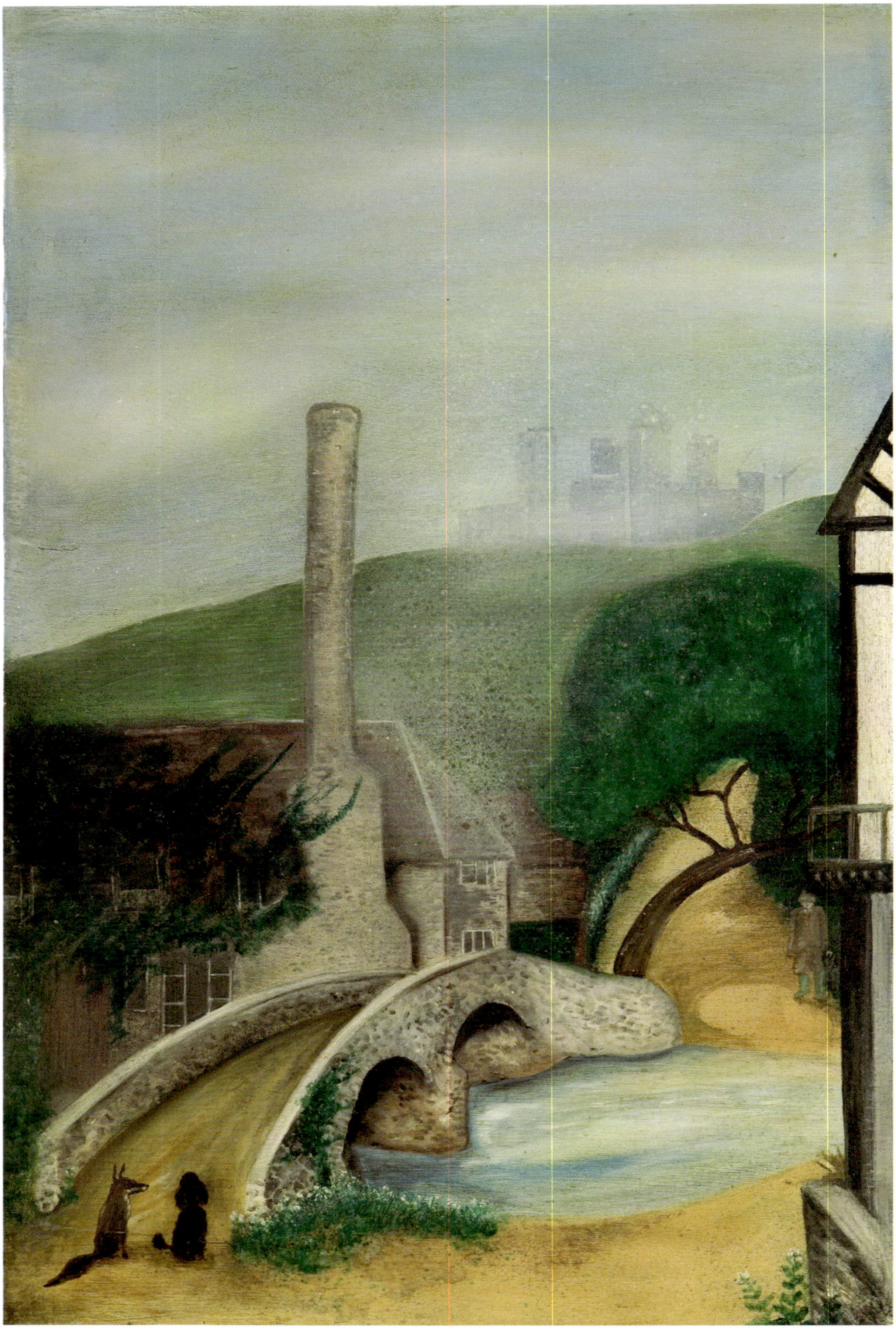

Jack by the Hedge, 2004
Oil on wood, 67.5 x 44.5 cm

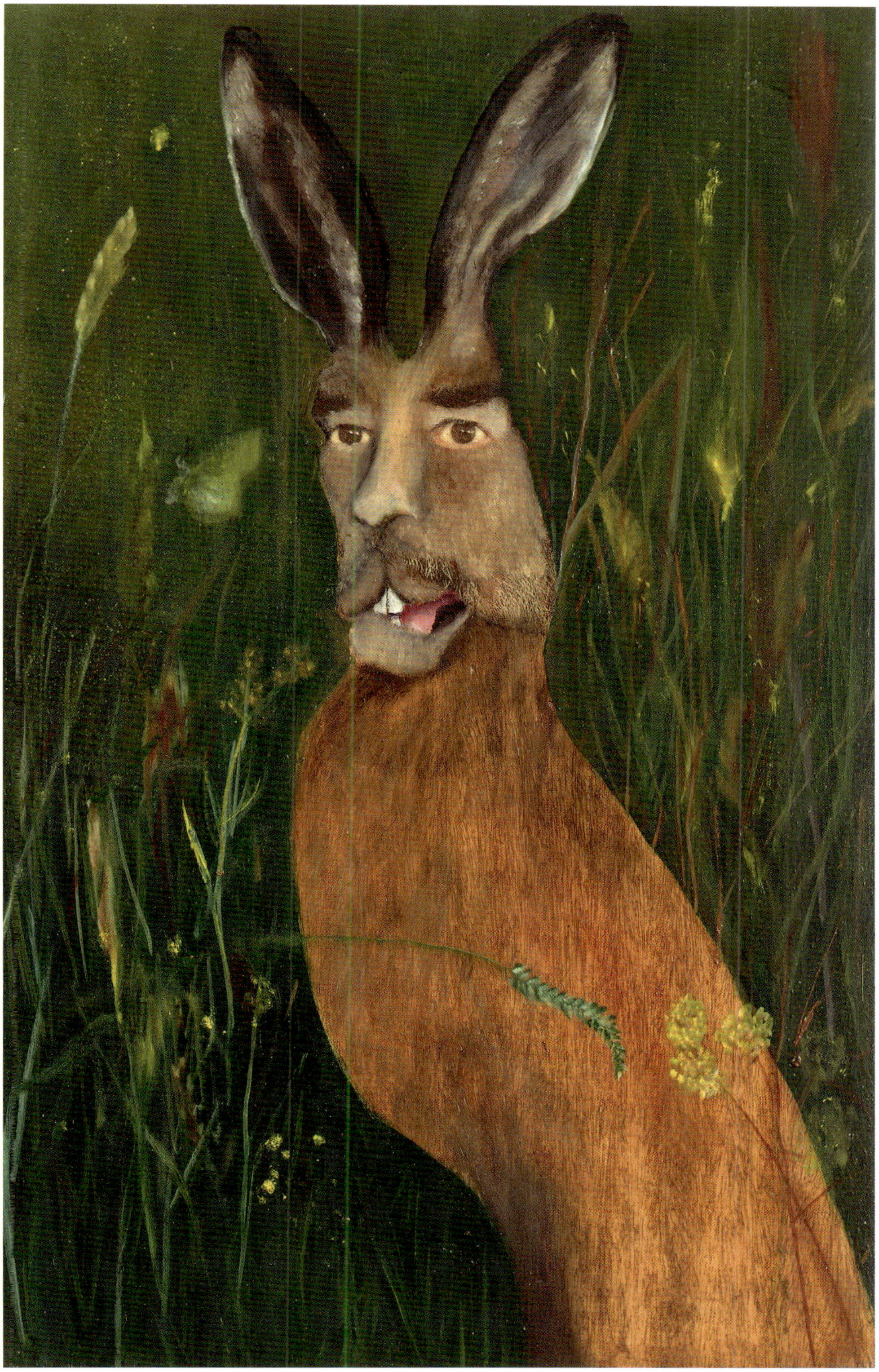

Saddam Haresain, 2004
Oil and collage on wood, 61 x 38 cm

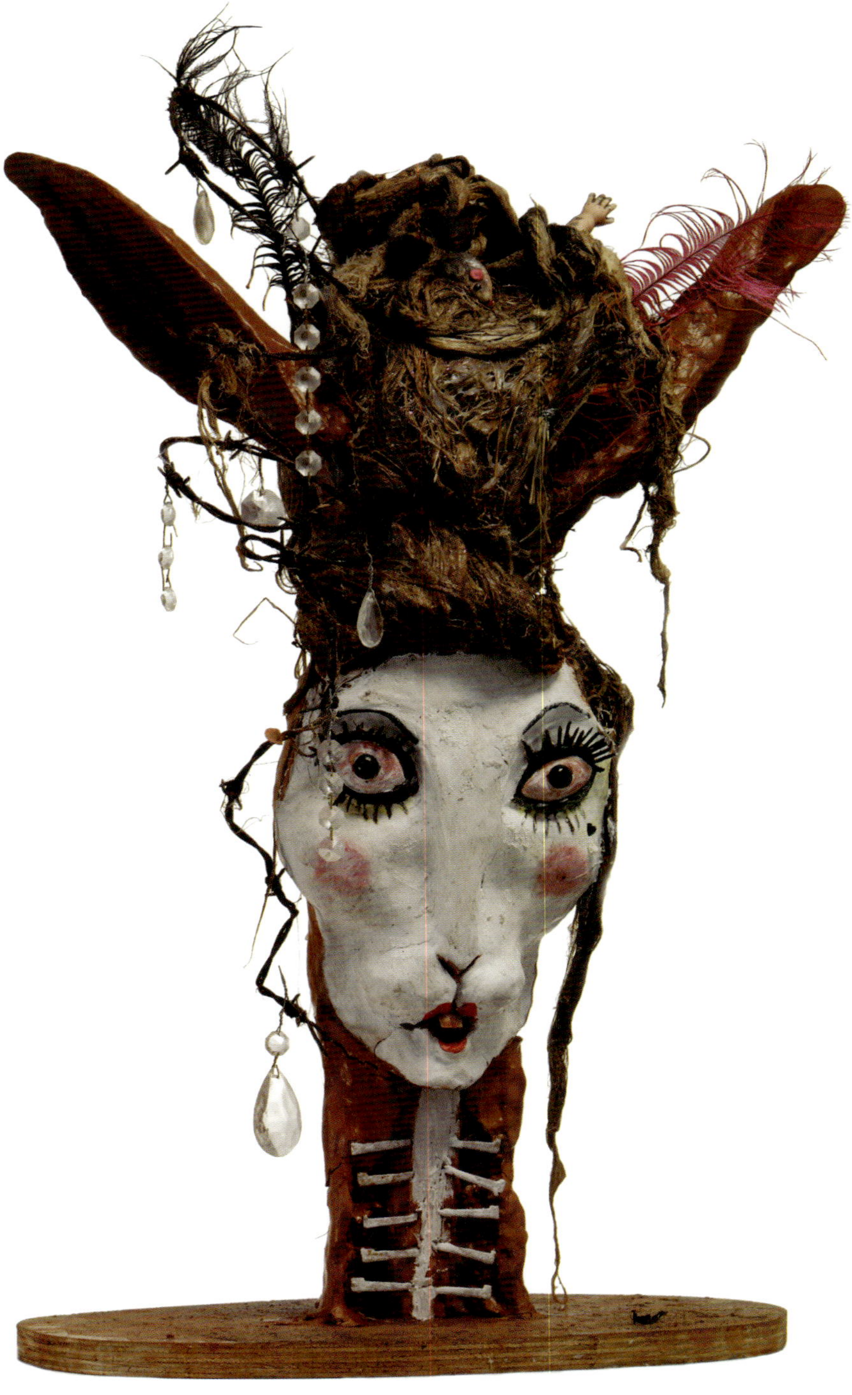

Changeling, 2008
Mixed media, 77 × 50 × 24 cm

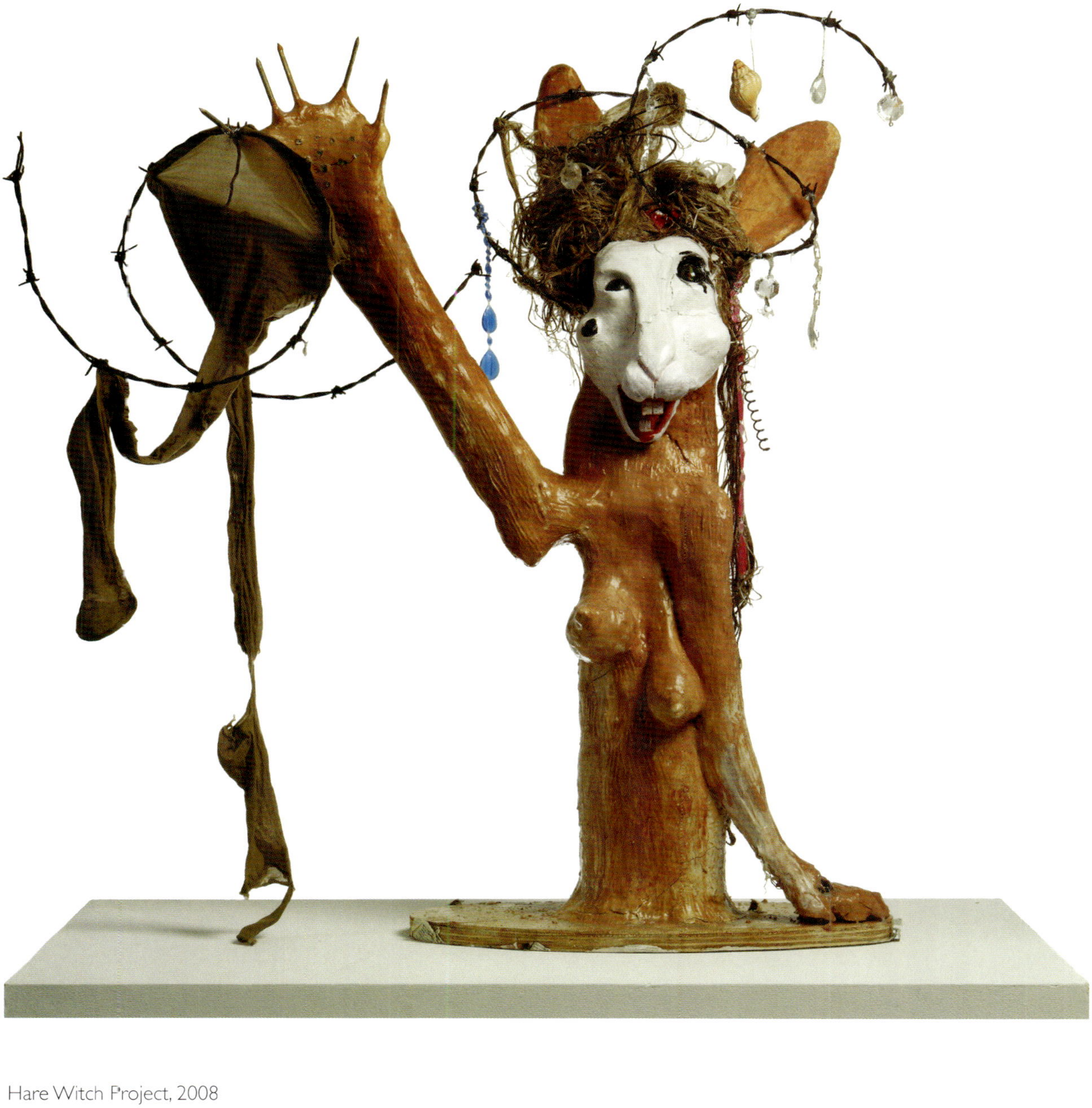

Hare Witch Project, 2008
Mixed media, 92 × 87 × 36 cm

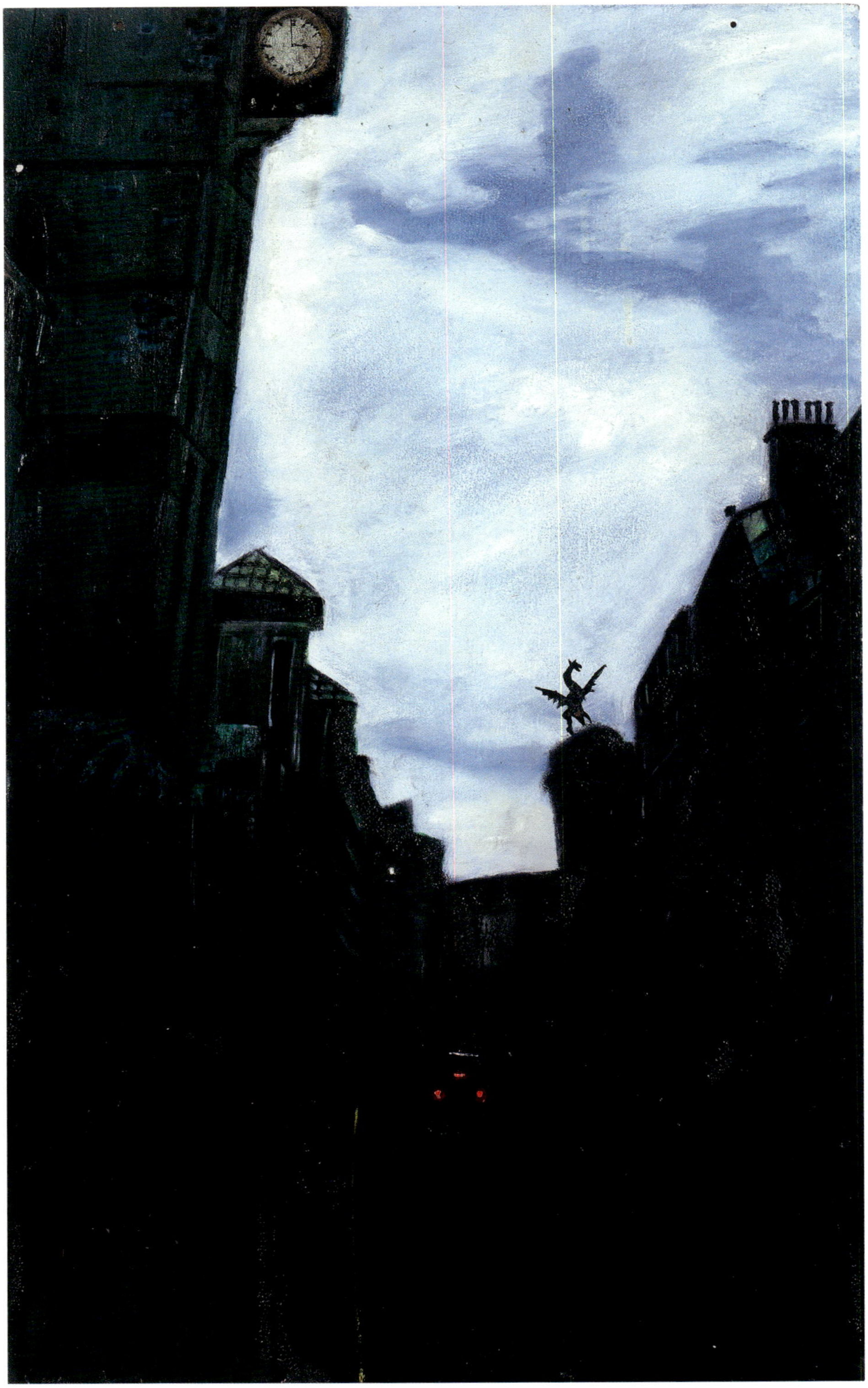

Timeless City, 2004
Oil on wood, 66 x 40 cm

Timeless City

Life in London is a game which, by definition, only a few can win.
Peter Ackroyd, *London: The Biography*

NATURE IS HARRISON'S primary concern in both art and life, yet rather than being confined to the countryside, it is also abundant within the city. If we imagine that humans control the city, it is only because other species have been squeezed into the corners humans have relinquished control over. Though Peter Ackroyd's quotation above originally referred to the competition between each of us for space and for prestige, in Harrison's world the eternal competition is between species and species, for territory and for survival.

London, as the artist's place of birth and residence, is clearly the inspiration for his cityscapes. It should be seen, though, as the space in which Harrison creates extravagant visions, just as it was for Blake, Dickens or Ackroyd. London provides the artist with the materials to transform numerous sites of memory into the settings for modern-day fables. Though recognizable sights appear, Harrison's city is an allegorical space. As the title of one of his most emblematic works – *Timeless City* (2004) – suggests, what we encounter in his work are fictionalised spaces that exist outside of ordinary chronologies. Rather than performing prosaic activities, his characters are seen acting out monstrous or wondrous desires. Harrison's tactic is to take London's characteristic features and failings, and transfigure them into the settings for his fictional, mythologised world. As well as depicting buildings possessed of architectural drama, Harrison transforms his city into a psychologically charged space, with some scenes inviting our sympathy and others seeming to behave aggressively towards us.

The area around King's Cross, which is the site of one of the finest Neogothic buildings in Britain, St Pancras Hotel, has assumed a special significance for Harrison. The area is a short walk from his studio and, at one level, offers us some insight into the harsher sides of urban life. One of the artist's early works, *King's X Boogie Woogie (*1995; overleaf) brings together Piet Mondrian's austere Modernism (based on the grid pattern layout of Manhattan) with the messier face of London. King's Cross is filled with human subjects who are objects of decay or dereliction.

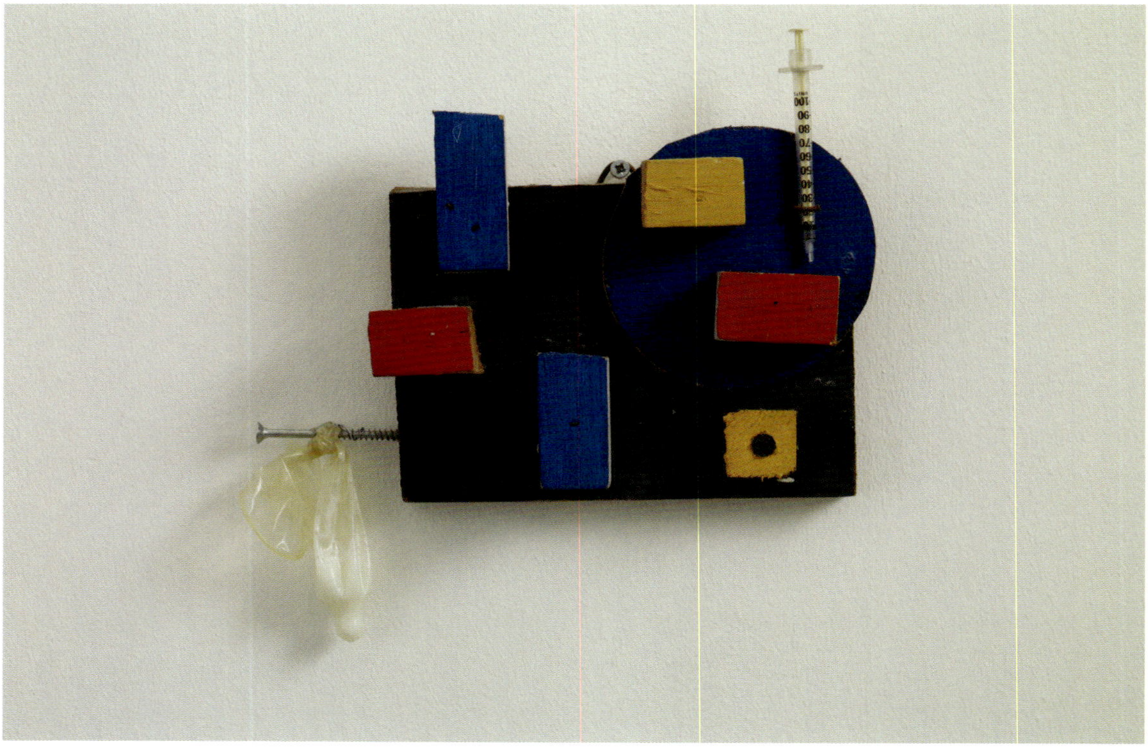

King's X Boogie Woogie, 1995
Found objects and oil on wood, 20 x 24 x 8 cm

King's Cross Fairies (1998), marked a turning point in Harrison's development, in as much as it is a canvas where real and fictional characters mingle. Both, however, have become possessed by the spirit of King's Cross. George Gilbert Scott, the architect of St Pancras Hotel (which is behind him), is here metamorphosed into a Gothic winged griffin from the façade of his own building. The creator becomes his own creation. The implication is that, for Harrison, art is a litmus test for true character. In addition, his own painting's composition is designed to pay homage to the simple, friezelike compositions of Gothic revival painting and sculpture: it is as though Harrison's own artistic idiom has become possessed by the spirit of the site too. Scott is, then, the presiding genius of the area, supervising a cast of other half-human, half-mythical figures. A drunk and horny faun lies prone on the pavement hugging a crack can: the grandeur and squalor of modern life sit cheek by jowl. However, even in

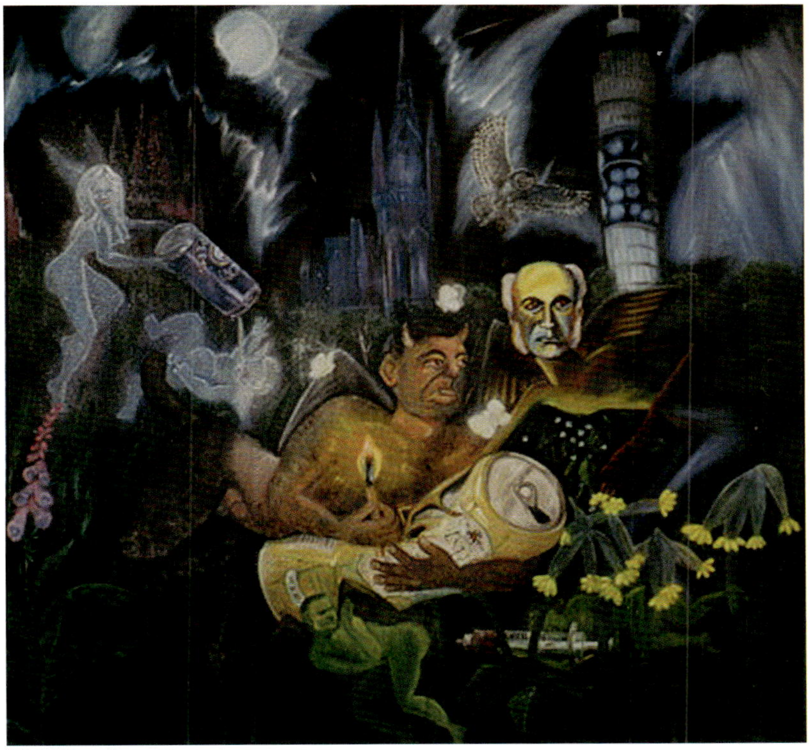

King's Cross Fairies, 1998
Oil on canvas, 152 × 183 cm

the midst of majestic architecture and half-human, half-animal casualties, nature finds a way to flourish. In the midst of the darkness, cowslips thrust upwards and outwards in every direction, signifying the first flush of spring and heralding new life. The flowers are a symbol of hope. They also intentionally confuse our sense of time: the wintry light is offset by a spring bloom. As Harrison has noted, many of his works break the idea of dramatic unity of time, and in the case of this painting, his intention was, amongst other things, to make concrete a prophecy expressed in the *Book of Zechariah* (14:6–7), where it is said 'It will happen in that day, that there will not be light, cold or frost ... but it will come to pass, that at evening time there will be light'.[1]

In several of Harrison's more complex compositions, we are pointed away from the scene immediately presented towards another time and place. His method of

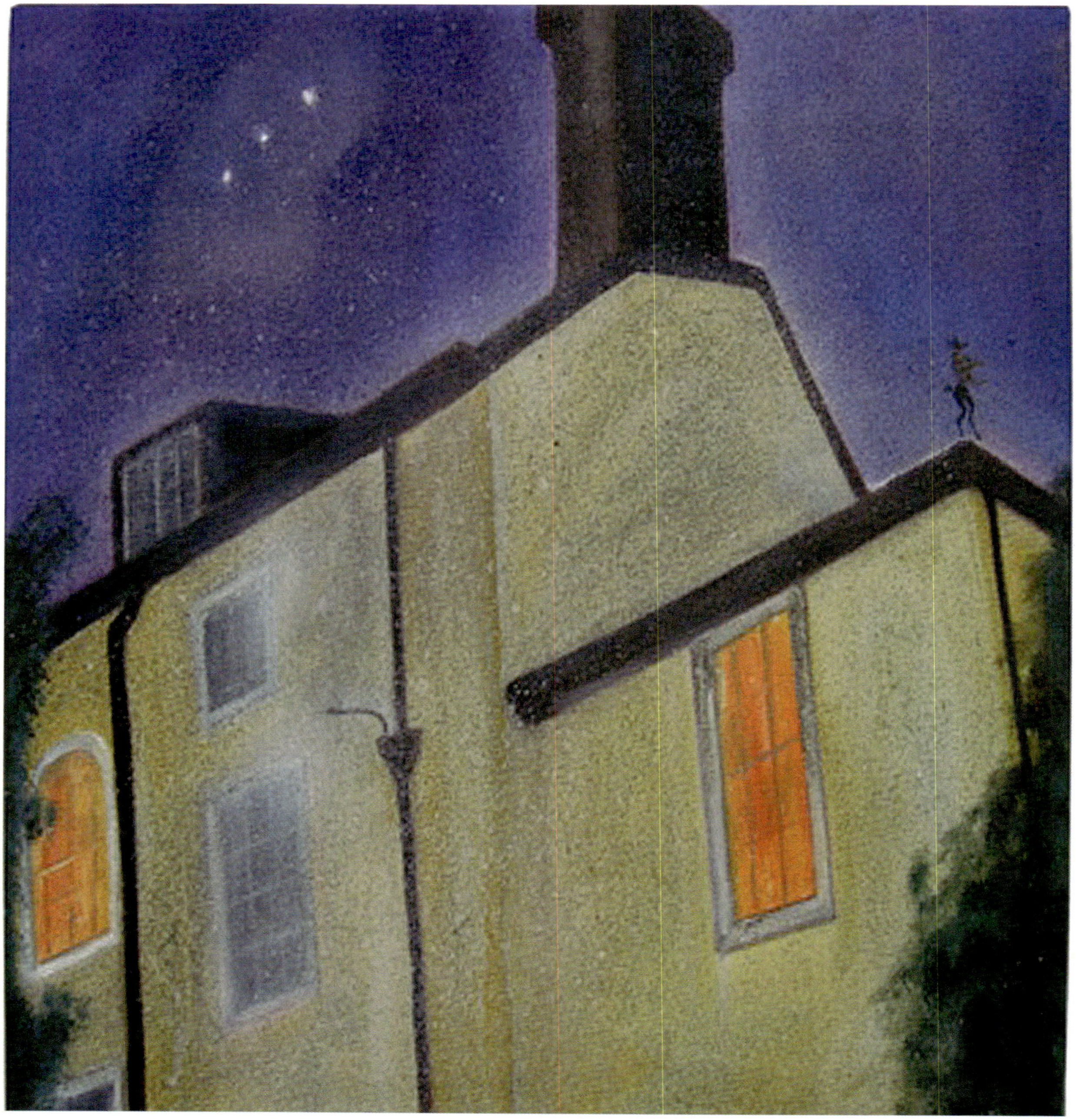

Leave the Lights On, 2006
Oil on canvas, 37 x 37 cm

interweaving the art historical, the mythical and the personal has become the principal means of making his entire imagined city magical. We might also say, however, that Harrison has progressed over the years from portraying individuals as alarming spectacles to representing the entire city as possessed of its own peculiar life-force, and that this is also a significant source of the magical air that animates many of his works. In his more recent works, every inanimate object seems possessed of *anima*, the breath of life. The very fabric of the city – the stone, clay and glass out of which it is made – seems to be rendered animate, and each building is given a distinct personality. In pagan mythology, the world is rendered animate by life-force, or spirit, emanating into all inert matter: in Harrison's recent works, each element is knitted into a whole in which animals, the built environment and human beings are possessed by a determinate force. Harrison extends the device that John Ruskin termed 'pathetic fallacy' to every class of object. *Leave the Lights On* (2006), for example, presents us with the exterior of an ordinary terraced house, but the way in which it is presented suggests not only that it is alive but also that it is aggressively hostile towards us. The scene is rendered highly emotive by Harrison's brilliant manipulation of atmosphere and perspective. We might first notice the unnatural ferocity of the orange light radiating from the windows, or else the devilish imp leaping from the roof. But only more gradually are we likely to observe how Harrison has carefully constructed the picture so that the building appears to possess an independent life, whilst at the same time remaining entirely realistic.

Leave the Lights On is an exceptional painting, and worthy of our attention for other reasons. The scene is established so that we feel akin to a predator or mischievous interloper; the unexpected corollary of this is the idea that the house is somehow retaliating. The angle it occupies defies the laws of perspective; it expands towards the roof, being largest at the point it is furthest away from us. The implication is that the house is looming over us, like an animal raising itself on its hind legs to protect its turf. It is the contrast between the ordinariness of the subject and the strangeness of its treatment that is crucial here. Two passages from Freud's essay *The Uncanny* condense many of Harrison's concerns: 'the uncanny is that species of the frightening that goes back to what was once well known and had been long familiar', and 'everything we now find "uncanny" meets the criterion that is linked with ... remnants of animistic mental activity and prompts them to express themselves.'[2]

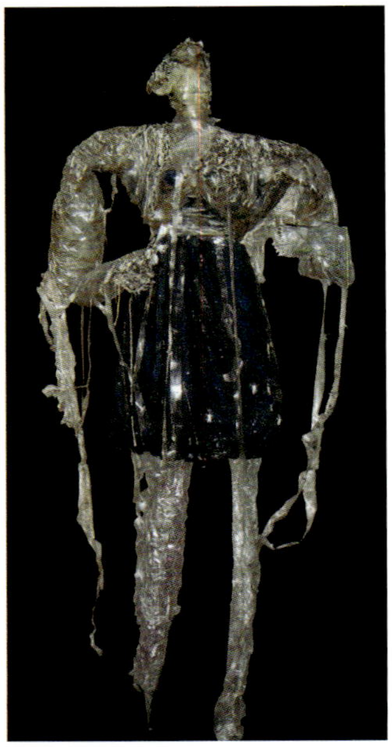

Skeletape, 2005
Found objects and sellotape,
213 x 122 x 25 cm

Harrison's sculptures similarly combine the domestic, and so the familiar, with the mythical. They adapt cheap, prosaic materials and even rubbish recovered from the street. When conjuring the textures of flesh and its decay in a work like *Skeletape* (2005), Harrison's dexterity with materials creates tension between his medium and message. *Skeletape* exemplifies how a single work can embody several ideas. It alludes to the wastefulness of consumer society, to the brevity of beauty, and to art's ability to create the illusion of life. Such density of allusion comes directly out of the artist's inventive play with materials. When new, Sellotape has all the characteristics of the cheapest type of plastic: it is shiny, crisp and physically (as well as metaphorically) tacky. Over time, its decay is almost theatrical: it becomes brittle, it yellows, and it crumples and wrinkles like flesh. Perversely, it is precisely because the work is made of something as ordinary as office stationery that it strikes us with the power of something like a votive offering from an early culture. It is like a shocking artefact from a day-of-the-dead celebration. As with his paintings, the work possesses an alarming, talismanic potency and an iconic simplicity. *Skeletape* performs the

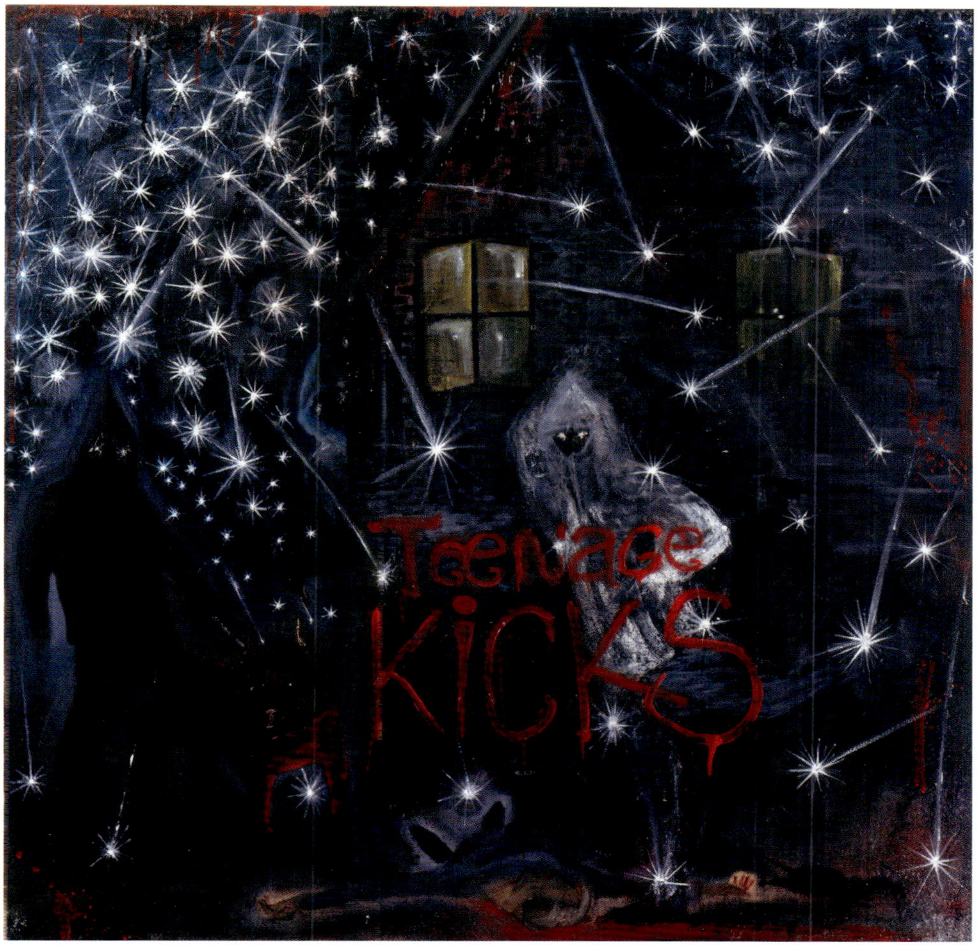

Green and Pleasant Land (Teenage Kicks), 2007
Oil on wood, 60 x 60 cm

ritual functions that primitive art forms once did. Yet despite this, the work is also about our own time. The figure adopts a pose drawn directly from fashion magazines: she is a victim of our own obsession with obsolescence. Her head is topped by rotten silk flowers – both symbols of romance and, here, of youth turned to decay. Such wilful contradictions characterize Harrison's mature style in all media: a sense of threat always accompanies wonder; charm always sits alongside dread.

Like *Skeletape*, *Green and Pleasant Land (Teenage Kicks)* (2007) evokes oppositions of all sorts. Two hooded figures are caught in the act of vandalizing the picture plane that we are

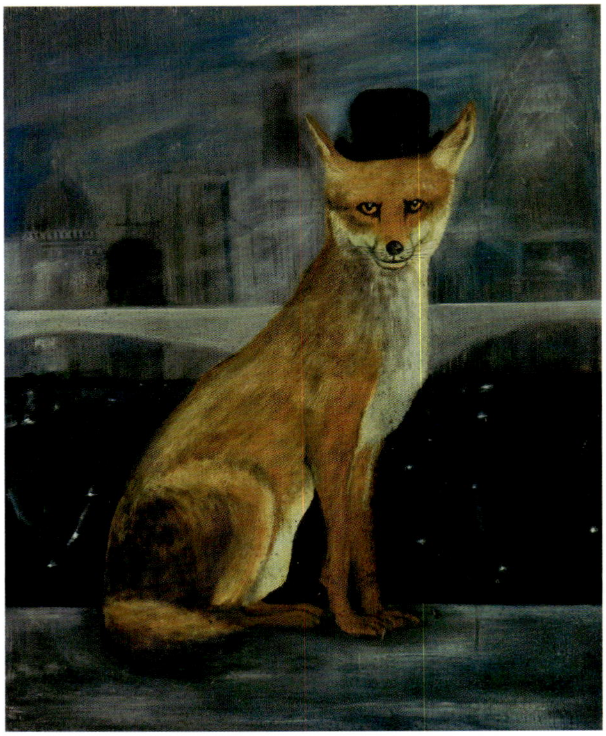

City Gent, 2005
Oil on wood, 57 x 45.5 cm

viewing: they spray graffiti out of the canvas at us. Their scrawled writing resembles fresh blood, dripping across the painting's surface. The painting exploits the idea that painting is a 'window' onto another world, with a sheet of glass separating our space from the work's illusionary one. It is as though this glass is being defiled by the figures inside the painted space as we are watching, and in so doing we become witnesses to a violent act. But it is their own space that the teenagers are desecrating: they are unable to recognize their own interests. This pictorial device also unifies the composition, acting as a 'frame' for the vortexlike composition behind. Shooting stars fly in every direction around the teenagers, though rather than being symbols of good fortune, the stars are 'violent, like bullets flying through the air', in Harrison's words.[3] Their trajectories draw our eyes in every direction, creating an atmosphere of disorder, threat and reckless energy. In the artist's words, the teenagers are

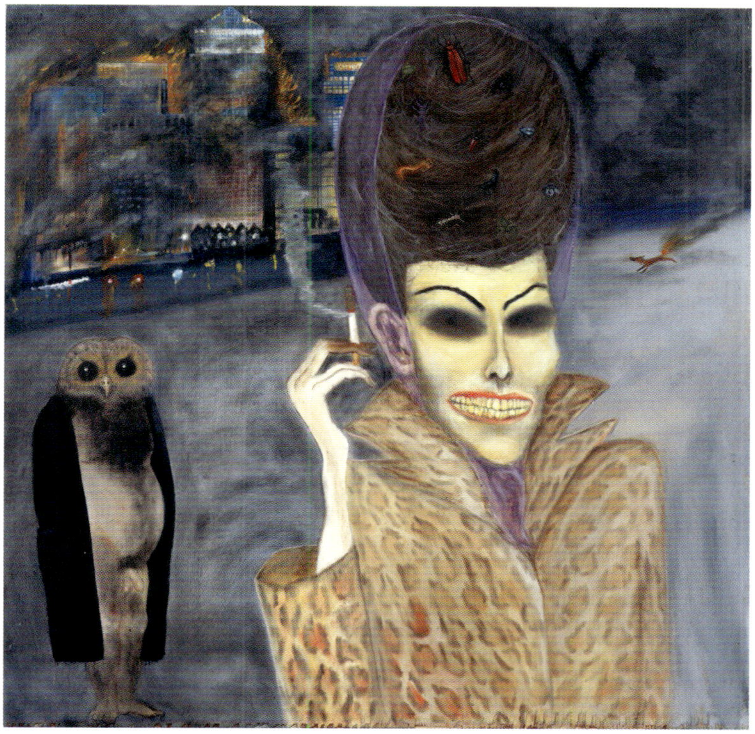

Spectre Lady, 2007
Oil on wood, 60 x 60 cm

rendered 'cartoonlike',[4] with shady forms and a lack of features. Though the title suggests the figures are teenagers, they are portrayed as evil spirits or embodiments of ill will, as bestial rather than rational beings. It is as though human violence and chaos were a perpetual threat to the order of the natural world.

Comparing Harrison's depictions of humans and animals reinforces the impression that humanity is unaware of the majesty of its environment. Harrison often reverses the roles of humans and animals in the way that Jonathan Swift did in *Gulliver's Travels*. For Harrison, as for Swift, humans are analogous to bestial Yahoos – violent, aggressive, in thrall to base instincts and ruinous of their world; animals, on the other hand, are almost analogous to Swift's Houyhnhnms – wise, dignified and able to invite our imaginative empathy.[5] The works *City Gent* (2005) and *Spectre Lady* (2007), illustrate these dramatic distinctions. *City Gent,* is almost a portrait of an urban fox, a treatment that Harrison rarely extends to his human subjects. Whereas the adolescents seeking thrills in *Green and Pleasant Land (Teenage Kicks)* are ill defined, the city gent is sharply individualized. Similarly, in *Spectre Lady* there is an improbable metamorphosis between animal and human. Whilst the spectre lady is rendered inhuman by her lack of eye sockets, her naked companion has an owl's head, transforming him into a harbinger of doom, as well as a symbol of wisdom. His appearance, akin to that of a character from an Hieroynmous Bosch, compliments the flame-scarred scene behind them. It is as though nature were taking revenge on man for his stupidity. This is also suggested by the lady's hollowed-out head, which has become a habitat for insects: her beehive hairstyle has become infested. Even in the city, nature abhors a vacuum.

If *Spectre Lady* is dark in tone, its companion piece, *Spectre Lady at Home* (2007), is positively macabre. Just as in *Pan Has Risen*, the floor sweeps out towards us, skewing the laws of perspective so that we are immediately enveloped into the scene. Again, the lady is oblivious to the nightmarish cityscape beyond, here revealed in her window. Behind her, 30 St Mary's Axe is engulfed in flames, as though it were under attack, though the perpetrators are not identified. This is an almost apocalyptic vision. Inside, her flat is filled with an unnerving and unnatural atmosphere. Through his masterful handling of colour and texture, Harrison conjures an ambience filled with dread. Hot and cold colours sit in immediate proximity: an old television emits a shrill blue light that seeps across the floor of the room like an escaping gas; on the right, an electric fire is hellish red, leaking liquid vermilion. In between, the lady's walls are rendered in off-colour versions ofVictorian bottle green and Georgian baby blue. By rights, both colours should confer dignity, but here they shroud the space in an oppressive gloom. The impression is of an unearthly or deathly space, in which the presence of life itself is jarring. One further idea defines *Spectre Lady at Home*: that of the confusion of dates and times of day. This is also a preoccupation running through Harrison's paintings of the city. In *Spectre Lady at Home*, most aspects of the lady's furniture and costume are datable to the 1950s, though Norman Foster's Gherkin sets the scene in the present. The contrast is between postwar austerity and brash, millennial architecture. The two periods evoked should be read as historical parantheses encompassing the artist's own lifetime: the painting is about the city's biography during the second half of the twentieth century.

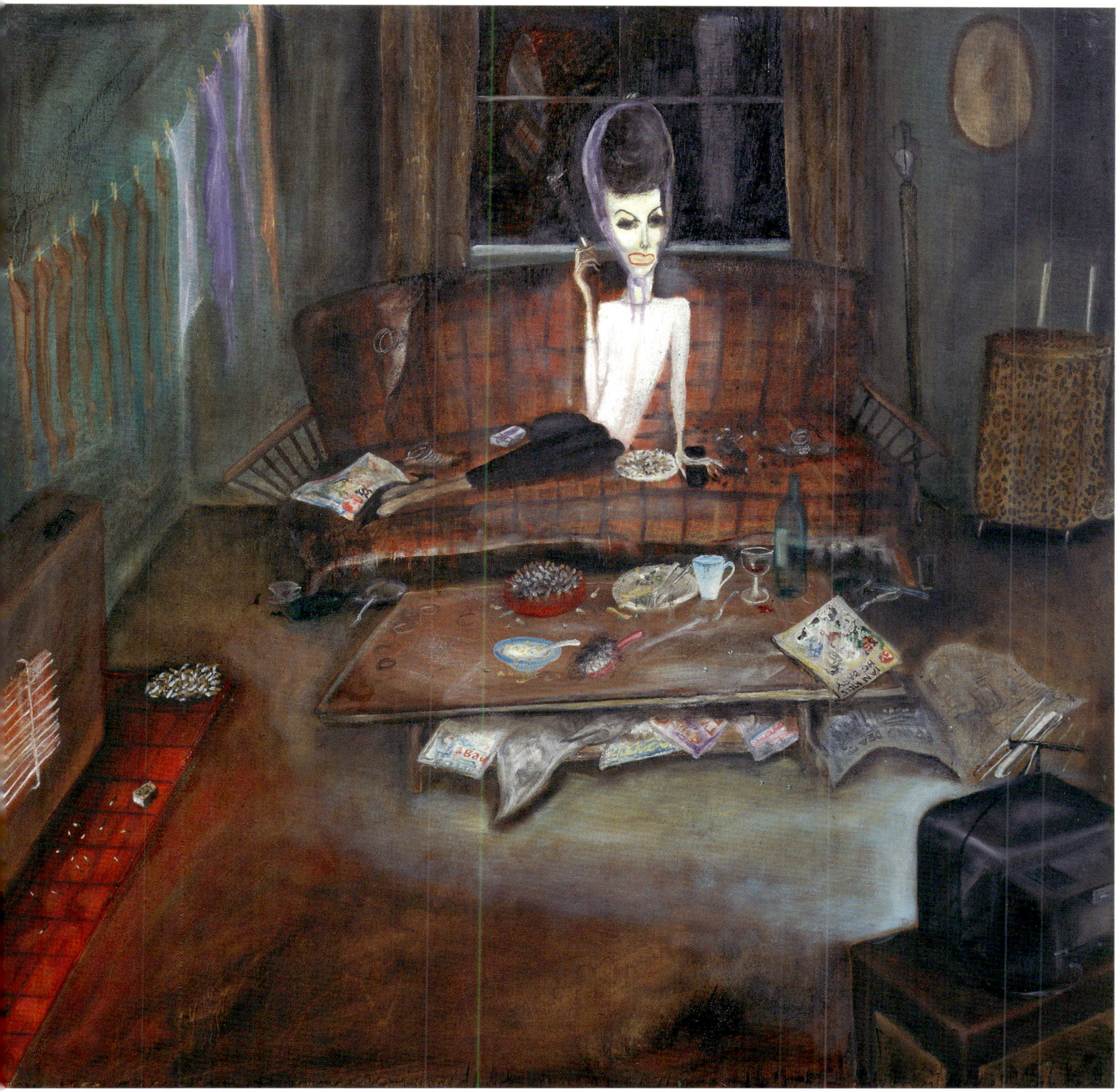

pectre Lady at Home, 2007
Dil on wood, 60 × 60 cm

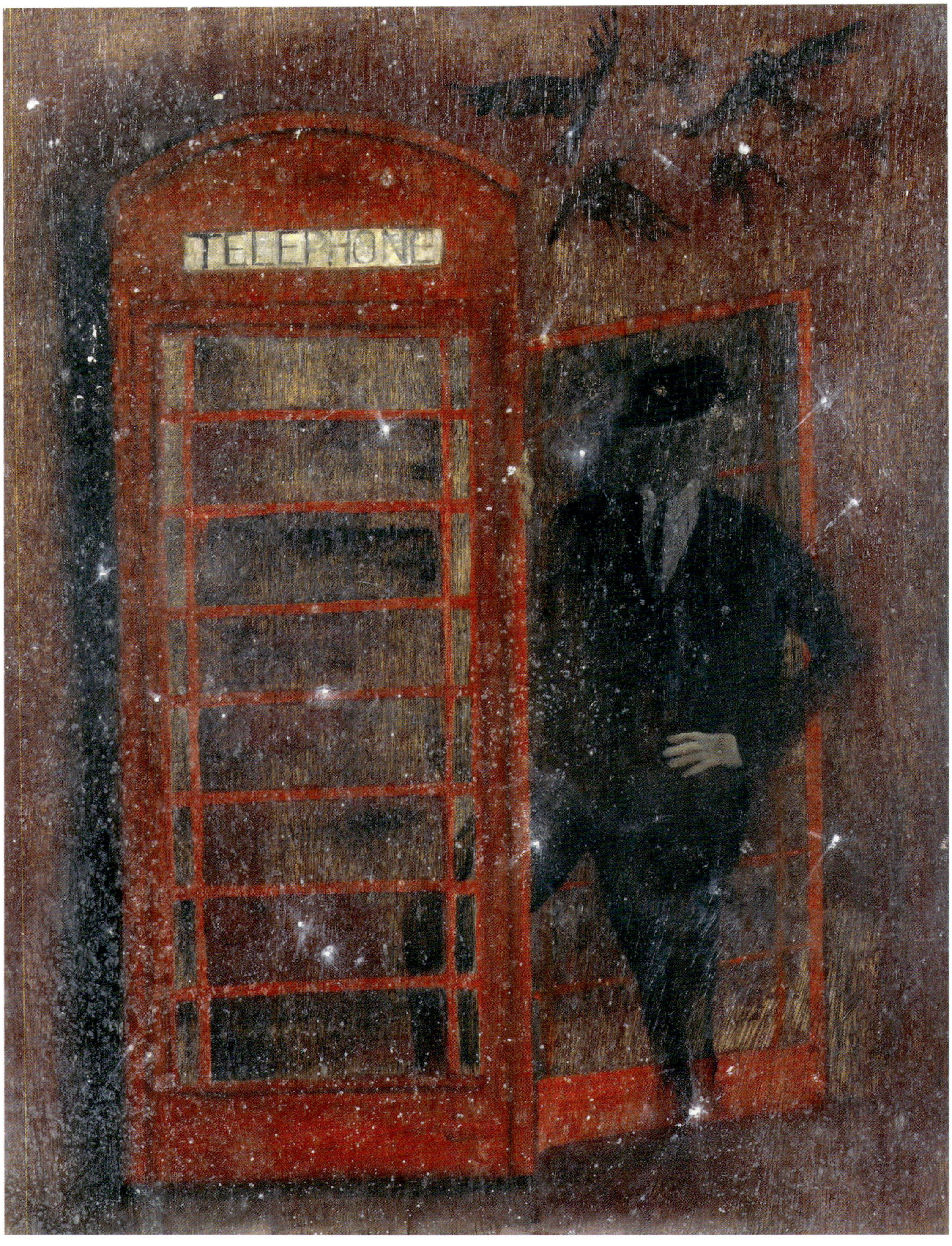

Disappearing Worlds, 2004
Oil on wood, 41 × 30 cm

Harrison's images of urban life grow out of a lifelong appreciation and affection for the architecture of Victorian, Edwardian and interwar Britain. The great achievements of these eras, like Scott's St Pancras Hotel, provide the settings for many of his works. Harrison's love of prewar architecture is also inferable from some of the more modest but equally iconic structures that populate his iconography. The red K6 telephone box, designed in 1936, is the central motif for one of the artist's smallest but most poignant works, *Disappearing Worlds* (2004). This image in particular is an elegy for a world we have lost: a world of beautifully crafted, individualized buildings and grand, elegant public spaces. Though *Disappearing Worlds* is not set at a fixed point in time, the man's costume is, arguably, from the 1960s, the time of Harrison's childhood. The generosity and grandeur of our ancestors' world is evaporating in front of us.

Timeless City (p. 56) is another painting that confuses both dates and times of day. Most obviously, the painting borrows Magritte's technique of representing a daytime sky over a nocturnal cityscape.[6] The top half of the image is bright blue, the lower half set in darkness, punctuated only by a taxi's red rear lights. The taxi functions to set the scene somewhere near the present; without it, the vista could be dated to any point in the last hundred years. Only a single dragon – guardian of the city of London – provides another focal point. Here, Harrison shows us the city as a stage set, in which each building and sculpture is an actor. *Timeless City* points us towards the conclusion that the city is far from simply a place of tawdry pleasures and degradation. Harrison's imagined city also contains moments of beauty, serenity and drama. These moments, however, are mostly seen in the absence of humans. Indeed, the best of the city is often seen in its sculptures, or spaces that are stilled and exude a chilly, or chaste, grandeur; it is seen in parts characterized by heroic geometries and the dignity of order.

Harrison's *Isokon Building* (1999), which depicts Wells Coates's Modernist block of flats, illustrates these ideas. For Harrison, drama and theatricality are the determining principles of all powerful design and art alike, and the Isokon building embodies both. The painting reveals the artist's mastery of creating atmosphere through the subtle play of light and colour. Initially, Harrison's admiration for the building is obvious. The perspective chosen echoes those used by Modernist photographers who celebrated the beauty of the machine age. Seen from below, the building's staircases thrust upwards with a dynamic force. The building is seen as a heroic, monumental sculpture, and yet, paradoxically, as

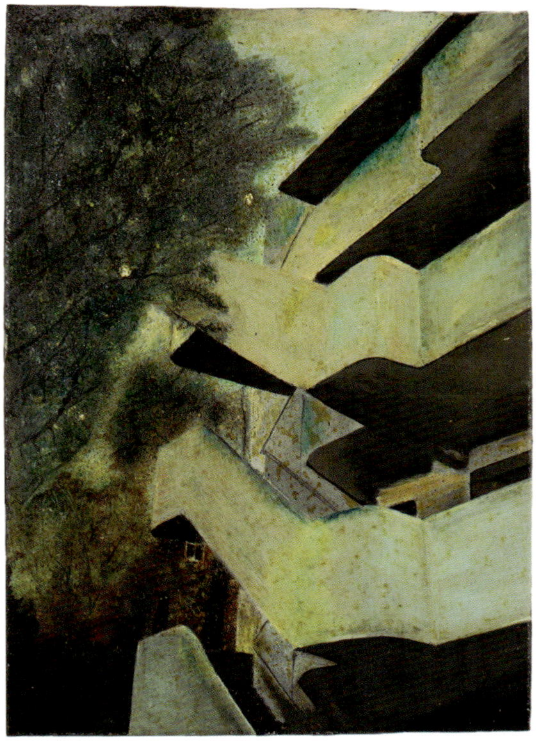

Isokon Building, 1999
Oil on wood, 43 x 33 cm

possessed of those very qualities that Winckelmann attributed to the best of classical art: 'noble simplicity and calm grandeur'.[7] Harrison's world here aspires to an ideal where the historical and modern are as one. It is perhaps for this reason that, whilst the artist captures the sculptural magnificence of the building – conveying its weight, mass and volume – he also suggests it is strangely outside of time. The structure is seen in what is both a convincingly natural and yet fantastical half-light. The sky is suggestive of a cool spring morning, but the trees appear to radiate the heat of a midday sun, and the staircases are seen in a raking evening light, albeit one with sharp lemon highlights and blue shadows. It is as though the building were a ghostlike object, outside of its expected time and place, and without human inhabitants. Harrison's Romanticism is, then, some way from Coates's Modernism.

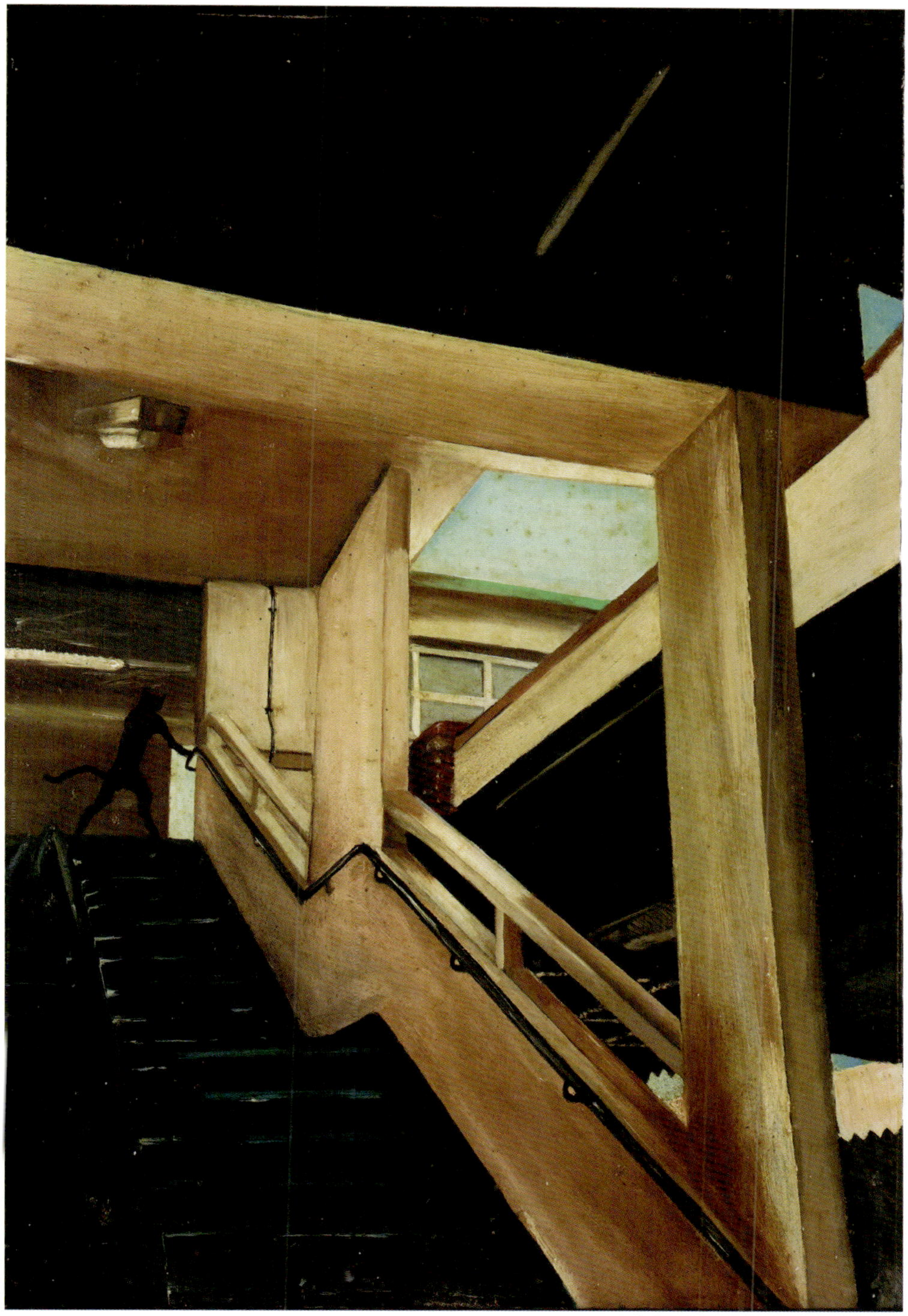

Station Staircase, 1999
Oil on wood, 43 x 33 cm

Other works have recapitulated these themes in other keys. *Station Staircase* (1999), for example, reveals a public space charged with menace as well as grace. Such a work reiterates the sense that London is the home of dark spirits, which only a few of us can ever sense. The artist underlines this by picturing such a spirit in one of London's finer achievements: an underground station of the late 1940s. Even within clean, rational Modernist forms, we are haunted by spirits keen to regain their territory. A catlike spirit inhabits this station, itself smothered in a sickly, green fluorescent light even when the midday sun is out. Magritte's device of throwing the buildings of a cityscape into night-light is here used to new ends. Even in the finest parts of England, there are reasons to be fearful: as our senses are dulled, we cannot register how enchanted our cityscape is.

For Harrison, as for Peter Ackroyd, London is a city where the past is eternally played out, despite material changes. The settings of *Timeless City* and *Station Staircase* are a London of the imagination, deliberately outside of time, yet they nevertheless both conjure an evocative sense of place. Indeed, we might well use the words of J.K. Huysmans, describing the activities of the antihero Des Esseintes in his novel *Against Nature*, of Harrison himself: he 'seek[s] out evocative works which would transport him to some unfamiliar world and point the way to new possibilities, shaking up his nervous system by means of erudite fancies, complicated nightmares and sinister visions ... [his works are] ardent aspirations towards an ideal, towards a distant beatitude'.[8] Even though Harrison's imaginary city is unfamiliar, complicated and sinister, it is a place in which we are all invited to share.

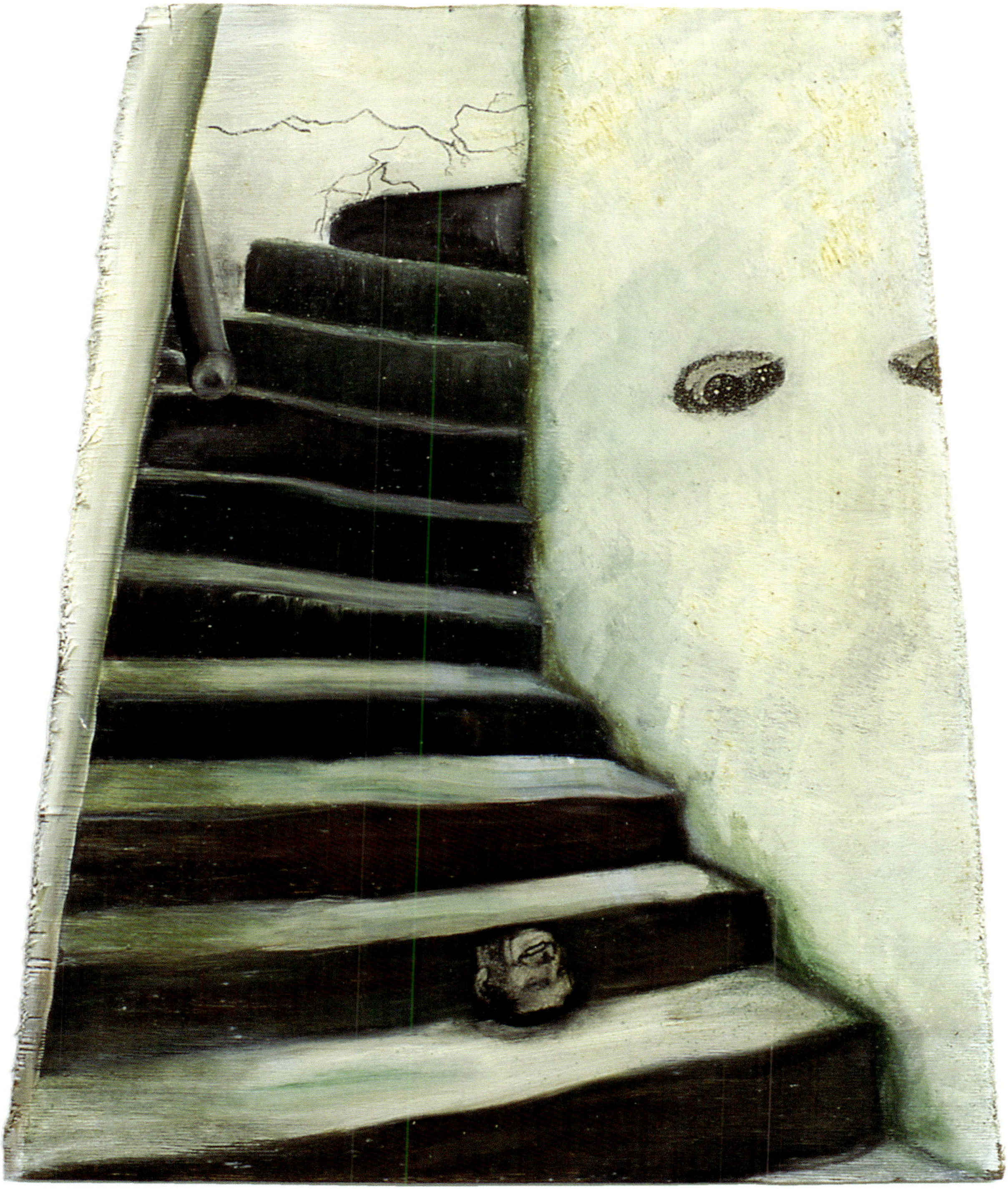

Haunted Stairwell, 1999
Oil and collage on wood, 55 x 40 cm

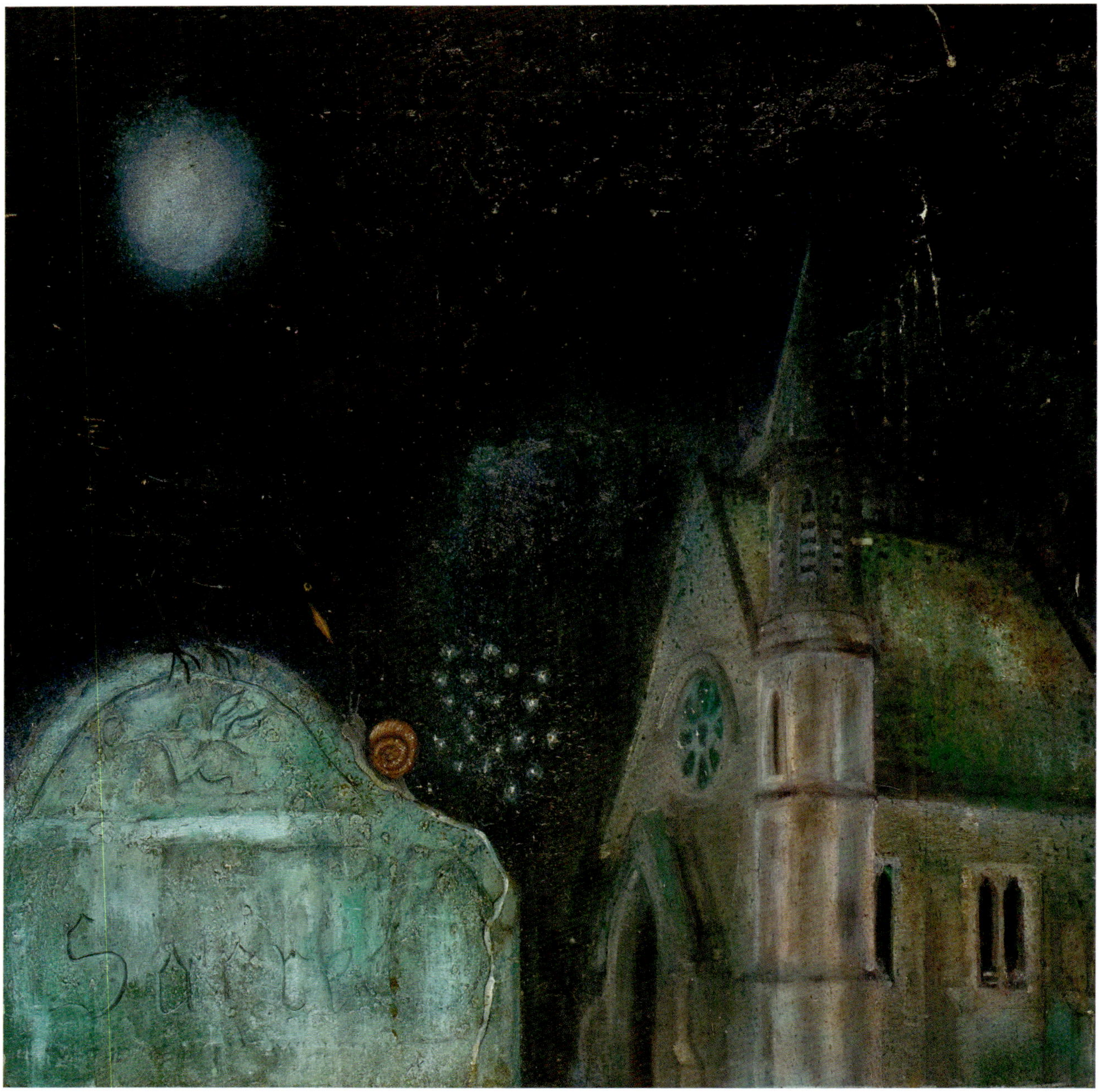

Sacred, 1998
Oil on wood, 45.5 x 52 cm

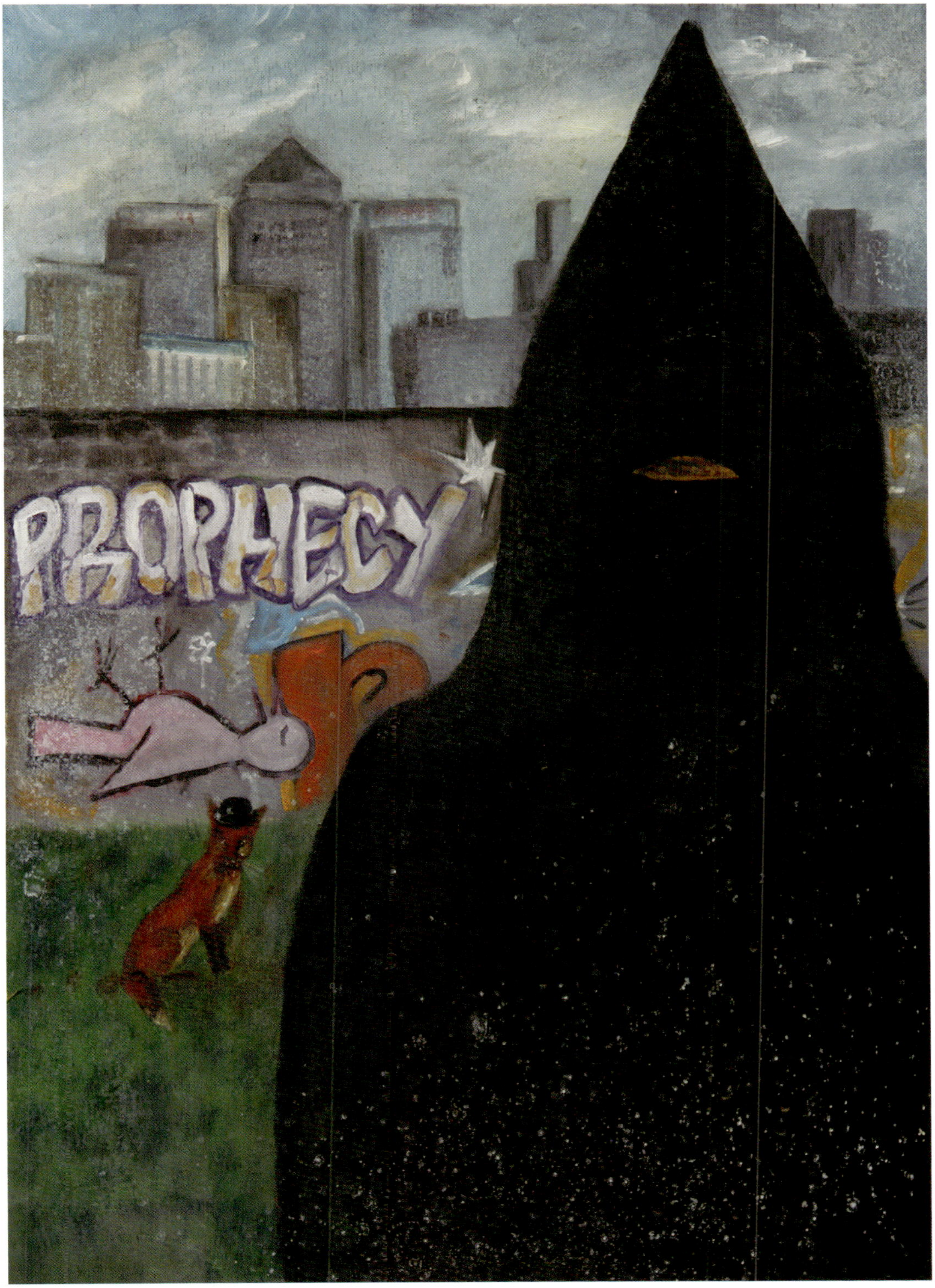

Prophecy, 2006
Oil on wood, 43 x 31 cm

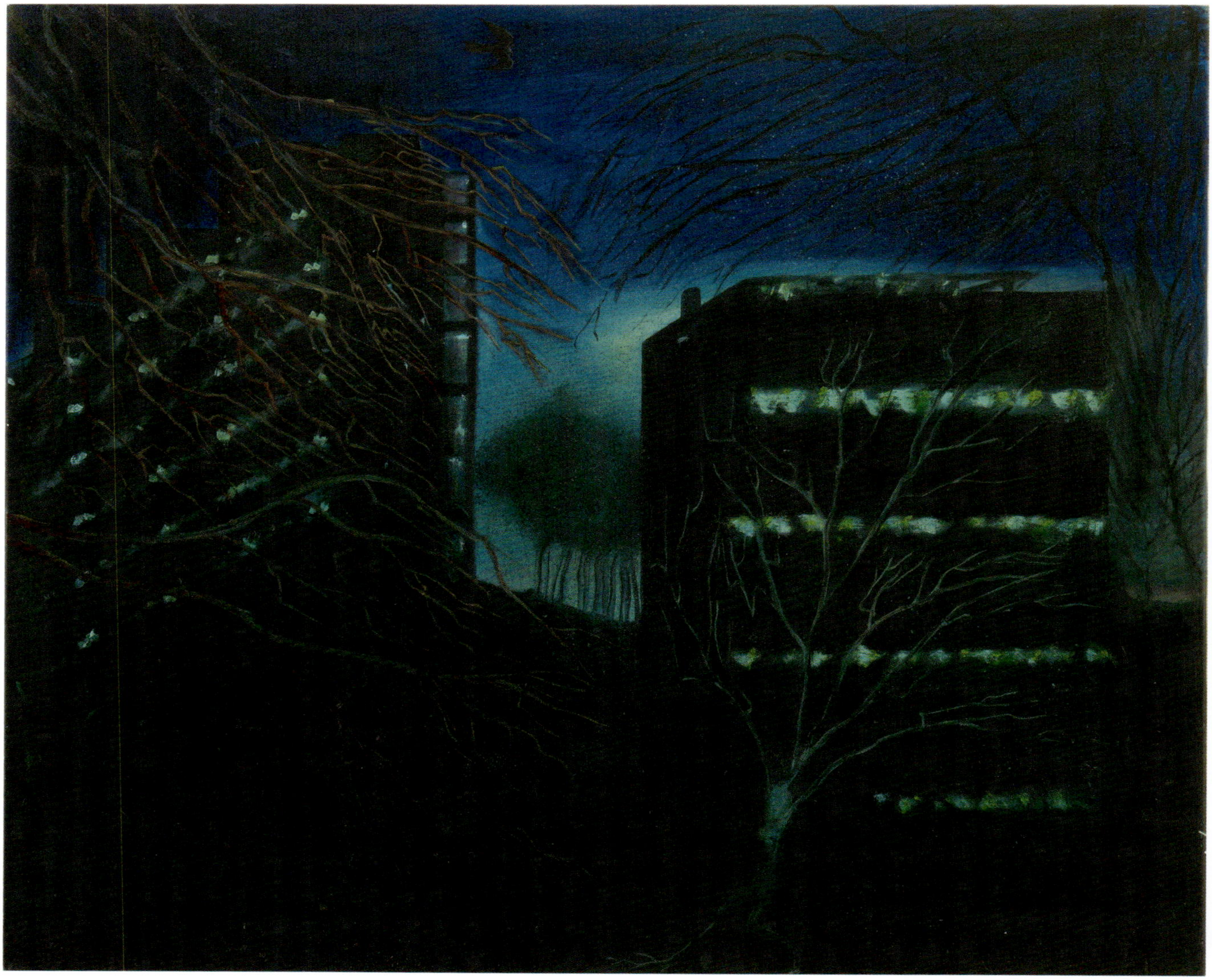

Daphne Chaste, 2000
Oil on canvas, 76 × 92 cm

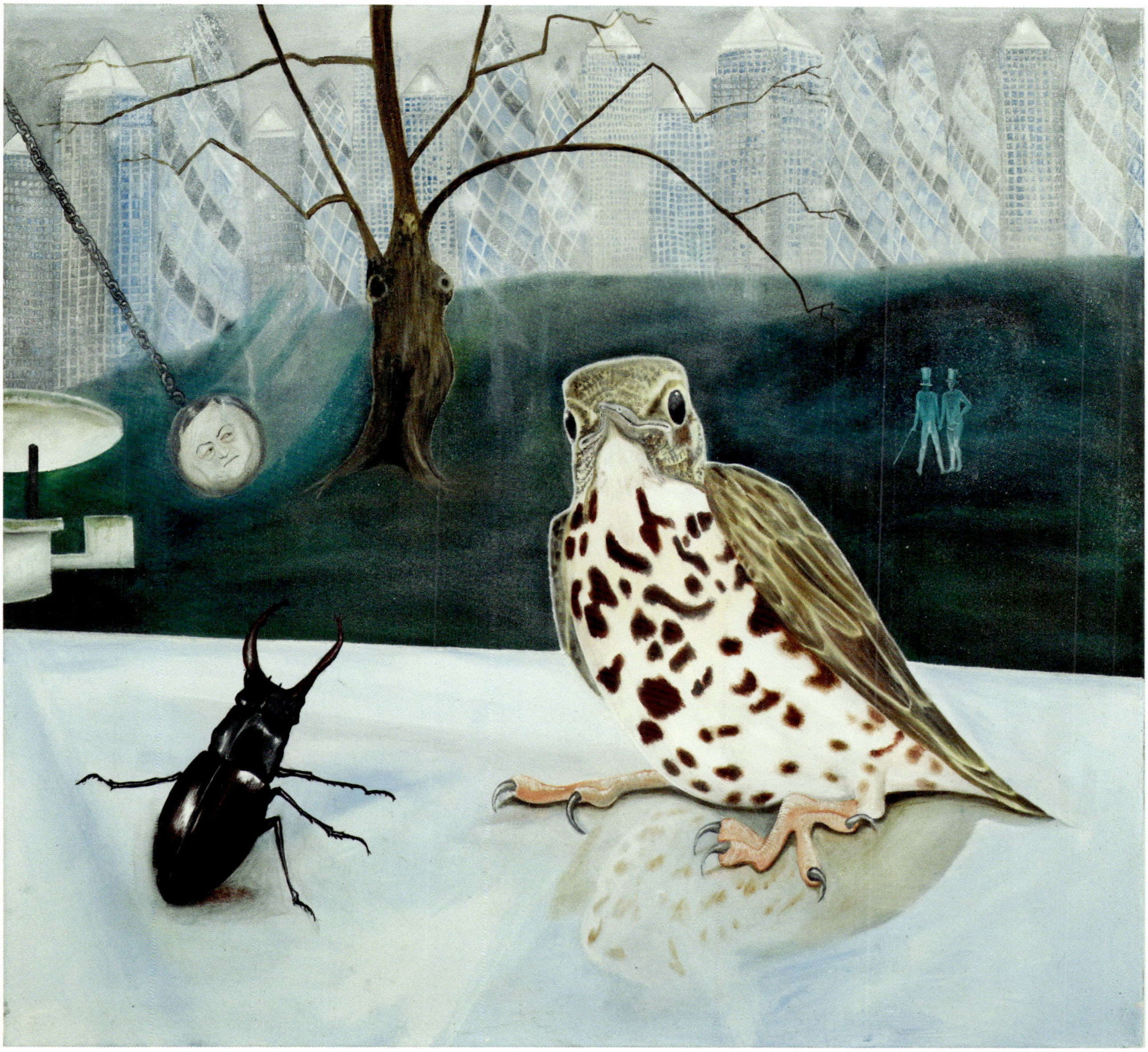

Farewell My Lovely, 2005
Oil on canvas, 76 x 91 cm

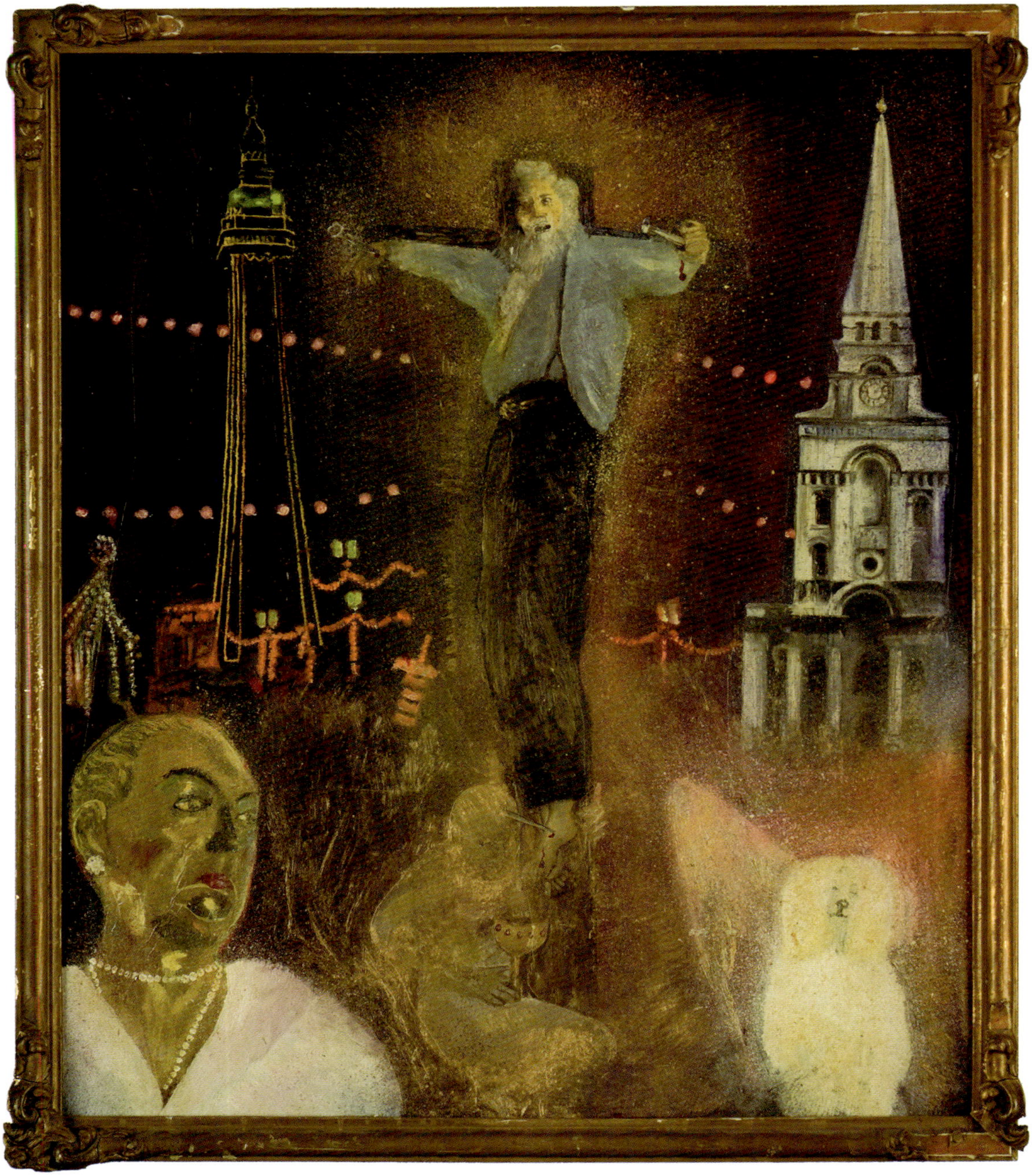

Hawksmoor in Drag, 1999
Oil and collage on wood, 64 x 54 cm

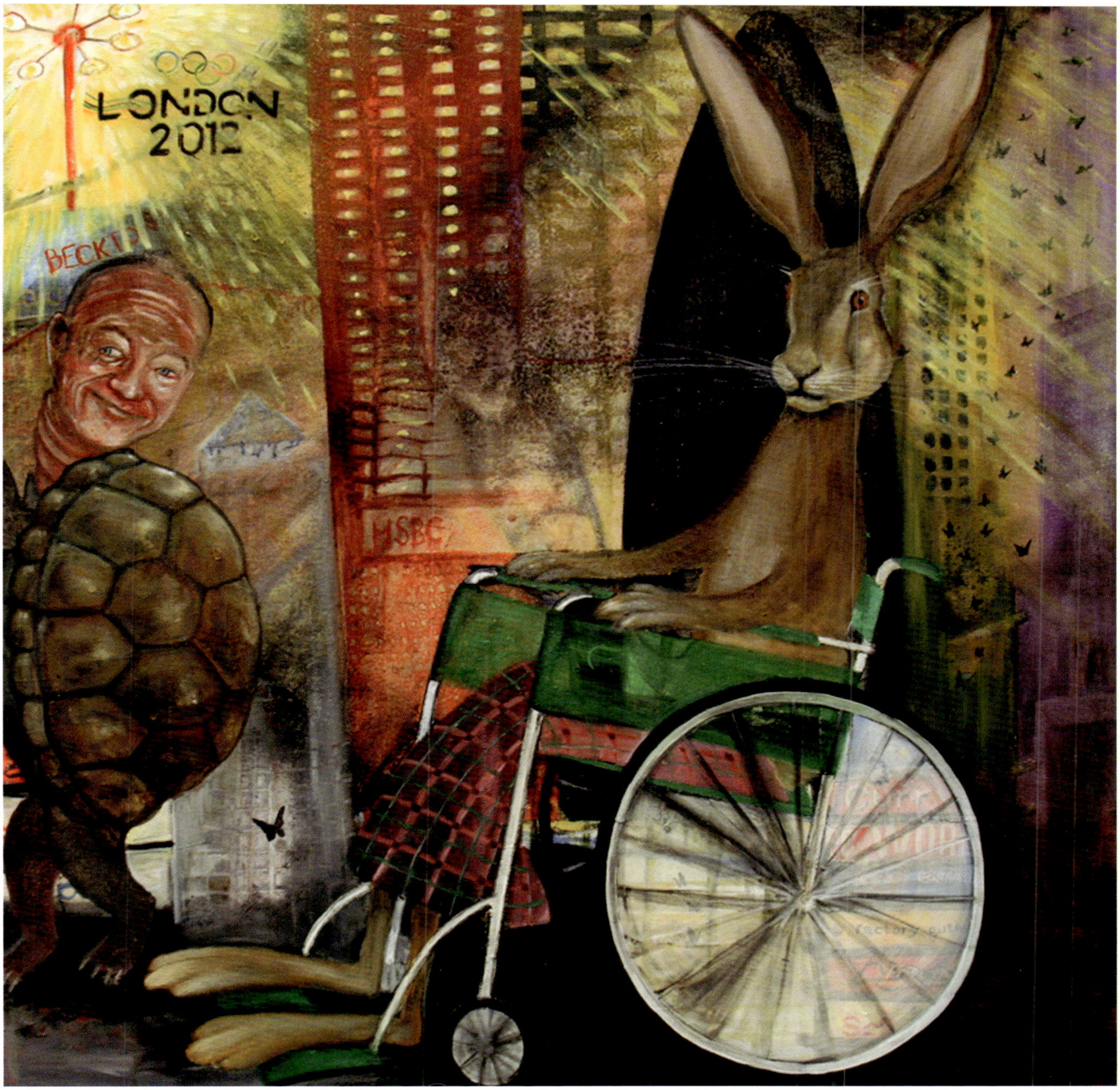

Disabled Hare, 2007
Oil on canvas, 66 x 66 cm

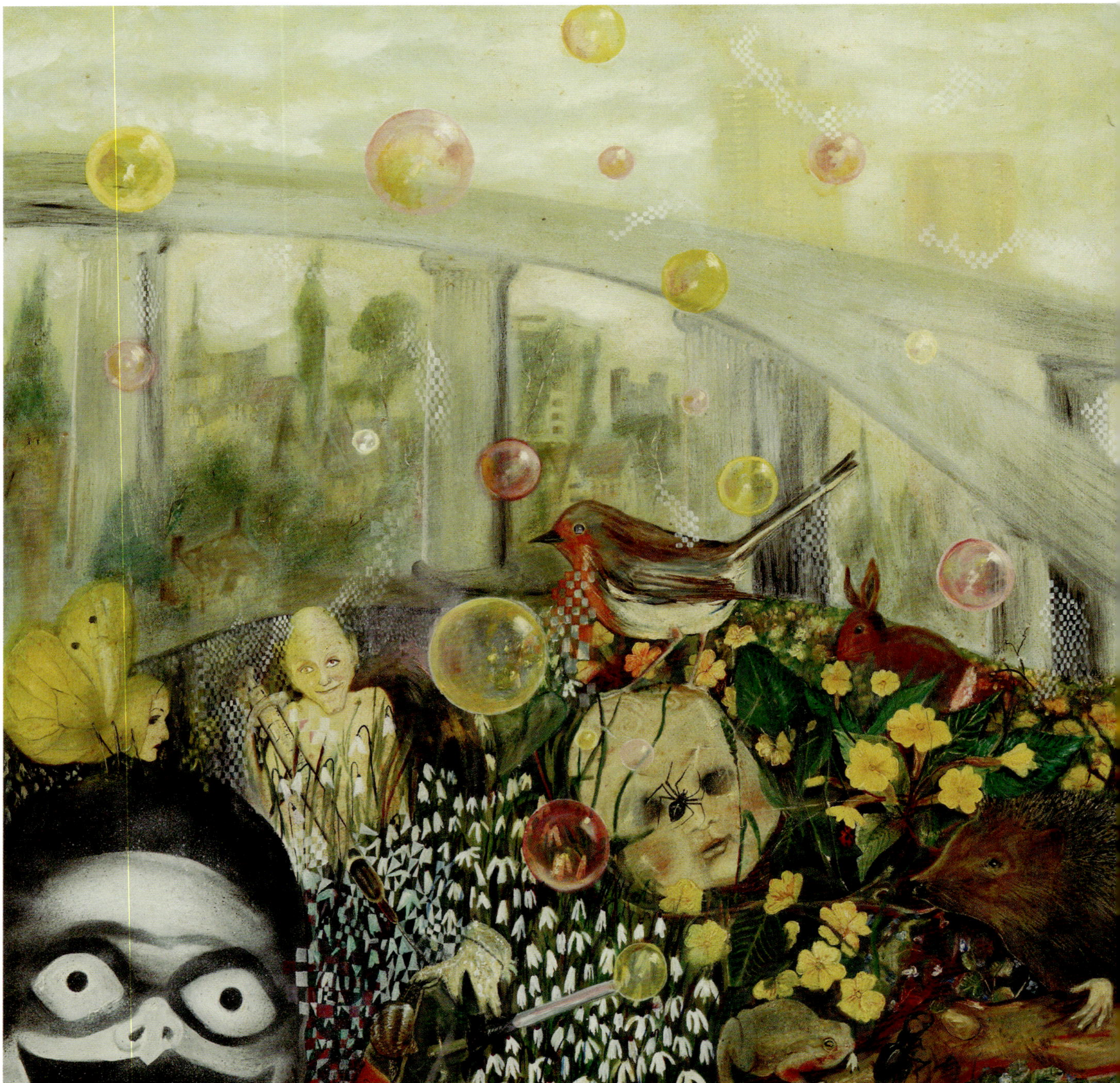

On Some Faraway Hill, 2001
Oil on canvas, 91 x 91 cm

Bad Fairies

In the dark recesses of our mind we all believe in image magic.
E.H.J. Gombrich, *Symbolic Images: Studies in the Art of the Renaissance*

HARRISON'S LATER WORKS feature an array of symbolic characters and artefacts that appear and reappear in different guises. Several of his most ambitious works may be seen as elaborate fantasies – modern day fairy tales – in which large casts of characters are assembled. In such scenes, supernatural and mythological characters hold precedence over humans. Indeed, the artist has described these works as akin to fairy stories. He has remarked that in his work, just as in fairy stories, 'the natural and the supernatural go hand in hand, whether in *Alice's Adventures in Wonderland* or the *The Wind in the Willows*, *The Master and Margarita* or Gogol's short stories'.[1] Such a strategy is a high risk one, with obvious perils attached: How does one render fairy stories muscular in tone, cosmopolitan in spirit and contemporary in style? It is the artist's employment of what could be seen as a whimsical mode of storytelling that allows him to conjoin contraries, and to treat both new and old subjects in each work.

Harrison's solution to the problem of creating convincing fairy tales has been to reintroduce subjects outside the mainstream of modern art, and to locate common ground between them. Several works join together ideas from baroque allegory, Victorian melodrama and contemporary gay subculture, for example. One area of common ground between these three is the iconography of vanitas painting, which alludes to the brevity of human life, and sets beauty in contrast with death and decay. Vanitas imagery, whose name is derived from the Old Testament phrase 'vanity of vanities ... all is vanity',[2] is primarily associated with baroque painting in seventeenth-century Italy and Holland, though later artists made frequent use of its stock of symbols. Artists such as Salvator Rosa developed an armoury of symbols for the transience of life, based around the genre of still life, which Harrison has directly drawn upon. His works are equally overloaded with diverse symbolic imagery, though he is concerned to juxtapose the modern and conventional elements of this imagery in order to reanimate the tradition, rather than faithfully recreate it.

One of the most complex of Harrison's works is *On Some Faraway Hill* (2001). Here, we encounter a profusion of symbols of both eros and thanatos – the erotic drive to procreate

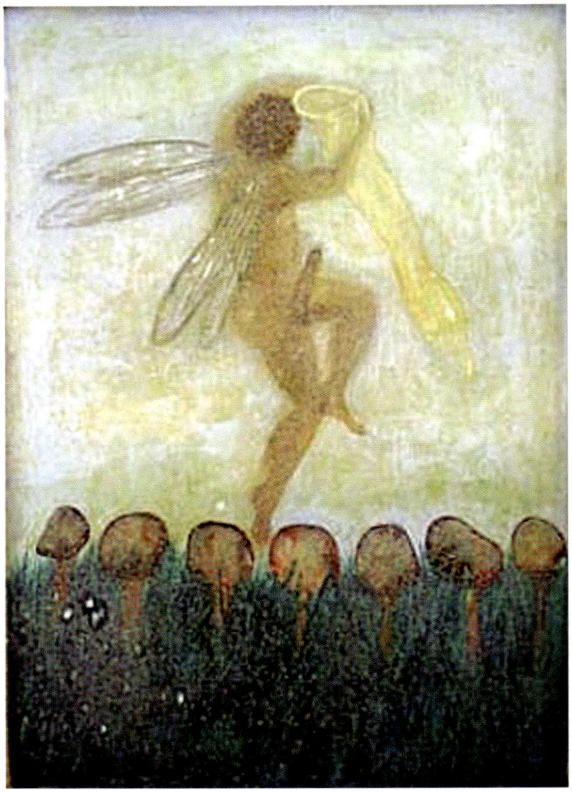

Faerie Ring, 2004
Oil and collage on wood, 36 × 26 cm

and its complement – crowded into the claustrophobic, shallow foreground of the work. For Harrison, each being is composed of competing, contradictory impulses. Even the title of the work embodies this view: though we expect a location far from the civilized world, what we are confronted with is a view of a mound by a motorway flyover somewhere on the city's fringes. Both individual symbols and their organization echo several moments from the history of painting, particularly those from the work of the Victorian fairy-painter Richard Dadd and James Ensor. The half-human butterfly at the bottom left of the painting recalls characters to be found in the work of Dadd; more generally, the intense, claustrophobic foreground of the scene recalls the intensity of Dadd's most famous work, *The Fairy Feller's Master Stroke*, where half-human, half-fantasy creatures fill our field of vision. On the other hand, the character at the bottom left recalls James Ensor's half-clown,

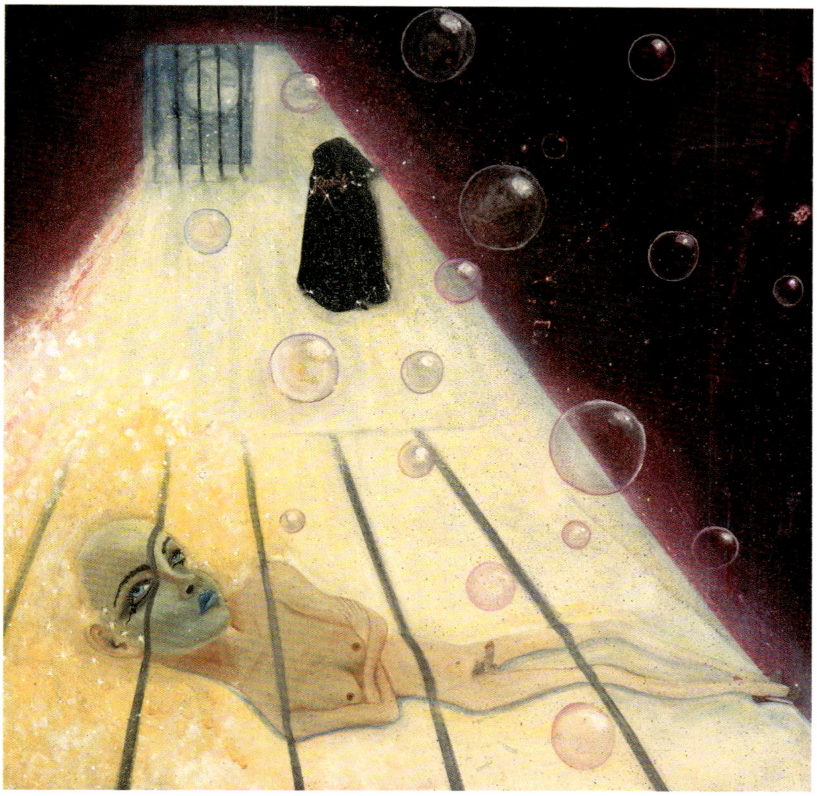

Roxy Needles, 2006
Oil on canvas, 76 x 76 cm

half-death-mask characters. Their expressions illustrate this idea: they are somewhere between a beaming smile, a rictus grin and a scream. The facial features of this character, however, also recall those of the late Leigh Bowery, whose loves and excesses were legendary in 1980s gay subculture. Bowery's role here is to be our intermediary to this other world, and a witness to the story unfolding behind.

One of the central motifs in the painting is soap bubbles, which feature prominently as a vanitas motif both in baroque painting and Victorian British art. Traditionally, bubbles have been used in vanitas art to symbolize the fragility and brevity of human existence, and the image of a child blowing bubbles, often accompanied by the inscription 'Who will escape?', is common in engravings from the sixteenth century. Indeed, the bubble became such a strong symbol of the transience of human life that during the sixteenth century the

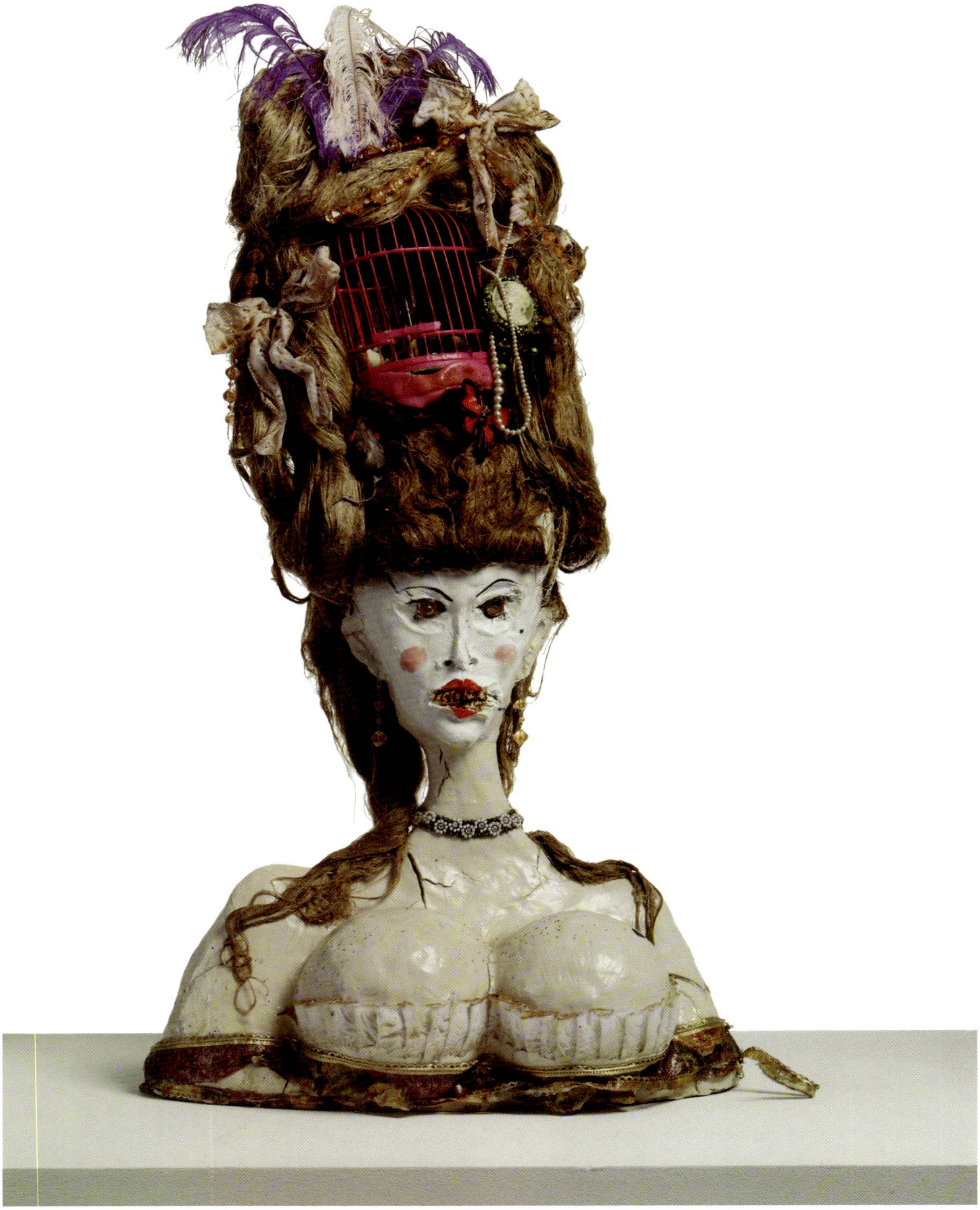

Dead Glamorous, 2008
Mixed media, 90 × 50 × 24 cm

expression 'homo est bulla' ('man is but a bubble') came into popular linguistic usage. Salvator Rosa's *L'Umana Fragilità (Human Frailty*; c. 1656), for instance, features a looming skeleton and a baby, representing the two ends of the human life-cycle, as well as bubbles floating skywards, which are intended to instantiate the work's title. John Everett Millais, on the other hand, reoriented the motif with an altogether sweeter message in his painting *Bubbles* (1886), which depicts a young, golden-haired boy watching a bubble rise above his head, and was made famous by its use in advertisements for Pears soap. Harrison's work causes these two uses of the motif to clash. His bubbles, unlike those of his predecessors, are rendered in acidic yellows and saccharine pinks, colours that signify both the morbid and light-hearted use of the motif over the years. Harrison's gift, then, is to reorient traditional symbols to his own ends, providing them with a new and natural home.

Even in the midst of death, however, life is present too: a red-breasted robin, radiant with colour, is situated at the centre of the composition, offering us a sense of renewal even when perched atop a clay skull. Harrison provides us with the sense that nature, even surrounded by human folly and destruction, will triumph. The immediate proximity of the robin and skull makes clear that the picture is, at least in part, a battle between the competing forces of hope and tragedy, decay and regeneration, life and death. Accordingly, a butterfly – another motif common in vanitas art – is pictured at the bottom left of the painting. This is significant because the butterfly symbolizes both the fragility and transience of human life, given its relatively short life-span, and rebirth and regeneration, given the way in which it comes to be what it is: its transformation from a caterpillar, through the mediation of a chrysalis, into a completely new creature. As such, it perfectly embodies the duality of the painting's themes. However, Harrison's butterfly is no ordinary butterfly: it has acquired a human face. The themes of life and death that pervade the painting are now explicitly related to man.

Harrison's sculptural works also include vanitas motifs, and adapt premodern formats and genres. In Harrison's hands, a portrait bust is seldom just a representation of an individual. *Dead Glamorous* (2008), his bust of Marie-Antoinette, for example, is a burlesque parody of traditional sculpture, an assault on the senses that simultaneously elicits horror and charm. She is a glorious symbol for our rapacious consumer society, a society that, in blithe ignorance, pillages the natural world and is enthralled to trinkets of one sort or another. Yet it is Harrison's distinctive use of materials that both brings the image to life and evokes death. Scanning over the object, we are first likely to see its inhuman attributes. Marie is assembled from found objects and rubbish: her appearance is abject. Her rotten teeth are made of rusty nails (having been corrupted by a taste for the finer things in life), and her eyes of old corroded batteries, decayed sources of energy. Such materials seem comically inappropriate for a woman who chose to be portrayed in bucolic fantasies. They also reflect Harrison's own immediate environment: all of his materials are 'locally sourced'. He suggests that instead of elegance we create entropy, instead of grace, disgrace, though he does so in a work that is filled with both morbid horror and mordant humour.

The artist's reuse of cheap or discarded materials serves several purposes. Firstly, it points our attention outwards to the external world. Here, specifically, it asks us to compare Marie's and our own obsessions with twisting nature into ever more absurd and artificial forms. Marie's wig glistens, luridly. It is constructed from flowers and hemp, then sealed in glue to make it both repellent and alluring. From one angle, it recalls waxy flaxen locks and golden midsummer straw, from another, spews of glutinous molten fluids, underneath which mice labour to survive. As Harrison remarks, each of his works symbolizes the 'constant battle that mankind fights for dominance over, when we should instead be living in harmony with, nature.'[3] Under the wig, Marie Antoinette's face is ashen-white: a naturalistic portrayal of period make-up and a death-mask alike. Her cosmetics cover sunken cheekbones and decayed flesh, the results of man's conflict with nature. The last feature of the work we notice, and which any other animal would notice, is that the bust smells strongly of perfume, a scent that is designed to conceal the stench of rottenness underneath.

Other works reinforce the idea that what animates us is always accompanied by its opposite. *Still Alive* (2005) reveals a robin above a mysterious and threatening head. The figure is little more than a pair of bloodshot eyes emerging out of the darkness. The mesmerizing gaze exerts a gravitational pull on our own. Harrison knows that the illusion of a gaze returned can be spellbinding: it can exert a power we might attempt to explain rationally, but which we will already have responded to by the time we do so. *Still Alive* enacts a form of modern witchcraft. Just as in Rosa's *L'Umana Fragilità*, the pictorial metaphor of glimmers of light emerging from darkness makes concrete how close we are to the primordial darkness of nonbeing. Lest we forget this, a rusty coil of barbed wire, portraying the subject as a mythical, Christlike martyr, thrusts out into our own space. This is fitting, perhaps, given Christ's relation to death and (re)birth, and the inextricable connection between the two in so many of Harrison's works.

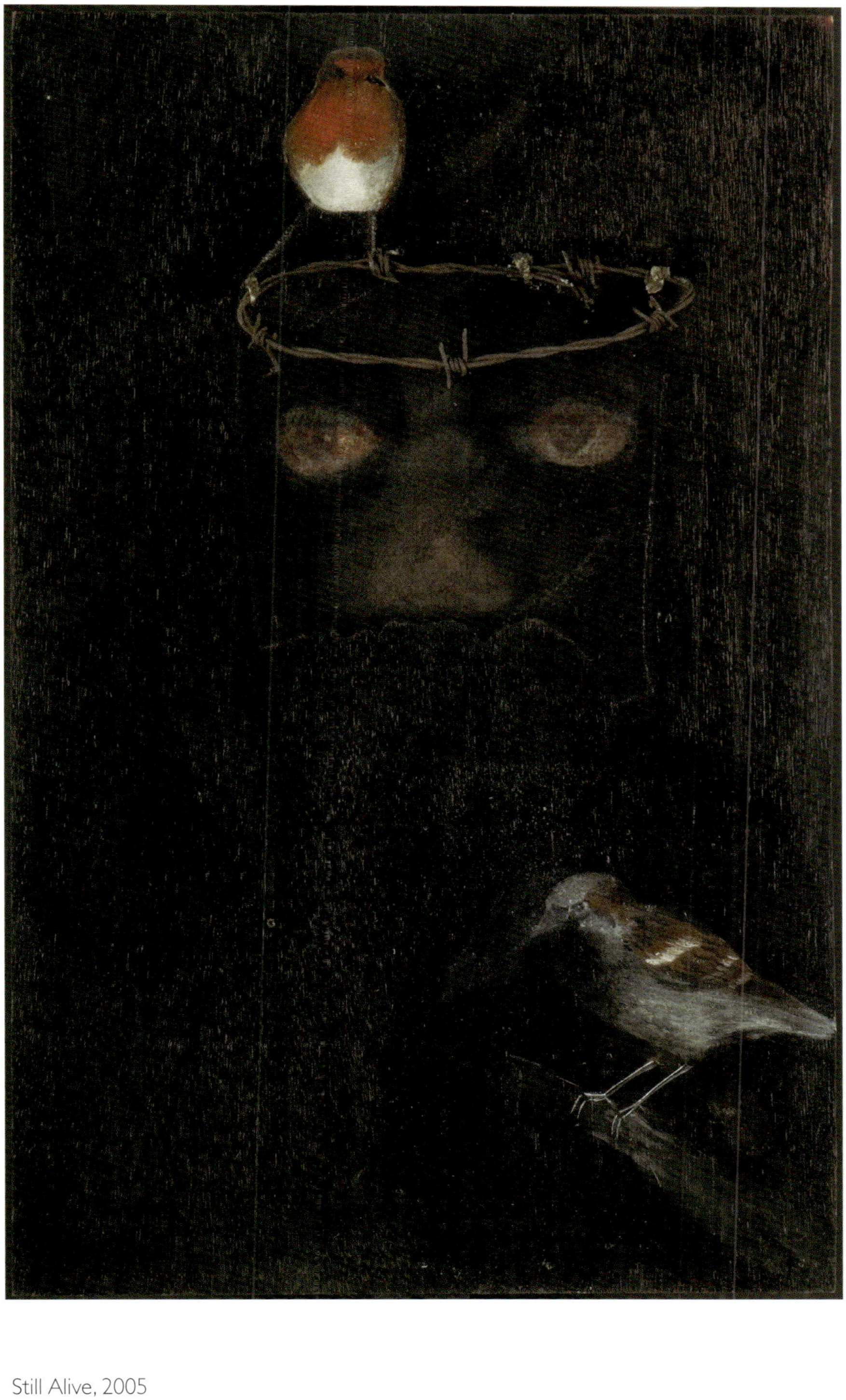

Still Alive, 2005
Found objects and oil on wood, 61 × 38 cm

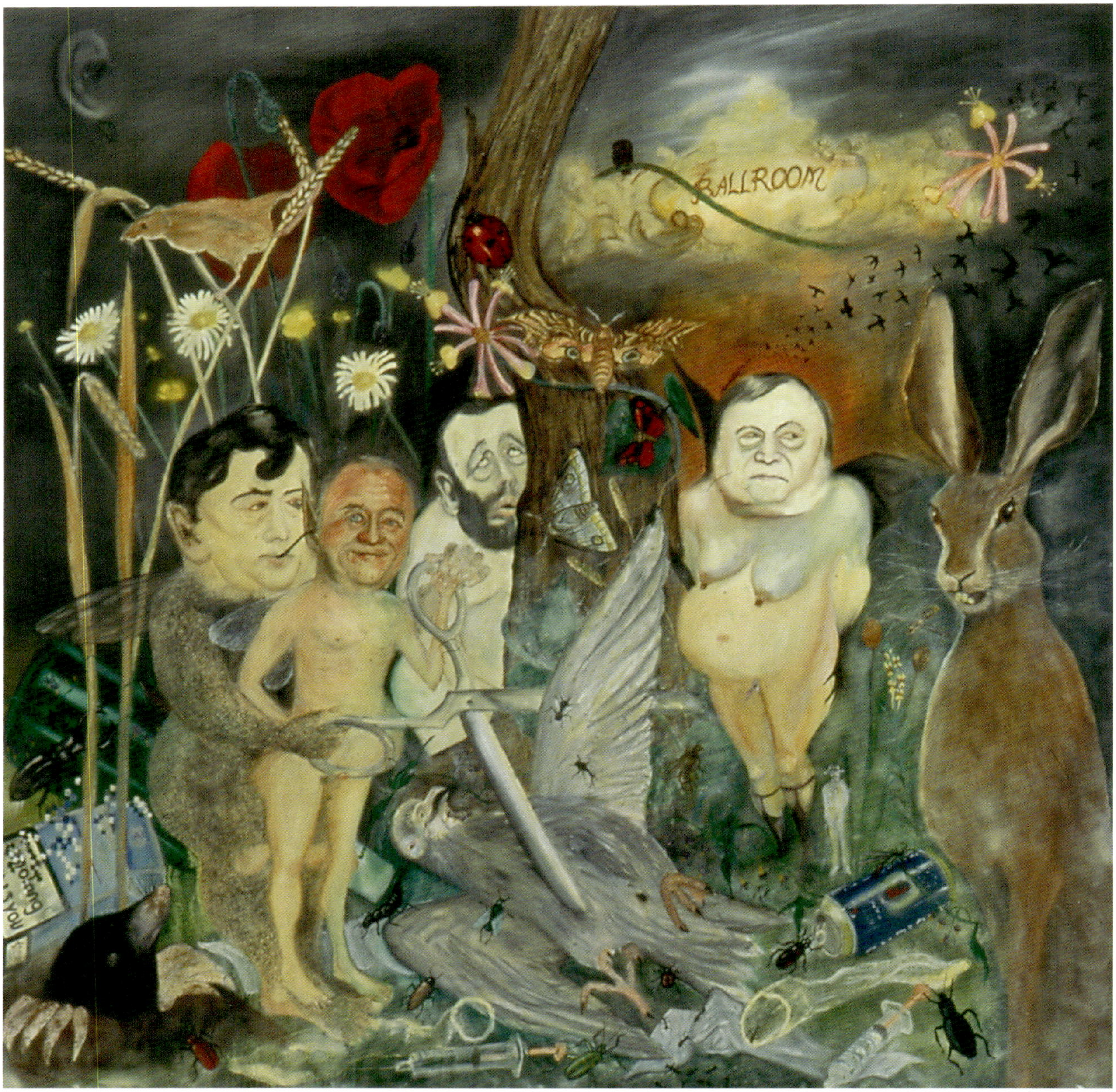

Bad Fairies, 2006
Oil on canvas, 92 × 92 cm

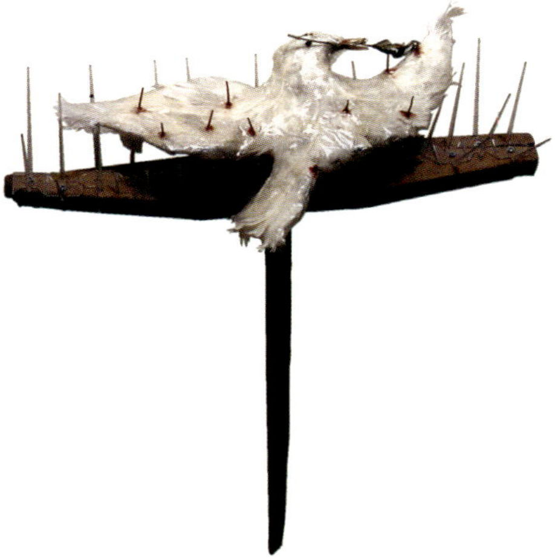

Back to the Ark, 2004
Found objects and sellotape, 92 x 30 cm

Across all of Harrison's mythological works, desire is scarcely suppressed even whilst death is at hand. In the comical *Bad Fairies* (2006), Gordon Brown and Ken Livingstone are pictured as malevolent sprites, naked and tangled in a homoerotic embrace, attacking a wounded pigeon, while Prokofiev's ear in the top left-hand corner is telling them to listen to nature. The pigeon, a bird that appears in several works, may be seen as a symbol for ordinary Londoners struggling to eke out a living. In the three-dimensional work *Back to the Ark* (2004), we also encounter a pigeon with an olive branch in its mouth constrained by Sellotape and spread across spikes used on buildings to prevent birds from landing. As the spikes puncture its flesh, the pigeon resembles a haggard and forlorn version of Saint Sebastian.

However, it is perhaps *Pan Has Risen* (p. 18) that best exemplifies the existence of desire even in the presence of death. Our first impression of the work is of a charmed world full of boisterous pleasures and of a gentle, picturesque landscape. Harrison knows that 'the picturesque' is a thoroughly English idea, but that it is also janus-faced. The first generation of writers to describe the picturesque, amongst whom was William Gilpin, saw the national landscape, in part, as wholesome, benevolent and nurturing.[4] By contrast, Harrison's work recalls the writings of the second generation of theorists who described the picturesque, Richard Payne Knight being a prominent proponent of this group.[5] Knight's view of nature is revealed in his 1786 work *A Discourse on the Worship of Priapus*, which covered how ancient fertility cults spanned East and West, and continued from pagan into Christian times. Payne Knight held both nature and eroticism to be sacred, and saw the two as inseparable, linked by a worship of 'the generative principle'. Harrison's beliefs are not dissimilar. For him, Pan is the spirit of true and unbridled erotic pleasure. Yet, as a god intimately associated with the countryside, he is pictured dancing wildly through fields filled with flowers and raising a half-empty bottle aloft. He dances across a carpet of superabundant flowers that creates a pattern of brilliant, over-intense blues, pinks and yellows. The collective purpose of these details, though, is to suggest that Pan is not merely drunk, but intoxicated with the fertility of nature at high summer. And well might he be, since the location pictured here is based on Porlock Hill in Somerset, a central place in English folk memory, as well as one well known to the artist. It is the place Cecil F. Alexander had in mind when he composed the words for the famous Anglican hymn *All Things Bright and Beautiful*, and clearly recalls the lines 'the purple-headed mountain' and 'each little flower that opens, each little bird that sings'. Harrison, of course, not unaware of the association, actually sought to incorporate it into the physical make-up of the piece by painting the scene over song sheets of the hymn.

If nature triumphs in his work, Harrison is an artist whose work nevertheless remains double-edged. For example, Pan is, improbably, a portrait as well as an allegorical figure. He is based on a builder whose powerful physique Harrison had admired from afar. The painting is, then, a paean to an object of beauty. But Harrison's Pan mixes allure with aggression: his size renders him confrontational, as well as fantastical. As in Payne Knight's pagan scheme, this god embodies the principles of creation, destruction and renovation. The fact that the perspective is subtly tilted towards us at the edge of the picture plane again makes us feel as though Pan is running out of the painting into our own world, and indeed at us. The effect is as exhilarating as it is threatening. Harrison's pictorial device suggests that this figure is not only a force of nature, but a force too strong to be contained by the square of the picture frame. Nature is an uncontrollable force, unruly and possessed of overpowering plenitude; it is a force that embodies the creative and destructive dualities depicted and symbolized in so much of Harrison's work.

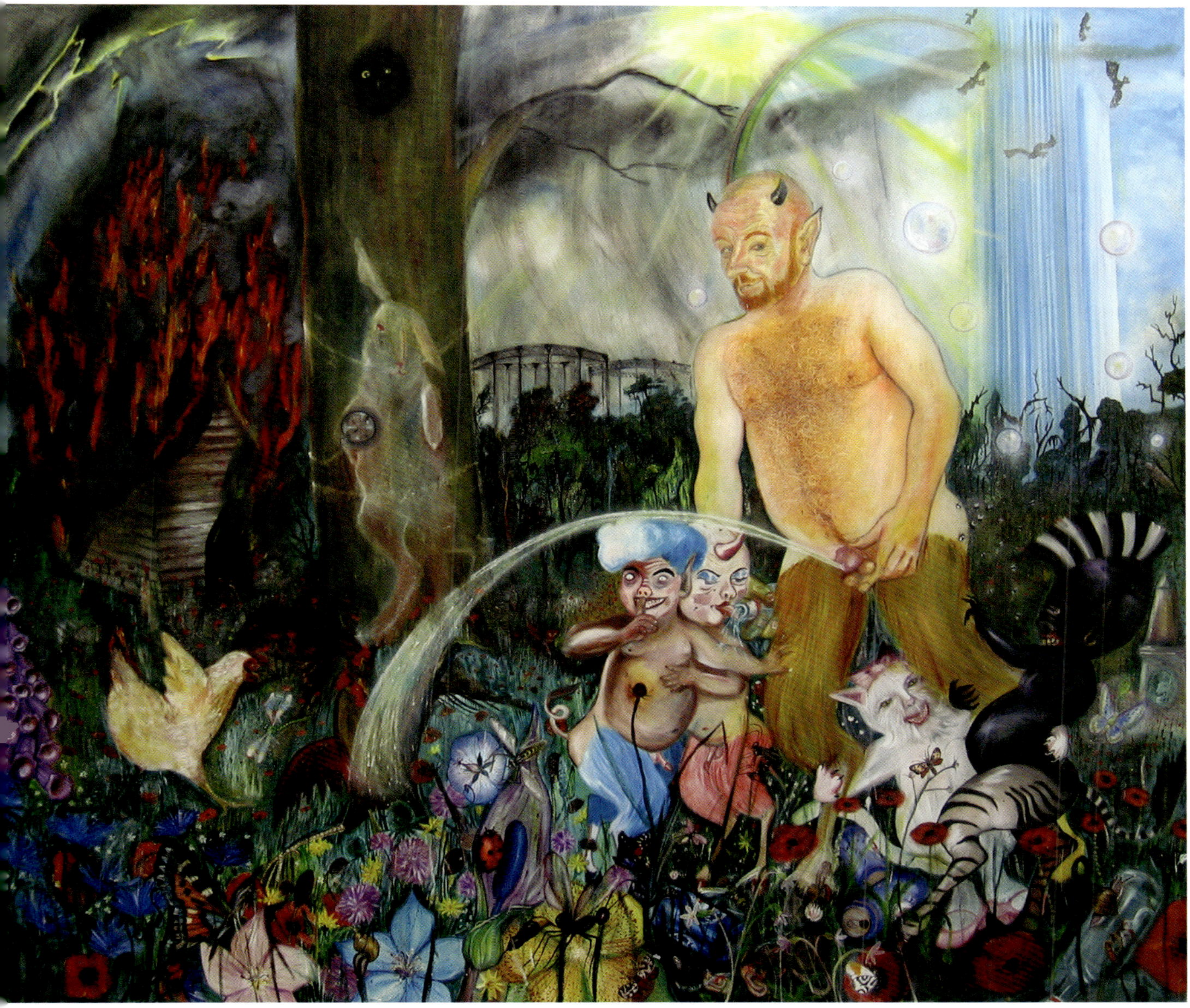

Exorcising the Red Demon, 1999
Oil on canvas, 60 x 72 cm

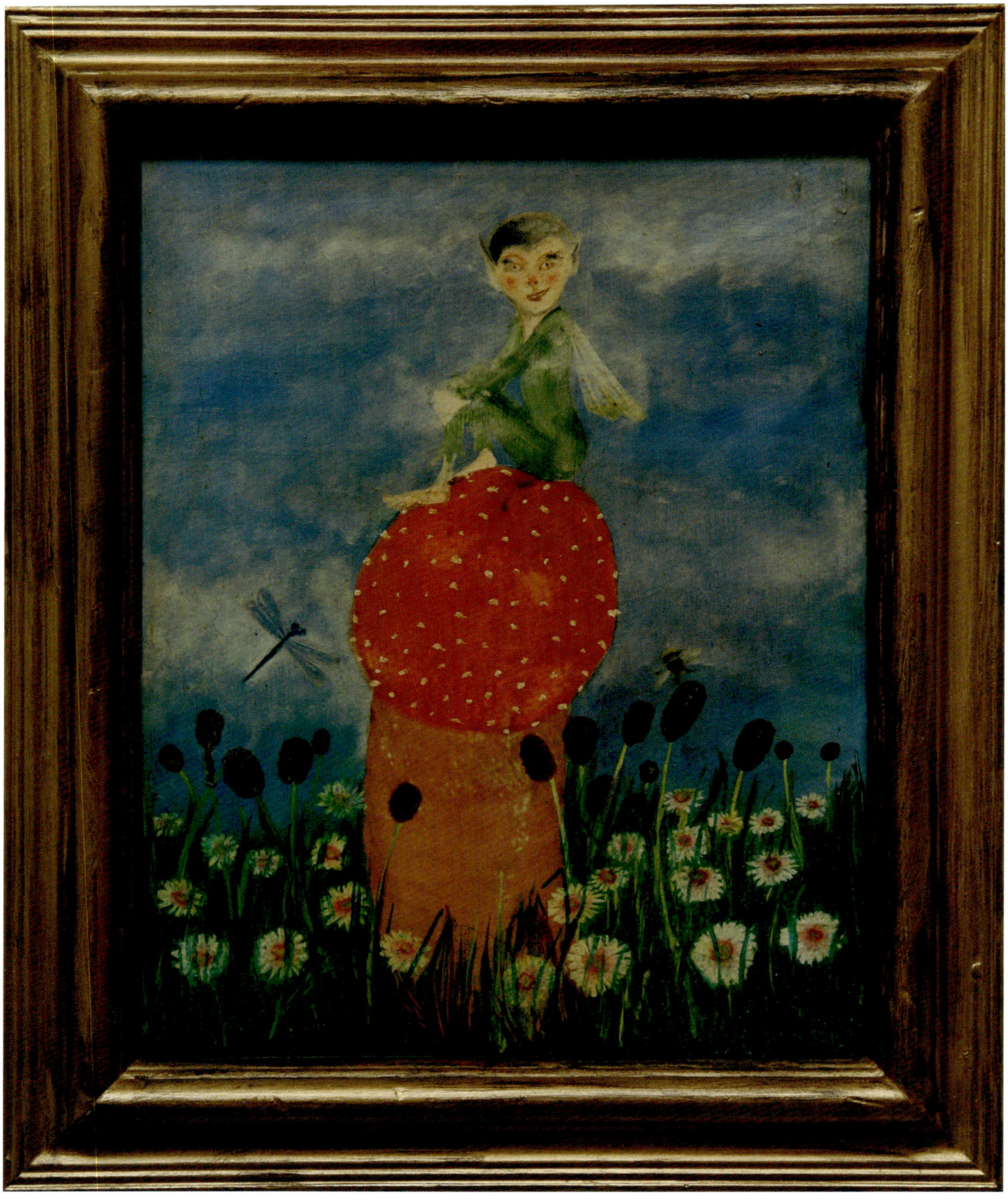

Pushing Up Daisies, 2004
Oil on wood, 36 x 28 cm

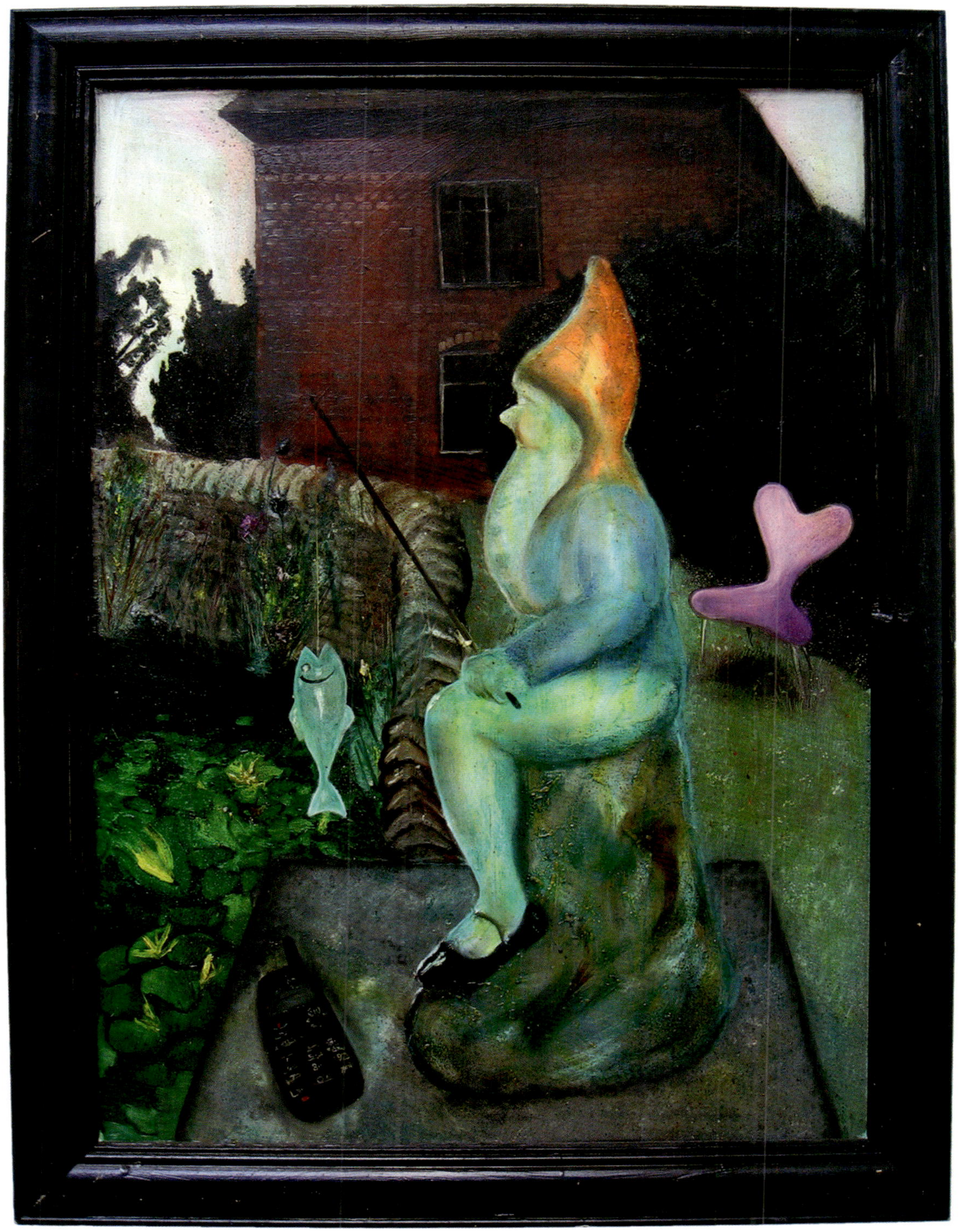

Country Life, 2000
Oil on wood, 60 x 46 cm

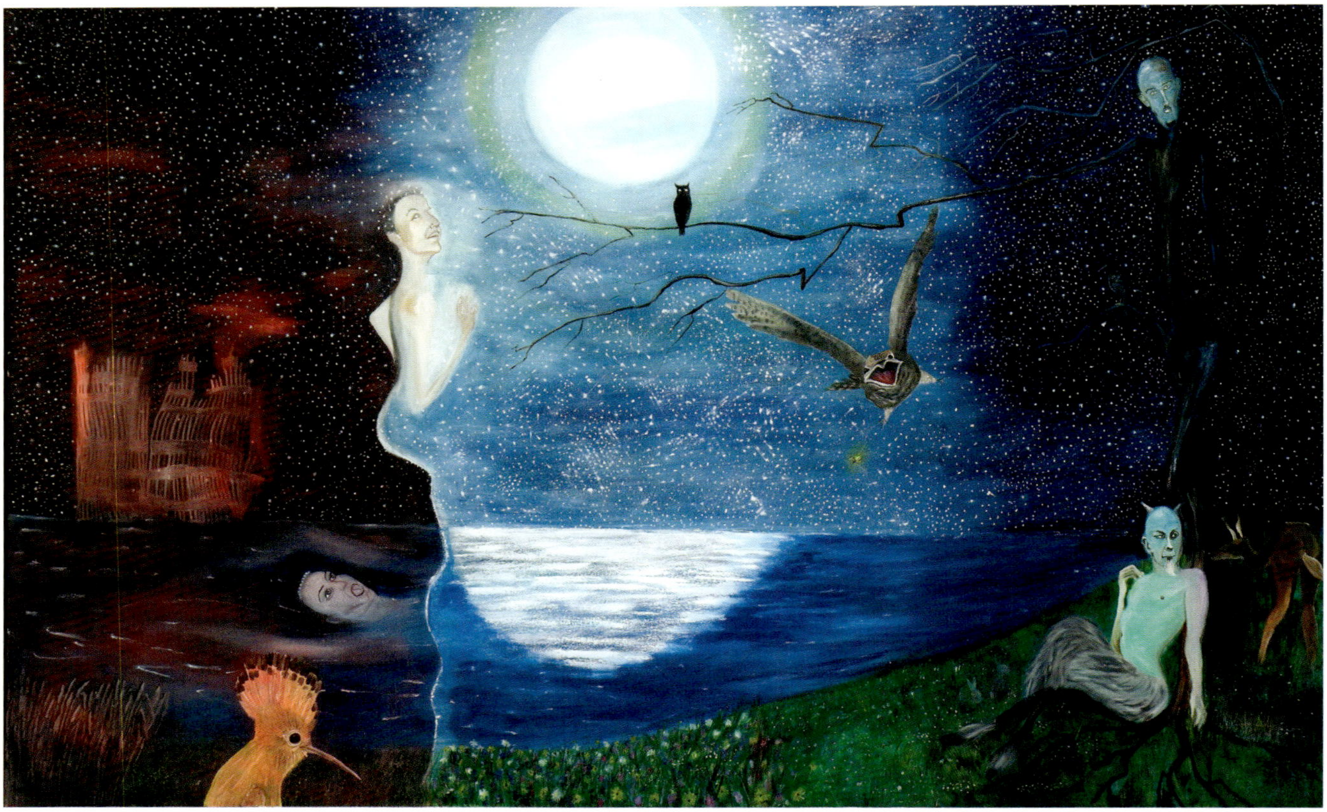

Spirits Drifting, 2001
Oil on canvas, 100.5 X 159.5 cm

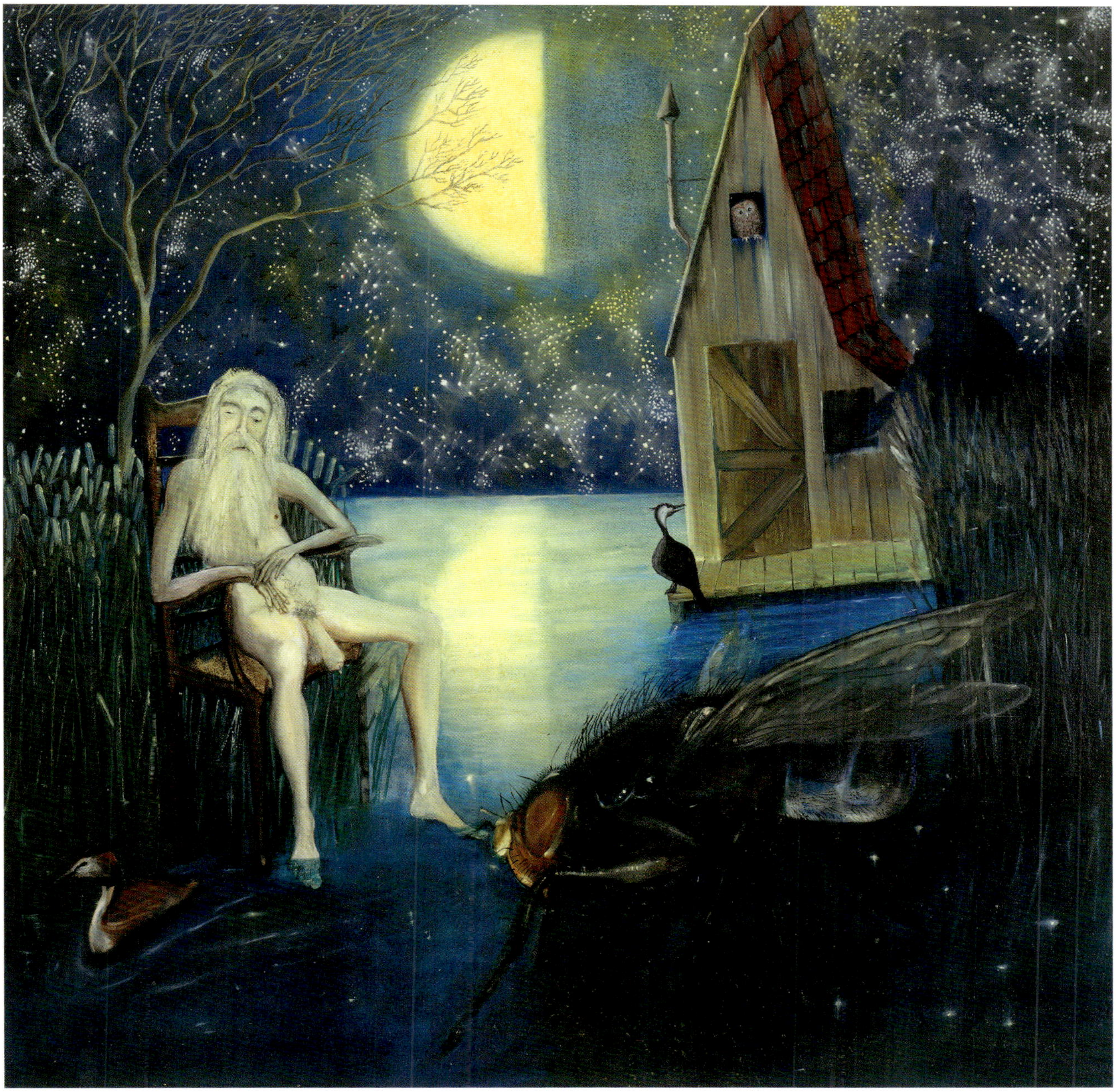

Moon and Dangly, 2004
Oil on canvas, 91 x 91 cm

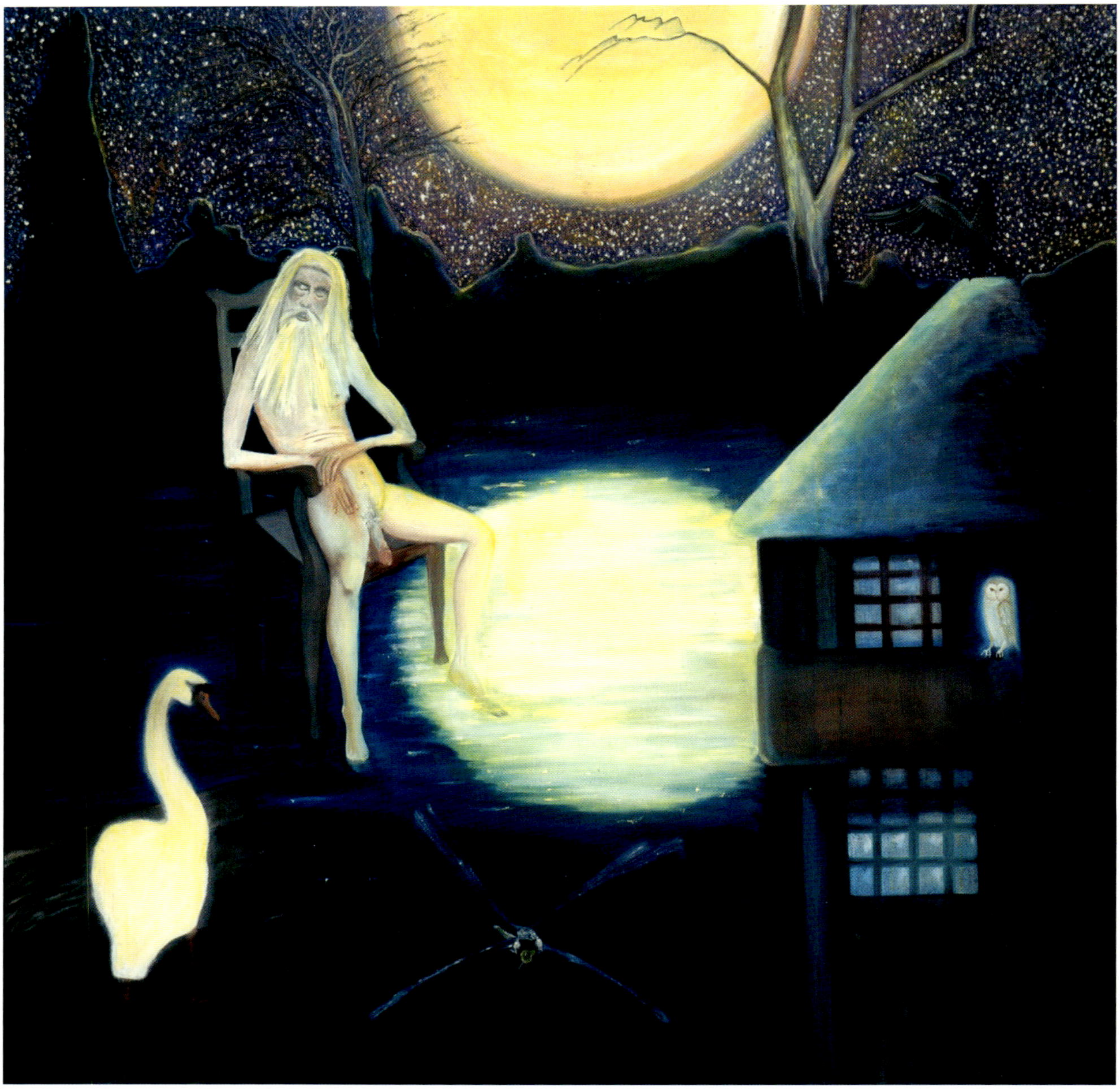

Other Half of the Moon, 2006
Oil on canvas, 93 x 93 cm

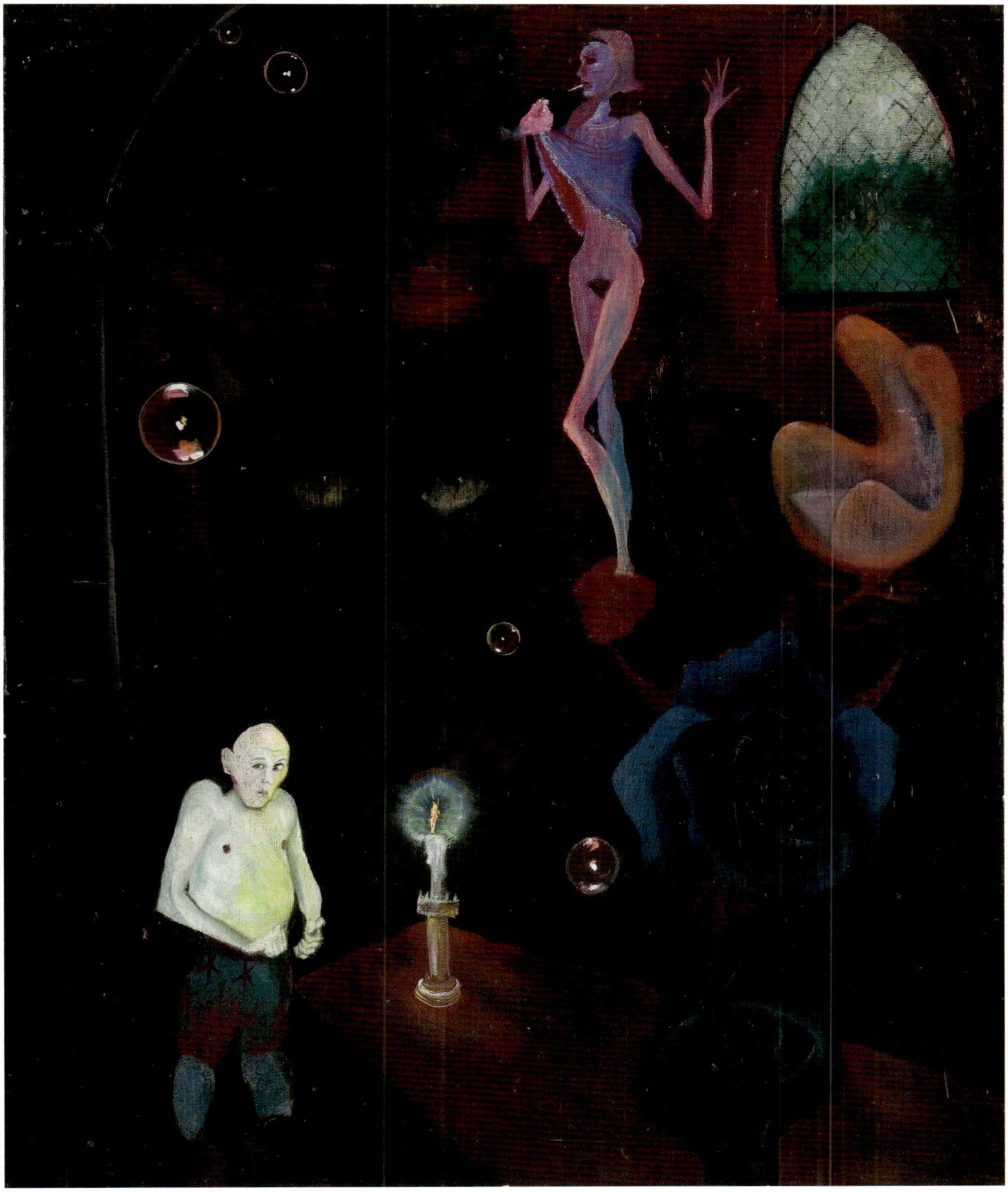

Through the Gothic Window, 2001
Oil on wood, 62.5 × 51 cm

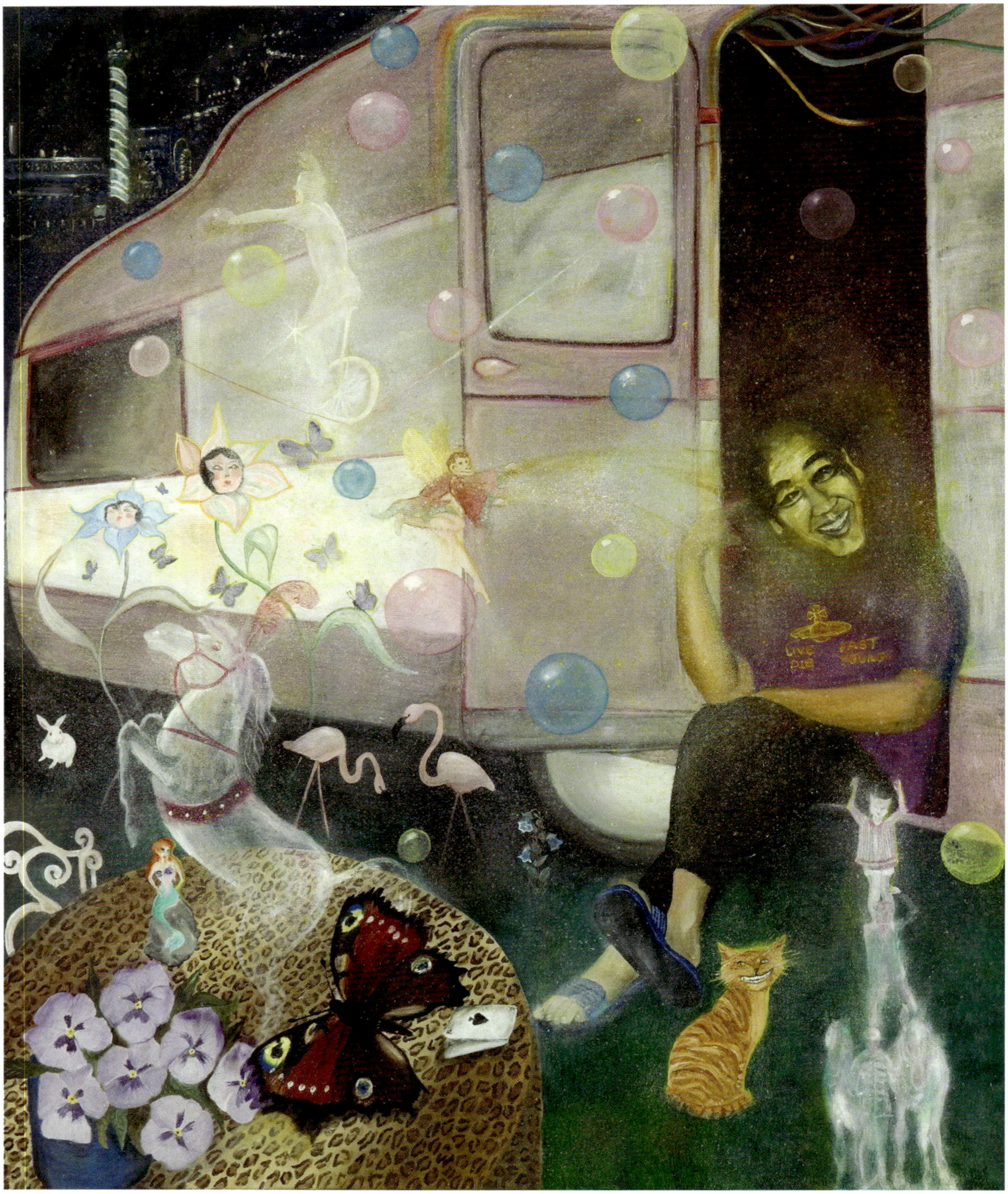

Miss Kitty in Paradise, 2005
Oil on canvas, 91.5 x 76 cm

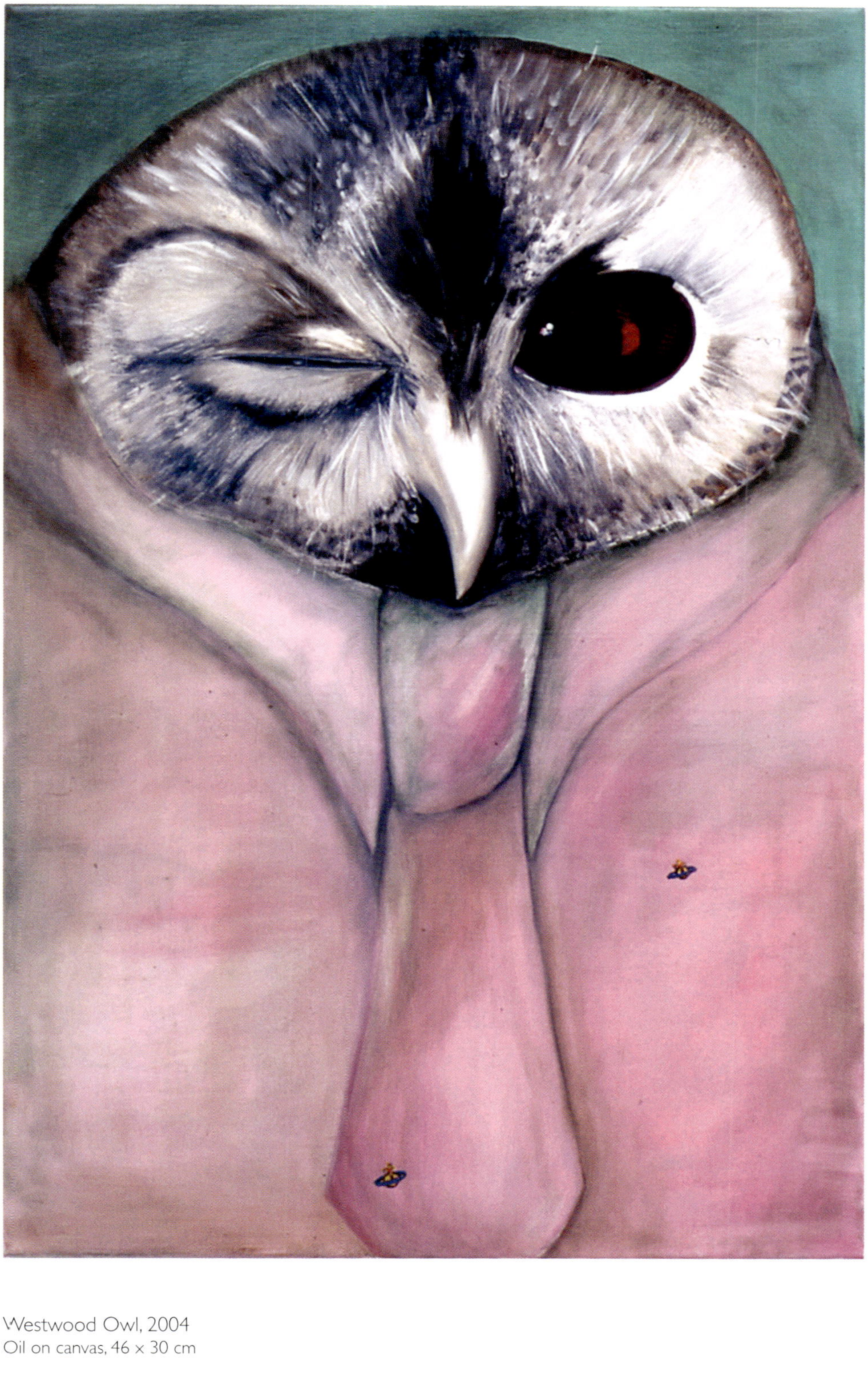

Westwood Owl, 2004
Oil on canvas, 46 x 30 cm

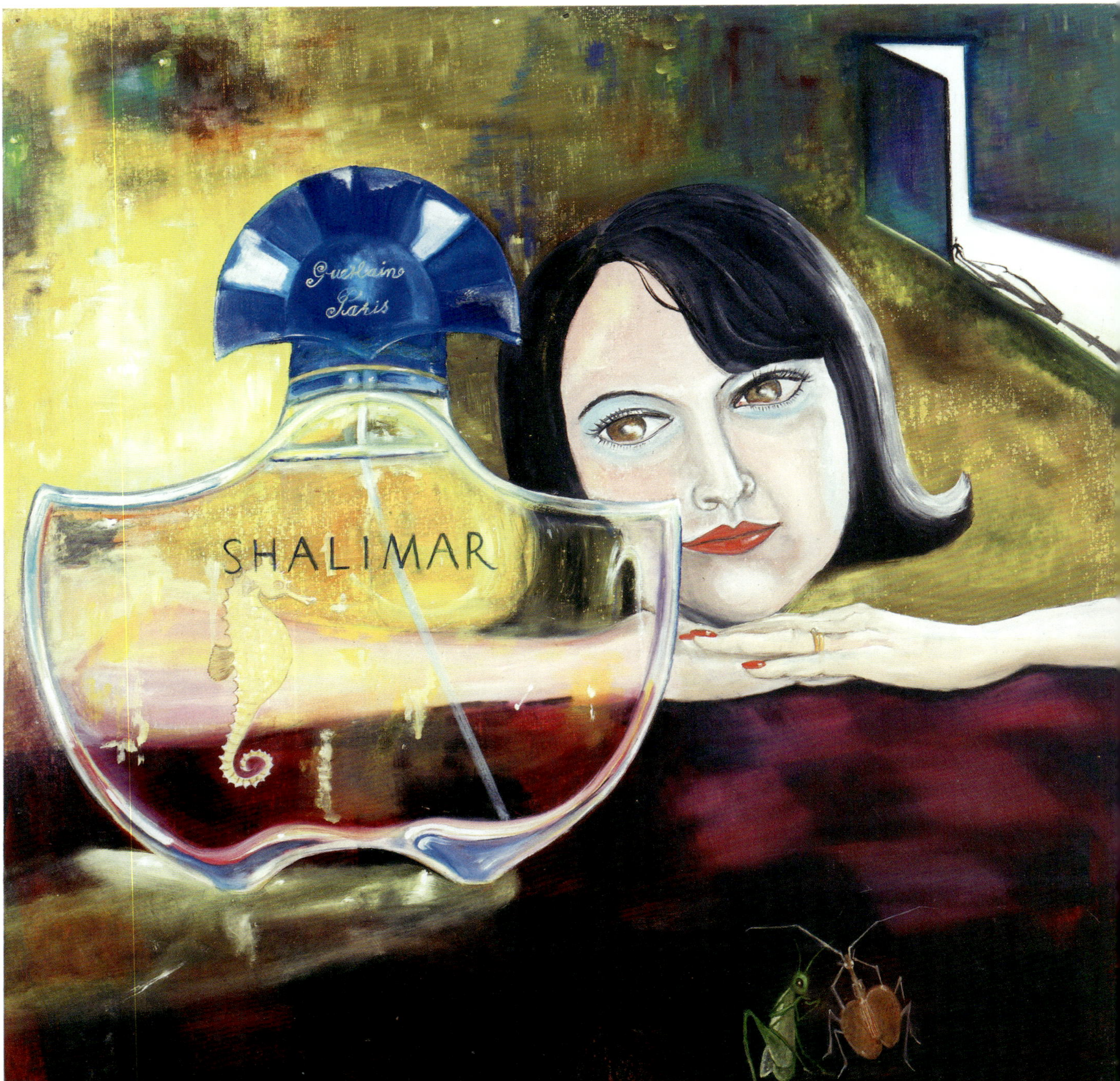

Once Upon A Time, 2007
Oil on wood, 60 x 60 cm

Existence

Like prolonged echoes mingling in the distance
In a deep and tenebrous unity,
Vast as the dark of night and as the light of day,
Perfumes, sounds and colours correspond.
Charles Baudelaire, *The Flowers of Evil*

HARRISON'S MOST RECENT body of painting and sculpture has the collective title *Existence*, signalling his aim to create a personal cosmology in the manner of premodern artists such as William Blake. *Existence* also significantly enlarges upon Harrison's previous vision of man's place in the universe. As in his earlier work, Harrison's cosmology is one in which past and present are scrambled; in which the realms of the fictional, personal and universal bleed into one; and in which the invisible is made visible and the tangible intangible. But beyond exploring how we have alienated ourselves from the natural world, as he does in his earlier work, Harrison also explores how we have lost touch even with our own senses.

Harrison's focus in *Existence* is on how our sense of smell can carry an astonishing emotive charge, and, specifically, on those aromas that enrapture us, namely those of 'flowers, sex and chemistry'.[1] His latest series of paintings takes as its starting point what Harrison calls the 'potency' of the perfumier's art.[2] Each begins with a scent created by arguably the greatest ever perfumier – Guerlain. All of the scents Harrison refers to were created in another age – ranging from Jicky, created in 1889, through Mitsuoko, Shalimar and Vol du Nuit, created in 1919, 1925 and 1933 respectively, to Habit Rouge, created in 1965. For Harrison, the art of perfume offers us some of the richest and most visceral sensory experiences, and, moreover, a way of rethinking our relationship with the world. *Existence* offers us an imagined place in which our senses can be revivified; it offers us a place in which, to use John Donne's words, 'Exstasie doth unperplex … and tell us what we love.'[3]

It is no coincidence that the range of perfumes the artist has chosen to represent is historical. In Harrison's view, our postwar pursuit of modernity has left our appreciation of the material world, as well as that of our imaginative world, degraded. Smell is, of course, commonly thought of as the sense most directly connected to memory. As the artist has noted, Proust is thought to have dipped his pen in Guerlain's Mitsuoko perfume before beginning to write each day, to release his powers of recollection and imagination. At one level, Harrison's concern in *Existence* is with how the ways in which we organise our sense impressions have changed over time. Anthropologists have called our perceptual relationship to the sensible world our 'sensorium', believing it to differ enormously from culture to culture, and time to time. For Harrison, the modern world has left us dumb to much of the natural world, and, importantly, to the power of scent. Our sense of smell has become weaker through constant exposure to regimes of hygiene and the battery of industrial chemicals they require. Surrounded only by artificial, man-made materials, we have become inured to a world of thin, faint scents. In consequence, the works in *Existence* can be seen as attempts to reopen what were once naively called our doors of perception to worlds we scarcely even know we have lost contact with.

Human beings have the least specialised sense of smell of almost any mammal. We rely on an absurdly narrow range of sense impressions, experiencing nature primarily through our powers of visual perception. Harrison's representations of other species alongside man-made scents suggest that we have become half-functioning beings with feeble powers of perception, and that the ability to smell is now really something only animals possess. Whilst we are scarcely conscious of the wider ecosystem in which we exist, the animal kingdom is only too aware of how we have degraded it: Harrison's work asks us to acknowledge how partial our view of the world is.

Many of Harrison's works in *Existence* recall Baudelaire's poems, certainly the greatest poet to versify on the hallucinatory powers of perfume, and arguably the greatest on the primacy of the imagination. Indeed, the series as a whole seems to exclaim a sentiment similar to one of Baudelaire's own: 'How far perfumed paradise, you are removed / from us ... where the heart drowns in pure voluptuousness!'[4] Like Baudelaire, Harrison asks us how far 'progress' has dulled our senses and stultified our imaginative powers, and invites us to reanimate them. He similarly deplores what the poet called 'this drab canvas we accept as life',[5] and instead finds inspiration in the supernatural, the erotic and the macabre. Moreover, the individual themes across *Existence*, as across Baudelaire's poems, intertwine sacred and profane love, metamorphosis and madness, the corruption and oppressiveness of the city, and innocence and eros.

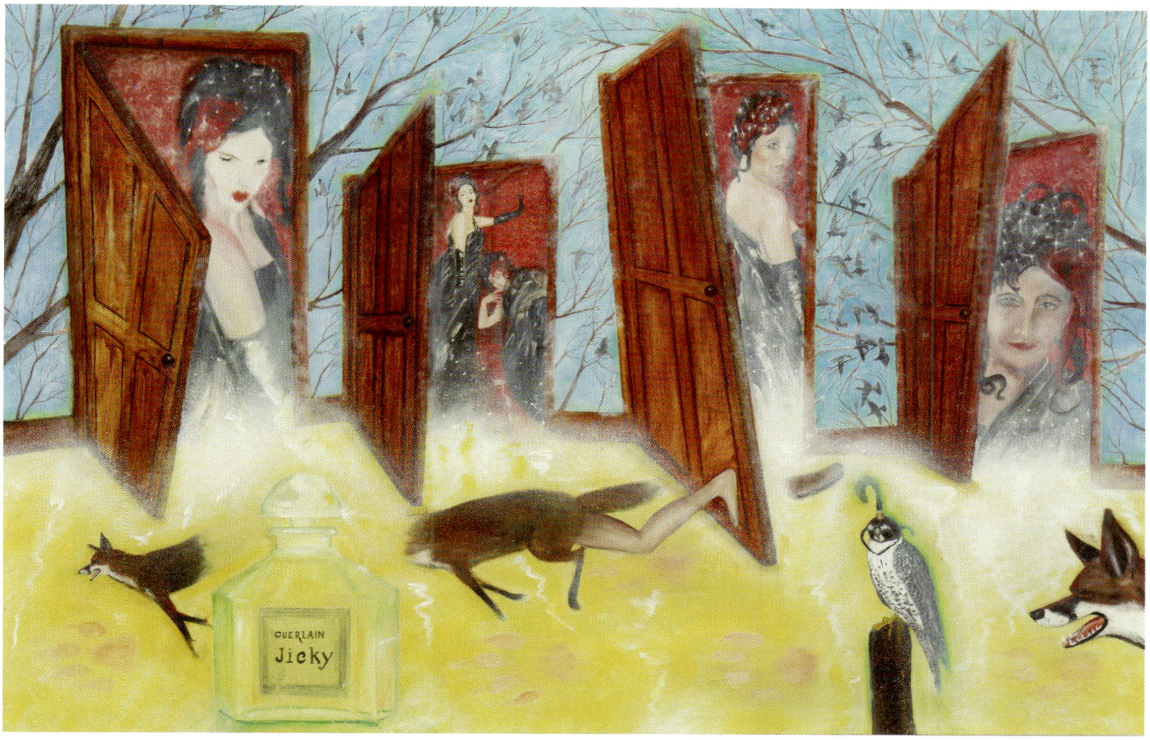

Hallucinajicky, 2008
Oil on wood, 81 × 122 cm

Certain works, such as *Hallucinijicky* (2008), explicitly offer us a Baudelairian sensation of 'joy in being possessed, in being overwhelmed, a truly sensual pleasure like that of rising in the air'.[6] *Hallucinijicky* conjures an atmosphere of almost narcotic pleasure and fin-de-siècle decadence, recalling the associations of the perfume. At the time of its creation, Jicky was described as having a druglike potency and was thought to be able to send its wearer into reveries. To recreate this idea, Harrison retired to bed one night wearing the scent, and did indeed experience vivid hallucinatory dreams, which form the basis of the painting. The work, then, is a homage to the art of the perfumier and his ability to intoxicate and delight. We encounter a swirl of doors that fly around a room, flinging themselves open to recall a *Through-the-Looking-Glass* world where we are almost asked to imagine 'six impossible things before breakfast'.[7] Each is like a portal to another possible world or another age – a perfumed paradise in which glamorous eighteenth-century prostitutes beckon.

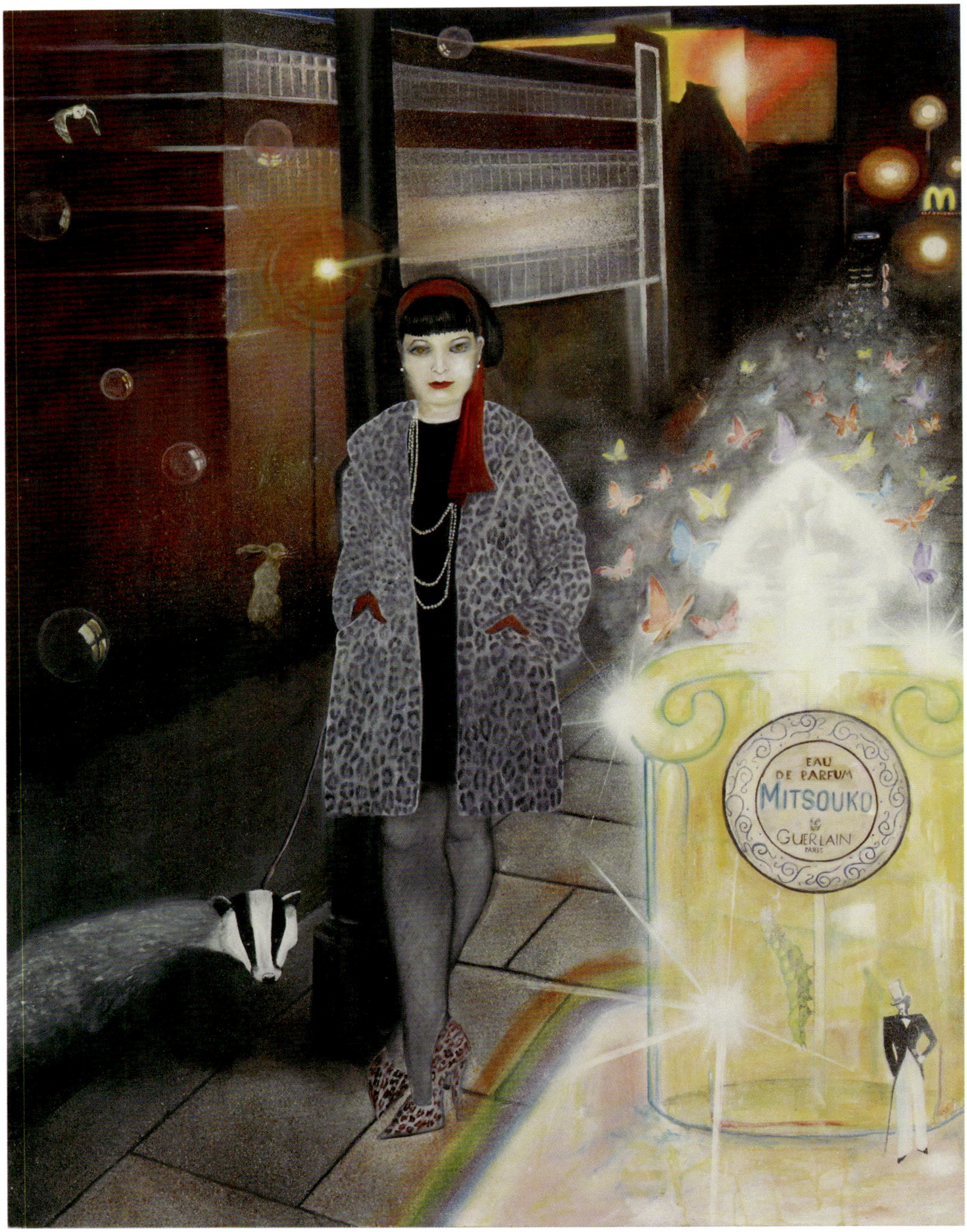

She's Not a Girl Who Misses Much, 2008
Oil on wood, 124 x 95.2 cm

Here, as in the Alice stories, time does not obey the laws of linearity; here, it is imagination, sparked by overwhelmingly intense perceptions, that throws open our doors of perception.

Hallucinijicky brings an individual's interior consciousness to life, evoking a stream of heightened sensations. The scene crackles with jolts of white-hot energy, as though unleashed by our newly-discovered senses. The flattened and luridly intense sky is more like dense, tangible matter than a distant canopy; it recalls Baudelaire's images in which 'sound and perfume swirl, in the evening air' against a 'sky [that] is delightful and sad, like a huge altar'.[8]

If *Hallucinijicky* creates an almost heavenly space, other works in *Existence* place us in a grittier reality, though an equally hallucinatory one. *She's Not a Girl Who Misses Much* (2008) suffuses a real location – Wharf Road in East London – with a crystalline, magical atmosphere. It is dominated by the two figures of a girl and an alarmingly large human-scaled bottle of Guerlain's Mitsuoko, to which the girl is seemingly oblivious. A caterpillar inside the bottle provides a playful symbol of the perfume's hallucinogenic power. It crawls skyward, recalling both the worm in Tequila bottles and the Hookah-smoking Caterpillar from *Alice's Adventures in Wonderland*, who suspiciously knows how to grow and shrink using only the mushroom on which he sits.[9] The caterpillar is also positioned close to a burst of rainbow-coloured butterflies, whose jewel-like colours throw light and colour over the slate-grey streets. These symbols of nature's power overwhelm our feeble attempts to interrupt the rhythms of night and day with fluorescent lights.

On the left of *She's Not a Girl Who Misses Much*, again we are offered an intermediary to the netherworld of the painting: a watchful hare bears witness to the wondrous events at hand. Harrison notes that throughout various cultures, the hare has not only held a special symbolic place, but has often, as in ancient Egypt, signified existence in its entirety. For Harrison, then, the hare is a timeless figure, in contrast to the evanescent butterflies and soap bubbles that float around him. Bubbles also appear in Baudelaire, who, like many other artists, uses them as a vanitas motif in his work, blending wonder and melancholy in equal measure:

> [Cupid] blows bubbles from his rosy cheek
> Which soar into the sky
> As if, beyond the blue, to seek
> The other worlds on high
> They ride with wondrous verve at first,

Reflect the sunny beams,
Then spit their flimsy souls, to burst
And fade like golden dreams.[10]

For Harrison, too, death and decay throw nature's life-force into relief.

The same contrasts animate *Cadaverina and the Apparition* (2008). Both the title and a demonic, grinning goat's skull create a sense of claustrophobic intensity and menace. Behind the skull, flamelike patterns swirl feverishly and a candle gives off a brilliant light. It is as though the whole painting has become possessed by the spirit of the woman within it. *Cadaverina and the Apparition* conjures both romantic love and death: youth and beauty are embodied in the spectral figure who exists, it appears, only as a reflection. Yet whilst luscious reds and pinks connote erotic passion and romantic love, might we imagine a more macabre intermediary than Harrison's skull, which also returns our gaze? As always, Harrison offers us both narrative and formal surprises. The *cadaverinae*, against expectation, are actually in the foreground, *cadaverina* being part of the name for the common bluebottle (*Cynomya cadaverina*). Here, they feed on the proceeds of death, dancing gleefully around the skull.

Across the paintings in *Existence*, a single figure reoccurs – the artist's 'muse', recreated as a figure possessed of an elegance from yesteryear. In both *Cadaverina and the Apparition* and *Shalimar Noir* (2008; overleaf), the muse is styled as a starlet from interwar film noir, although her symmetrical features lend her a timeless beauty and sphinxlike inscrutability. If in *Cadaverina and the Apparition* the muse has a phantom quality to her, in *Shalimar Noir* she resembles a monumental classical sculpture.

Harrison has described his work as enacting a form of witchcraft, and the central incident in *Shalimar Noir* is, improbably, the exorcism of a witch's cat by a wise old hare. A cascade of birds' souls spill from the cat's mouth – the souls of the creatures the cat has killed being freed from their purgatory, we may imagine. The conception is as strange and chilling as Blake's *Ghost of a Flea* (c. 1819–20). The world beyond our sensory perceptions is revealed through the hallucinatory, and thus imaginative, properties of the perfume. For Harrison and Blake alike, imagination renders the invisible visible. For Harrison, the reenchantment of nature can begin only after we are reconnected to the sensible world and the rapturous world of the imagination through realising the full potential of our senses. And as this suggests, for him our imaginative and sensible worlds are inseparable.

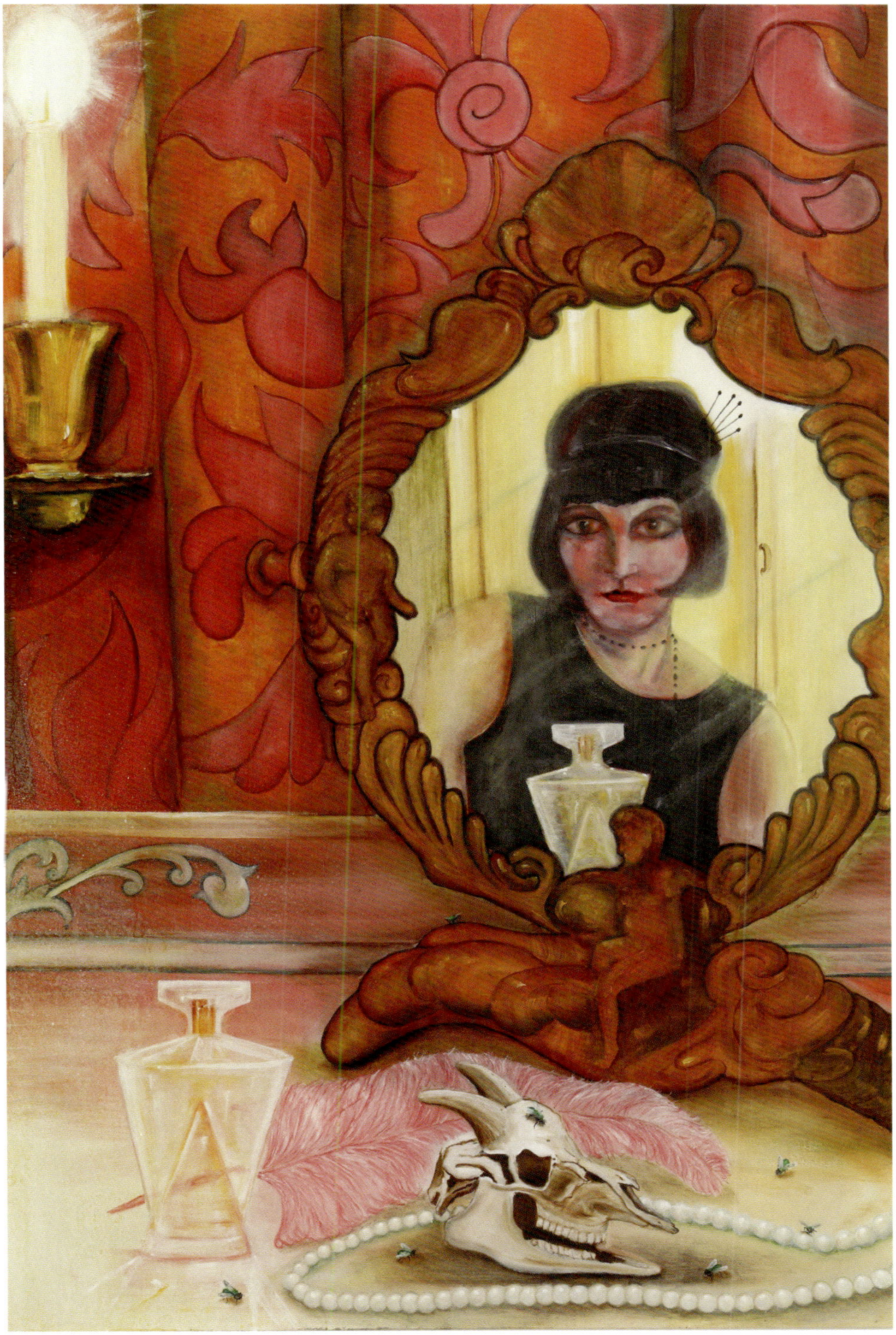

Cadaverina and the Apparition, 2008
Oil on wood, 122 x 81 cm

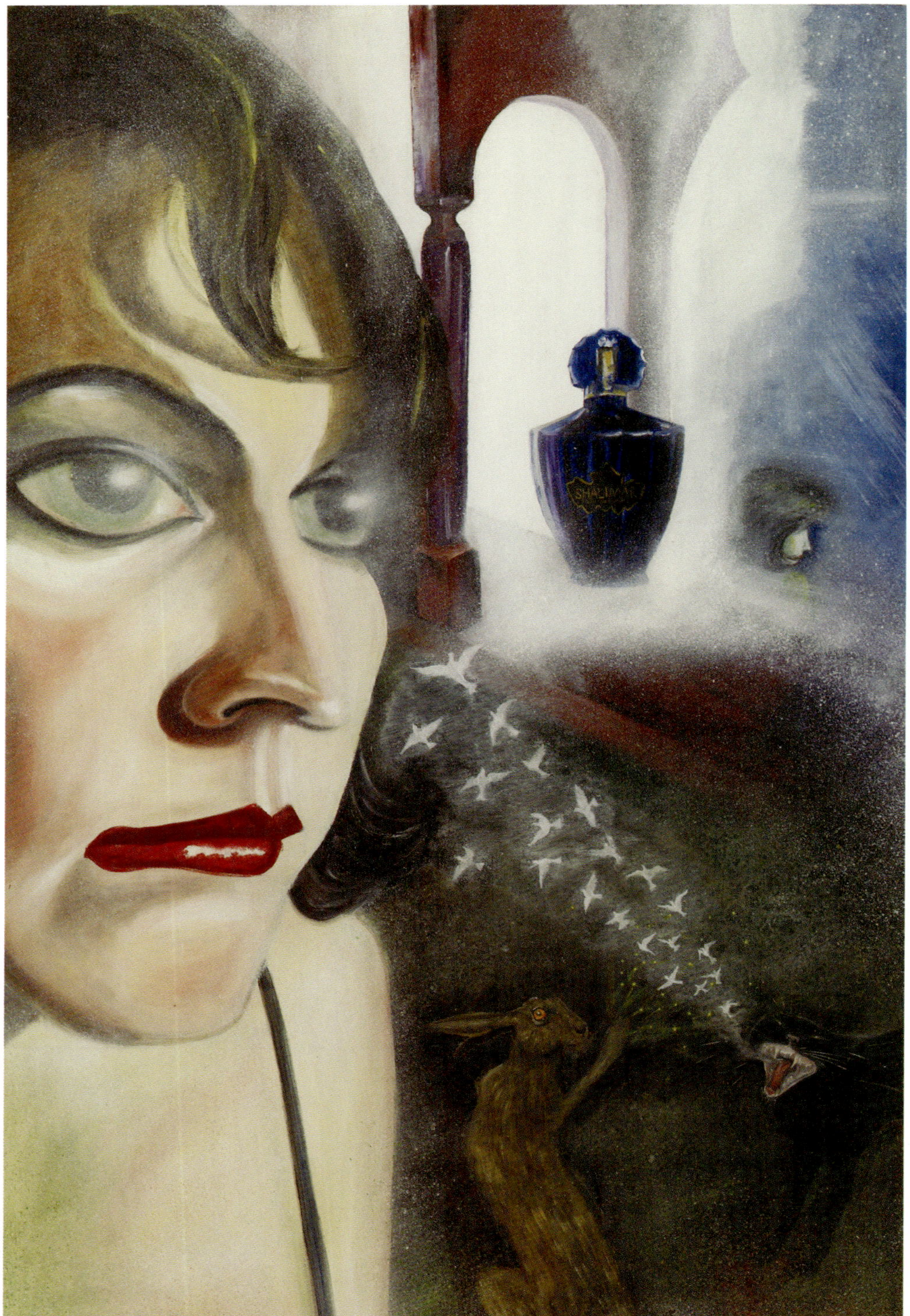

Shalimar Noir, 2008
Oil on wood, 122 x 81 cm

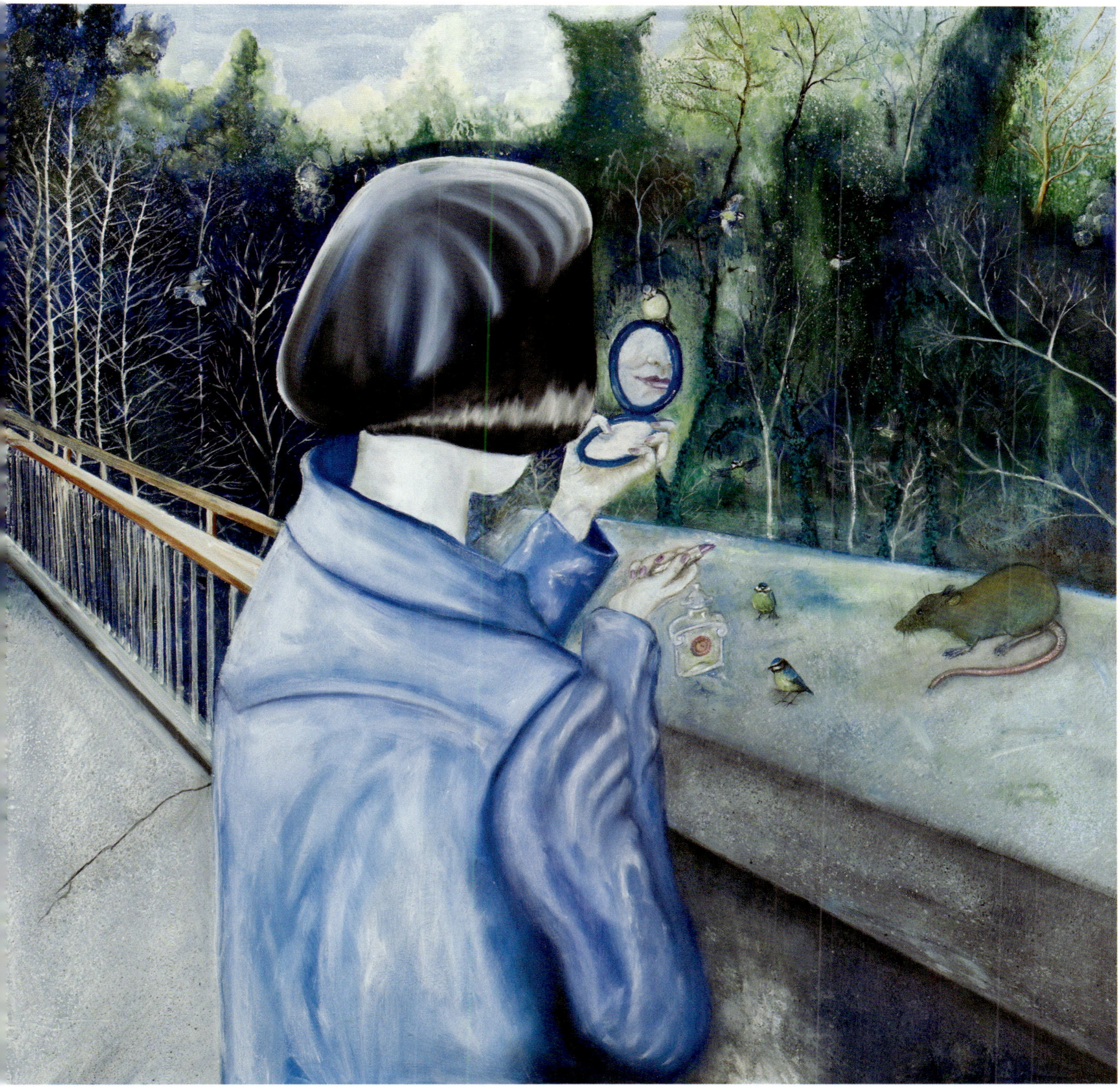

angled Up in L'Heure Bleue, 2008
Dil on wood, 60 × 60 cm

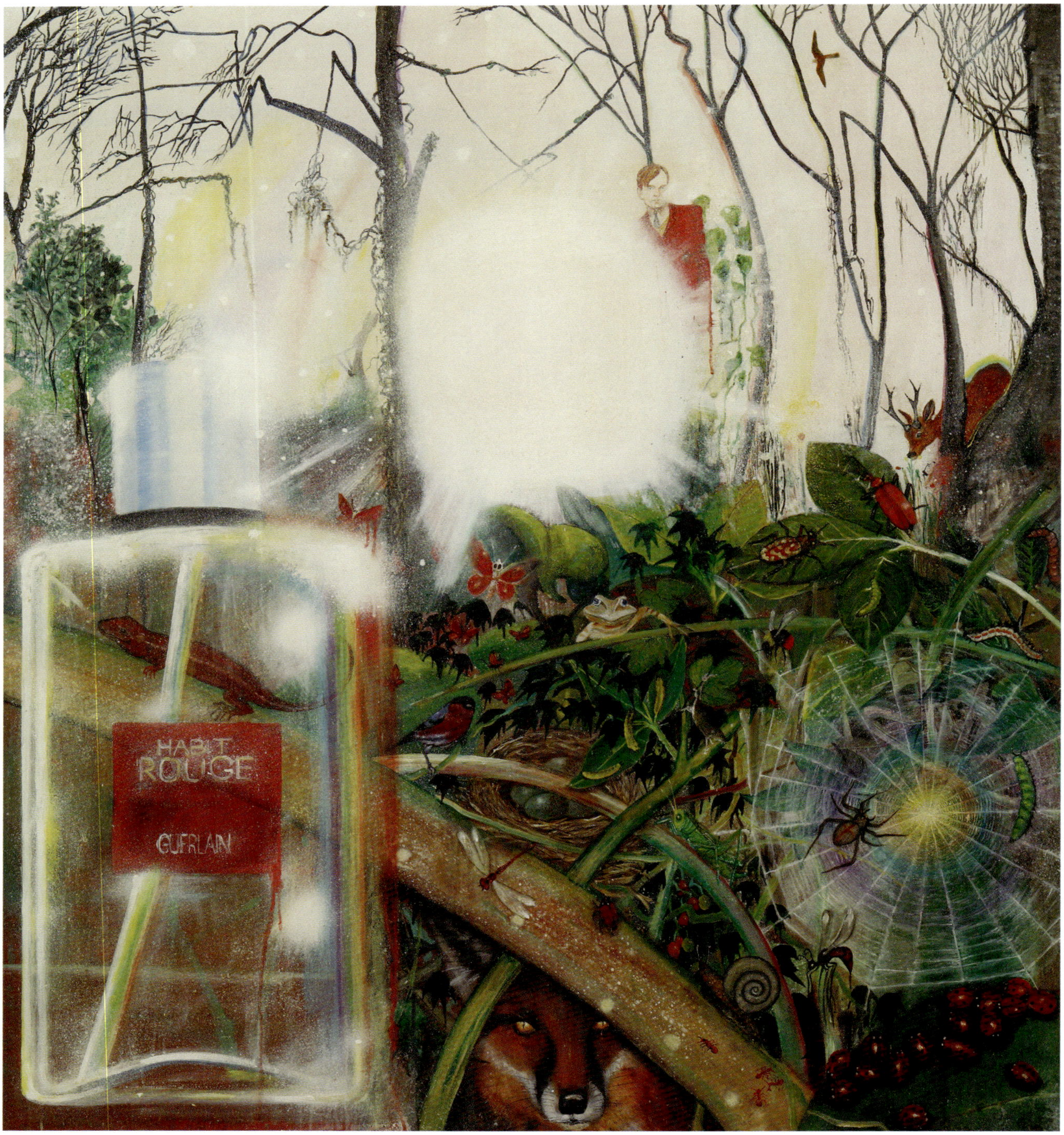

Red Jacket, 2008
Oil on wood, 110.3 × 100.2 cm

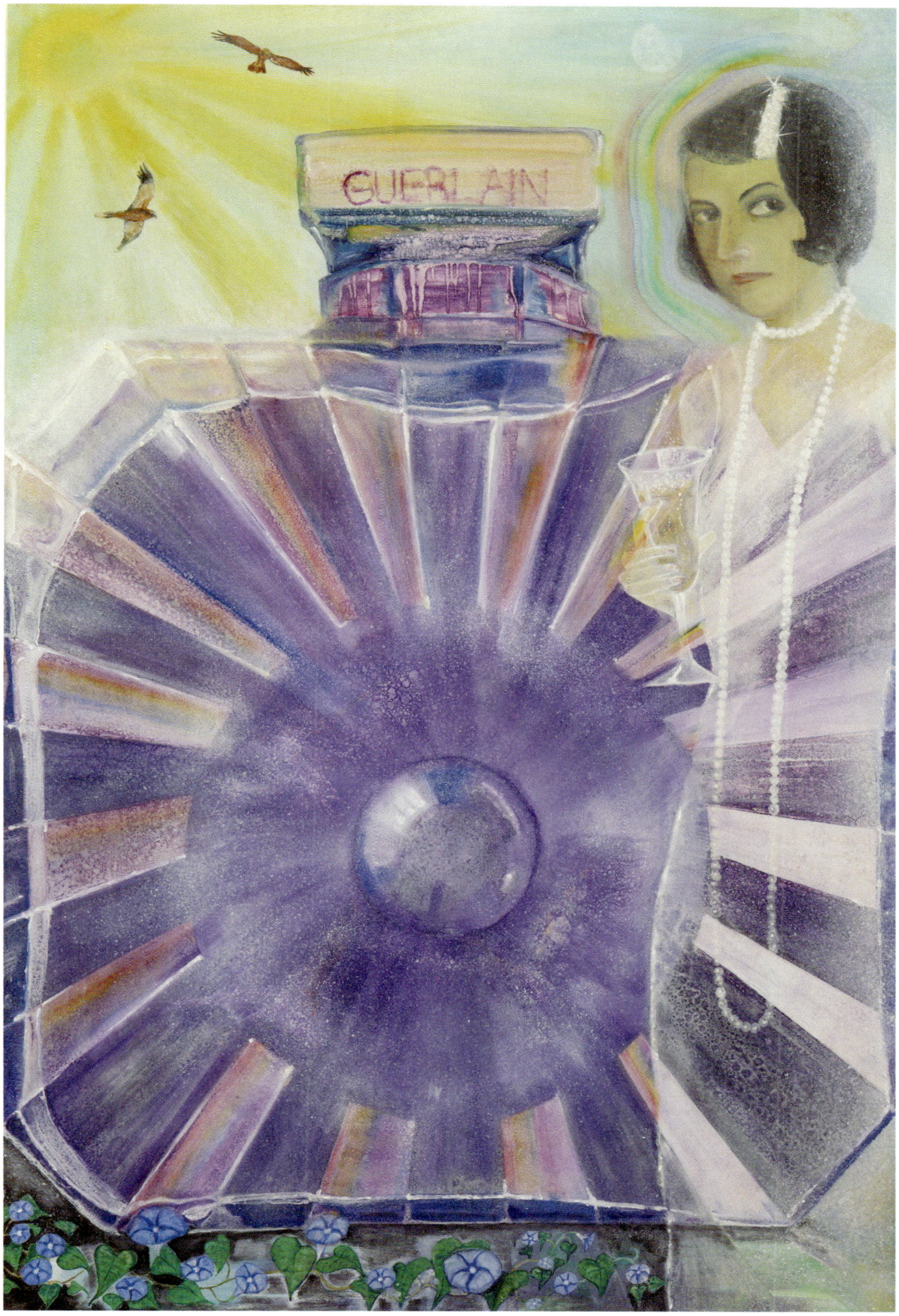

Night Flight, 2009
Oil on wood, 122 x 81 cm

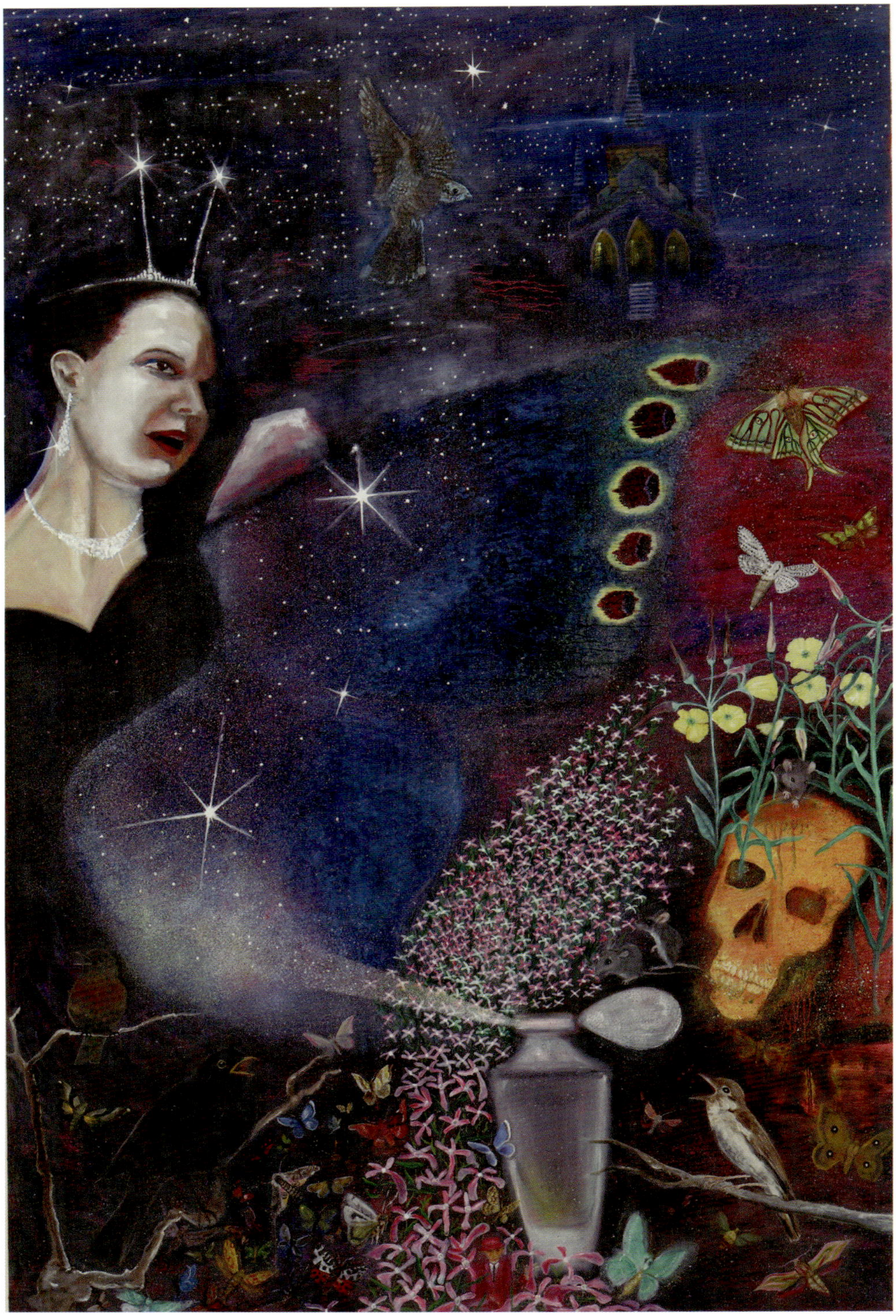

Midnight Butterfly, 2009
Oil on wood, 122 x 81 cm

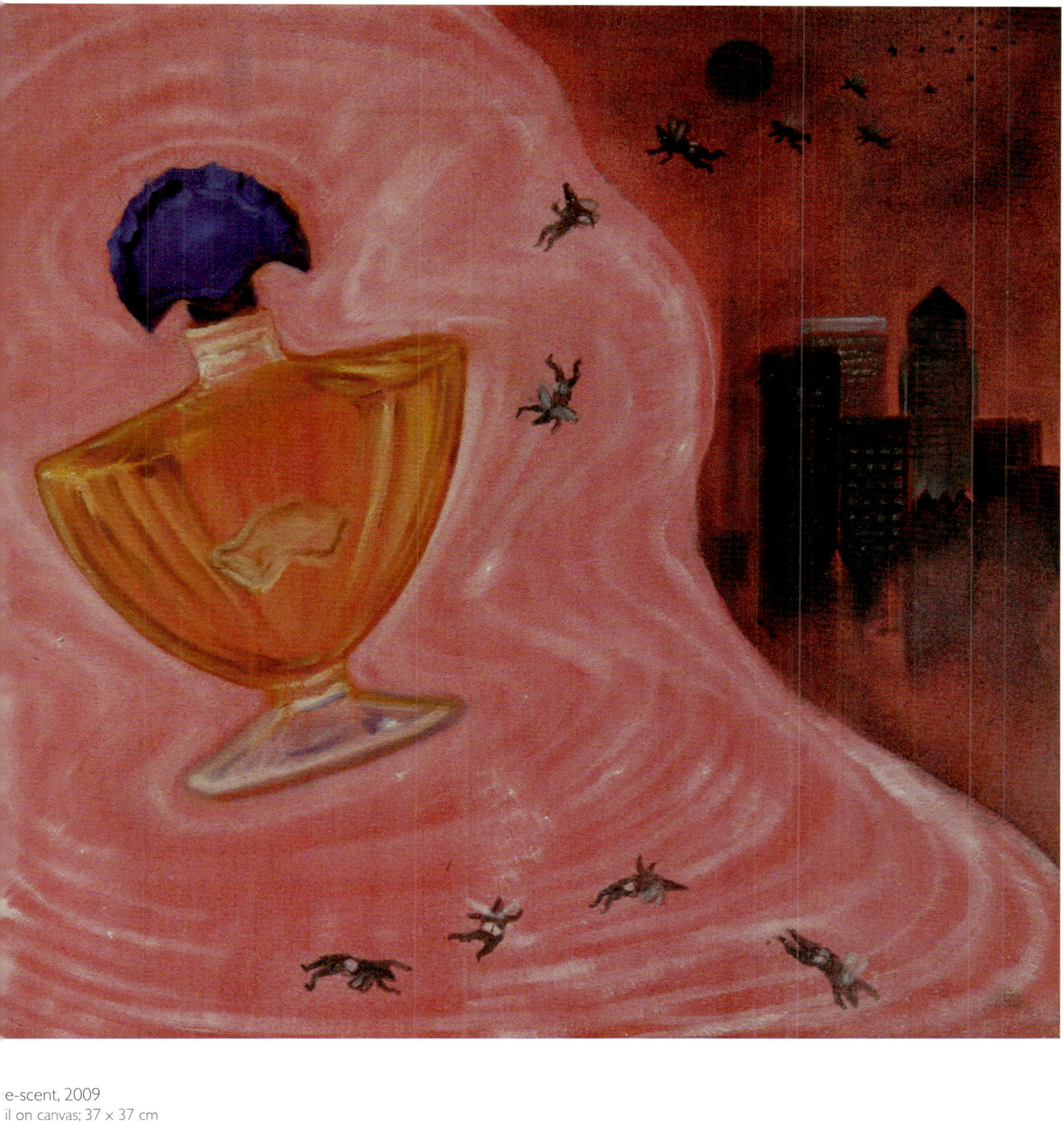

e-scent, 2009
il on canvas; 37 × 37 cm

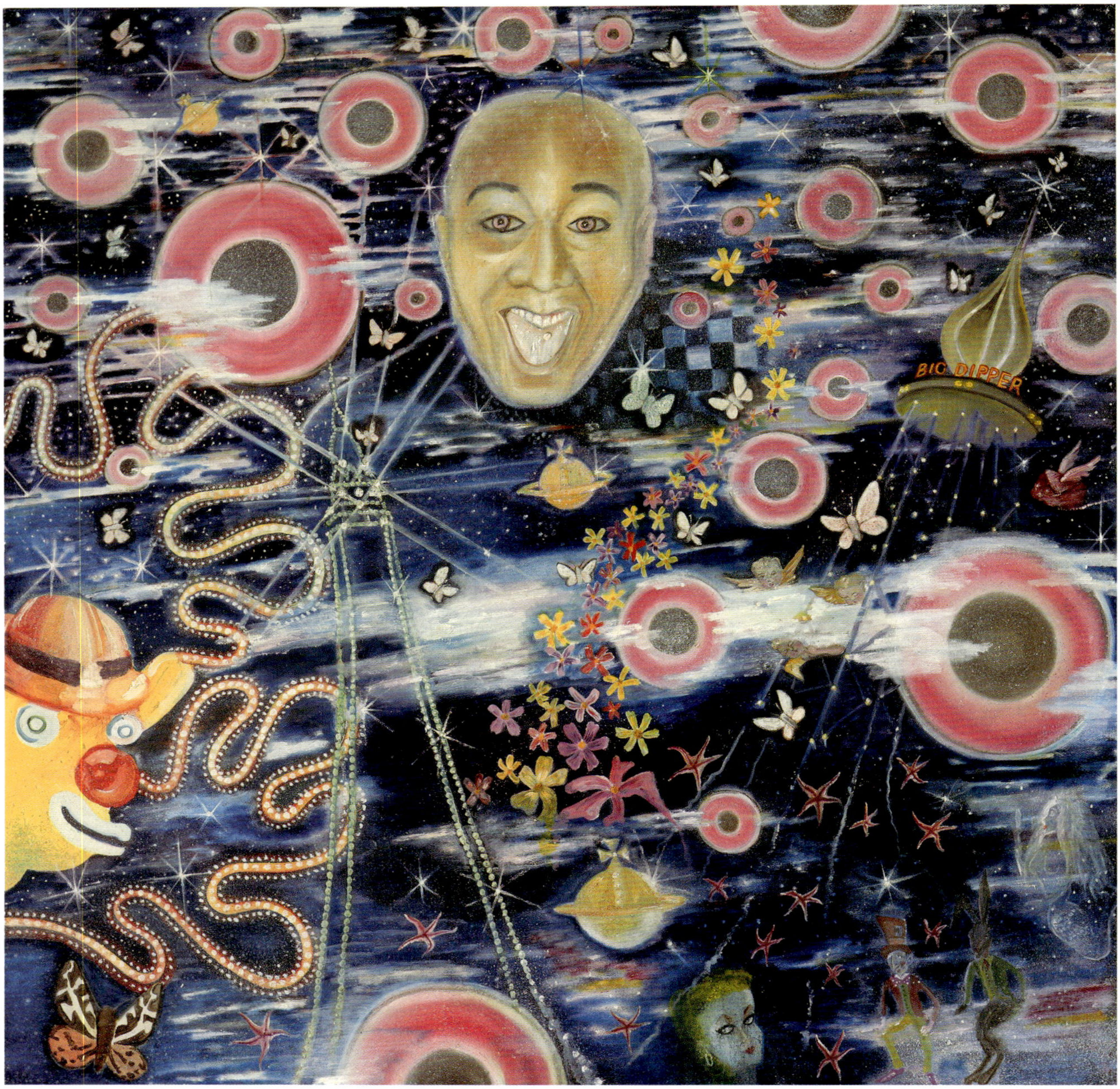

Mr Sparkle, 2006
Oil on canvas, 76 x 76 cm

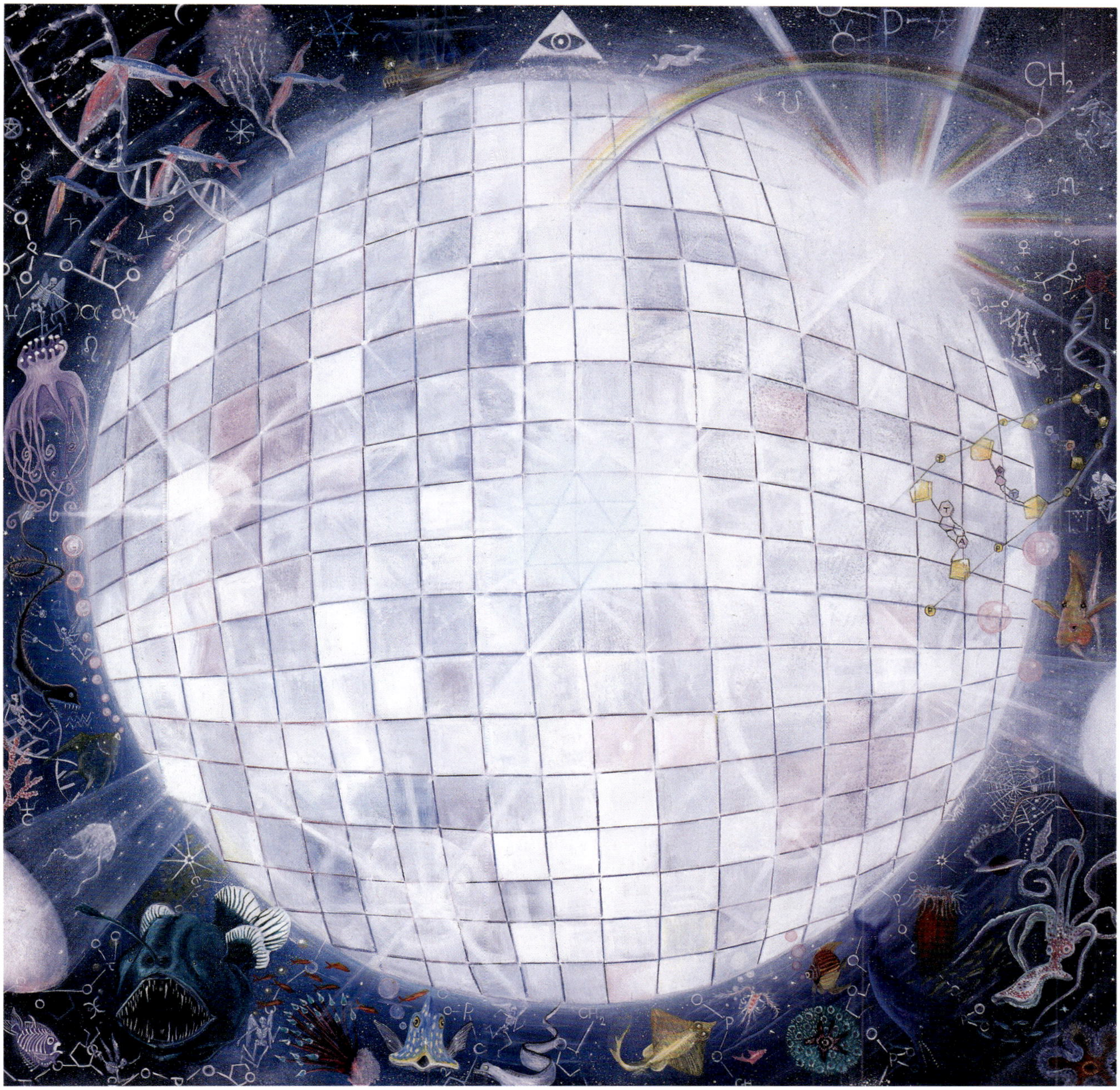

God, 2007
Oil on canvas, 91 x 91 cm

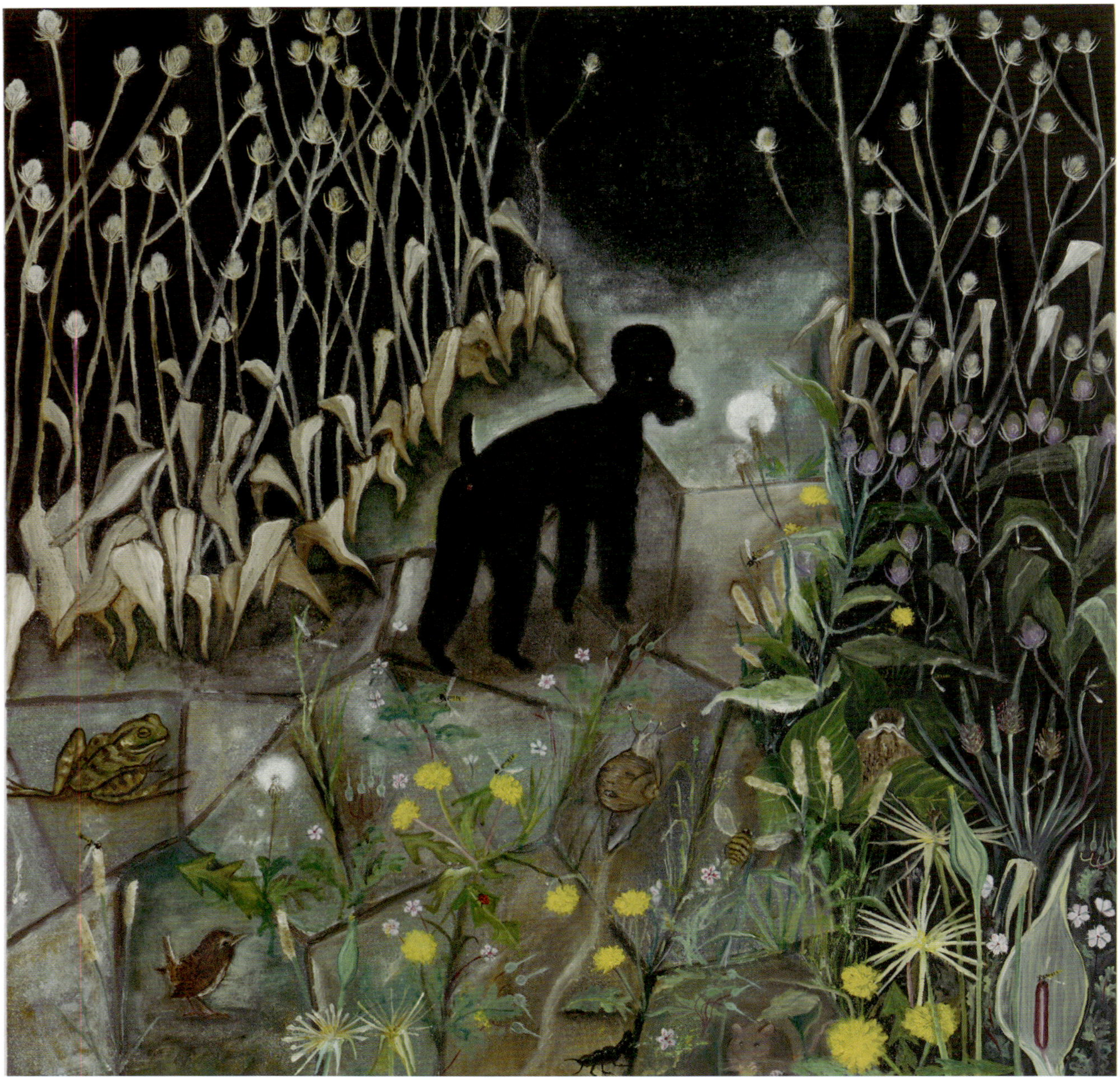

Up the Garden Path, 2007
Oil on wood, 60 x 60 cm

An Interview with Peter Doig

In April 2009, Peter Doig, renowned artist, friend and fellow student at St Martin's School of Art, met with David Harrison at his flat in North London. Sitting in the Hunting Lodge at the far end of the garden, they discussed art and life, interrupted occasionally by David's pet poodle Harrison barking at the host of birds flying down for their daily feed.

Speaker Key

PD Peter Doig
DH David Harrison

PD David, I wanted to start from the fact that your work seems to be about your life as a whole: acquaintances, interests, spiritual things. The private life and the work are inseparable.

DH They're inseparable.

PD Was there ever a single starting point?

DH I think it started as soon as I was conscious because I've always got overexcited about things. It's not enough just to like something: I have to gush. As far as life goes, I'm still gushing and I just hope that gush never stops. I think it's like constantly coming [laughs]. I do have a vivid memory from when I was two, though. I'd always try and get out of the pram, so my mum used to strap me in on my stomach. I'd be leaning over, watching the railings and the wall pass by, and I remember being consciously aware of their colour and pattern and texture.

PD Where was this?

DH This was where I was born, in East London. I used to have a trip from West Ham, where I lived, to Stratford where my nan lived.

PD What was it like growing up in the East End?

DH East London was like Gormenghast, it was full of eccentrics. *Everyone* was eccentric, so that was normal. And I was born into this world that had been devastated by war. Not that I thought about the war – it simply meant tons of space. You played everywhere; you could go on railway lines and old tube tunnels. The world was your playground.

PD Quite an outdoor life then, full of freedom?

DH I don't know if I had freedom. My mum was very, very strict. There was a lot of sneaking around.

PD Did anyone encourage you to make things?

DH No, there was nothing like that. As a child you just made your own toys. In our little gangs we'd get a whole derelict street with a house each. There were streets and streets and streets of abandoned houses. A bomb would have dropped on one and people fled, leaving all their stuff behind – clothes, furniture, everything. Once I went into a house and there was a perfect bedroom set up, except a tree was growing through the middle and on the mantelpiece there was a blackbird's nest with eggs in it. It was like a Magritte, or some mad de Chirico, although I didn't know that then. When I first started being introduced to modern art, I realised that I had been playing with it for years. Except the East End wasn't a dream world: it was real.

PD Yes, and in your work there is this mixture of nature, the built world and its inhabitants; no one takes precedence over the others. If this goes back to making your own toys and playing in abandoned houses, was there a point, at school maybe, when you started making things that might be considered to be, um...

DH Art?

PD Art [laughs].

DH Well, I think that was going to school, although, again, no encouragement there. I did lots of drawings. My dad used to work for Odhams Press, and he used to bring home lots of different types of stationery. I had all this posh stuff that no one else had – pencils and pens, rulers and putty rubbers. Dad was always bringing home loads of sellotape, which I made animals out of, to play with. Sellotape became a major material. It's nostalgic for me now.

PD But then I met you at St Martin's. How did you end up there?

DH Well I wasn't very good at school. I was very bad at school, in fact. When I was fifteen they decided to expel me. They called mum (she dealt with that sort of

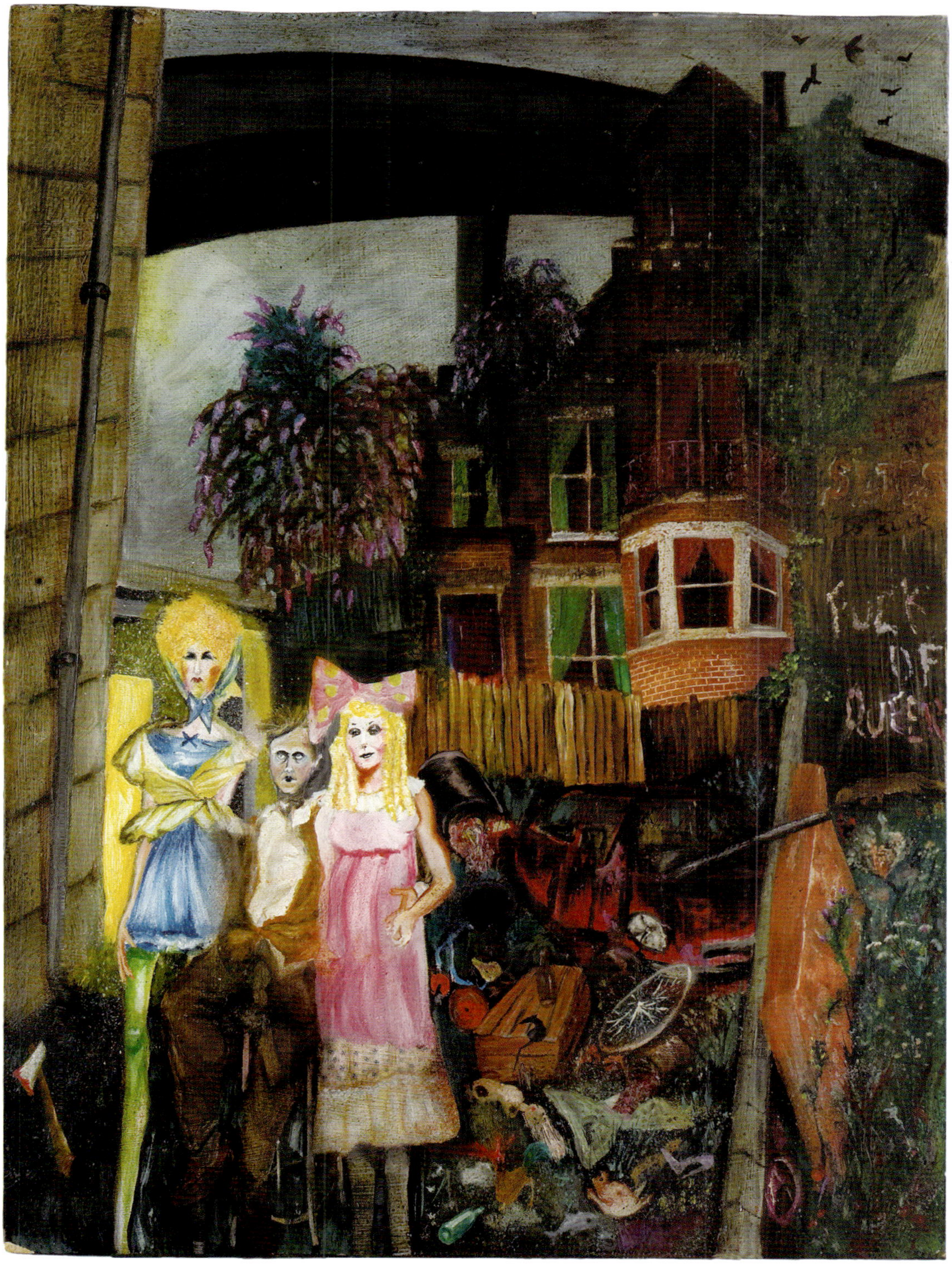

God Bless Our Happy Home 2001
Oil on wood, 69 x 51 cm

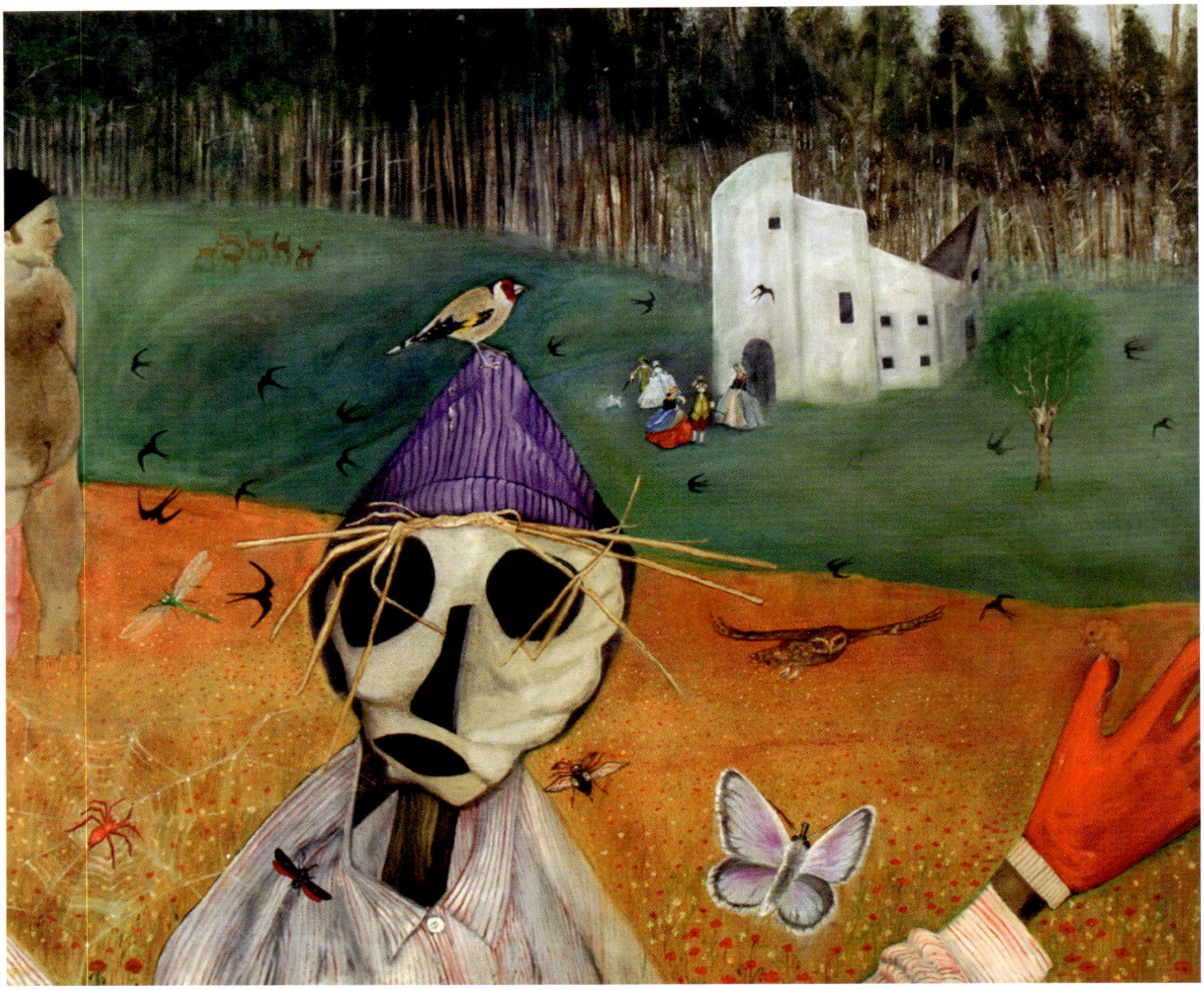

In Every Dream Home a Heartache, 2005
Oil on canvas, 76 x 91 cm

thing) and said 'We need him to leave school. He's got absolutely no ambition, he's never going to do anything, he's a bad influence.' And she said, 'David wants to be an artist.' They just said, 'You don't become an artist. Maybe David could go into graphics?' So that kind of put paid to that. It was a very working class thing. Dad was working for IPC magazines at the time, and I went to work there, for *Birds of the World* magazine, as an illustrator. It was because I was always good at drawing that when I was about sixteen they started sending me to a day release school, to learn to do proper drawings.

PD So how old were you when you went to St Martin's?

DH Well, I was a 'mature' student, which is a funny word as I was only in my mid-twenties, but among loads of very young people.

PD Why did you decide on St Martin's?

DH When I'd finished my day release, *Birds of the World* folded. By then I'd started mixing more in the London scene and I decided to leave IPC because I didn't want to have that kind of 'career'. I started working in the shop called Nostalgia, one of the first to sell what's now called 'vintage', but we used to just call them 'old clothes shops'. I met a whole different bunch of people then and they said I should go to art school. It sounds really dumb, but I didn't even know which school was an art school. Anyway, I started doing evening classes at West Ham College. A lovely lady called Rose Humble ran the art class and it was her who helped me sort out my A-levels and tried to get my portfolio together. She picked out a few colleges to apply for, and I saw that St Martin's was in Soho, so I went for that.

PD That's how I chose St Martin's as well, purely geographically. I had no idea about its history.

DH I must say when I went to look at St Martin's, there was something beckoning about it. I walked in the door – it felt warm, it smelt like an art school and looked kind of tawdry, like an old clothes shop. I loved it. The interview at Central was more like going into a fussy art shop, all talk of brushes and paper thickness.

PD And when you got there, what was most distinctive for you about the St Martin's experience?

DH Well, Soho was such a fantastic place; it was a village and it had something for everyone. There was a real gay scene going on. And there was no elitism – no VIP lounges. You could just wander about.

PD You had licence to go to all these little places that were actually quite exclusive – not because they were expensive, but because most people didn't know about them. But what was it like being at art school for you?

DH I was shocked by how suburban it was. I was surprised that my antics could shock the so-called wild and whacky people – lots of little rich kids. I thought everyone was going to be having orgies – though maybe orgies are too suburban.

PD In terms of trends, though, I think it was a time when you were able to develop your own work your own way. Young artists now are much, much more aware of outside pressures and influences than we were.

DH I wasn't aware of the outside world at all, in a career sense. I knew nothing about galleries. Being at art school wasn't an apprenticeship; people didn't take themselves too seriously.

PD It was all very in-house, wasn't it? It was about making work for your contemporaries within that building.

DH It was a protected environment. You could pop into each others' studios and talk about things.

PD I remember right from the beginning your work addressing your group of friends.

DH And the people were there when I was doing it.

PD There were always people in your studio, so if you hadn't painted whilst you had an audience there'd be no work! You even painted when you were talking – you're always talking.

DH And there was always something going on.

PD You went to the seaside on the weekend, you made a painting on Monday. You met

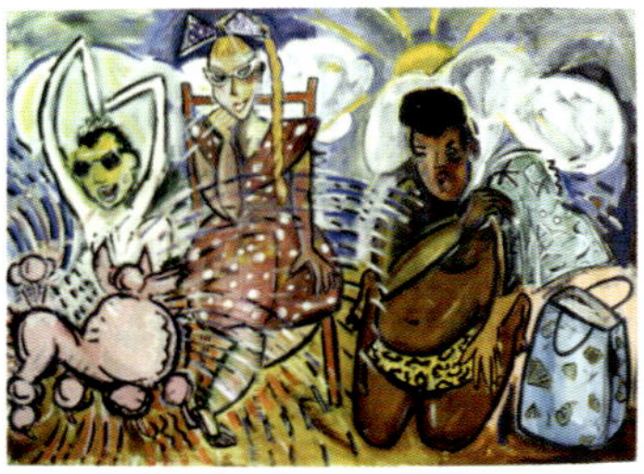

Fun On the Beach, 1981
Acrylic on canvas, 122 x 183 cm

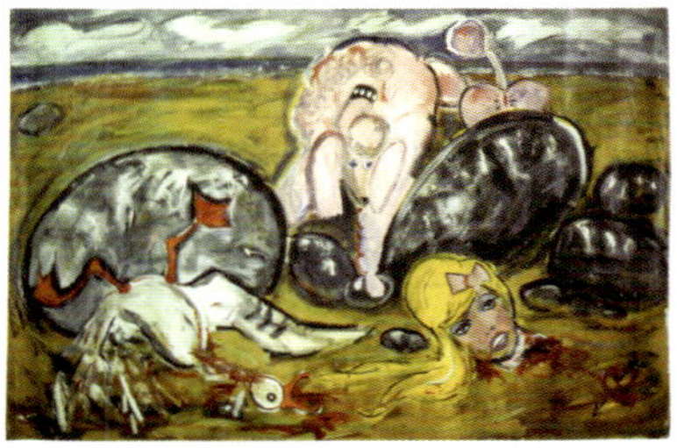

Hoover's Discovery on the Beach, 1982
Acrylic on canvas, 91 x 152 cm

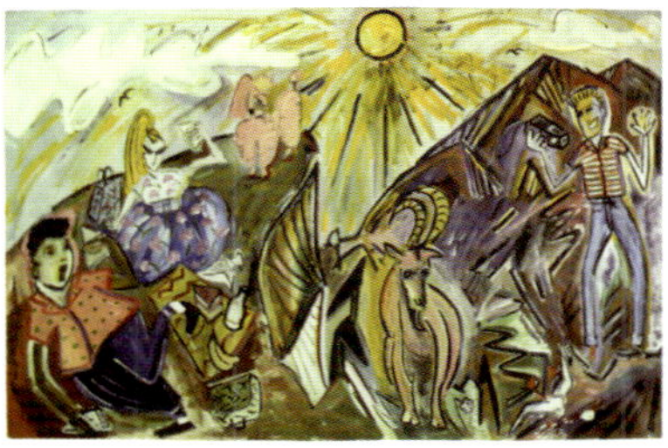

Picnic at Valley of the Rocks, 1981
Acrylic on canvas, 130 x 183 cm

someone and an encounter happened, you made a painting of that experience. You shared your life with us all.

DH It was like a book.

PD Yes, and it was open, happening and materializing before our eyes. It was almost like a daily cartoon in a sense, like a diaristic running commentary full of characters.

DH In those days, I was living in Foxley House with Jean and our two poodles, three cats and their countless kittens, three terrapins and a rabbit. A big party place. Me and Jean seemed a lot older, even though we weren't much.

PD From my perspective, you seemed to be a bit of a mentor.

DH Mums and dads [laughs].

PD To a group of us, not just students, your studio was always its own world.

DH There was a gathering of people all the time, the same as in the flat: people like Isaac would bring up others, and Joey would bring up all those rent boys and trannies. It was almost like the English East End version of the Factory, but without the self-consciousness.

PD No, it wasn't projecting back to the outside world. It was about doing things for us.

DH Oh god yes, it was almost a performance every night in the flat. If some of the things that went on there had been filmed they would have been so beautiful

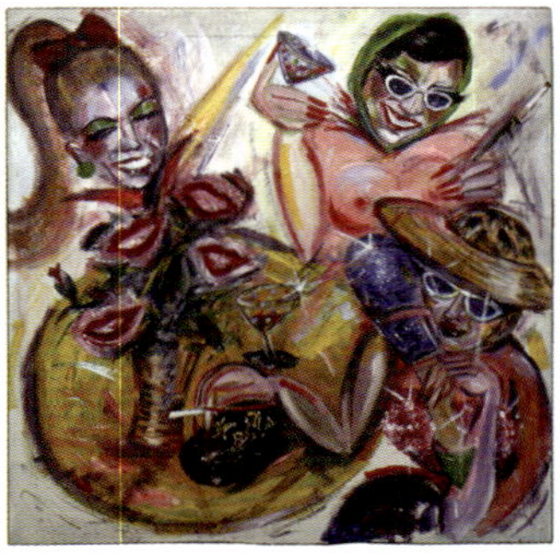

Jean, Ayshe & Narin, 1980
Acrylic on canvas, 100 x 100 cm

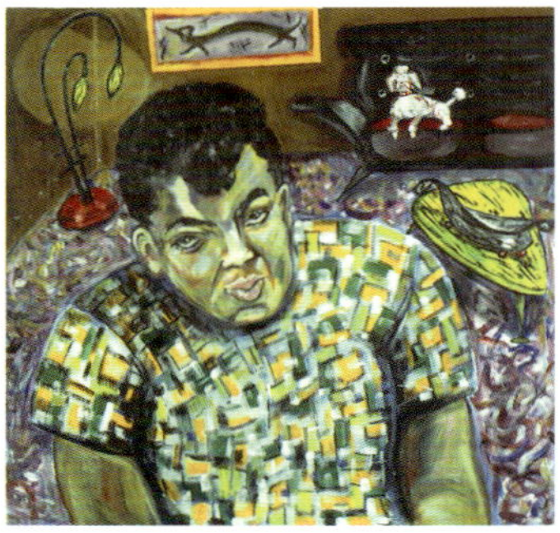

Joey, 1981
Acrylic on wood, 60 x 60 cm

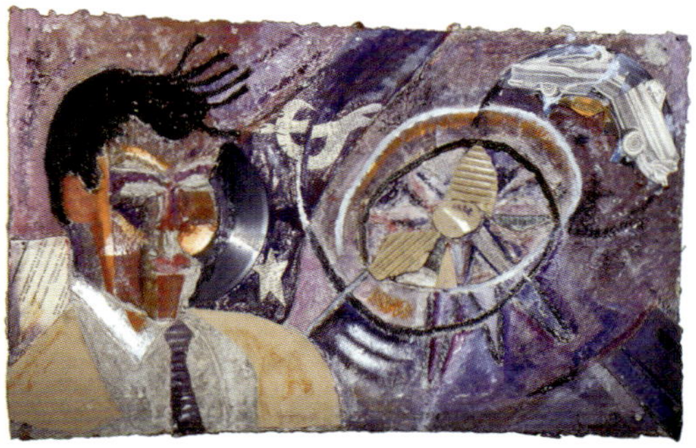

Isaac, 1980
Acrylic and paper mache on wood, 30 x 60 cm

now. I mean things like John dressing up as a woman and giving a little rendition when he was drunk, then we'd tie him up outside the pub [laughs]. Maybe they're more beautiful in the mind's eye.

PD Some people see everything they do as art and document it. Those early films of Derek Jarman and his group, for instance: they seemed to be conscious that they were making things to be shown.

DH None of us were there to be recorded – it was just a fleeting moment in time.

PD So in some ways even though your work has always been about your group, it's also been quite private.

DH But I do think that privacy was to do with being not all that confident. People think that I'm very confident and very mouthy or very showy, but most of the noise is because I am self-conscious and quite shy underneath. I know that if I don't make some kind of big noise at first then I won't make any at all.

PD I think it takes a brave person to be a brave artist. Maybe with you this is partly to do with being gay and having encounters with strangers, on occasion – I hope I can say that.

DH Yes. Not enough occasions!

PD An encounter with someone new, or a stranger, is a 'what if' scenario. What if they're psychopathic, what if they're immensely powerful and dangerous, what if they have no legs?

DH At least you could run away.

PD But take the paintings of Pan, starring the builder that you saw on the street. They're full of desire and danger; they're highly erotic and funny; but they're remarkable because they come out of putting yourself at such risk. You showed them to the builder, is that right?

DH Yes. He was horrified that I'd given him horns. He had a huge crucifix around his neck; maybe I should have guessed he was religious. He was Albanian and his English wasn't good. I just said, 'I painted you as Pan. You're the god of nature,' but he couldn't divorce it from the devil, which is sad, because they're very different. I had wanted him to come in and strip off, but he wouldn't. I do think there was a fear there; it's funny, what did this big, powerful man think I was going to do? Although I have to admit you can't divorce the sexuality from the art. I want to make the audience see what I'm attracted to, I suppose.

PD When did you first see John Waters's films?

DH I think I saw *Pink Flamingos* in about 1973, a year or so after it came out. I was in Paris; it was something to do. I think that they made more of an impact in England, though, because his imagery of trash culture was so new. I used to think Waters's films were tongue in cheek, but there's a serious worship of celebrity culture which is repulsive. [Barking].

PD I suppose I brought up John Waters because of how extreme the characters in his films looked and behaved.

DH In fact, I think Divine was the genius of it all. He had the look, the walk, the talk, the action. Waters sold him off as a freak, but he was a very, very clever man. The sad thing now is that every fucking woman walking down the streets looks like Divine – but without the carefully skilled make-up and the movement [laughs]. Back then, I recognized the Waters look from when I was younger. We used to go and follow women with bouffants. When I was about ten, there was a sensational biker bird called Angela Stavers (I loved the name), who lived round the corner in a cottage by the railway line. She was like our pop star. We used to sit on the steps to watch her come out in fantastic leather miniskirts, stilettos and chain bracelets, and fishnet tights that used to cut into her legs, so little blobbles bulged out. She had pearlescent make-up and this black hair in a big, high bouffant with a fringe in her eyes, and big black false eyelashes that were coated with kohl pencil. Her boyfriend used to park on the corner, and she would skip round – click, clip, boomp, boomp. And on top of all this glam, glitzy stuff, the boyfriend would put a heavily studded, chained jacket over her shoulders. Then she'd perch on the bike, and off it would go – VROOM! That was performance art.

PD You were always into the way you looked. I don't think I've ever seen you casually dressed, even in your studio.

DH Am I not casual now [laughs]?

PD You told me a funny story once about getting ready to go out for a night when you still lived at home. You were getting changed in your bedroom…

DH Ha, I had a pair of bright pink jeans on and a red t-shirt from Let It Rock, or Sex, as it might have been called then. It had two cowboys on the front facing each other, with very big cocks – a famous t-shirt now.

PD Where were you going?

DH I was just going to the local pub, I wasn't a great clubber. This was 1973, so before punk. Mum always used to pop out of the kitchen and she caught me on the stairs. I stood there, worried, because she must have seen the t-shirt, and she said, 'You're not going out like that, surely?' I said I couldn't see why not, and she said, 'You can't wear red and pink, it's a terrible combination!' I remember my answer: 'Schiaparelli said that you could in 1955 and she brought out a perfume called Shocking to go with the pink and red look.' The funny thing, though, was that mum stopped me because of the colours and not because of the porn – it's not pornographic now, but it was slightly porny at the time. Not long after, Malcolm McLaren got arrested for that t-shirt – he invited me along to court, so I sat in the dock for support, all along wearing the t-shirt. Nobody noticed! But it was only in 1967 that homosexuality was, um, legalized.

PD Decriminalized.

DH Or decriminalized [laughter]. Choosing an outfit was one of the road signs down a road that had never been followed before.

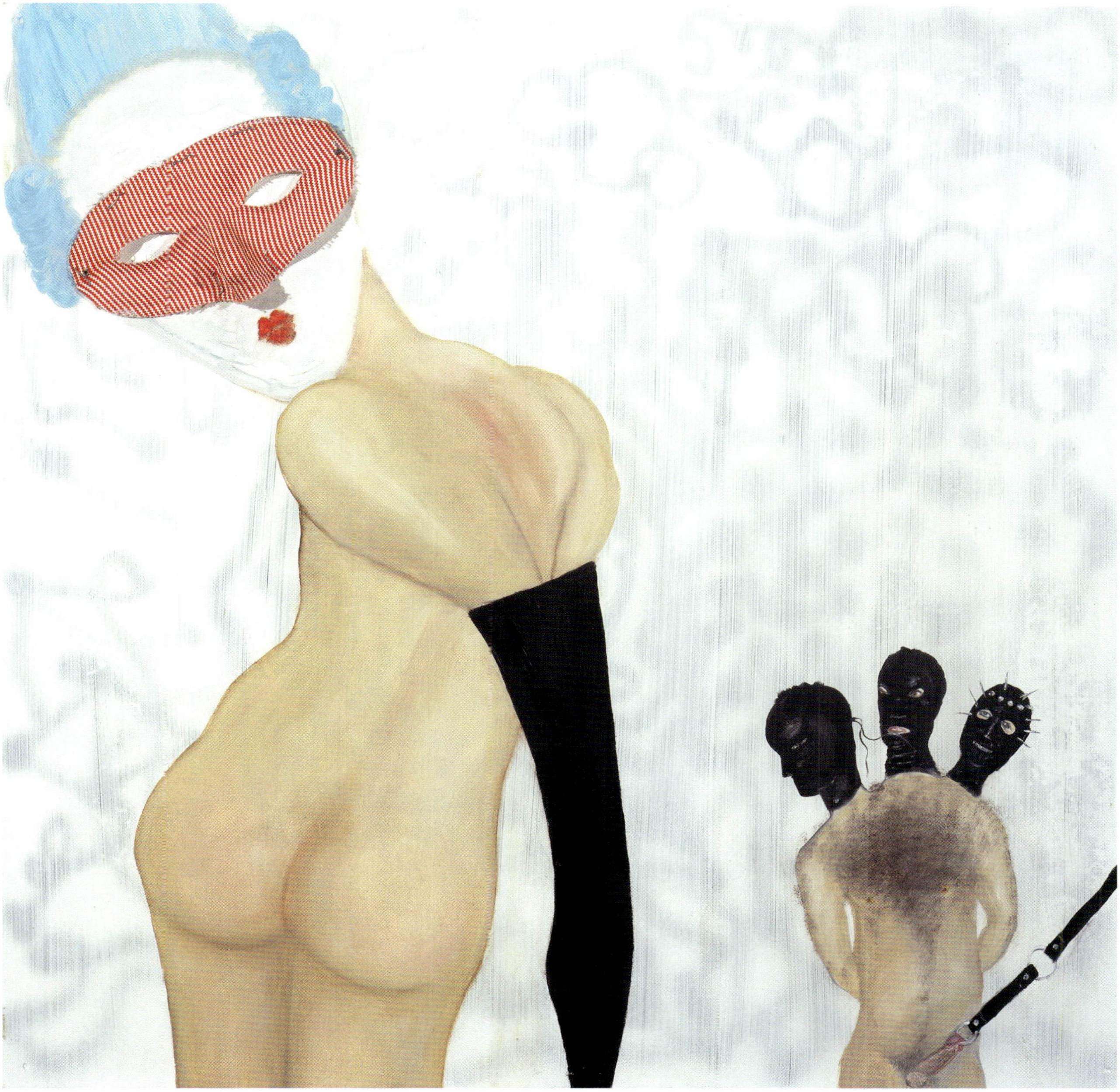

Persephone Tempts Cerberus, 2007
Oil and collage on wood, 60 x 60 cm

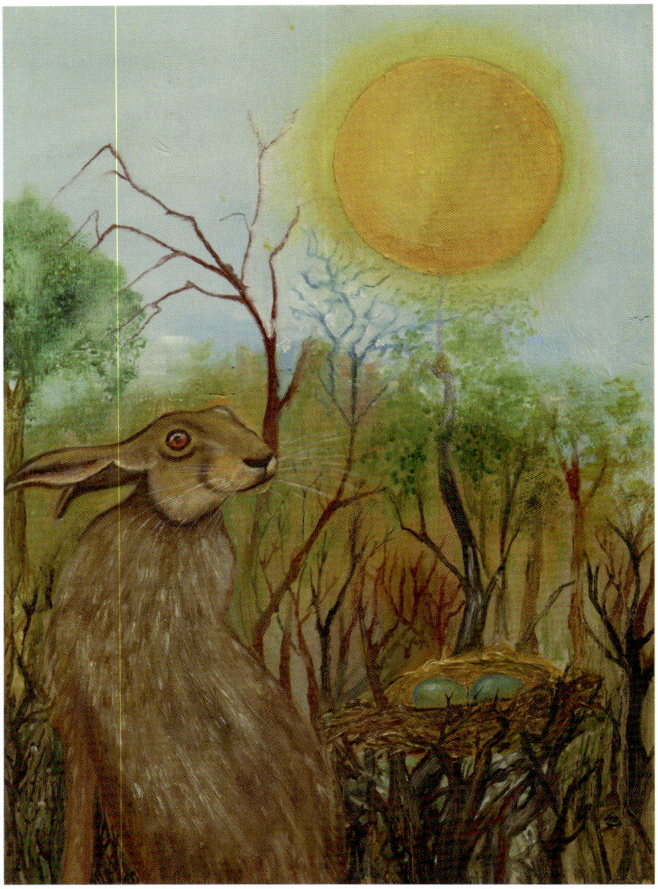

Hare Nest Day, 2008
Oil on wood, 41 x 31 cm

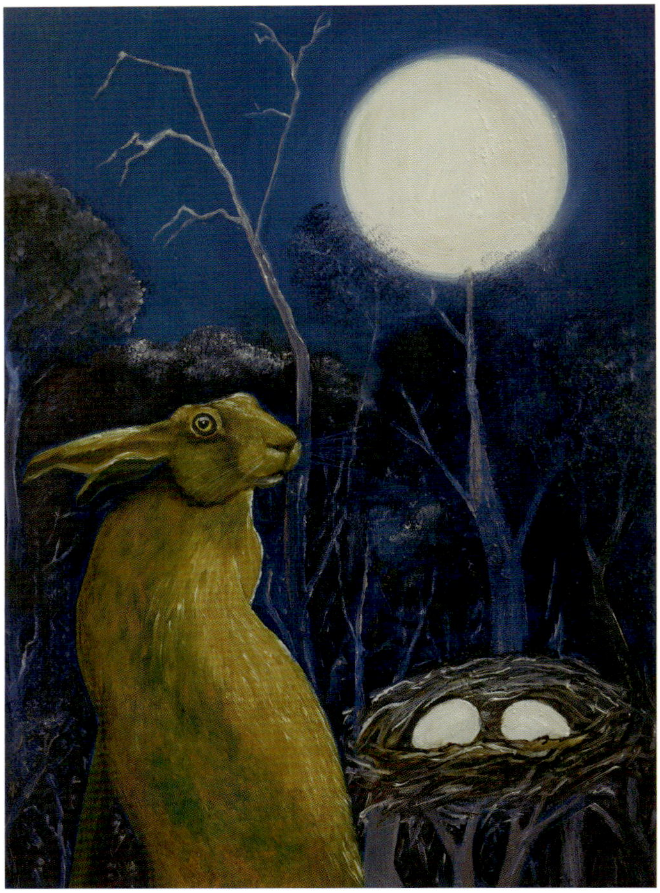

Hare Nest Night, 2008
Oil on wood, 41 x 31 cm

PD You didn't feel scared at all?

DH No, it was a different climate. I had never really been beaten up badly at that time. Provocation was fun and a bit of a joke, and also quite sexual, because most of the people that stopped you were big, hunky workmen: ''Ere mate, what have you got there?' You could tell they were getting a bit turned on by the ultra-open sexuality of it. But when you're young you feel indestructible, like Superman: my clothes were my cape [laughs]. I could fly through them.

PD So walking to the pub in 1973 in *that* t-shirt, did that attitude inform your work?

DH Oh god, yes. It was a 'fuck you' attitude. Remember too, I left school in about 1969, a little skinhead. Skinhead was very much an East London thing; it was the last true street movement before everything was crushed and manufactured.

PD You mean compared to punk? You could buy the t-shirt and be a punk.

DH Yes, punk was a completely made up look. Punk was middle class, really. Skinhead was about being from working class origins. When I was at school, if you were a bad boy the system sent you to Borstal. But being a bad boy in those days had an element of creativity to it – naughty ones were on top of things, always knew what was what, always inventing. So it was often the more interesting, clever, creative ones that got sent to Borstal.

PD They wanted to silence them because they had something to say?

DH Proper rebels did! There was one very handsome boy who was sent to Borstal, he created my first image of skinhead. When he came back, the school had been put into a brand new building made of lots of glass, so you could see the whole playground. He was driven in on a scooter by a friend; we heard it pull up and ran to the window, transfixed.

PD This sounds like another performance, like the motor cycle girl.

DH Exactly. At Borstal you had your head shaved bald. Now this boy made a feature out of it and cut a parting – it was almost surreal, having a parting in something that couldn't part. And he was wearing what's called a Crombie coat, with a spotted handkerchief and a pair of jeans rolled up high. And these big boots, what were called Rosie Reds: bright red workman's boots that were steel-toed, except the toe had been cut out so the steel was on show, and polished. It was everything that an English country gent would wear, except the other way round. Instead of polished shoes it was polished steelwork; a neat hairstyle cut into a bald head. He walked across the playground with such a stride, clutching records, and we all ran out and gathered round him like a gaggle of hens feeding off the farmer. He was like, 'Yeah what? I've just been away and I met all these black kids and they gave me these records. Have you ever heard of ska?' Straight away, everyone ran out and got all their hair cut off and pretended they'd been to Borstal [laughs]. Well, they hadn't.

PD How did this filter into your paintings at college?

DH When I got to college, I had fond memories of all these records and we used to go to Stratford Town Hall, which had reggae dances. Artists and DJs from Jamaica used to come over (there were no real DJ stars then apart from on the radio). Someone called Sir Coxsone came over once. All his old records were scrubbed out so you couldn't see the names of what was playing. It was like the opposite to promotion, rough and raw. The audience was a mix of little local skinheads and black people. That's the funny thing about skinhead, how it's changed round, because they were the first to start mixing with black people and that music culture. We also got strange bohemian types: big, fat black women looking just like something out of a Divine film, with loads of white powder on their faces and blond wigs, as if they were trying to look white. They came down from the West End with queers in flares who must have been pill poppers. They were the leftovers from the beatniks. They'd dance away to ska, because they'd known it from the mod clubs, from years ago. I wanted to celebrate that time because it seemed like it was a very special, small pocket of people.

PD This is ten years later, 1979.

DH Yes. I did quite a lot of paintings about ska culture – it was the avant garde in its way, with skinhead coming up in the middle of it. That's when I got interested in Edward Burra too, the paintings he made in Harlem in the 1950s. I did a painting of a big, black woman dancing, called *Return of the Ugly*. There was one record I loved by The Upsetters, which was called *Return of the Ugly*. I used to have a little record player in my space, remember? I used to leave the arm off so *Return of the Ugly* kept playing over and over again. But then we both brought our world into our work. Looking back to the paintings you were doing of King's Cross, with the gasometers and Greek statues, you were celebrating the place.

PD I lived in King's Cross for seventeen years and I couldn't prevent it entering my work.

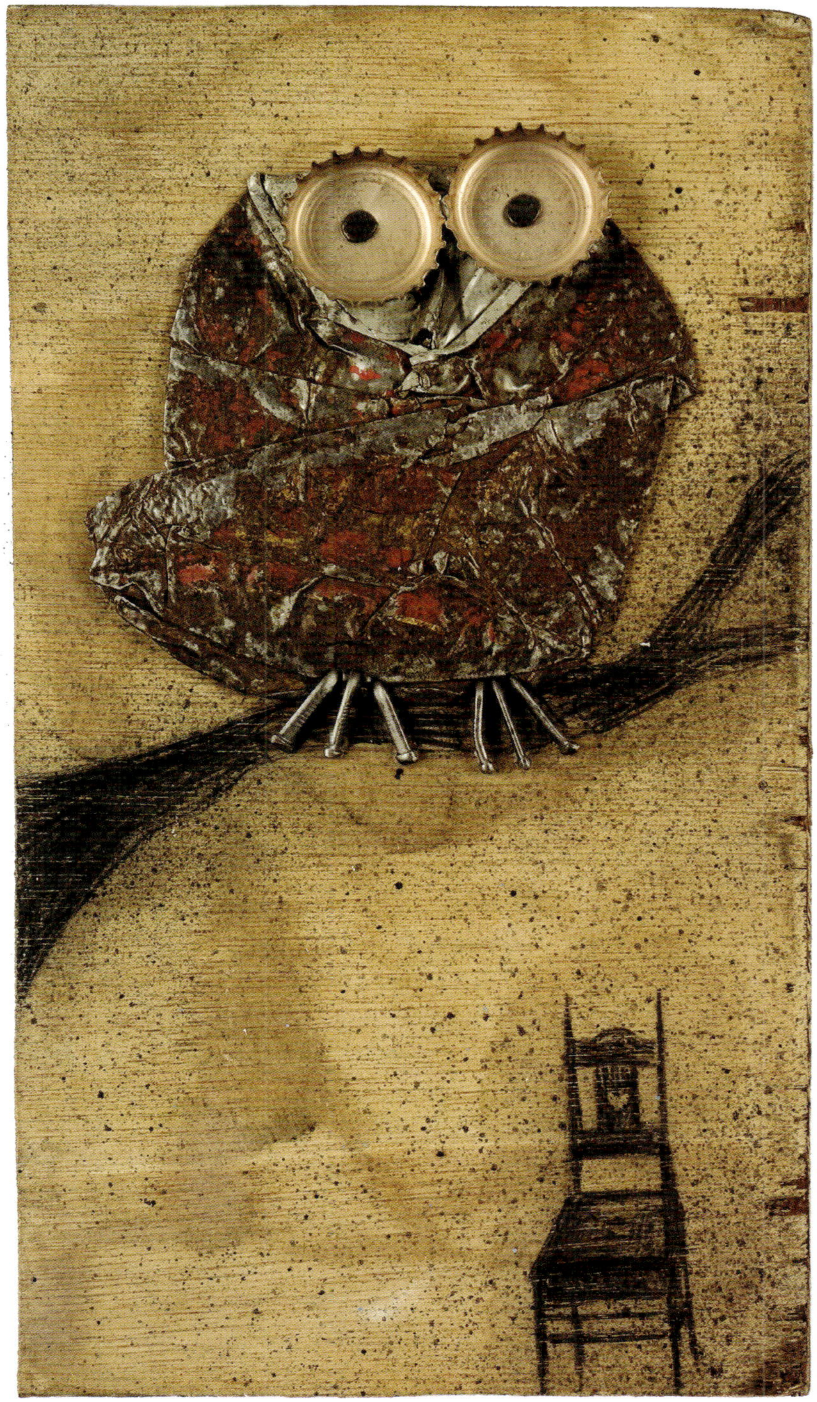

Fledgling Owl, 2002
Found objects and pencil on wood, 28 x 15 cm

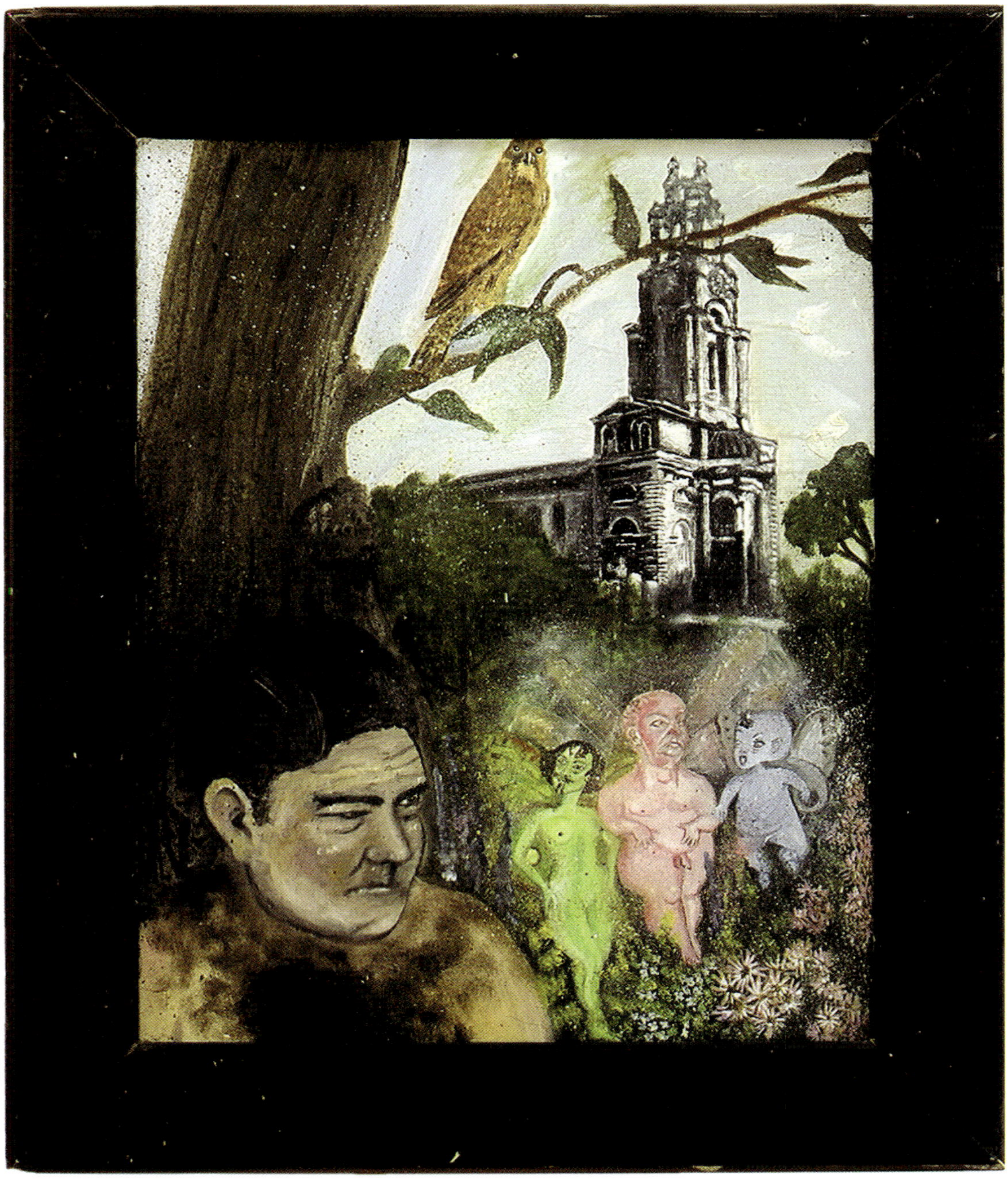

Limehouse Faries, 1998
Oil on wood, 60 x 46 cm

DH We used to do all sorts of things on your roof, and there was lots of parties, just a quid to get in to cover the costs.

PD The nightlife around there was such a potent world. As young artists, that was such an exciting thing in our lives, but it's difficult to make art about it. Edward Burra's paintings of nightclubs and Harlem and those Boston bar scenes are all the more remarkable for being so much of their moment. I think when we were both at St Martin's, our work was more similar in attitude than subjects. It was anti-painting, in a way. Maybe 'anti' is too strong a word, but it wasn't trying to be 'good'.

DH 'Flippancy' is the word for it.

PD I think young artists have to make a lot of art, even bad art, to get it out of their system. Otherwise, everything can get too precious and cautious too soon.

DH Or self-conscious. Learn to throw things away. Making work is like gardening. A plant will die down in the winter, appreciate it in the meantime.

PD Something else will happen next year, something better. And the paintings you made at St Martin's certainly had attitude in the way they were made, with their acrylic paint. As far as our tutors were concerned at that time, the dominant trend in British painting would have been called something like Lyrical Abstraction, or paintings that were obsessed with ideas about the sublime and fetishizing material. Your paintings were absolutely opposed to that, because they were made with plastic paint, very fast and direct. I could say garish was the immediate impression. But sometime after you left St Martin's, darkness creeps into the paintings, especially those of the 1990s, like in *Limehouse Fairies* and *King's Cross Fairies*. There's more literal depth in the surface, but there's also a lot more depth of thought. You changed materials and started to take a lot more time over the paintings. They became reflective, the minutiae and the details became stronger.

DH Yes. I moved to oil paint, which requires a system, unlike acrylics. When I used acrylics, it suited the fast-lived culture. I didn't want it to last; I didn't want that importance. Again, although it seemed aggressive, I always had a feeling of not being quite good enough to make a definitive statement. It's hard to see for myself where it went, but all the things

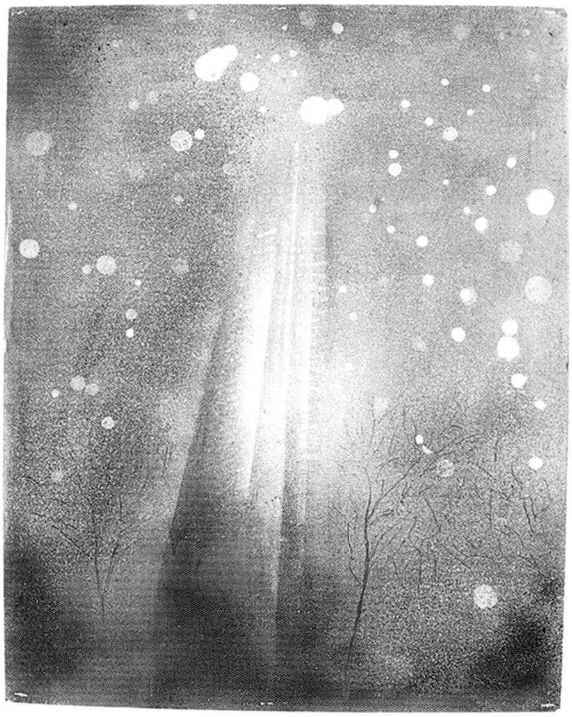

Barbican Tower, 2004
Oil and conté on paper, 65 x 49 cm

I took for granted were leaving my life. First of all there was illness and going to hospital, and then the realization that I'm not indestructible after all. I started to look at the world with a more curious eye.

PD At people?

DH Not just people: London. Although I was certainly enjoying London, I woke up one day and it started to disappear, bit by bit. [Barking] **Oh no Harrison, don't chase him off, you're so horrible! I said don't!** That's the only sparrows we've got left in London now. There'd be plenty of them if we just left them some space. Everything's so cleaned up and built over now that there's no voice for animals. Animals are treated as a nuisance in London.

PD I see the animals in your work as being almost like types of people that don't exist any more.

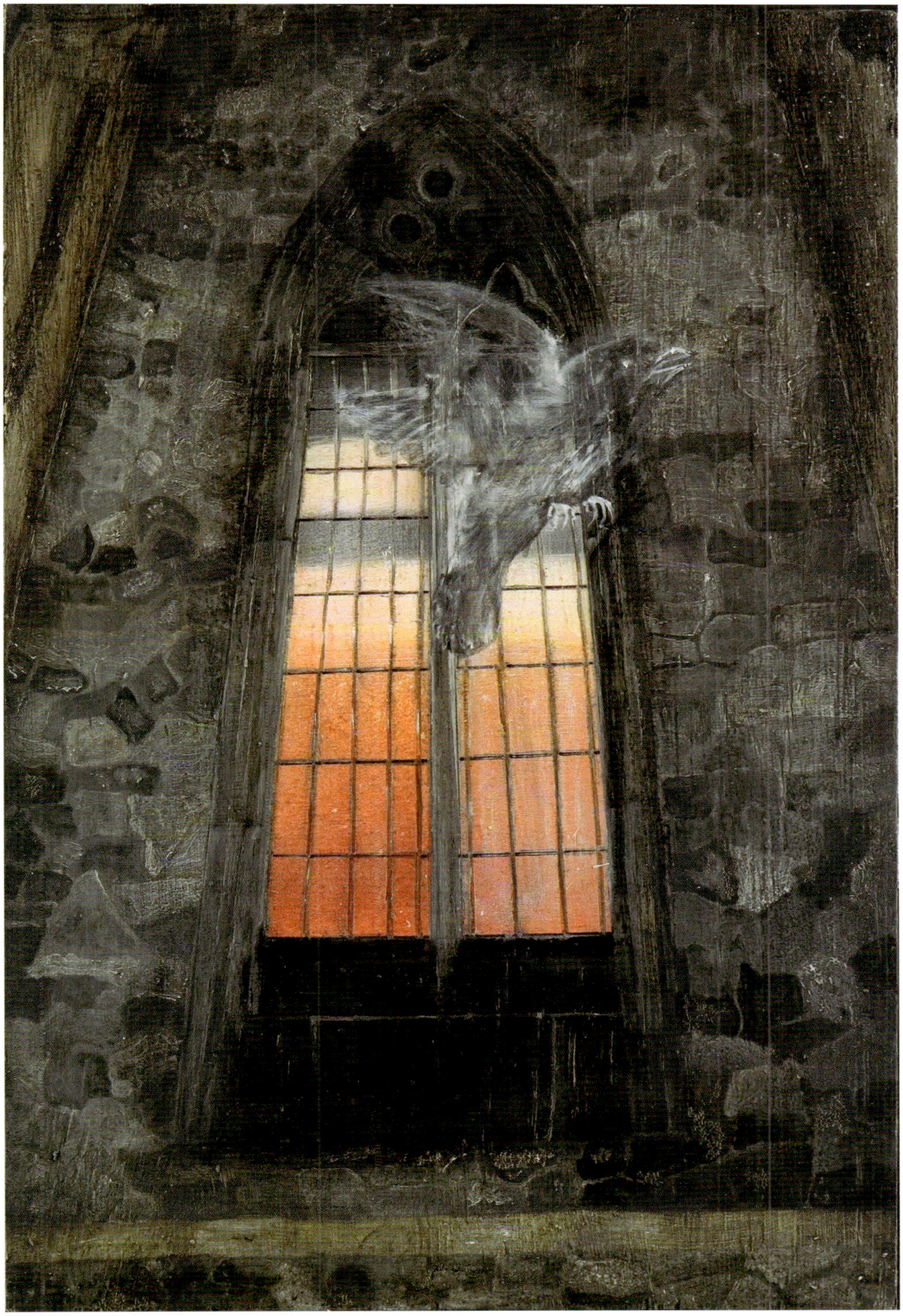

Shadow of a Sparrow, Requiem for Our City Birds, 2004
Oil on wood, 44.5 x 30 cm

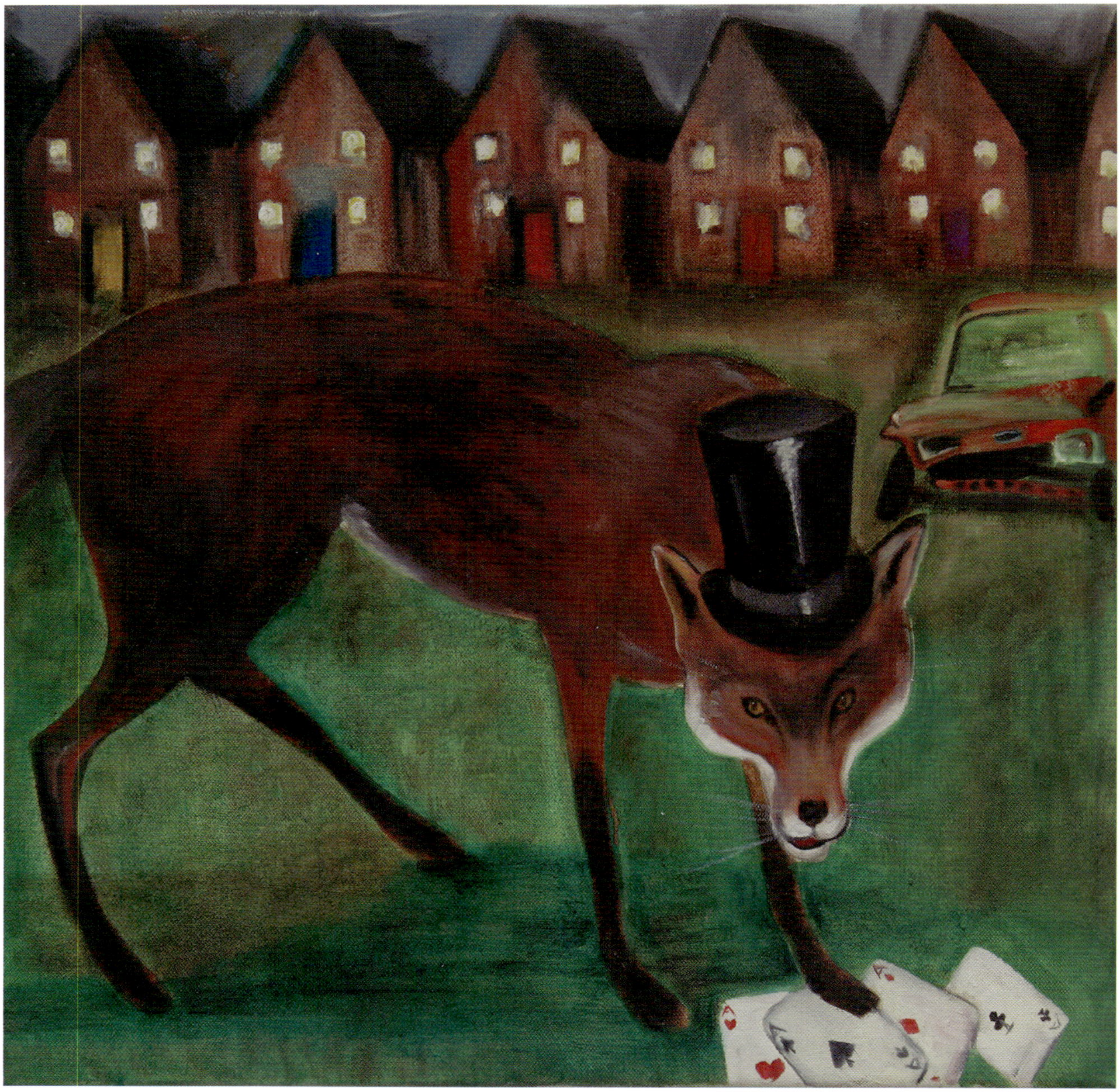

The Magician, 2006
Oil on canvas, 37.5 × 37.5 cm

DH The underdog, or the misfit.

PD They're too mischievous and canny for the underdog. The foxes and the owls and the hares have a lot of attitude.

DH Oh god, yes, it's as if those animals have a second sight, like fairy folk. They're all thinking more deeply than you can ever know, just to survive. Even pigeons – everyone hates them, but we're all made of the same materials really. Look at that one there, the male with all the colours, strutting along, and now another male has come up and she's in the middle. Look at the difference in colours: his neck is metallic green. How can they not be beautiful?

PD As beautiful as a parrot, any day.

DH If there was fewer, people might appreciate them. But it's sad that something has to be endangered before it's appreciated.

PD I think as a London painter maybe you have a keener sense of the place as a living organism, as something that is endangered. The way you look at London is like a lament.

DH A requiem [laughs]. You know, I think I would have been OK with growing old in the London of the past, but not the place it is now. I want to read you *De Egyptu*, a poem by John Cowper Powys:

Where the wet bank shines
With the celandines,
And the marigolds mock the moon,
Where the violets tender
Their deep hearts render
To the blackbirds' wistful tune,
Where the woolly sheep
In their hurdles sleep
And the rooks caw from the trees,
I must go; for the end
Is at hand, my friend,
And my heart is sick for these.
I must go; for the end
Is near, my friend;
We have lived. Let loose my hand!
I can get no ease
In my death, Felise,
If I die not in my own land.[1]

Beautiful, isn't it? Your own land doesn't have to be where you were born at all.

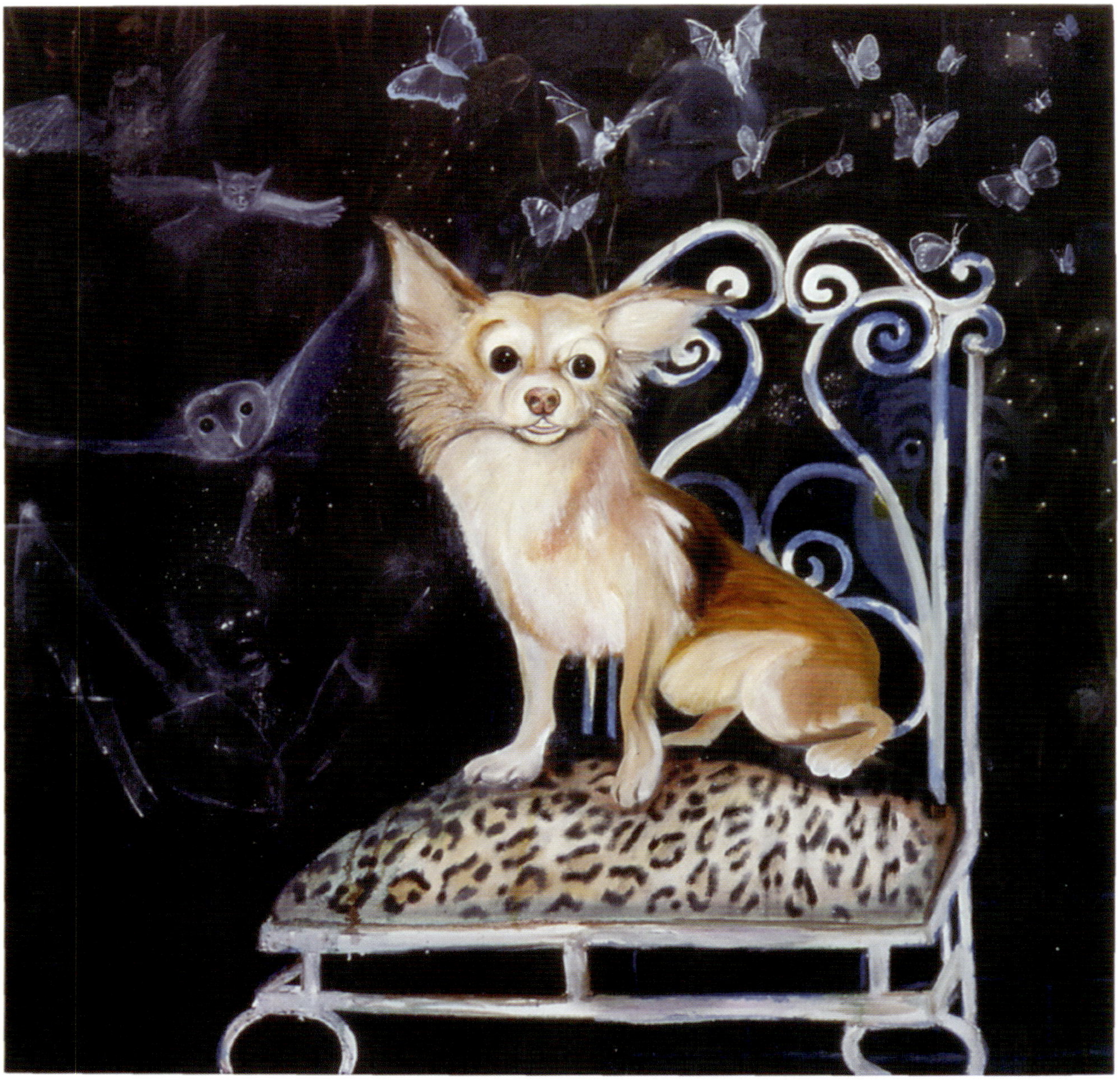

Behemoth Enters the Spirit World, 2004
Oil on canvas, 76 x 76 cm

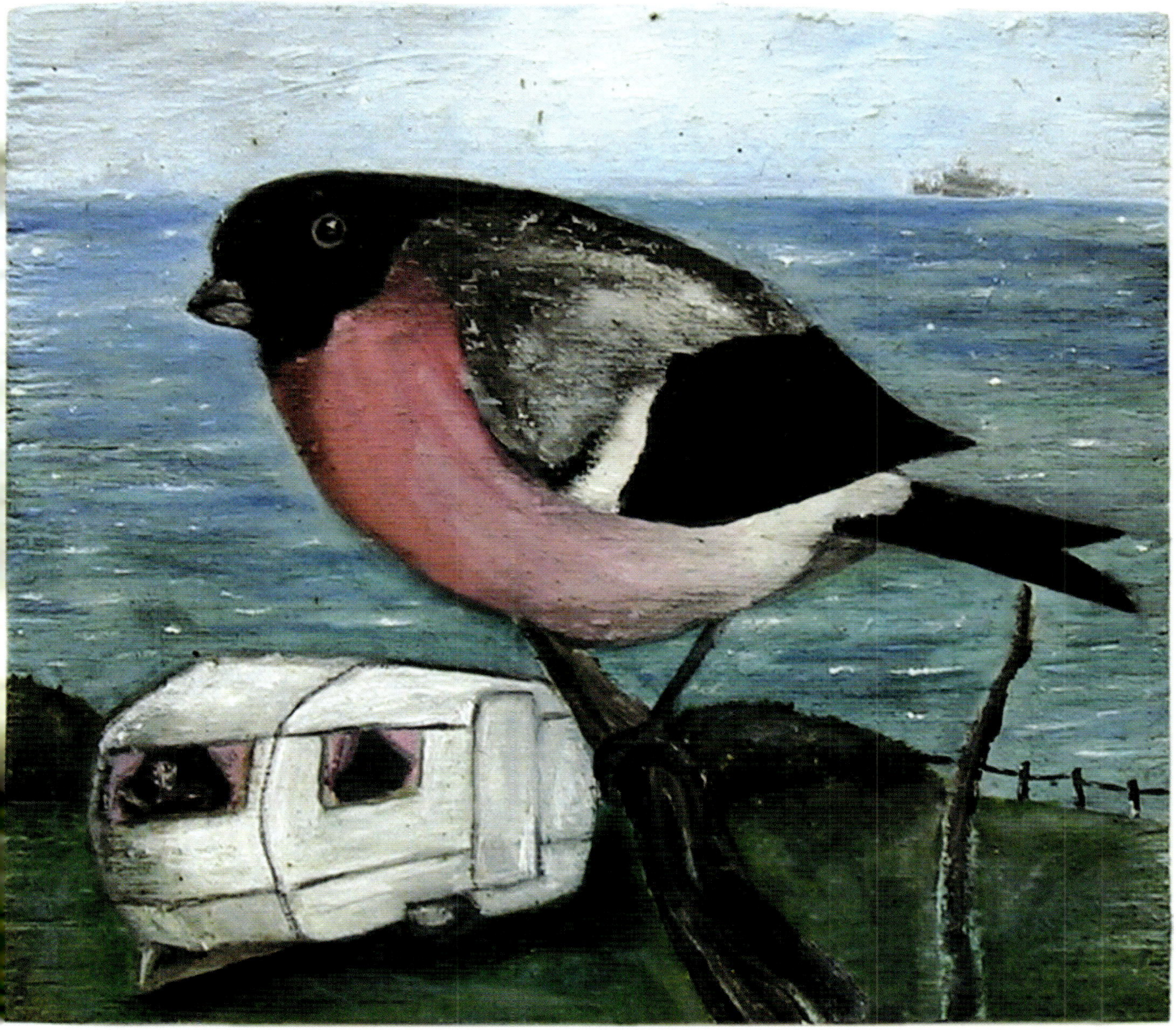

Beach Bullfinch, 2004
Oil on wood, 15 x 15 cm

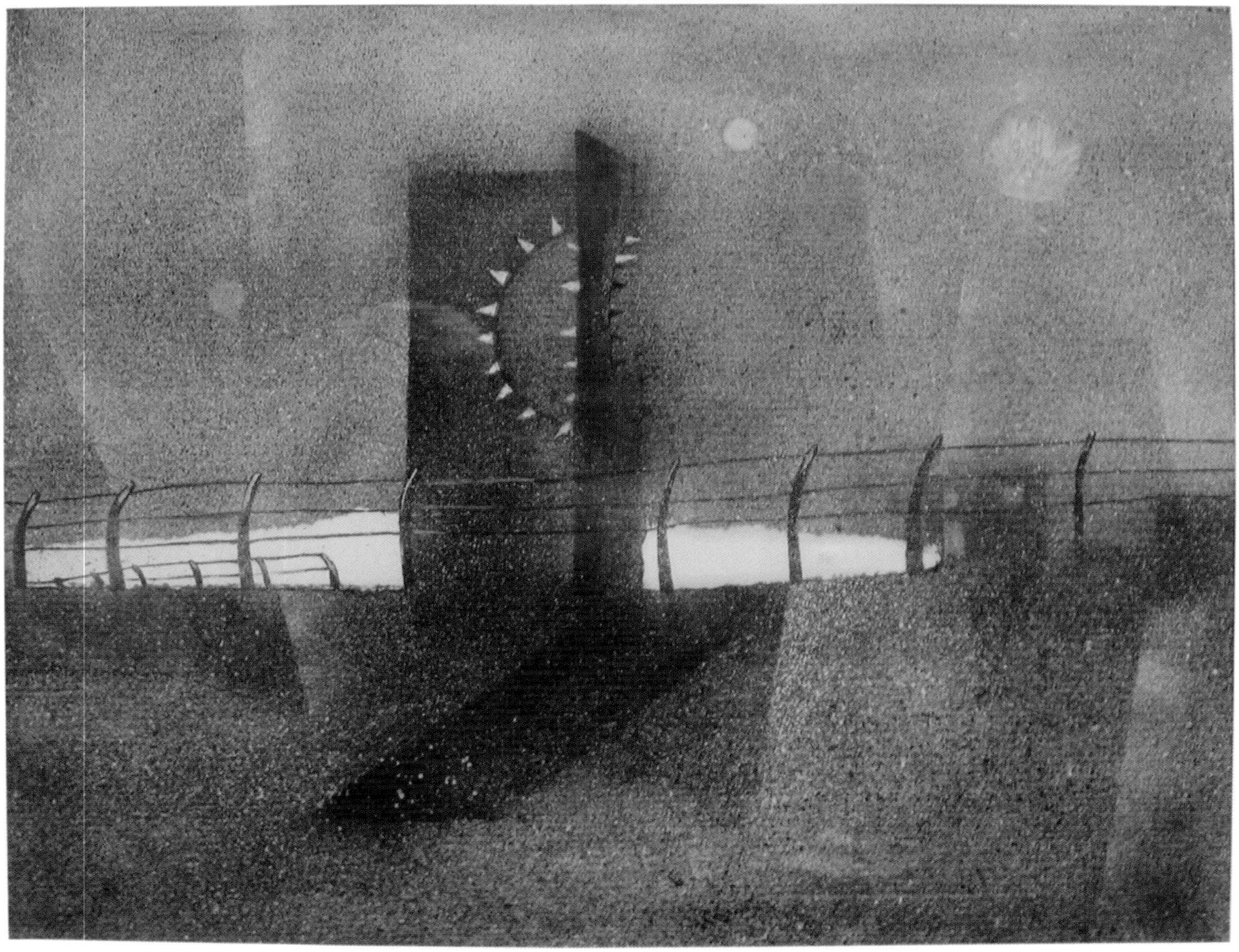

After Blackpool, 2004
Oil and conté on paper, 49 × 65 cm

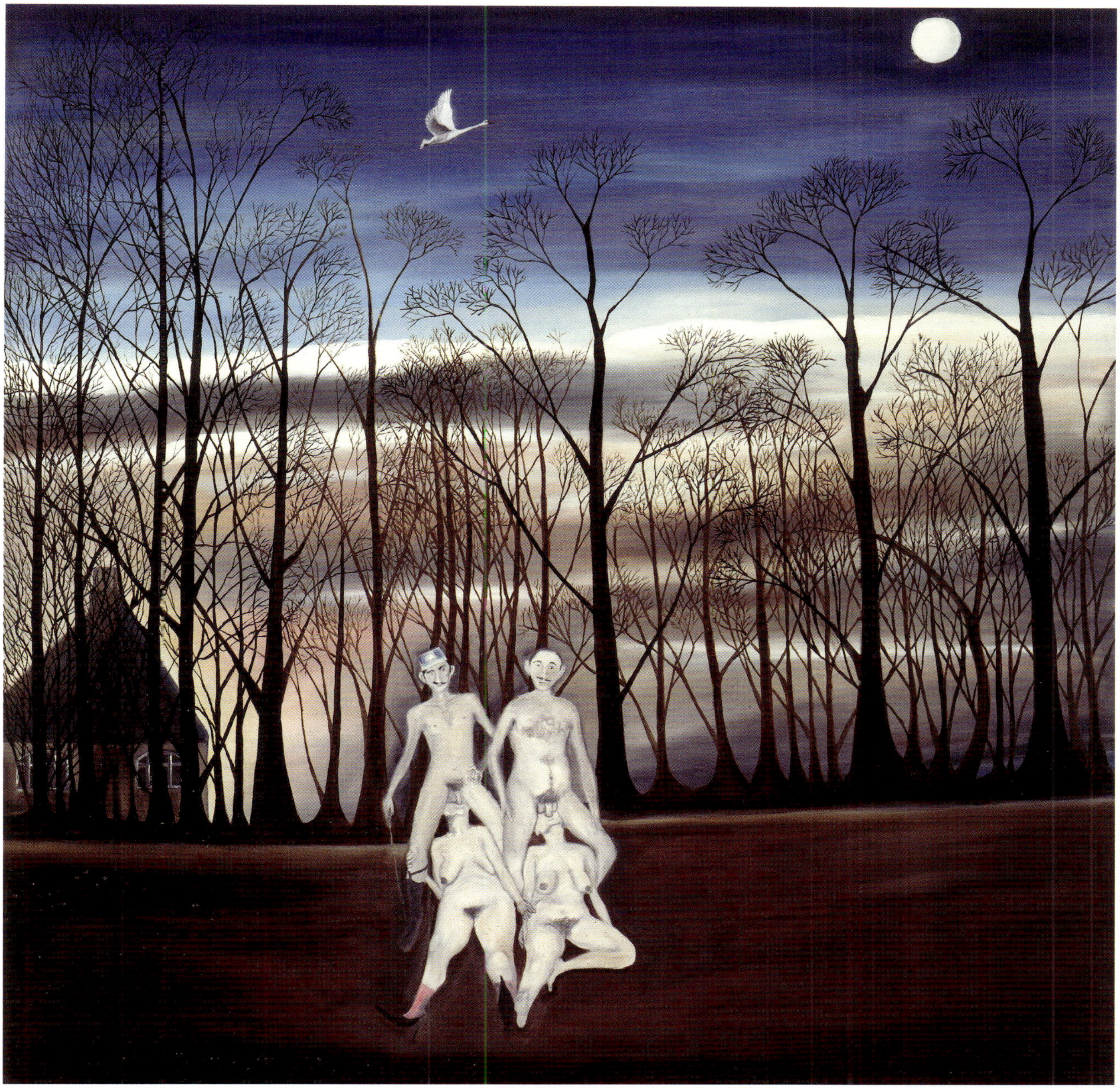

Swan Song, 2006
Oil on canvas, 80 x 80 cm

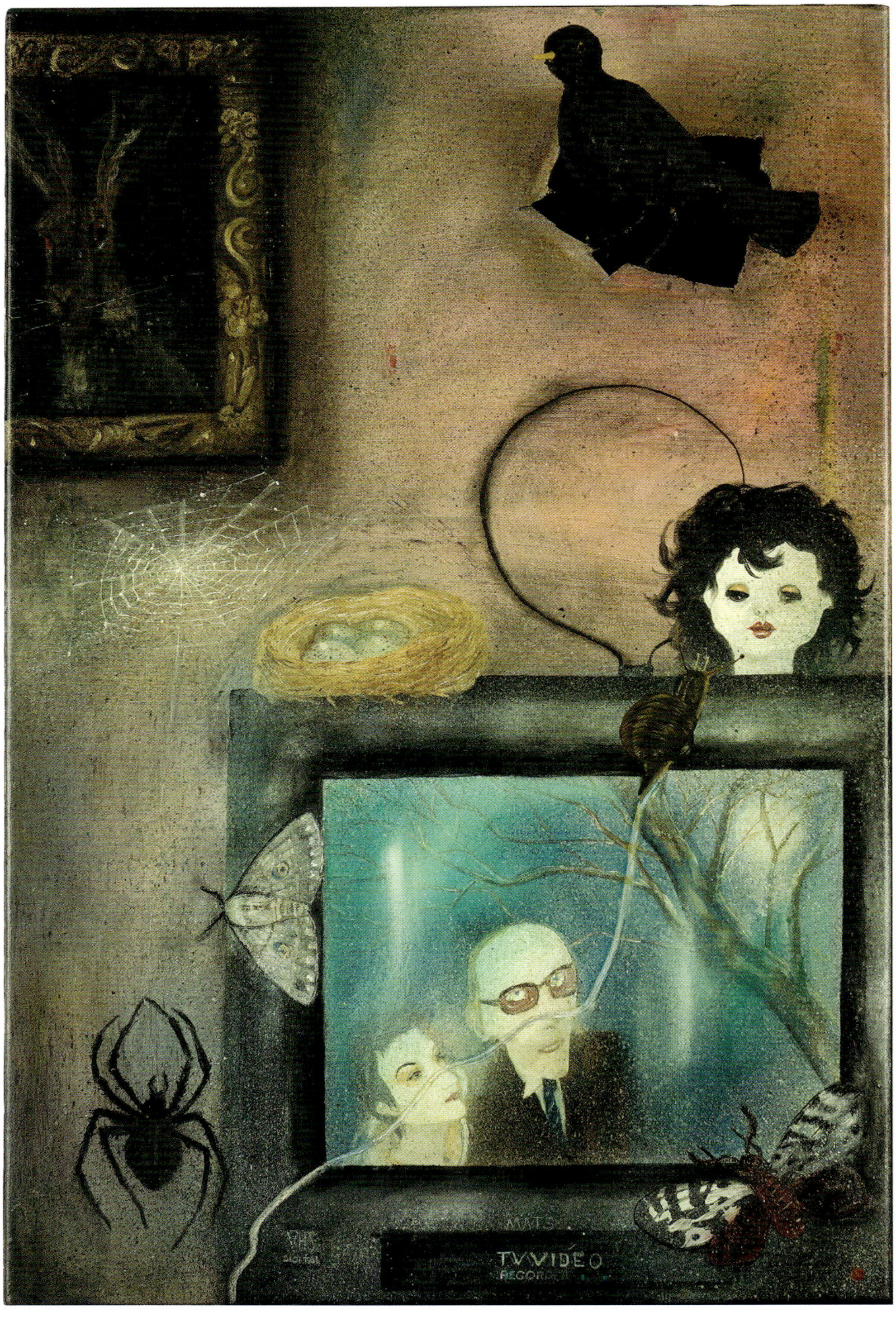

Do Not Adjust Your Set, 2004
Oil on canvas with wooden objects, 60 x 36 cm

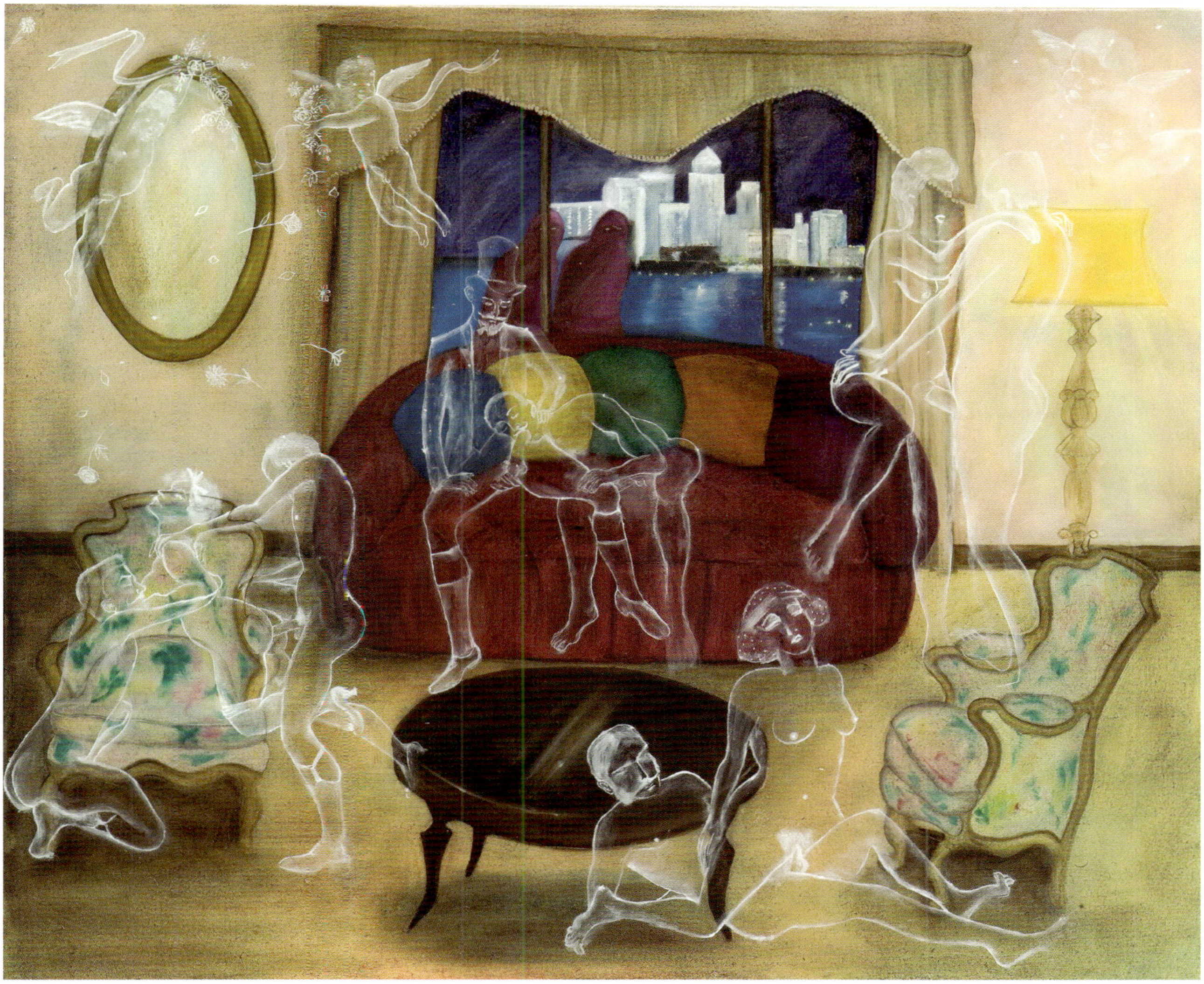

The Erotic Dead, 2005
Oil on canvas, 81.5 x 96.5 cm

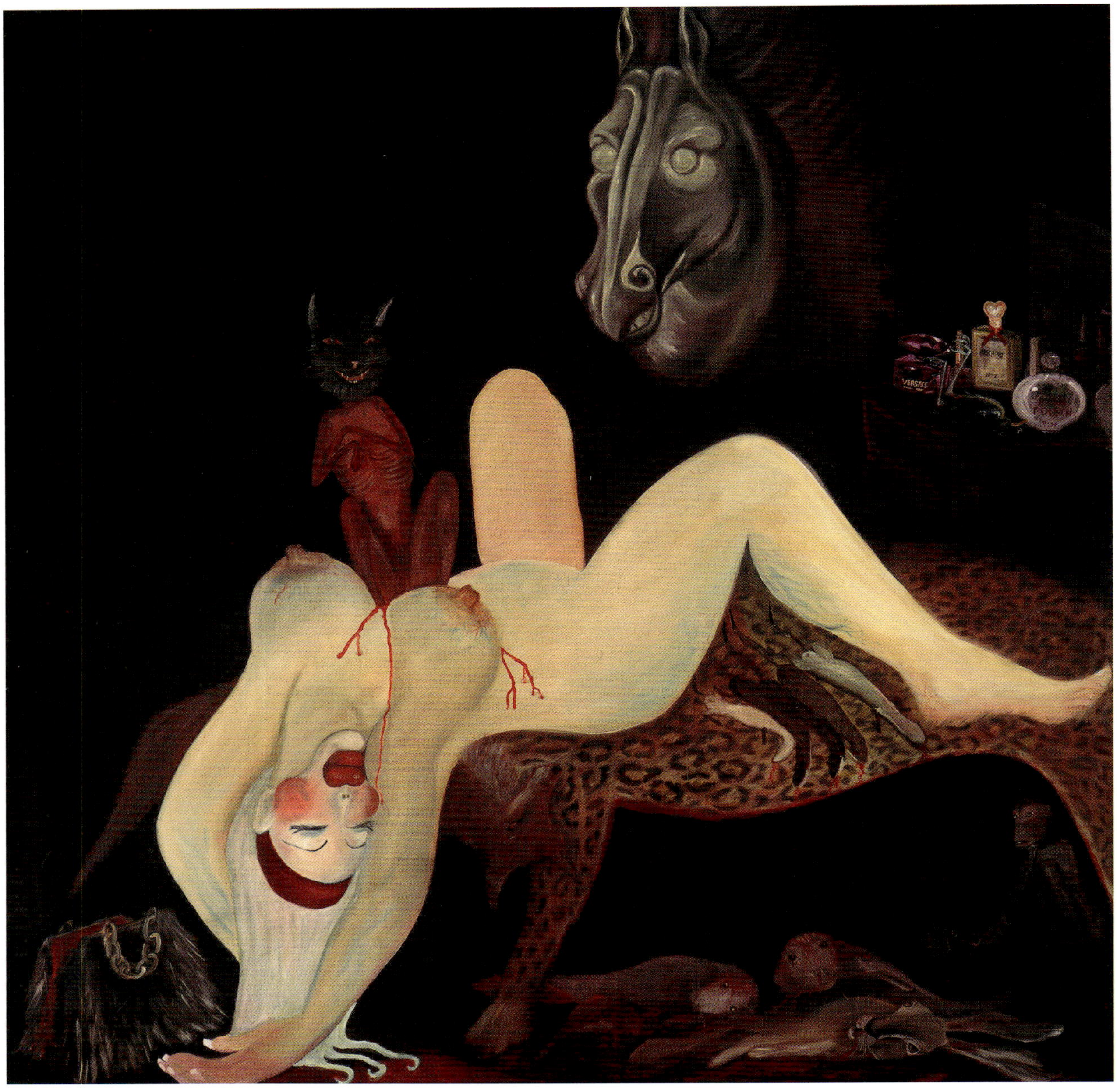

Cruelty Without Beauty, 2006
Oil on canvas, 91.5 x 91.5 cm

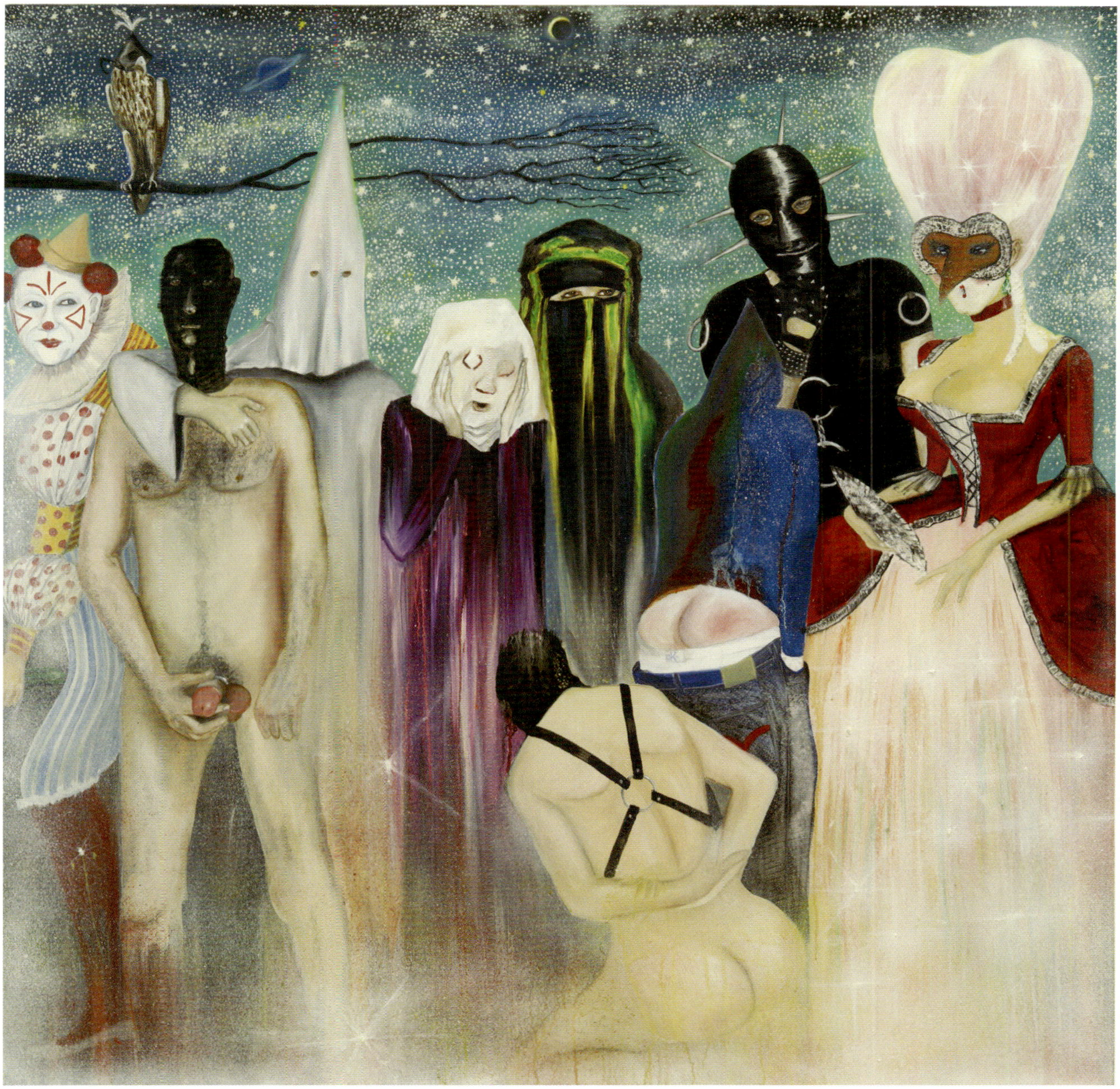

Masks, 2006
Oil on canvas 102 x 102 cm

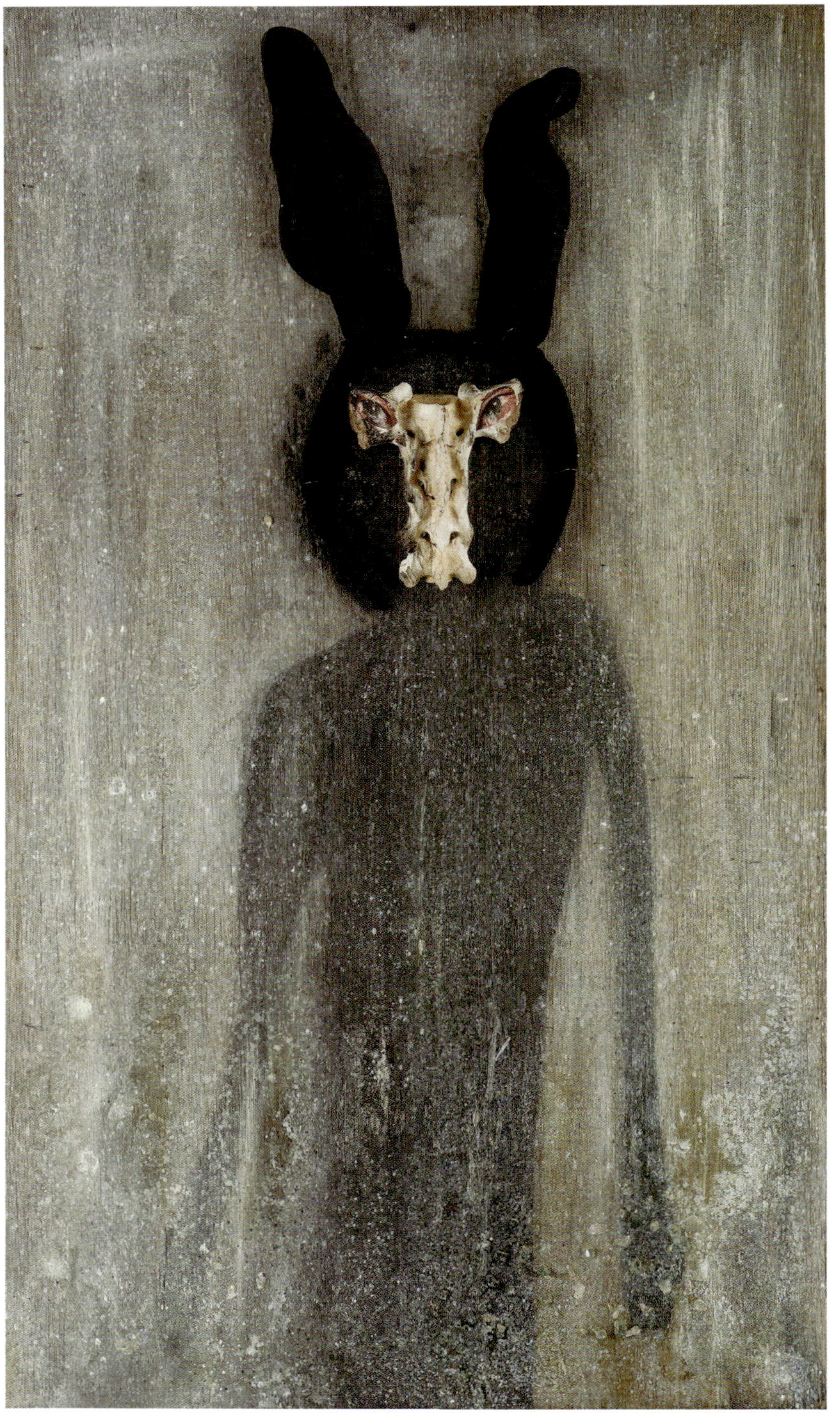

Hare Essentials, 2008
Oil and found objects on wood, 72.2 × 41.2 cm

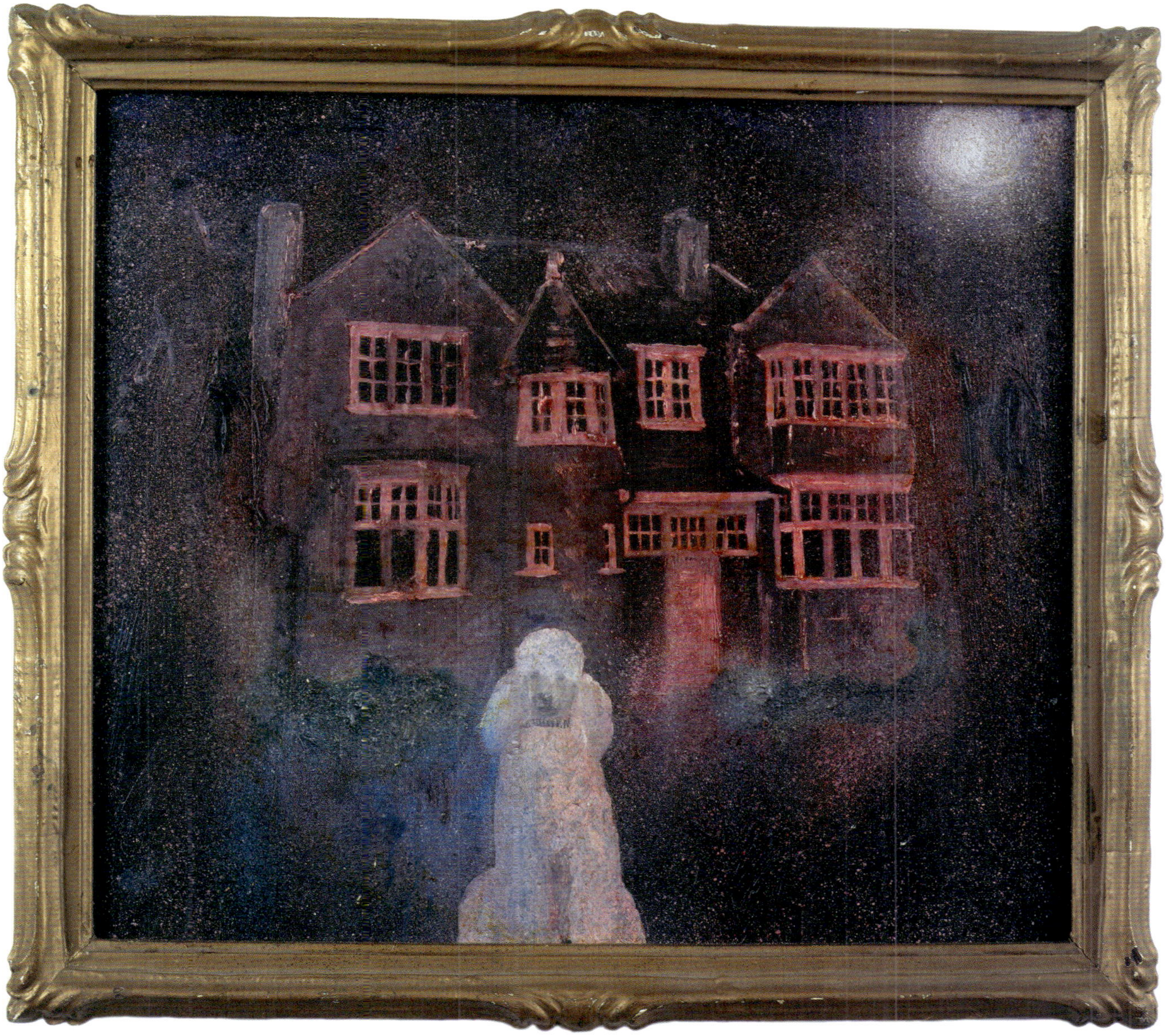

The Master That Never Returned, 1999
Oil on wood, 30 x 40 cm

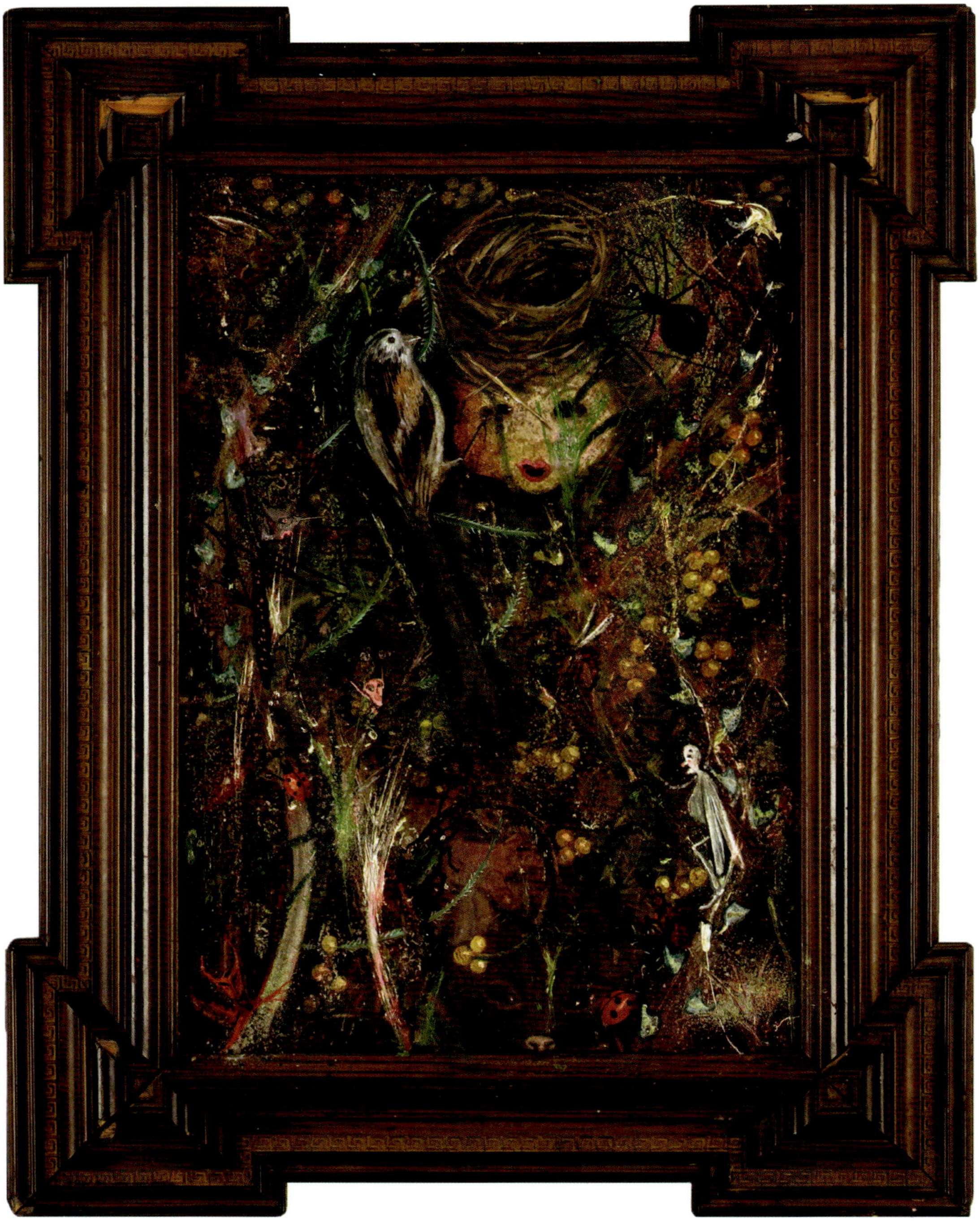

Hidden Nest, 1998
Oil on wood, 50 x 34 cm

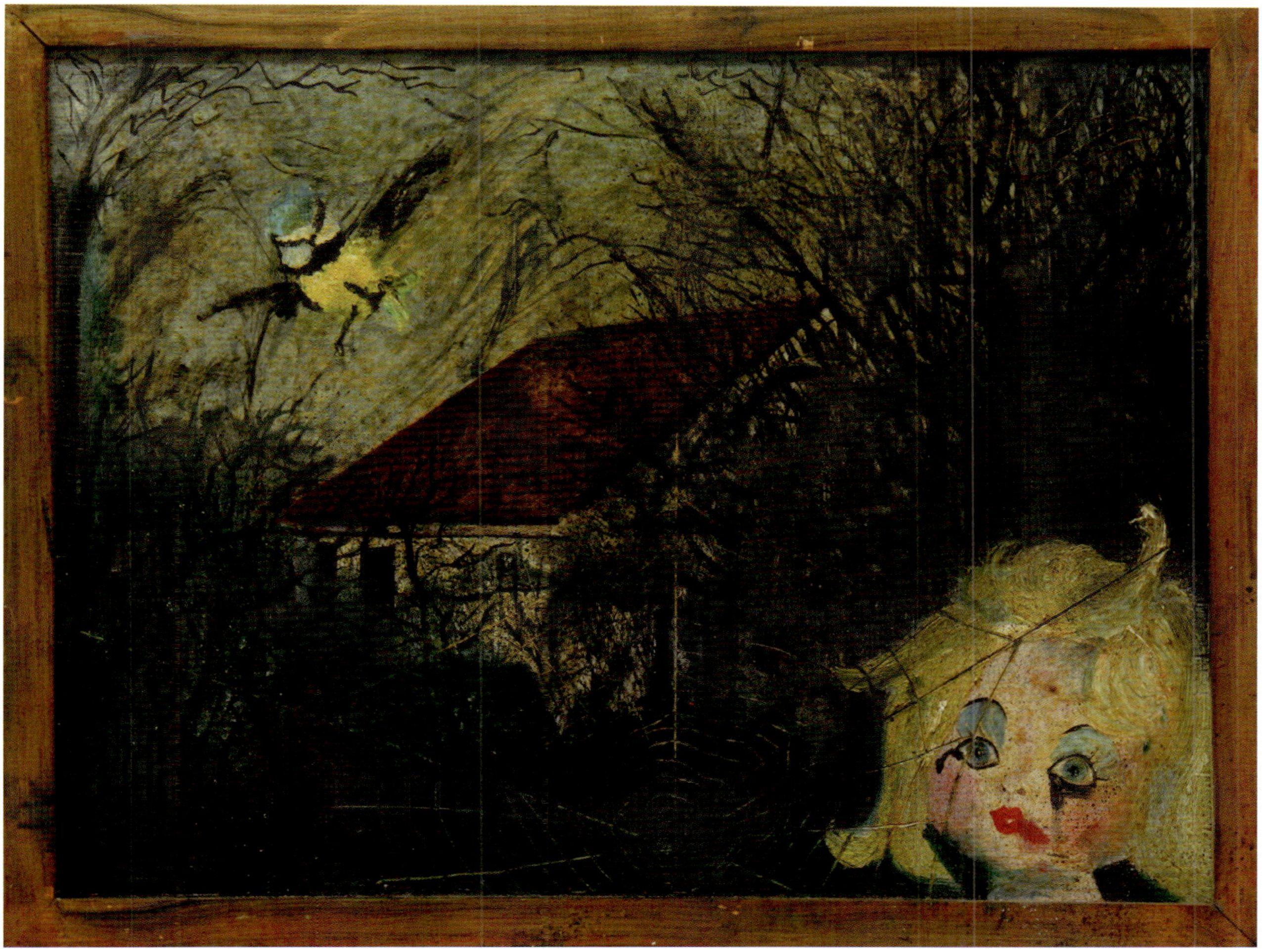

Dolly in Essex, 1999
Oil on wood, 25 x 30 cm

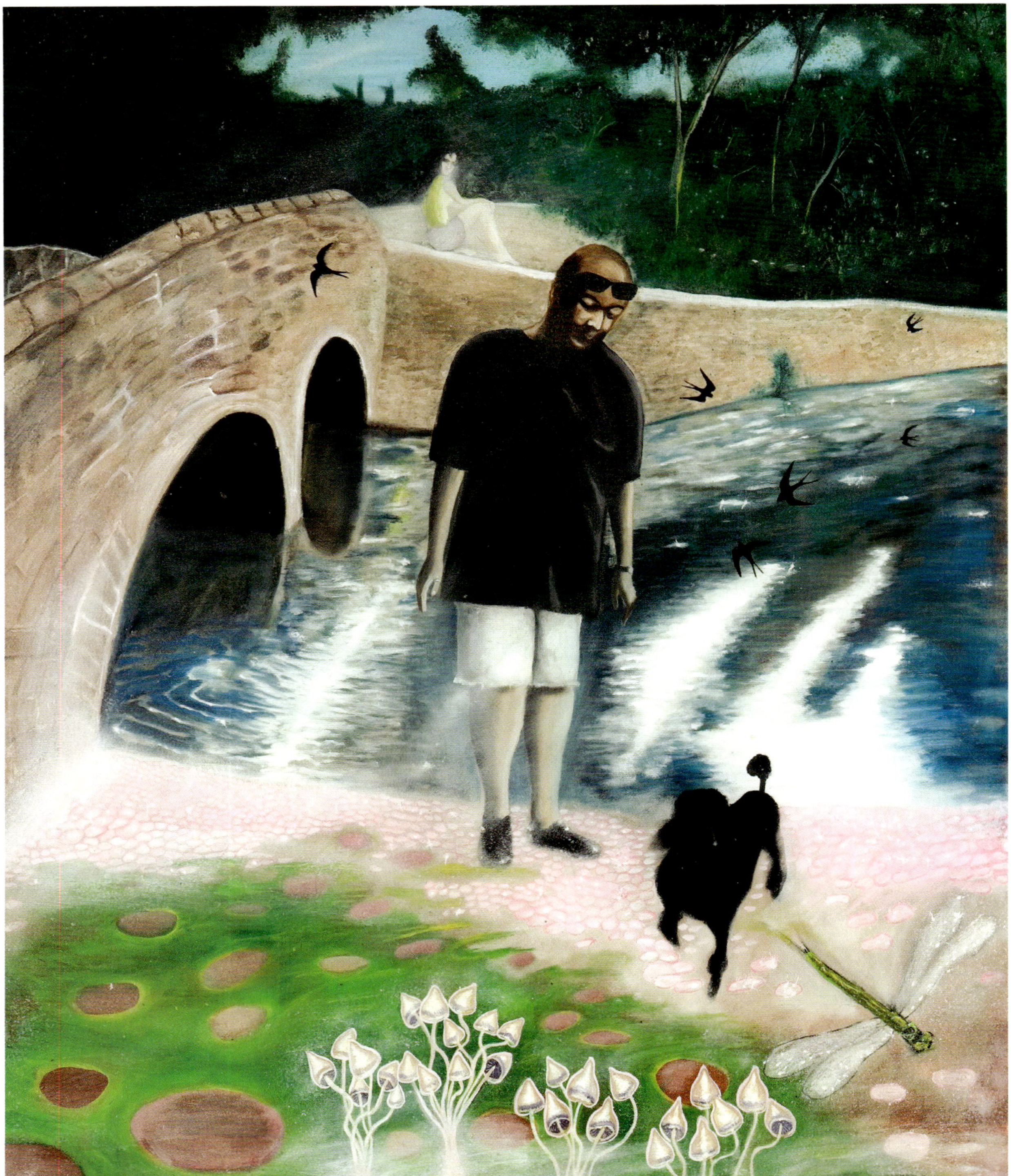

Magic Moments, 2005
Oil on canvas, 91 x 76 cm

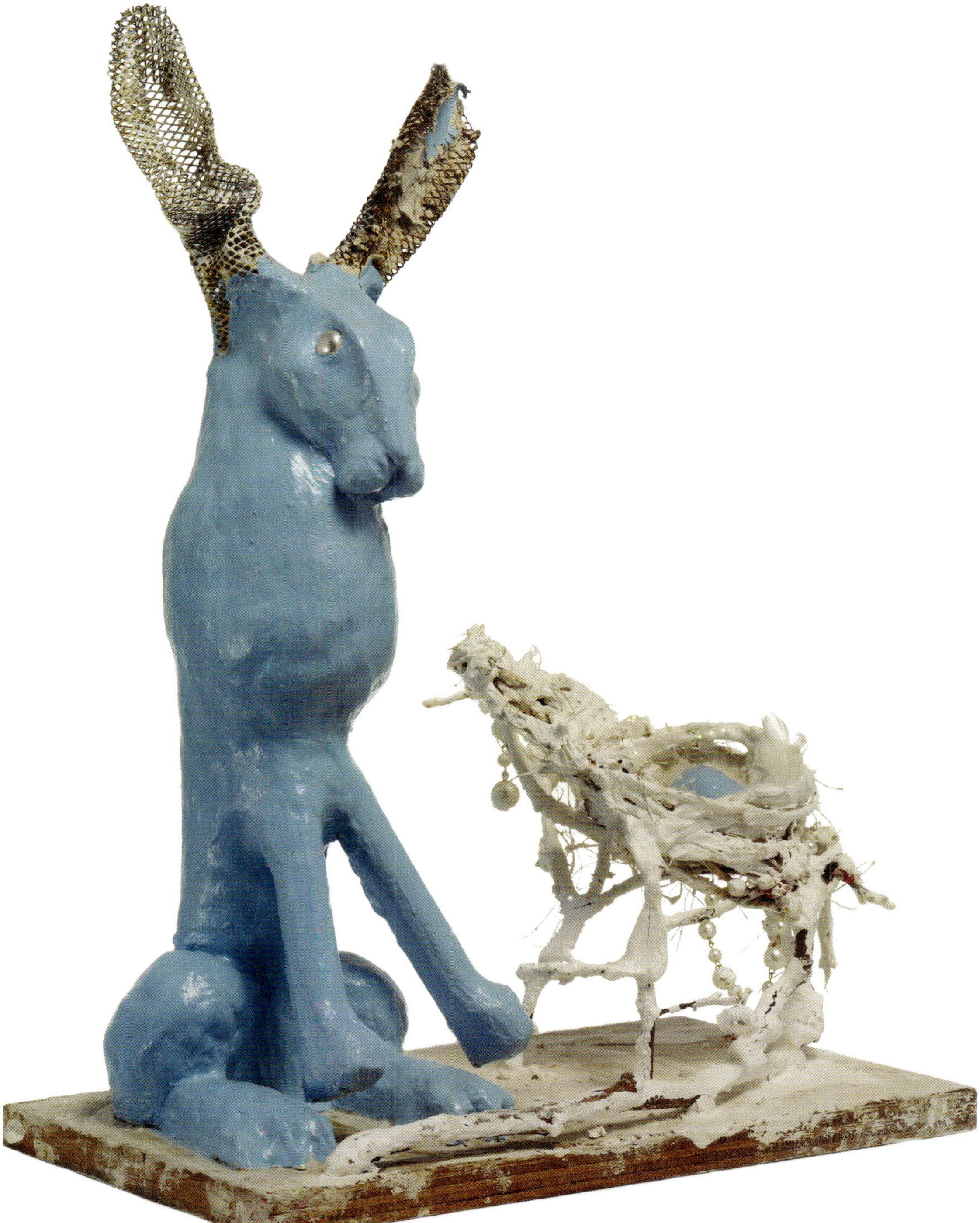

Blue Hare Nest 2009
Mixed media, 48 × 34 × 24 cm

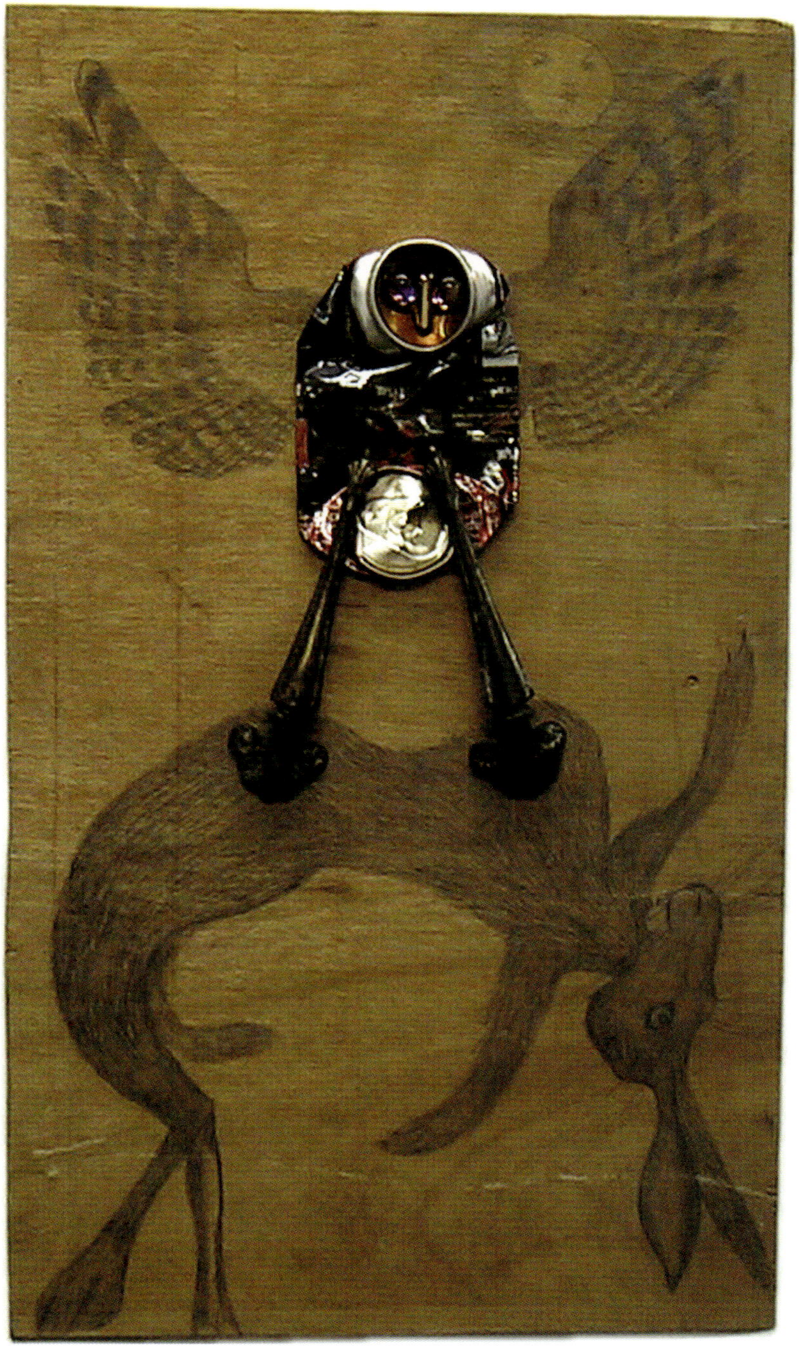

Hare Today Gone Tomorrow, 2003
Found objects and pencil on wood, 40 x 20 cm

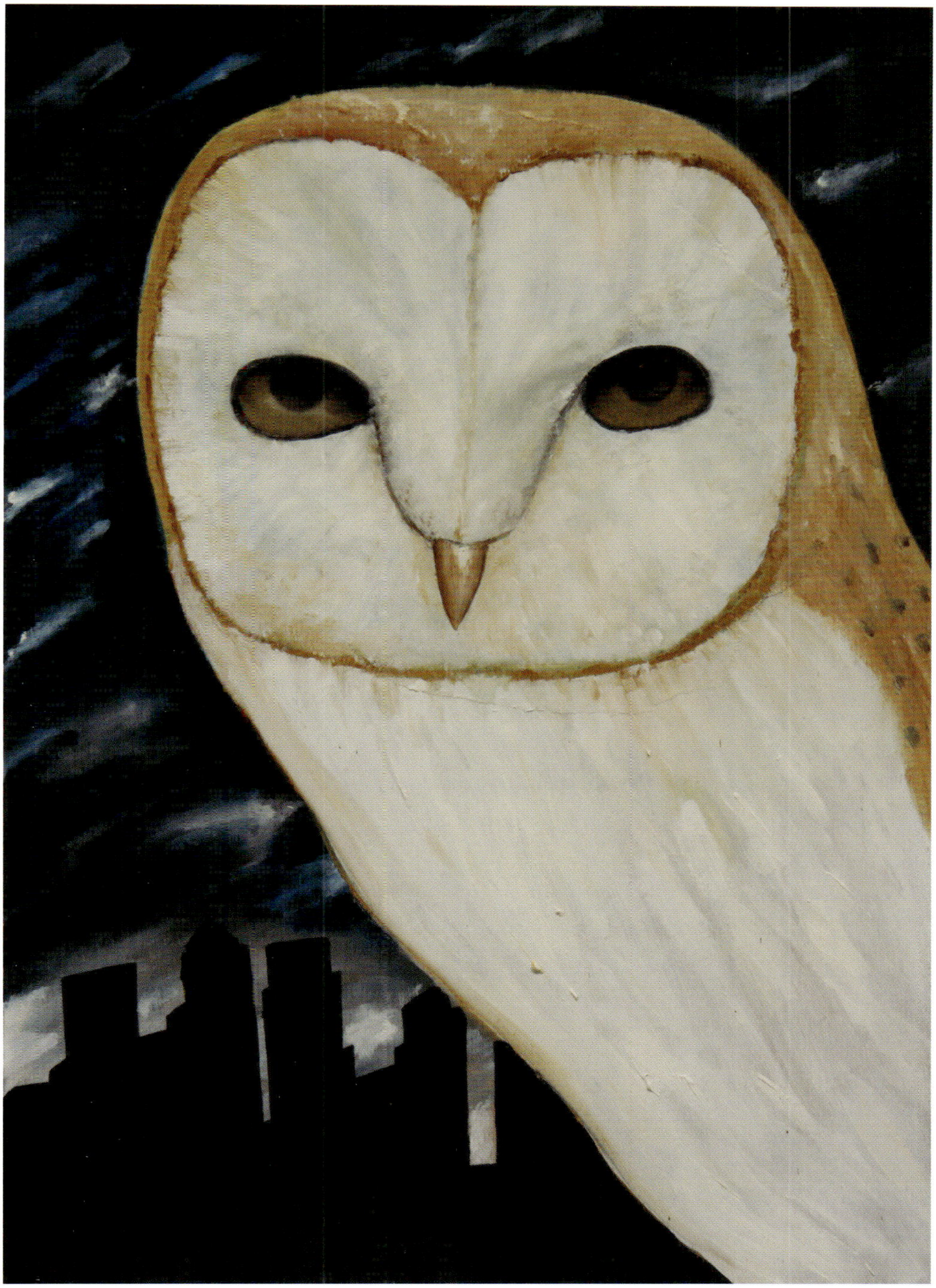

City Owl, 2006
Oil on wood, 43 x 31 cm

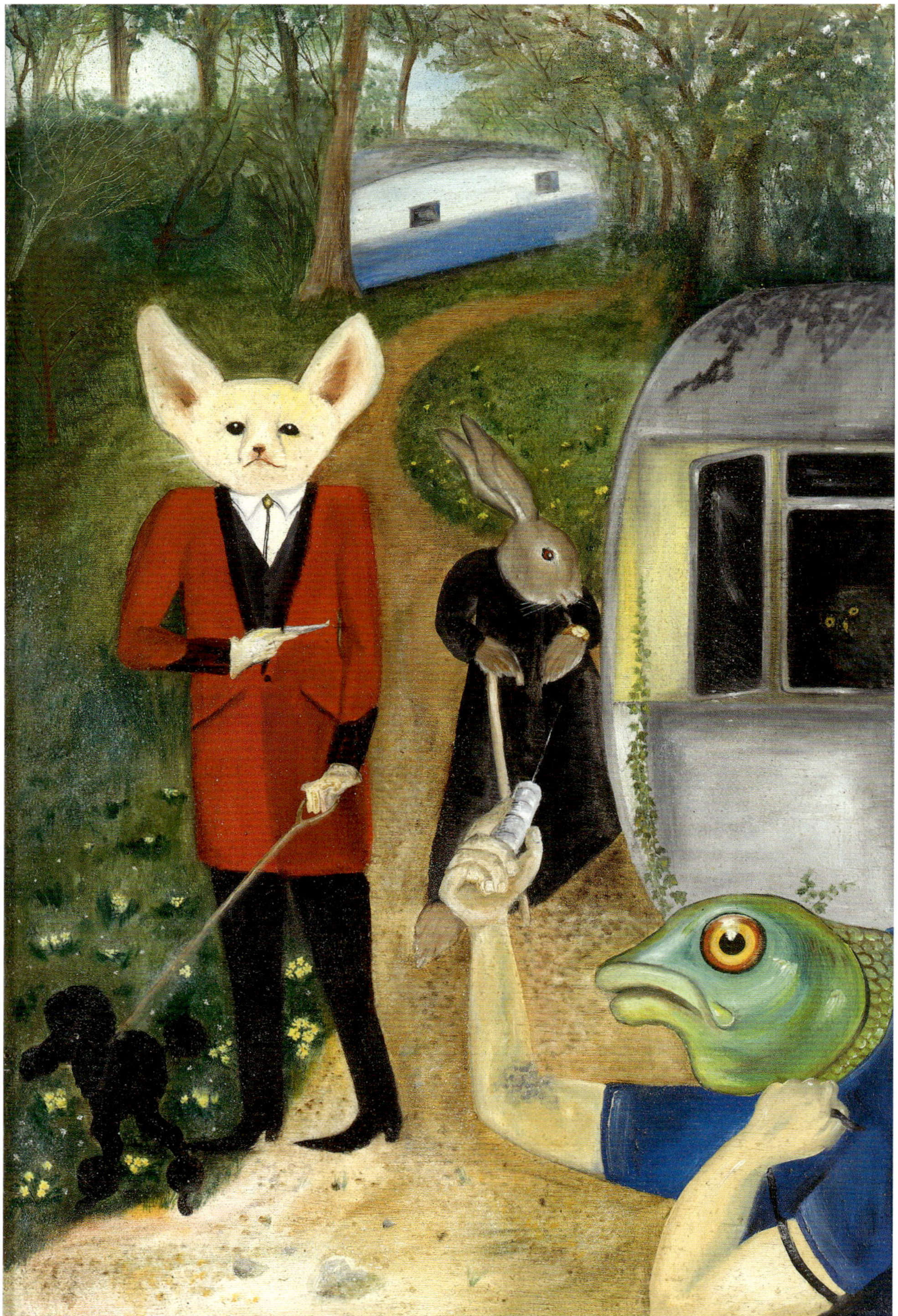

Bad Habits, 2004
Oil on wood, 46 × 38 cm

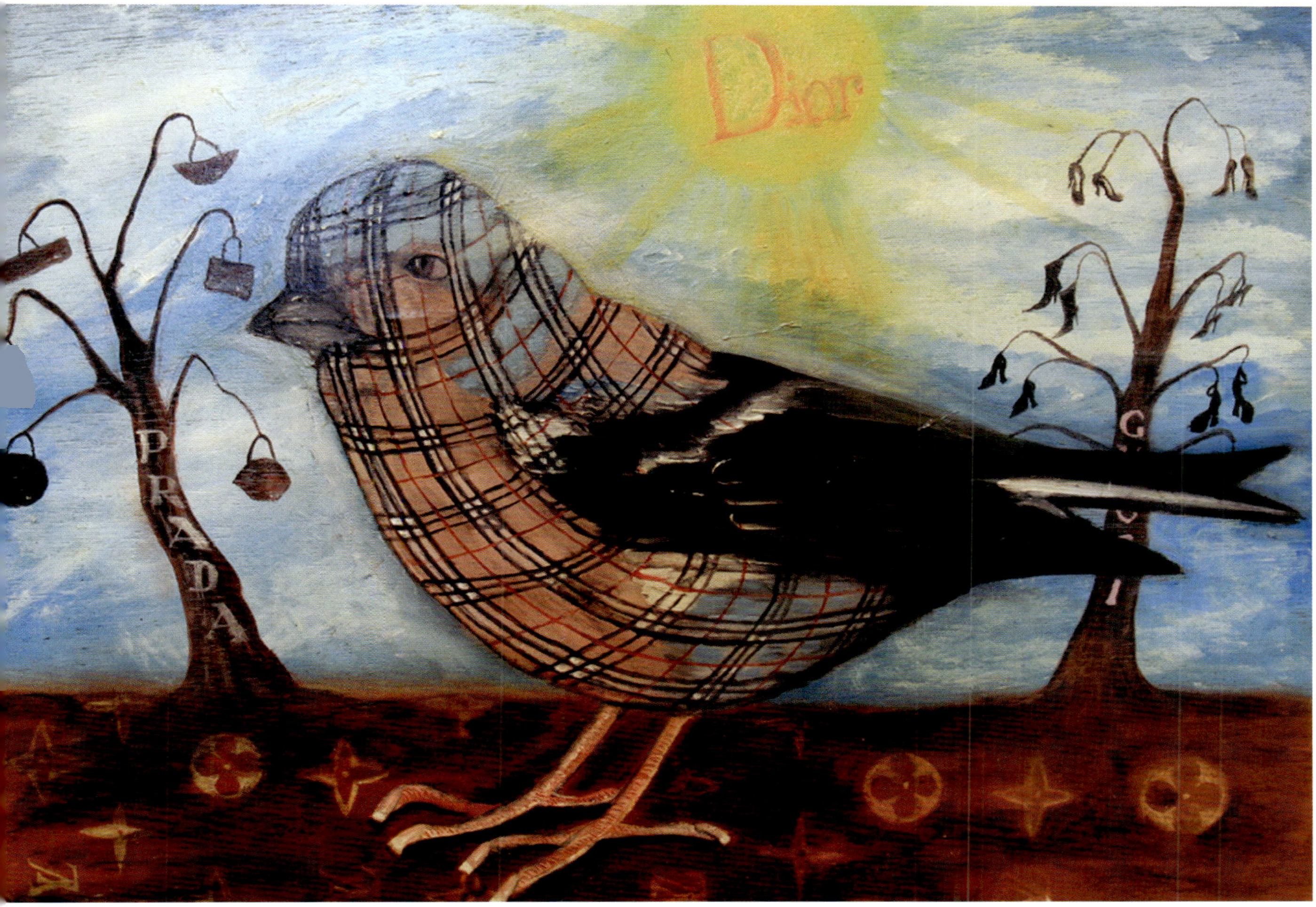

Chavfinch, 2006
Oil on wood, 30 x 43 cm

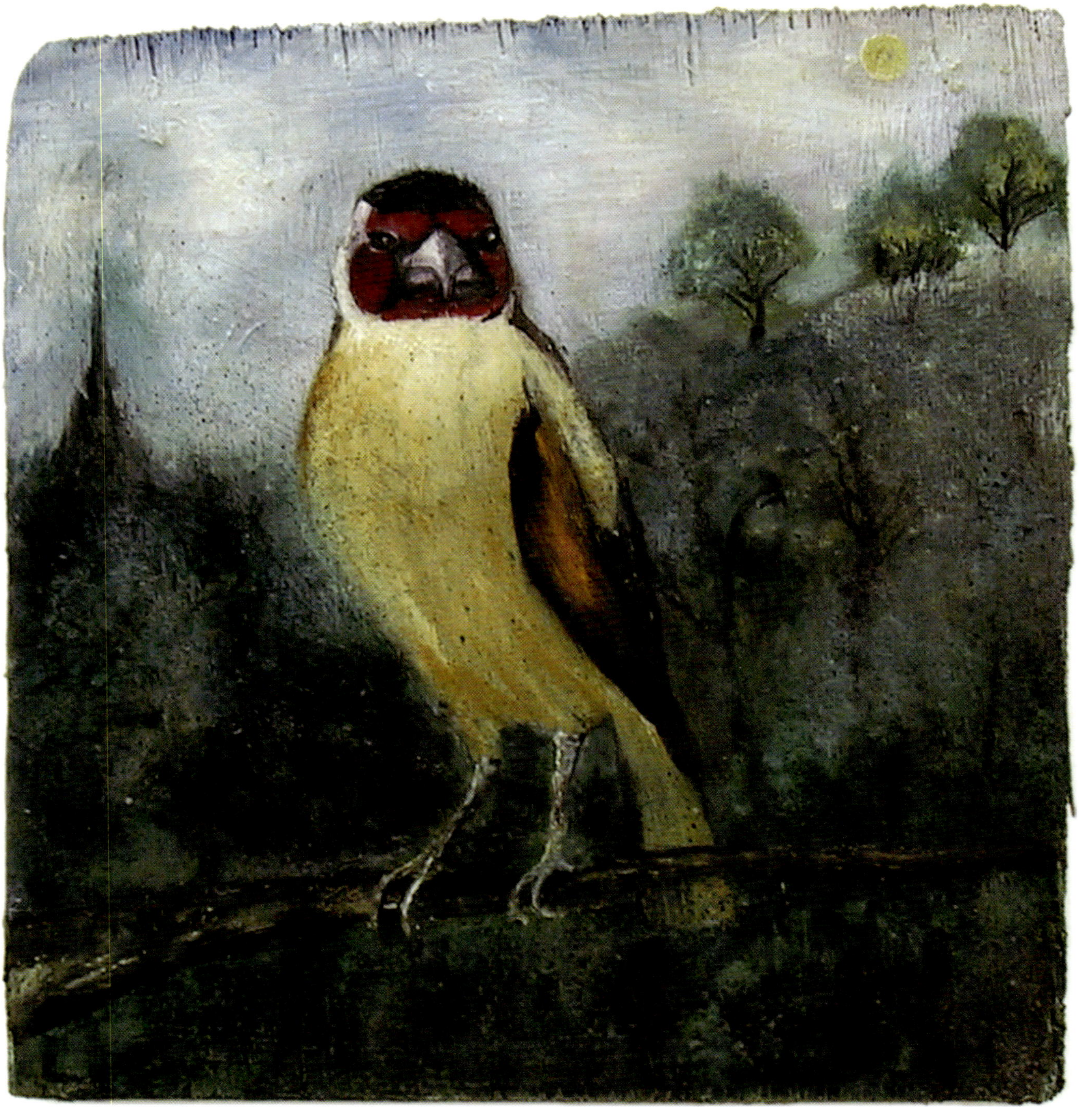

The Passion, 2004
Oil on wood, 15 x 15 cm

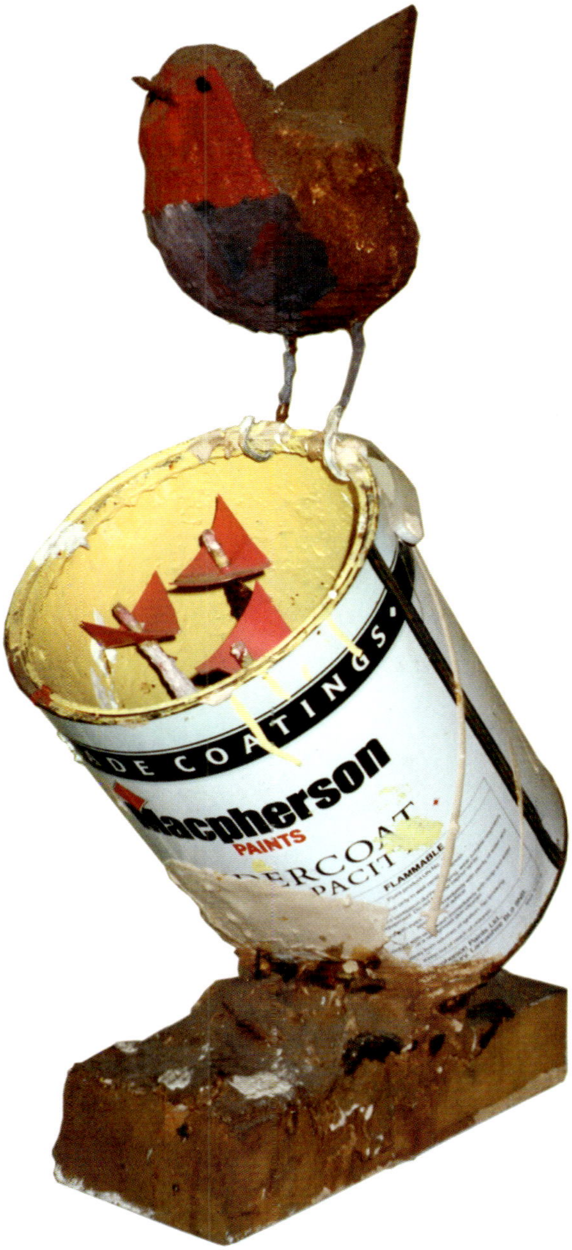

Robin at Nest, 1997
Found objects, 51 × 30 × 18 cm

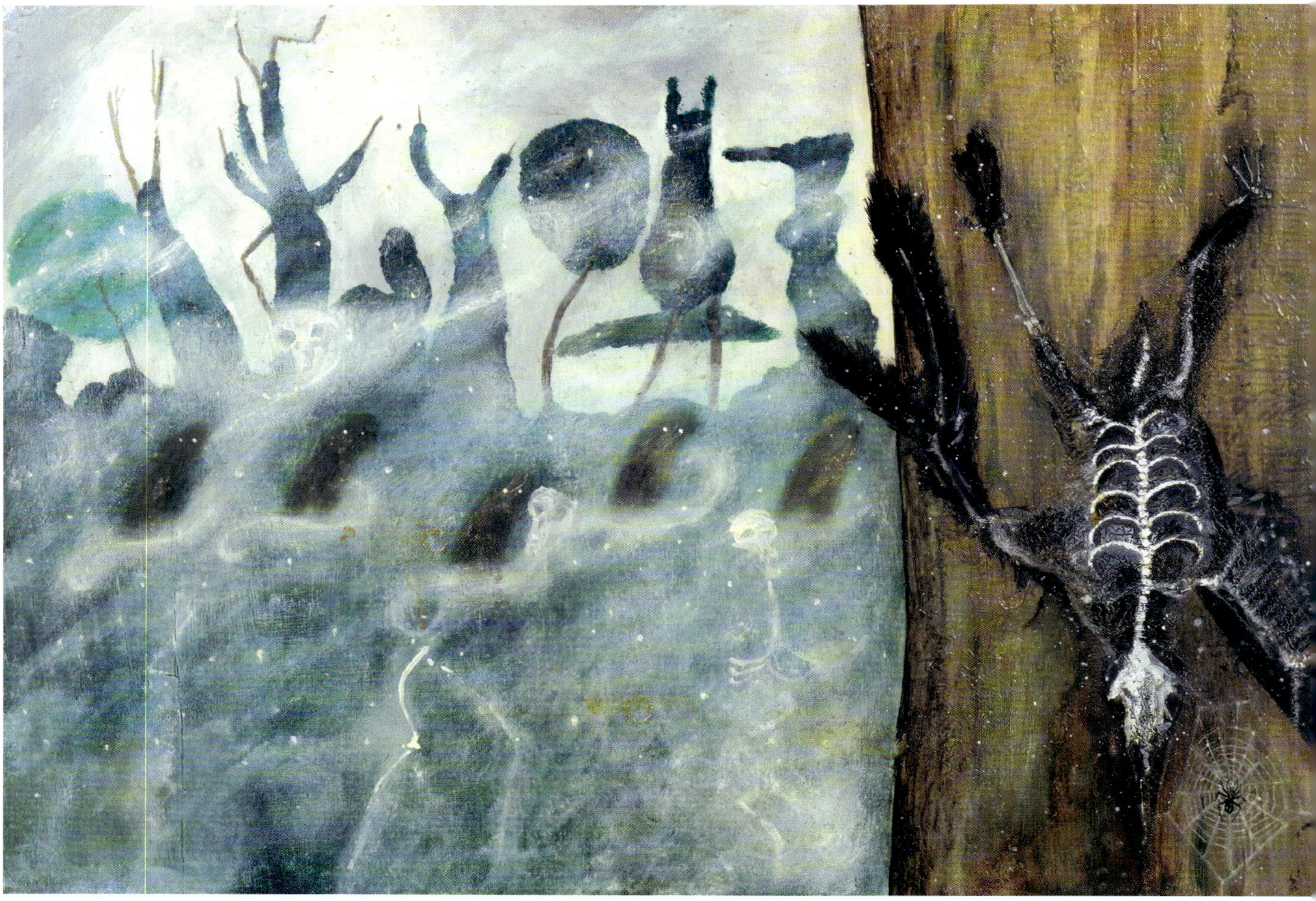

St Peter, 2005
Oil on wood, 32 × 46 cm

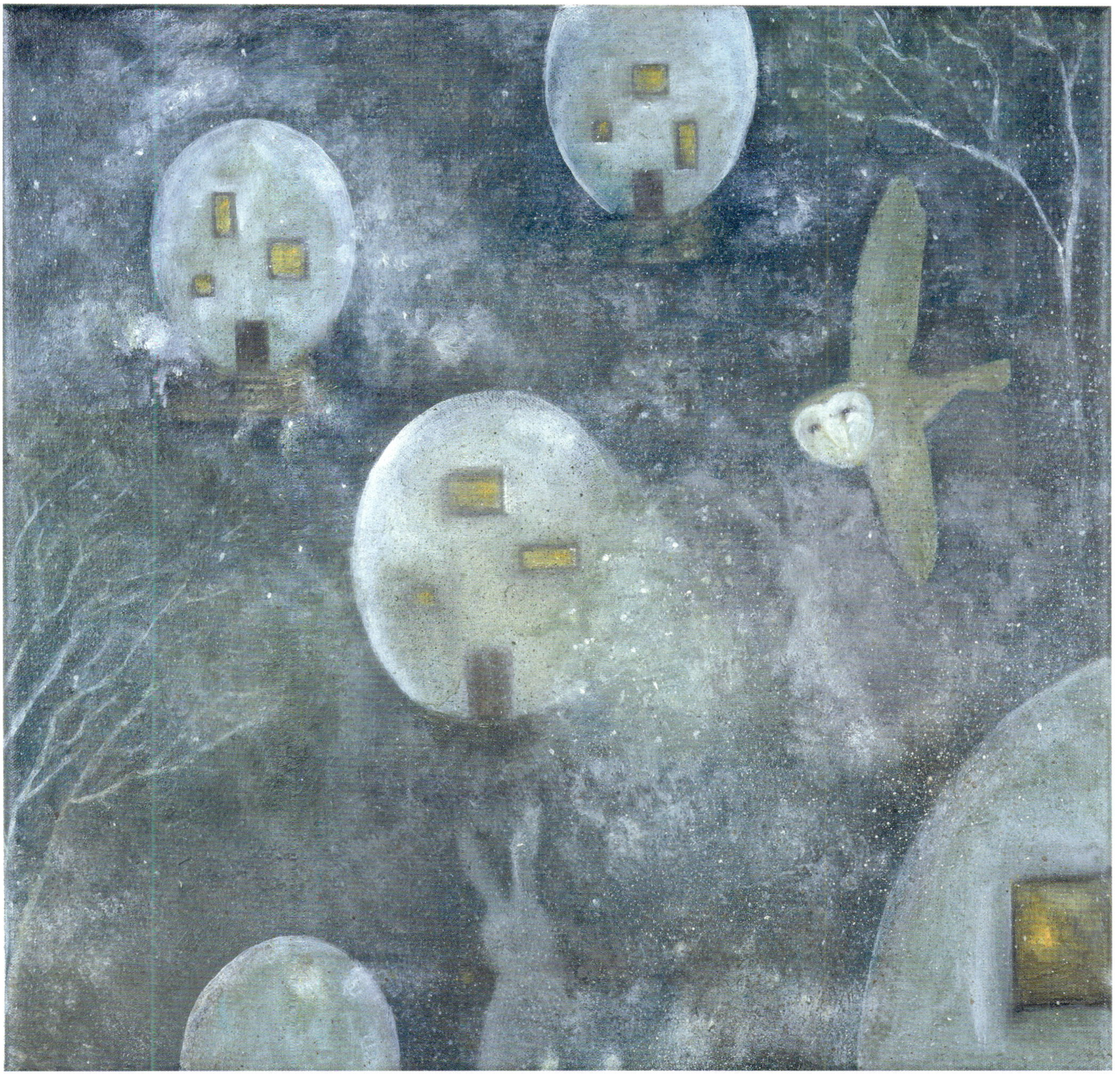

Egg Houses: A Natural Development, 2006
Oil on canvas, 37 x 37 cm

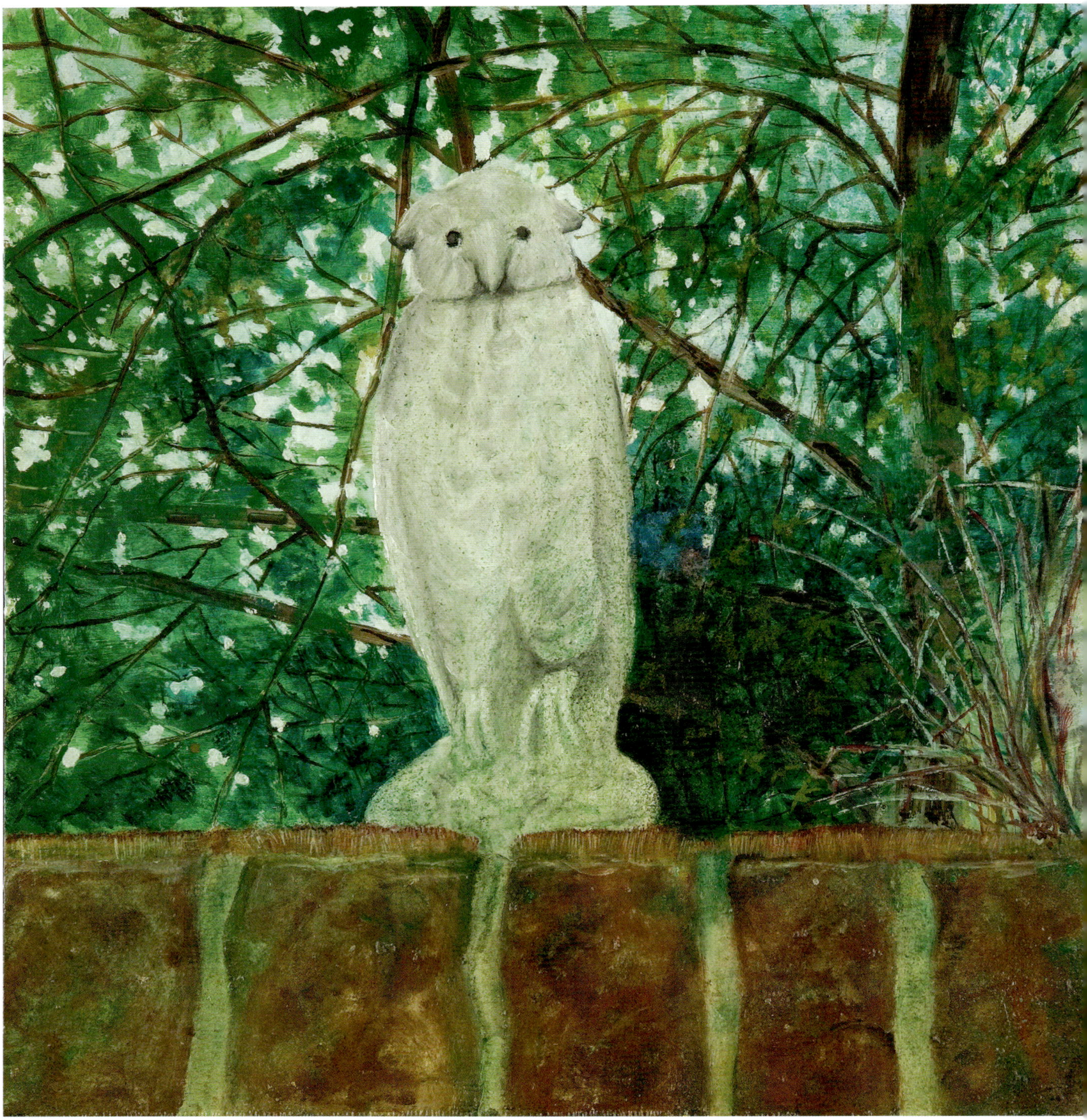

Stone Owl (Spring), 2003
Oil on wood, 47.5 x 44.5 cm

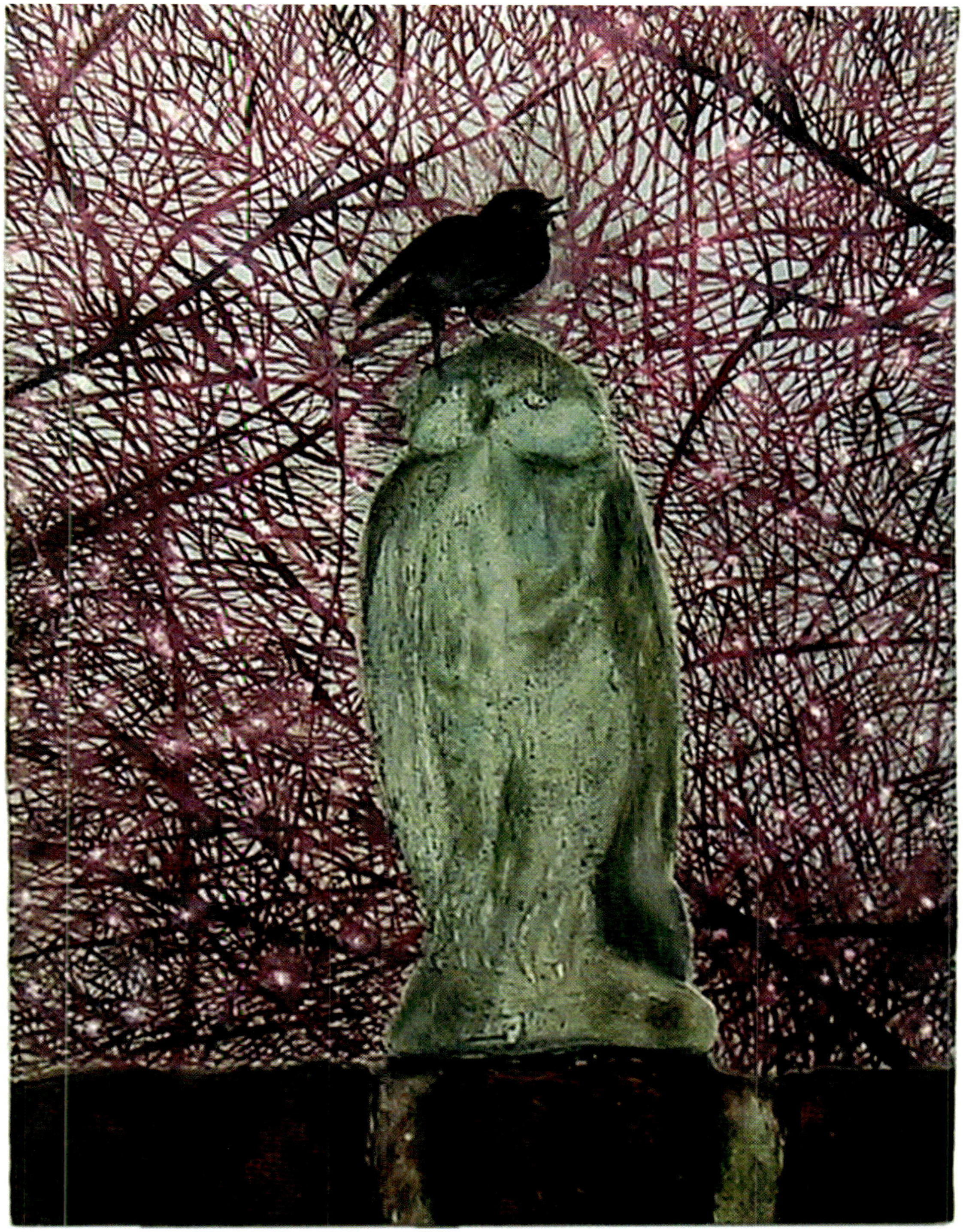

Stone Owl (Winter), 2003
Oil on wood, 30 x 25 cm

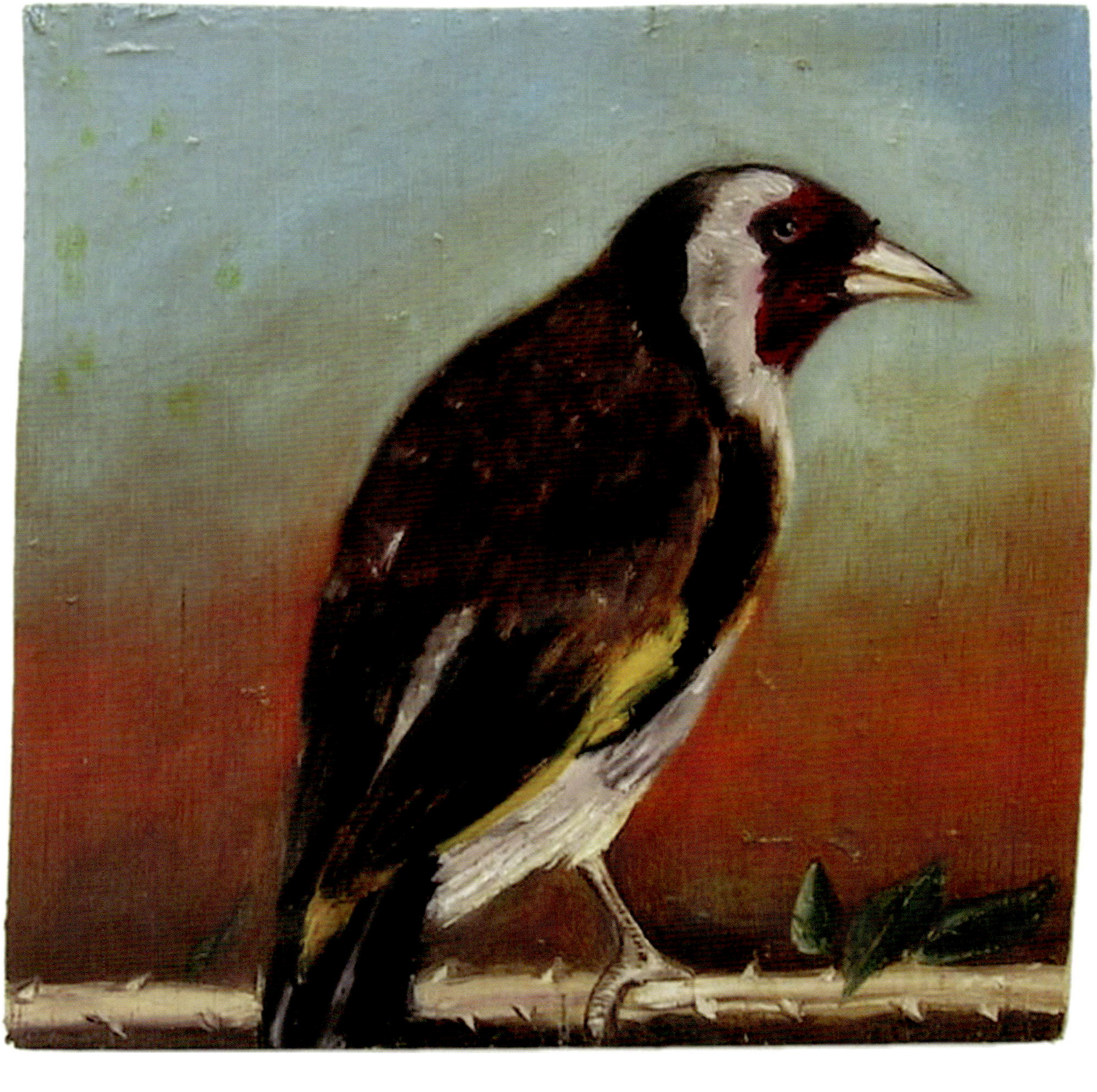

Destiny, 2004
Oil on wood, 15 x 15 cm

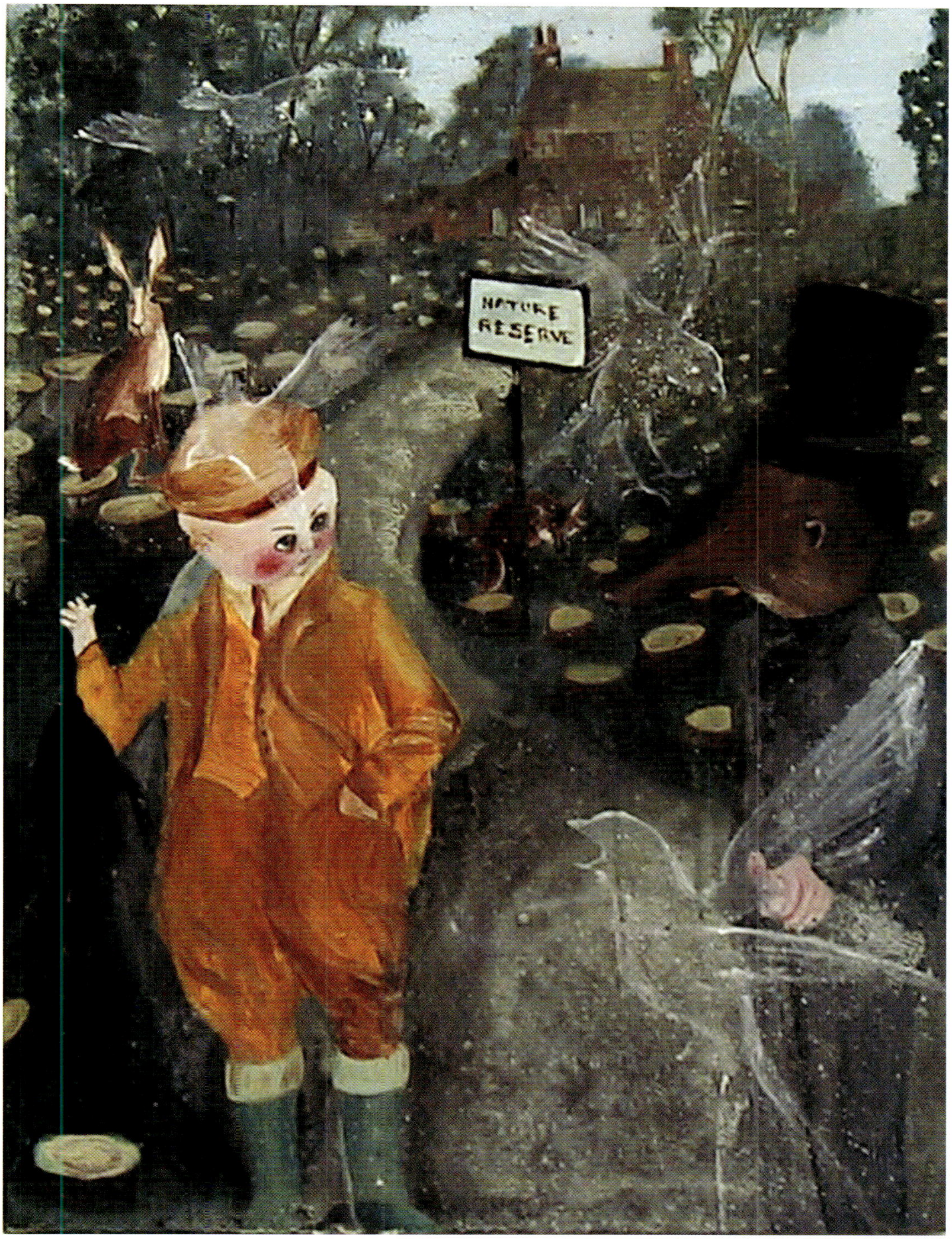

The Gamekeeper and the Councillor, 2004
Oil on wood, 46 x 30 cm

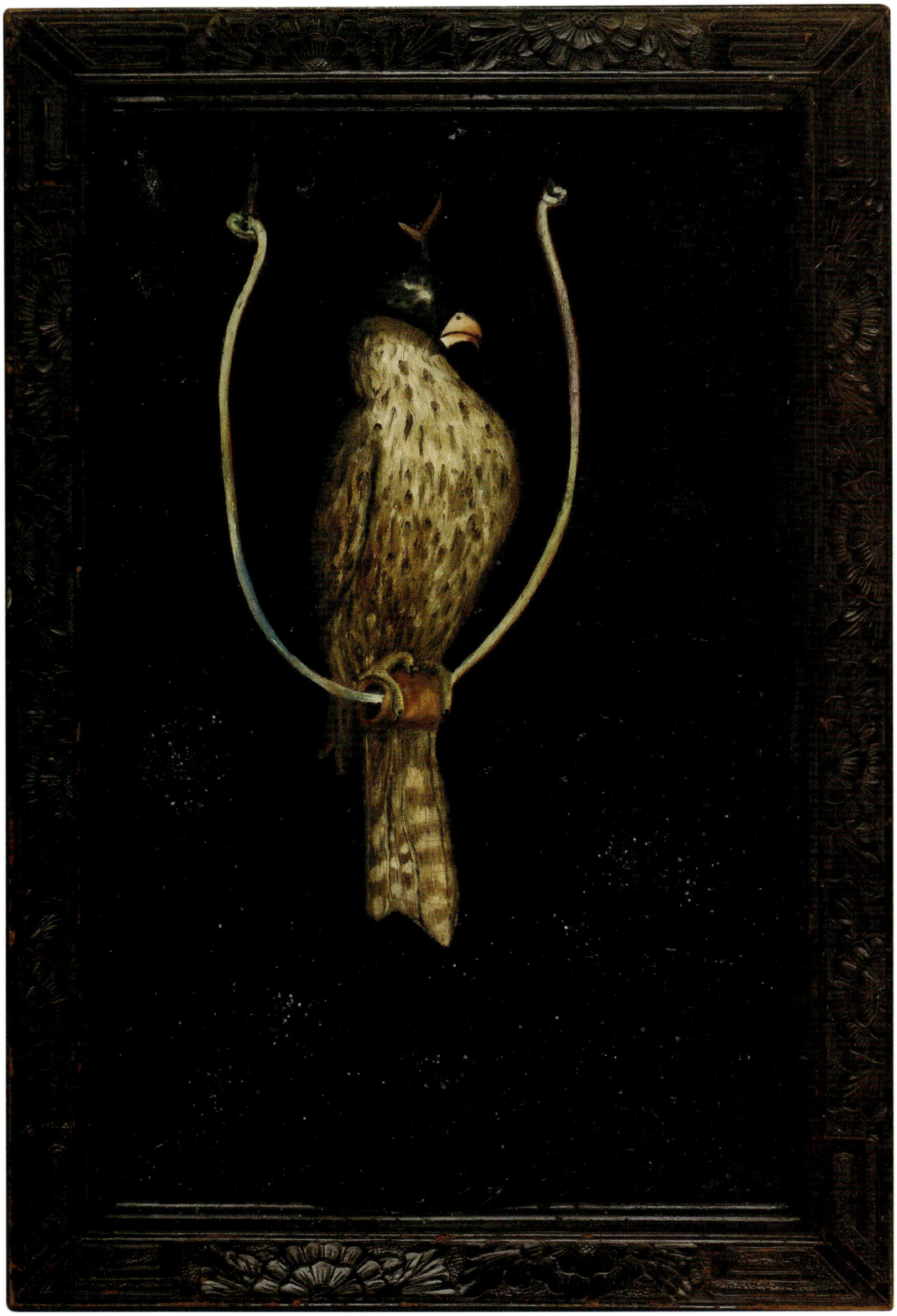

Masked Rapture, 2004
Oil on wood, 71 × 46 cm

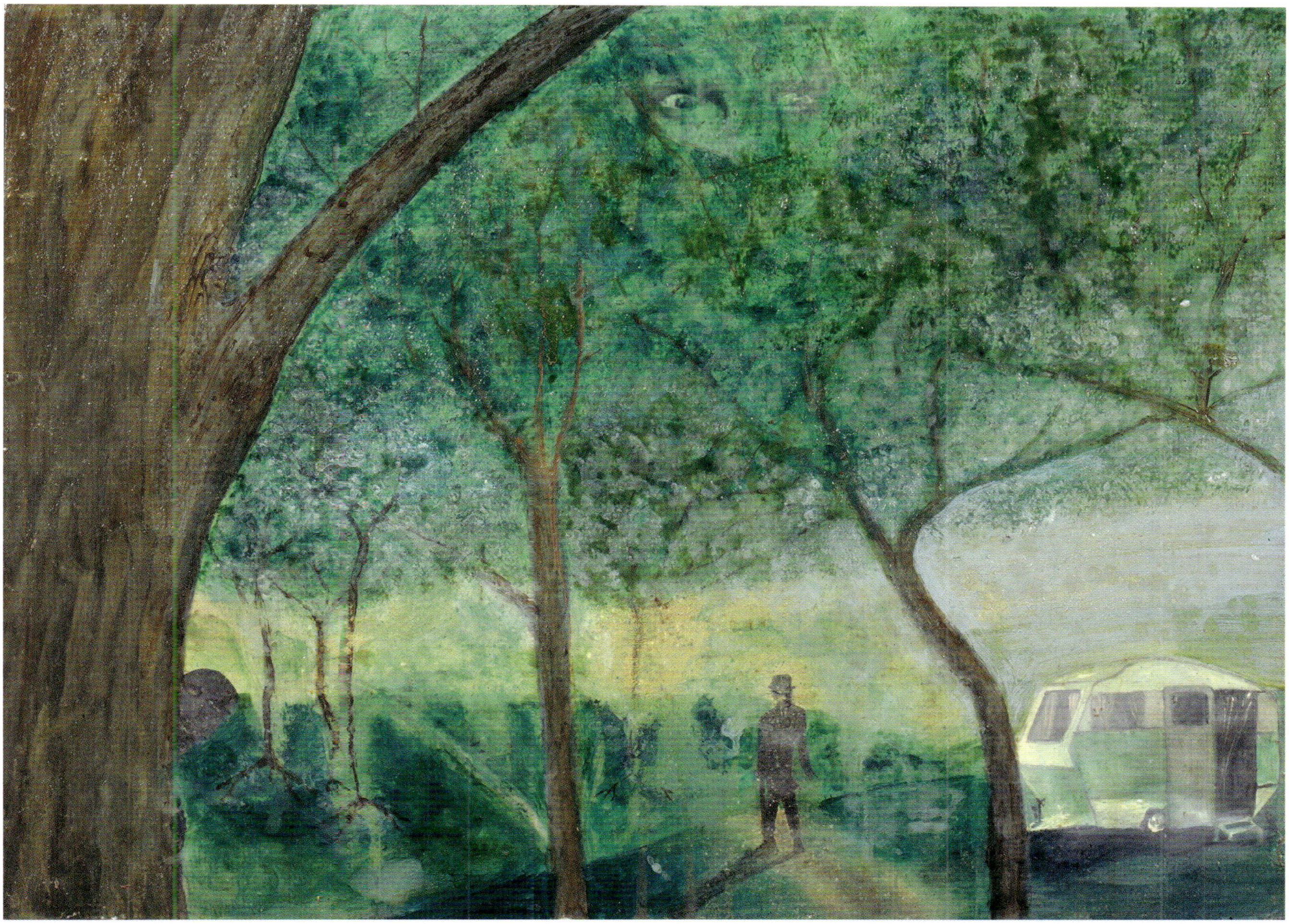

Honey I'm Home, 2005
Oil on wood, 33 x 46 cm

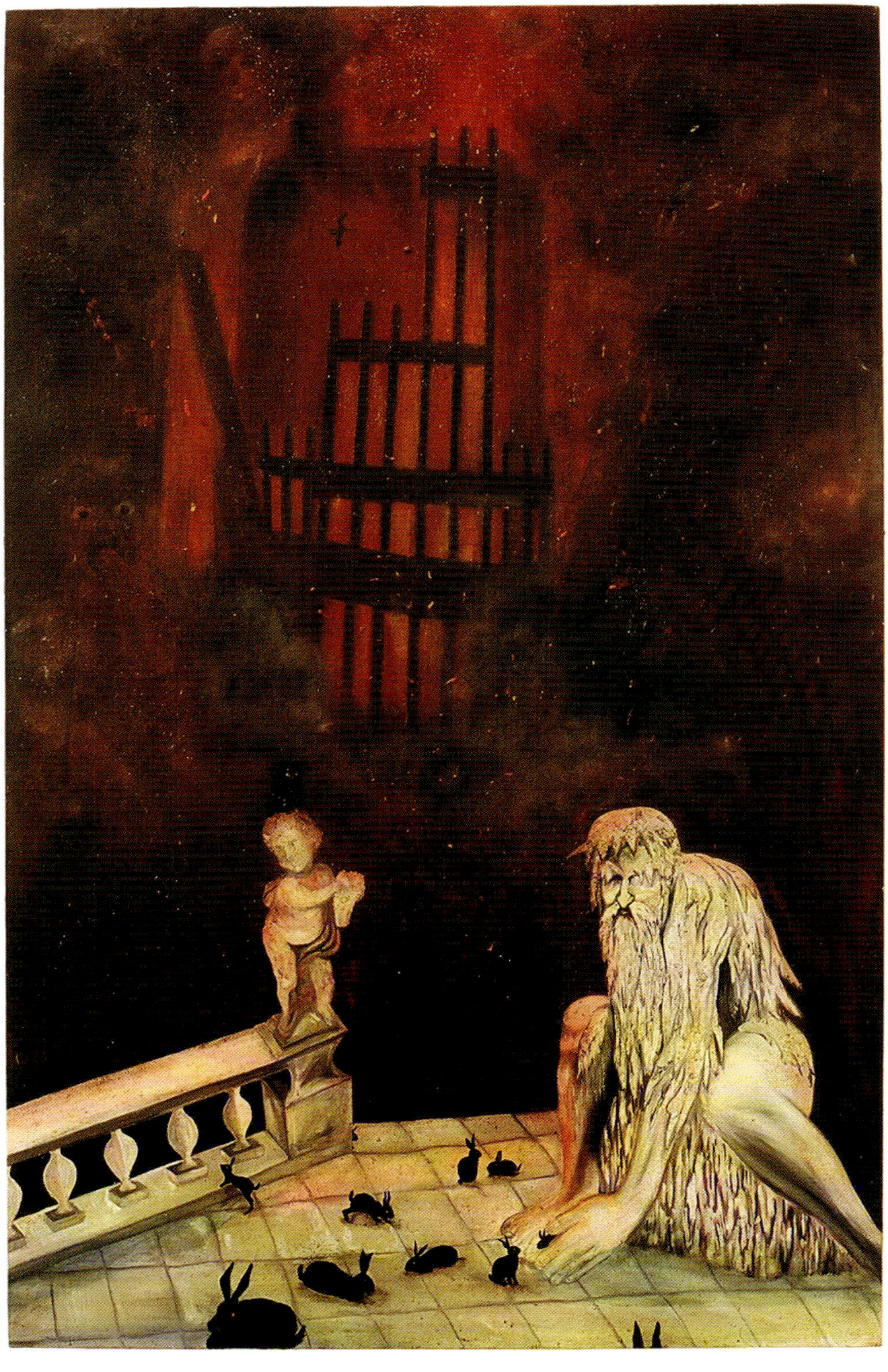

The Meek Shall Inherit the Earth, 2001
Oil on canvas, 122 × 91.5 cm

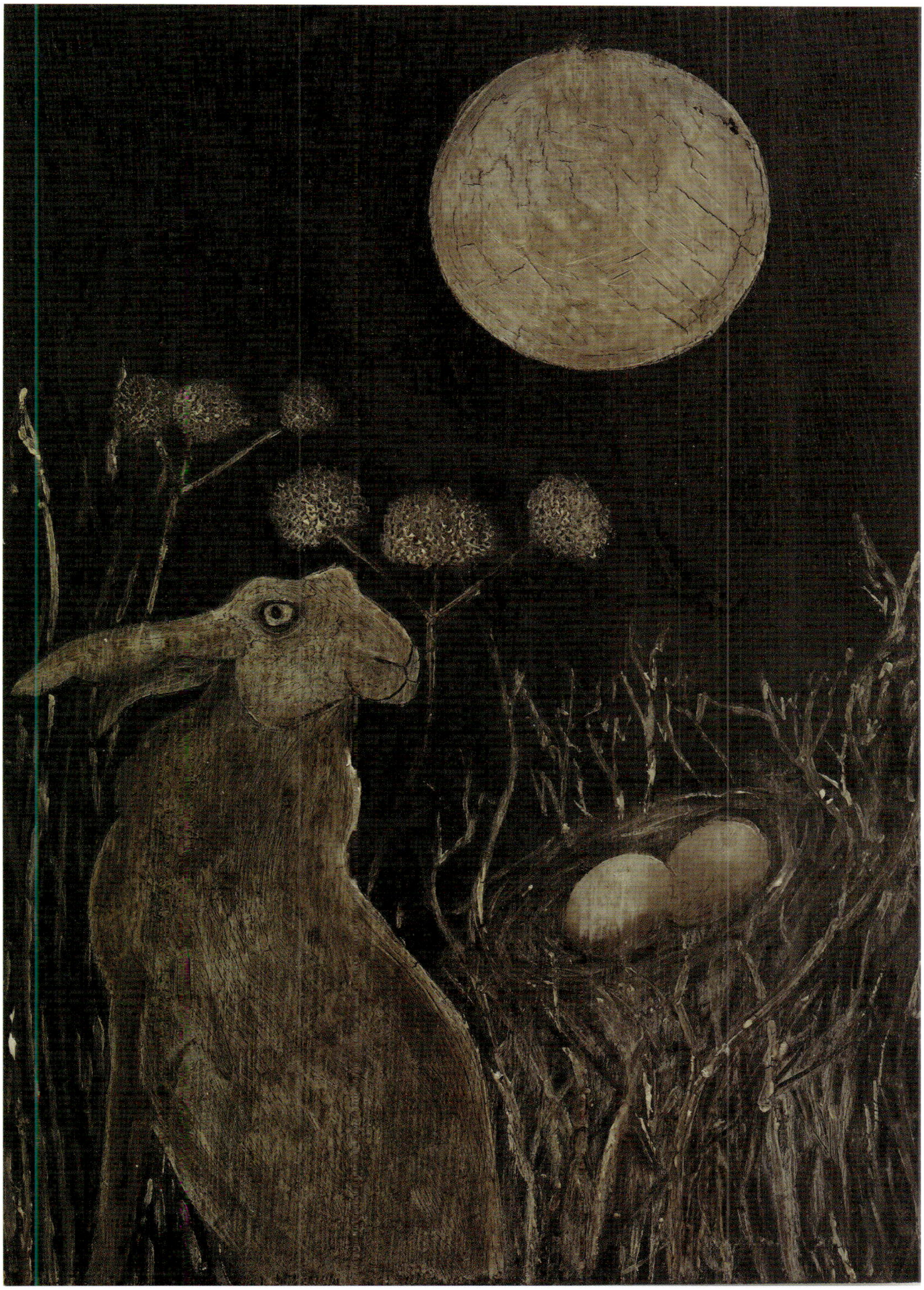

Hare Nest 2, 2008
Oil and bitchumen on wood, 41 x 31 cm

Moondrop, 2006
Oil on canvas, 37 x 37 cm

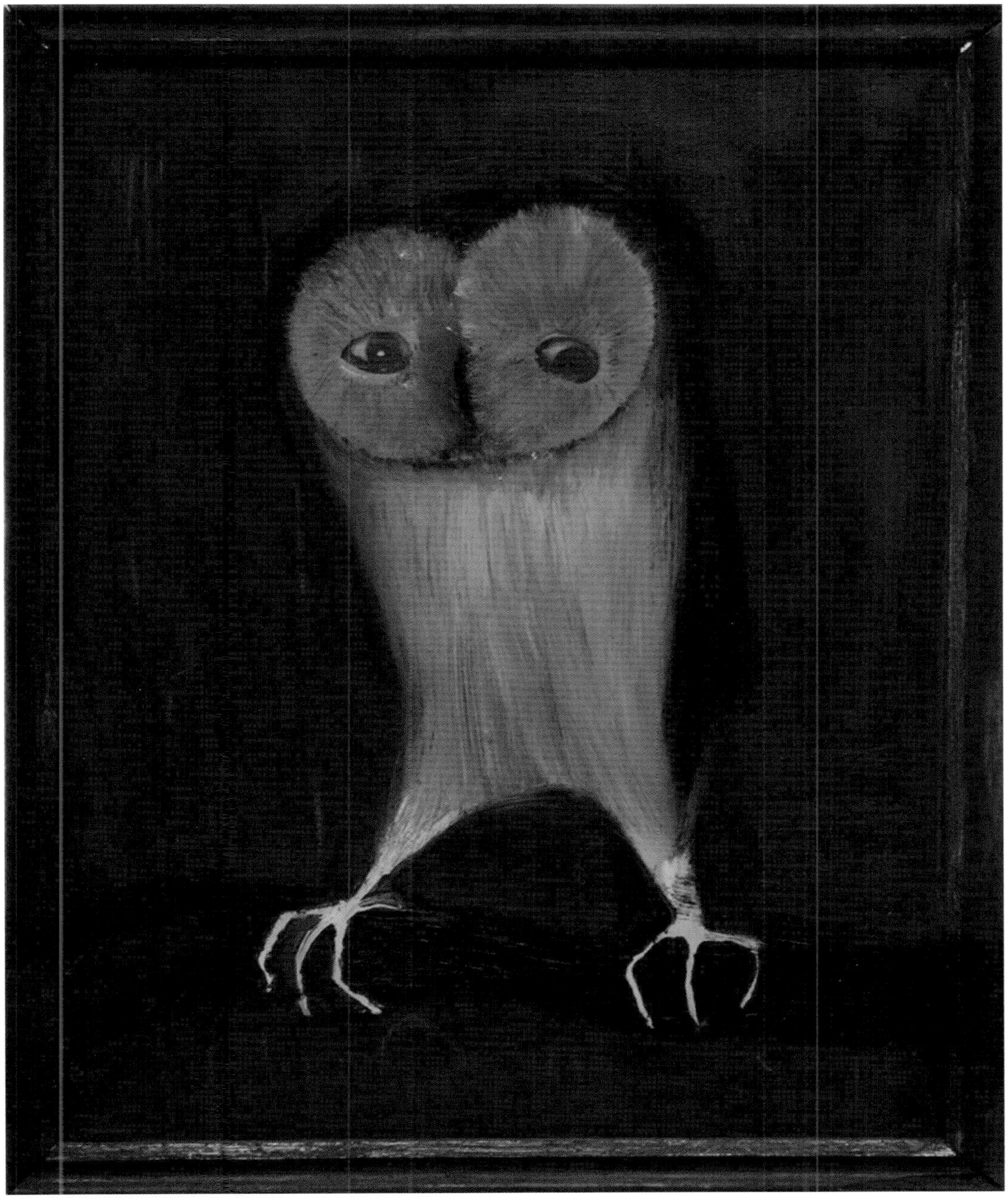

Purple Owl, 2005
Oil and collage on glass, 27 × 22 cm

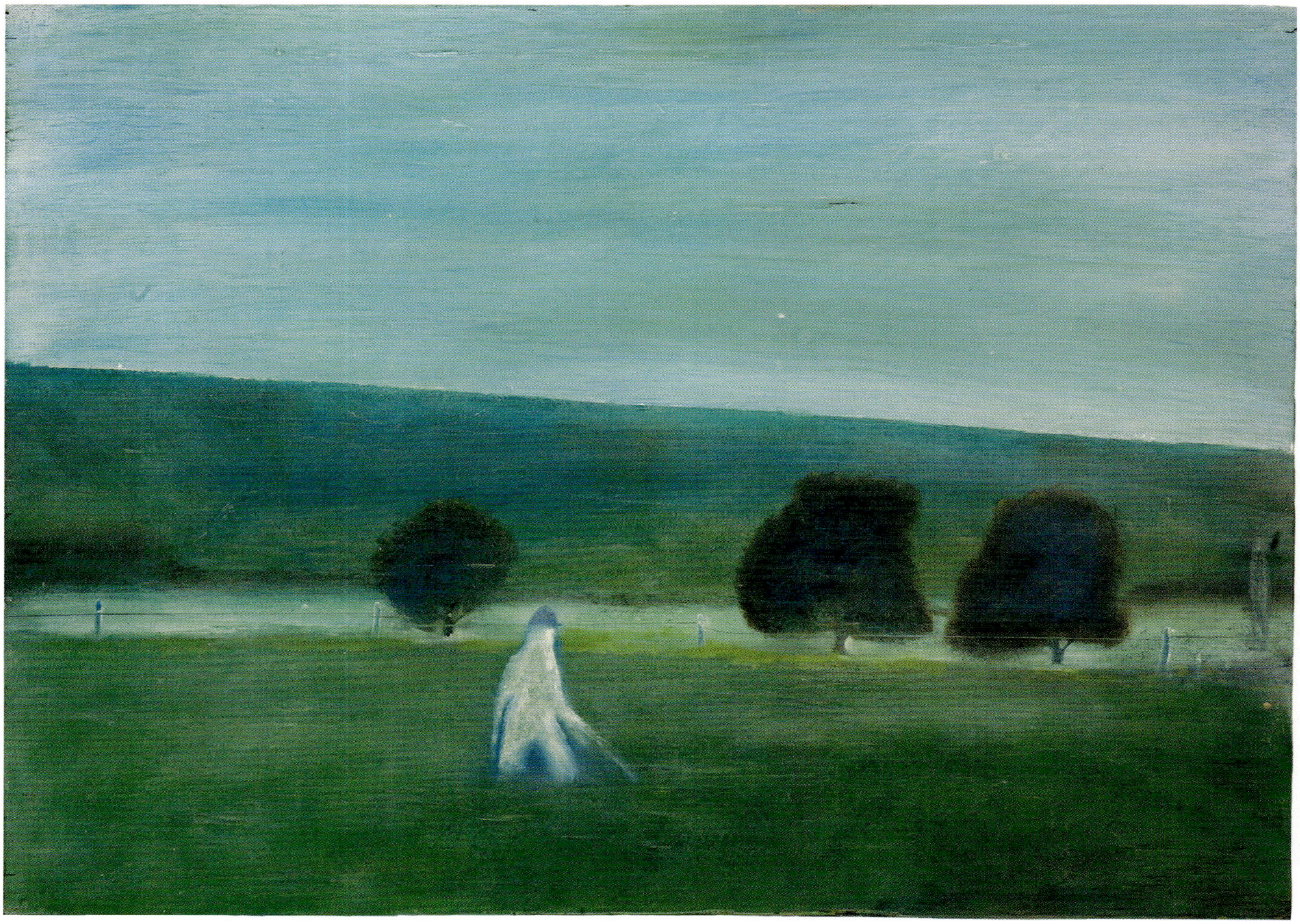

The Mawkin, 2008
Oil on wood, 48.4 x 66 cm

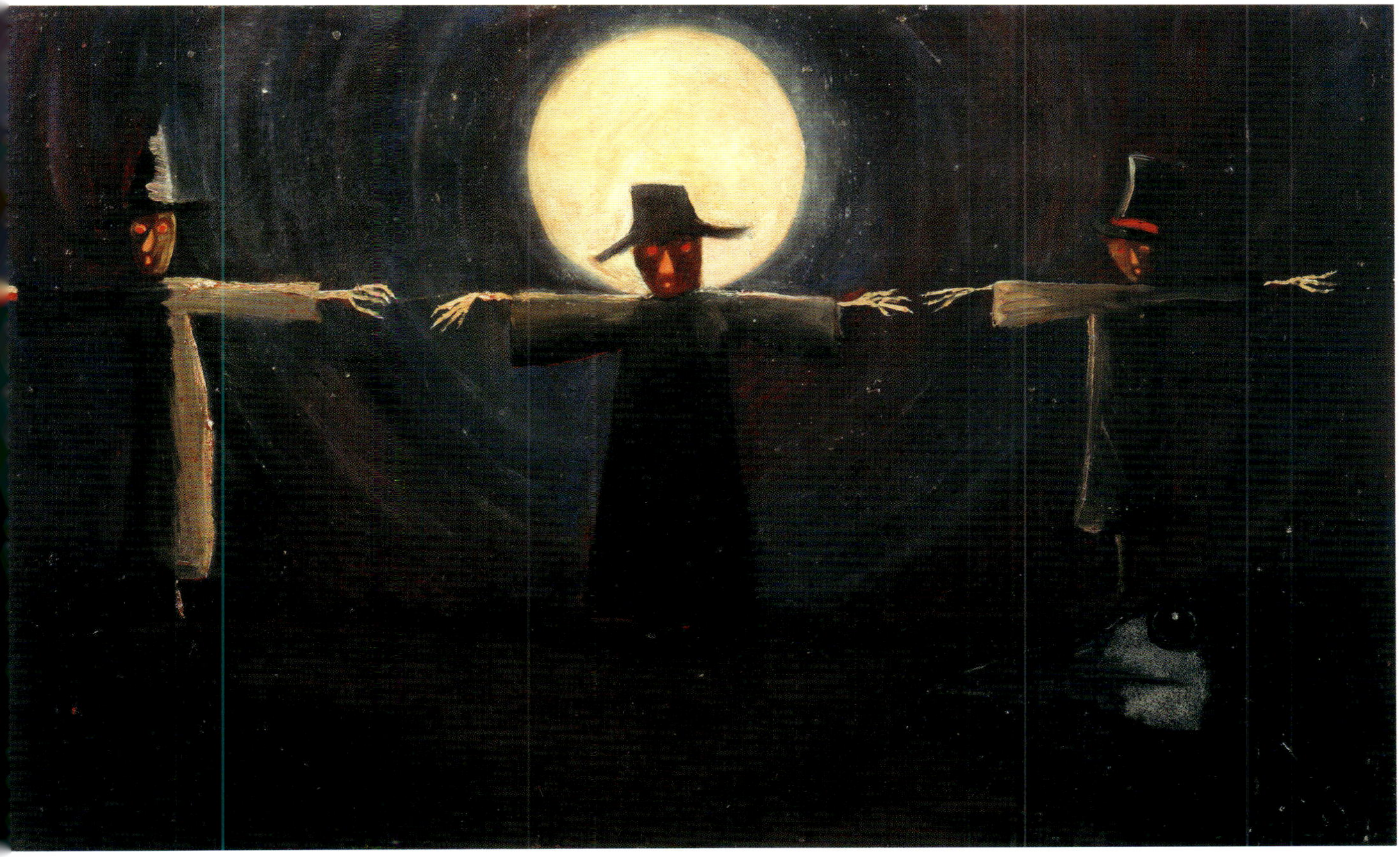

The Crucifixion, 2004
Oil on wood, 38 × 61 cm

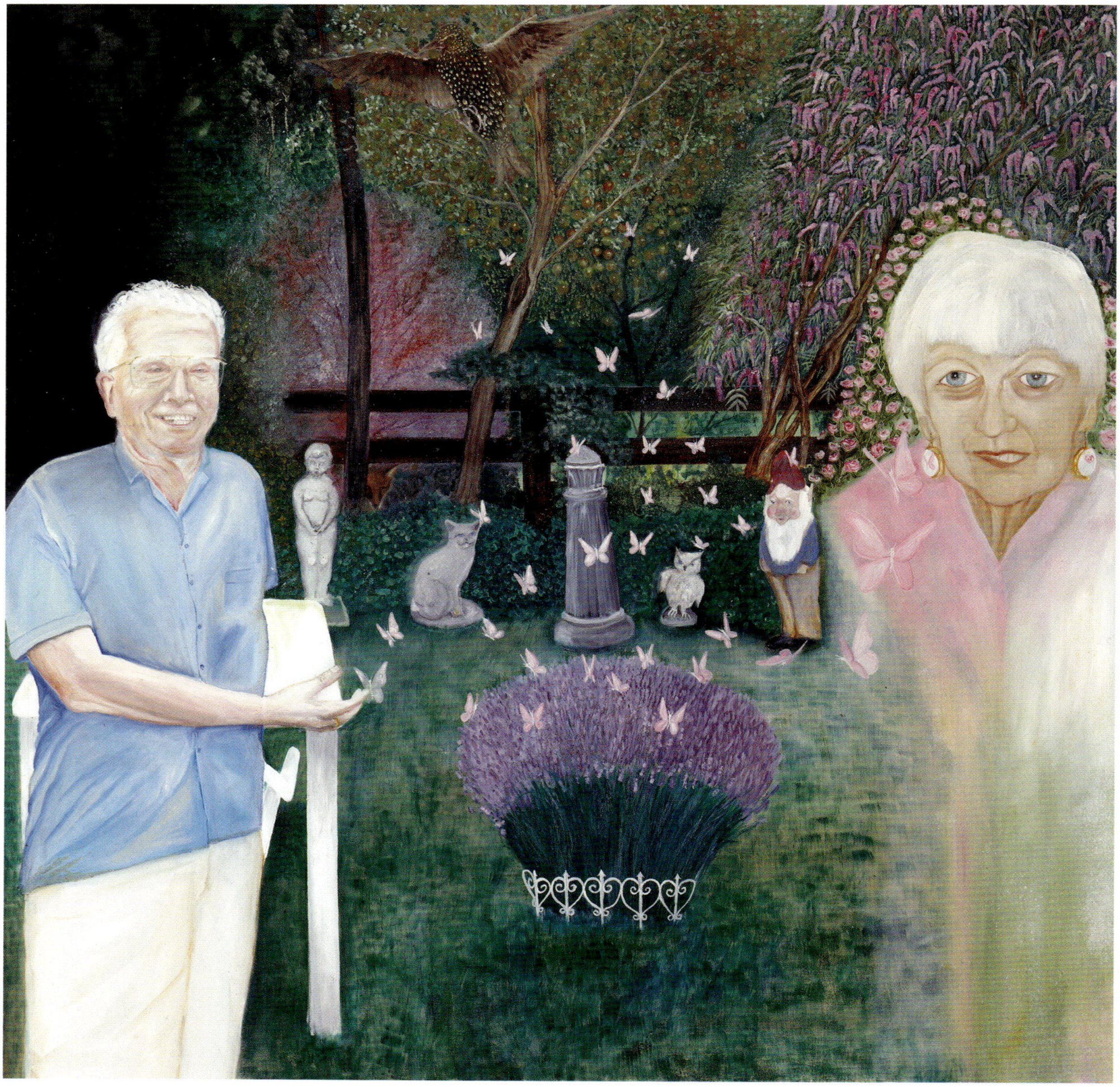

Emmie and Charlie, 2007
Oil on canvas, 91.44 x 91.44 cm

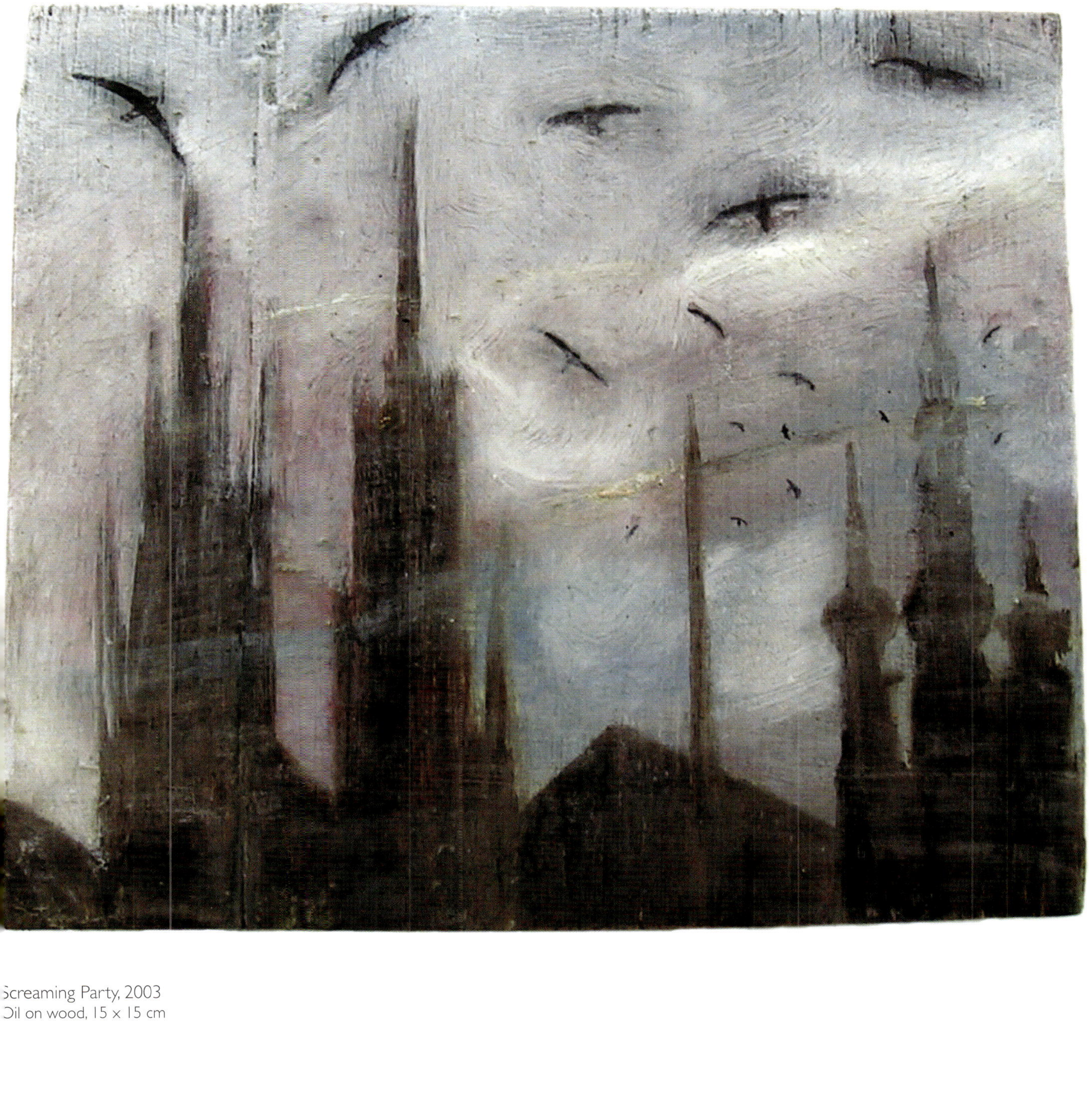

Screaming Party, 2003
Oil on wood, 15 × 15 cm

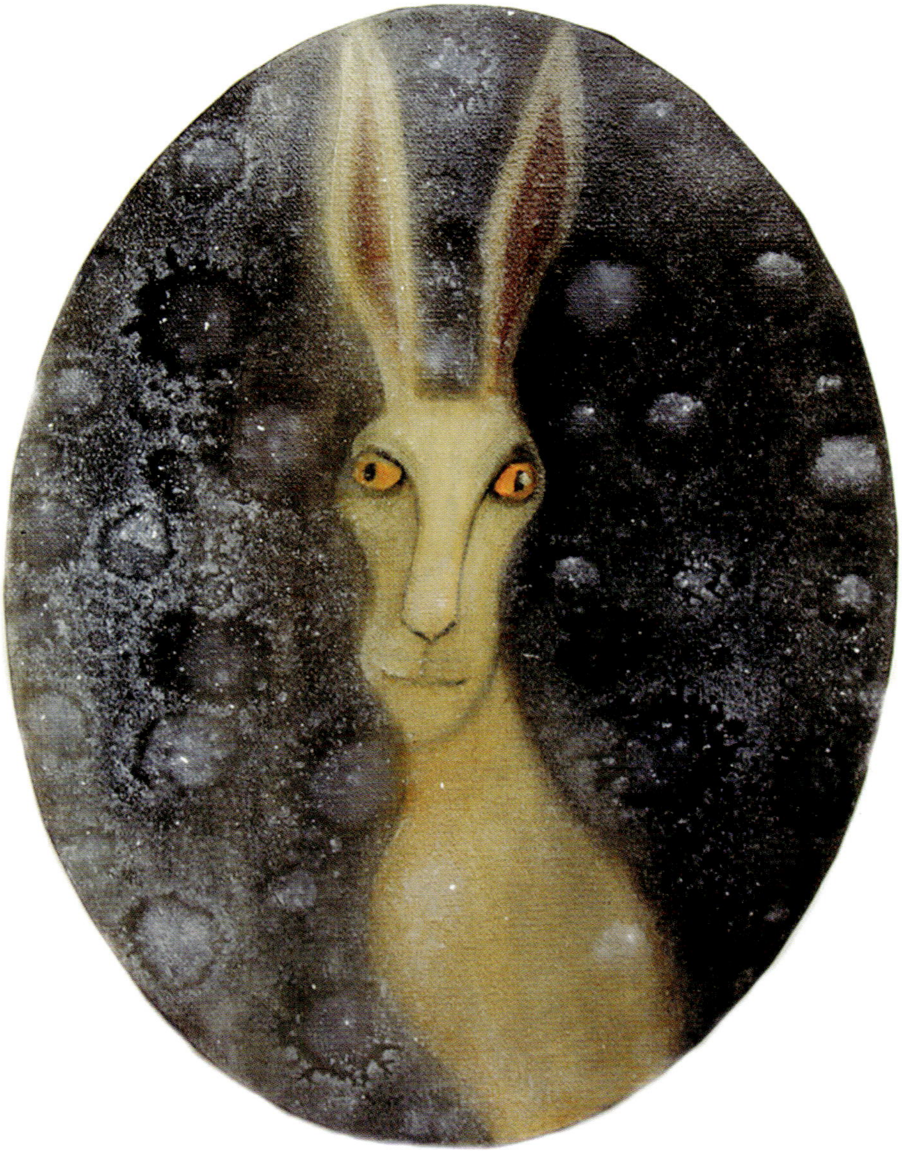

Goldeneye, 2008
Oil on canvas, 40 x 30 cm

Selected Catalogue of Works

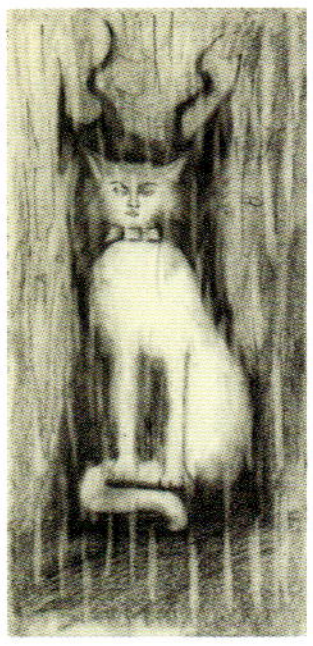

Mystical Cat, 2001
Pencil on paper, 29.5 x 14 cm

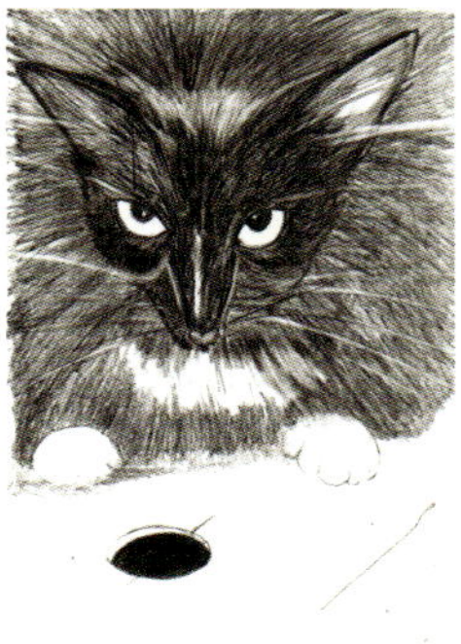

Tyrone Waits Patiently, 2001
Pencil on paper, 29.5 x 14 cm

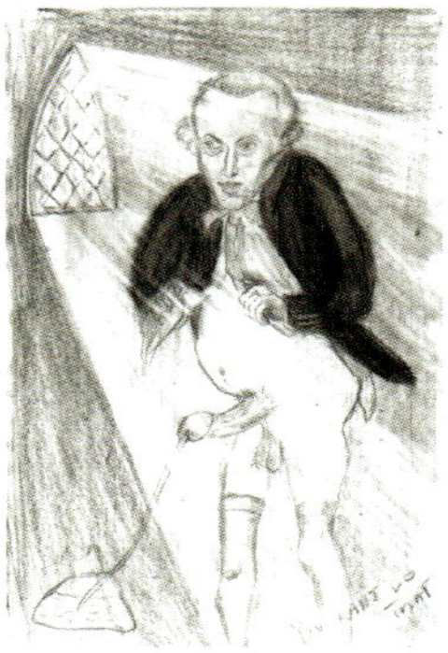

You Kant Do That, 2001
Pencil on paper, 29.5 x 14 cm

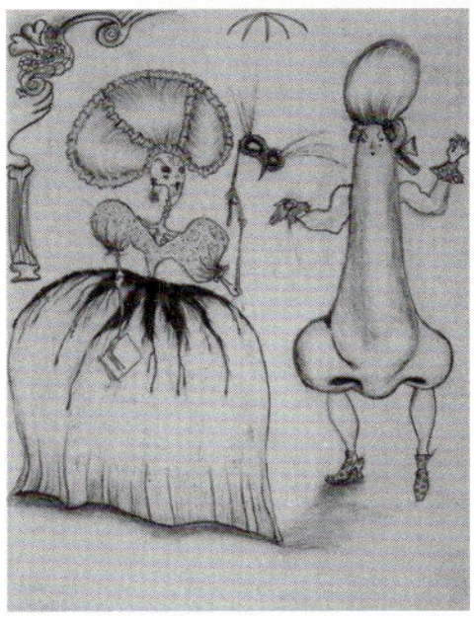

Nosegay, 2001
Pencil on paper, 33 x 25 cm

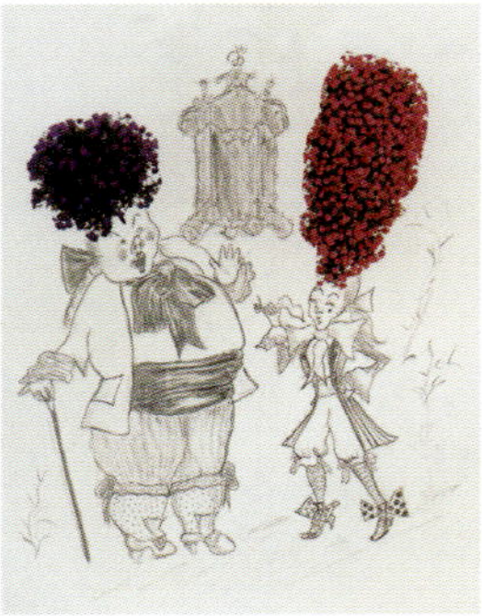

He Looked Ridiculous, 2001
Pencil and collage on paper, 33 x 25 cm

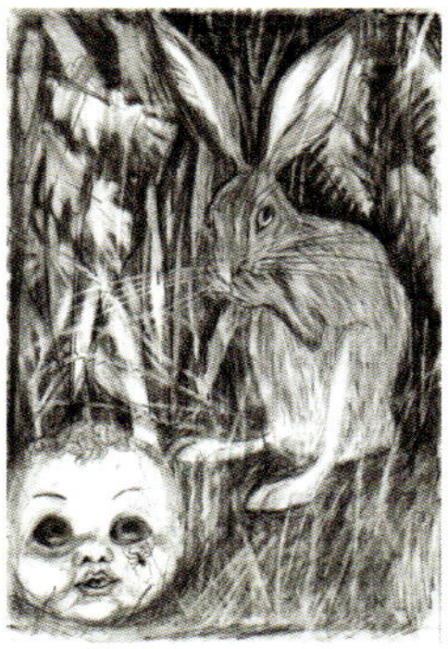

Head of Hare, 2001
Pencil on paper, 29.5 x 14 cm

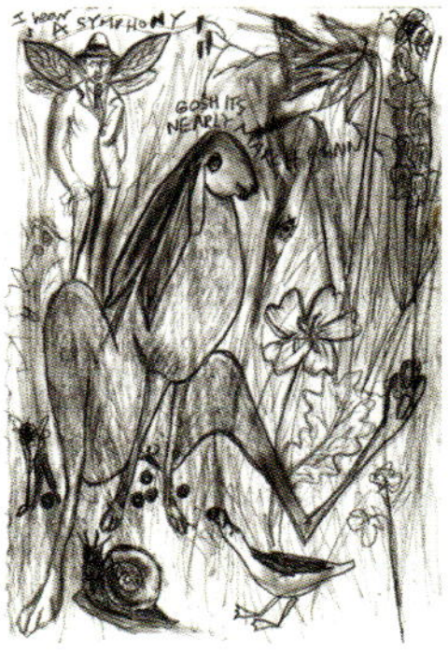

I Hear A Symphony, 2001
Pencil on paper, 29.5 x 14 cm

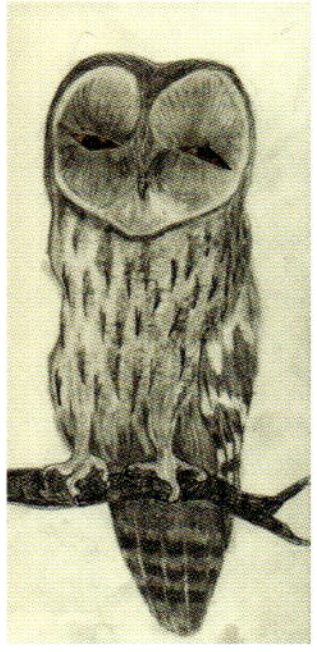

Tawny Owl, 2001
Pencil and collage on paper, 29.5x 14 cm

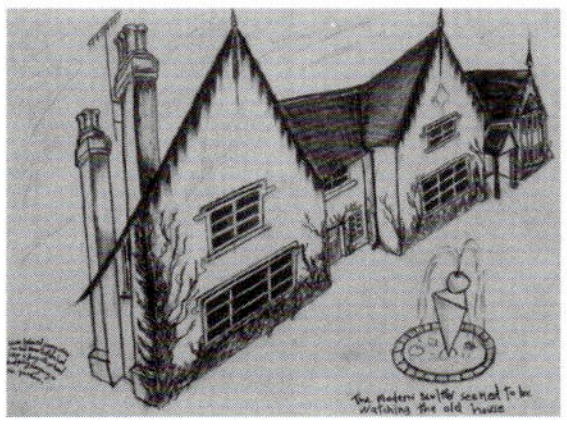

House and Fountain, 2001
Pencil on paper, 25 x 33 cm

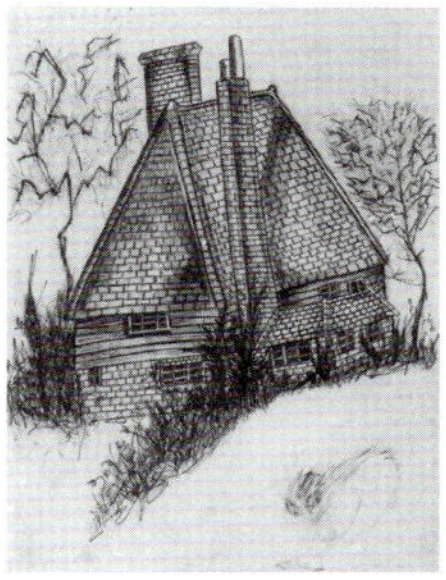

House in the Country, 2001
Pencil on paper, 33 x 25 cm

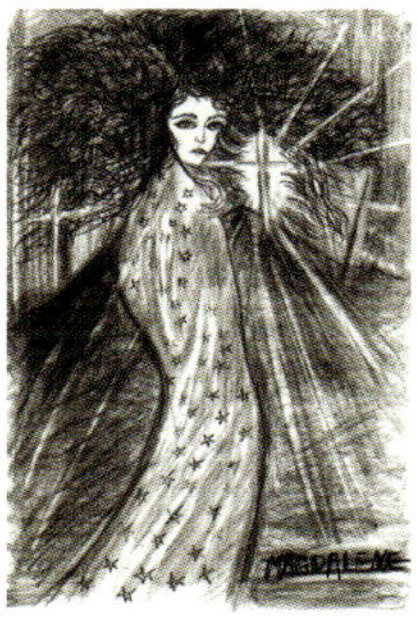

Magdalene, 2001
Pencil on paper, 29.5 x 14 cm

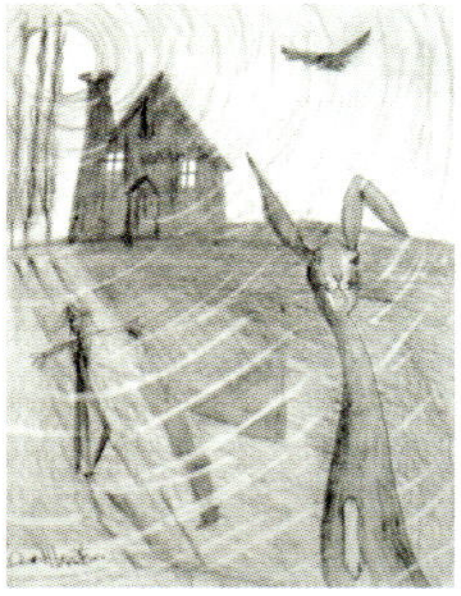

Hare and Scarecrow, 2001
Pencil on paper, 29.5 x 14 cm

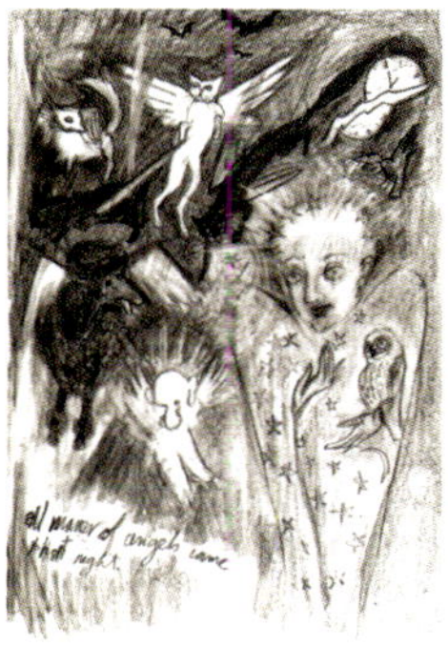

All Manner of Angels Came that Night, 2001
Pencil on paper, 29.5 x 14 cm

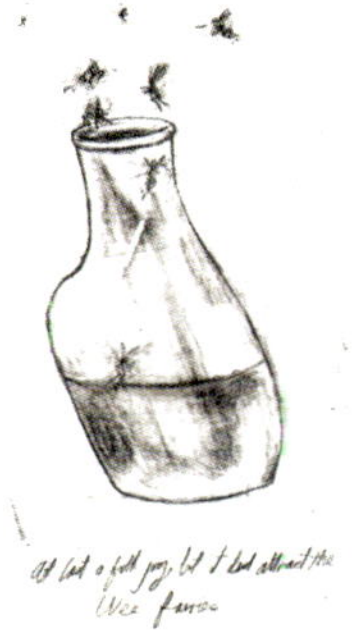

At Last a Full Jug, But it Did Attract the Wee Fairies, 2001
Pencil on paper, 29.5 x 14 cm

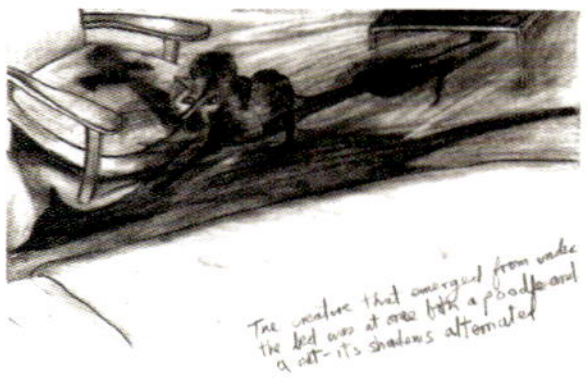

Catpoodle, 2001
Pencil on paper, 14 x 29.5 cm

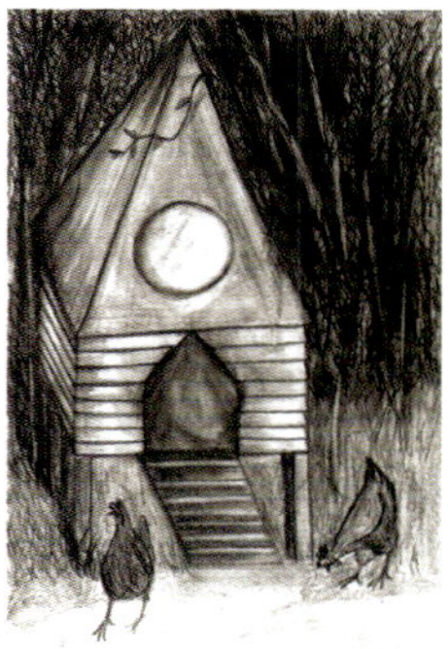

Chicken House, 2001
Pencil on paper, 29.5 x 14 cm

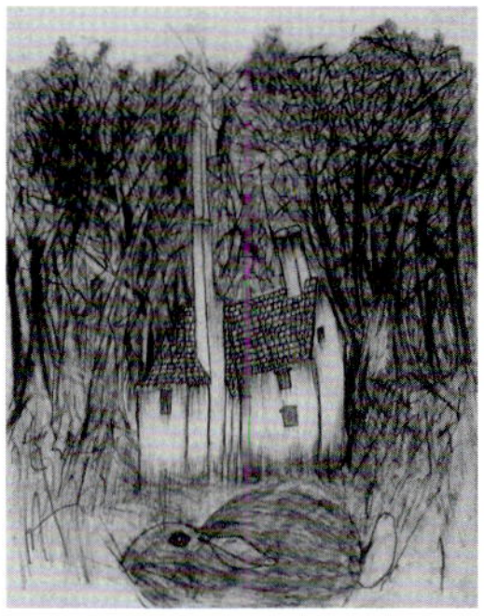

Country Life, 2001
Pencil on paper, 33 x 25 cm

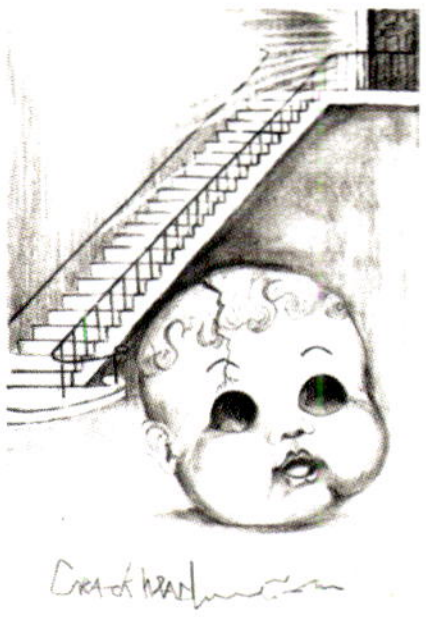

Crack Head, 2001
Pencil on paper,
29.5 x 14 cm

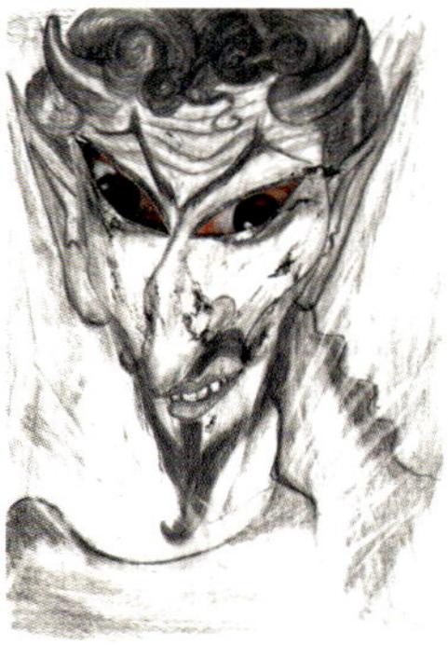

Devil Eyes, 2001
Pencil and collage on paper,
29.5 x 14 cm

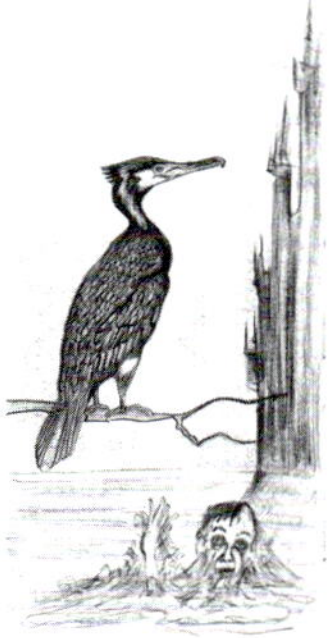

Drowning Man, 2001
Pencil on paper, 29.5 x 14 cm

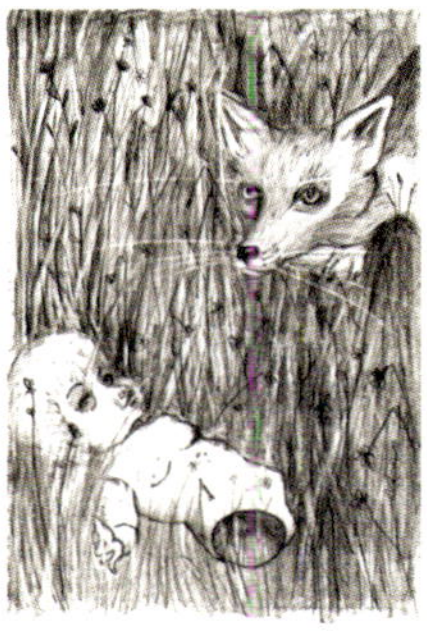

Fox with Doll, 2001
Pencil on paper, 29.5 x 14 cm

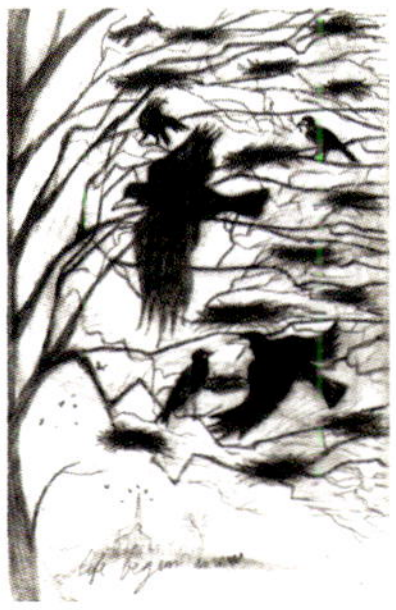

Life Begins Anew, 2001
Pencil on paper,
29.5 x 14 cm

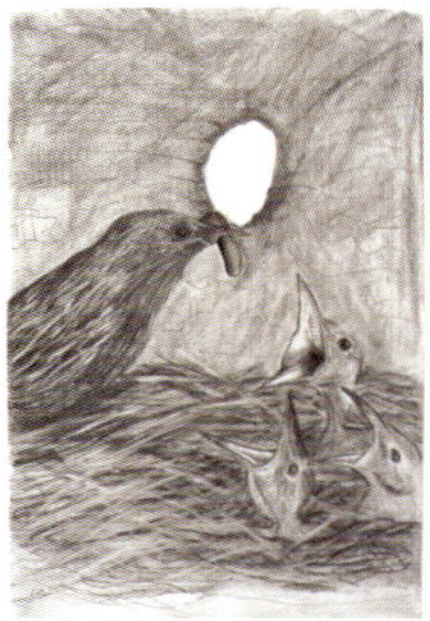

Birds in Nesting Hole, 2004
Pencil on paper, 30 x 21 cm

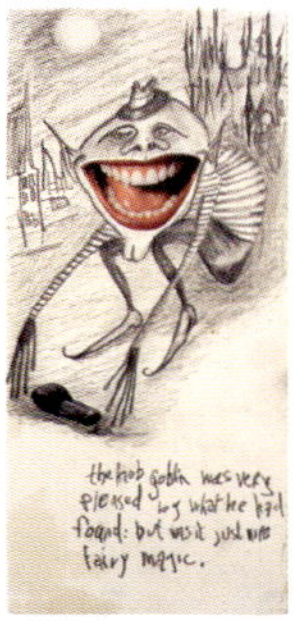

Cock Goblin, 2004
Pencil and collage on paper,
20 x 10 cm

Sculptures, 1982–2008

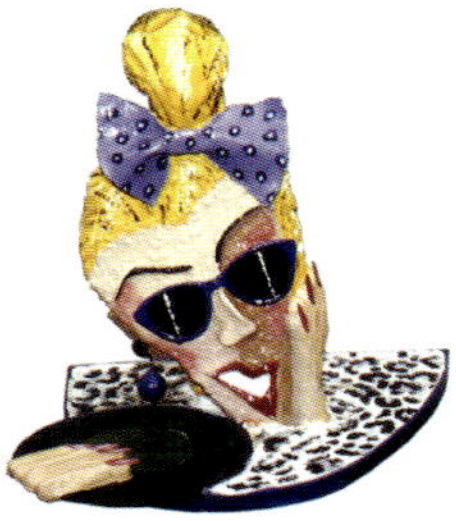

Jean's Favourite Record, 1982
Found objects and acrylic,
40 × 36 × 30 cm

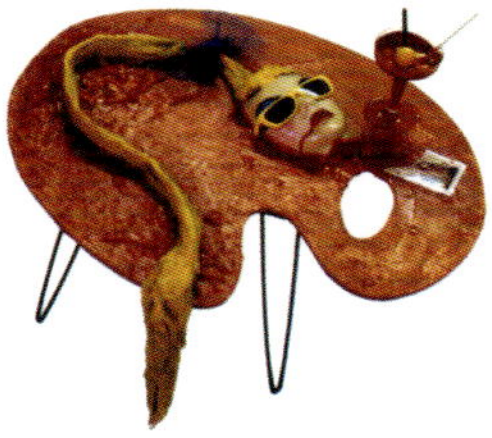

Table Sculpture, 1983
Mixed media, 60 × 60 × 60 cm

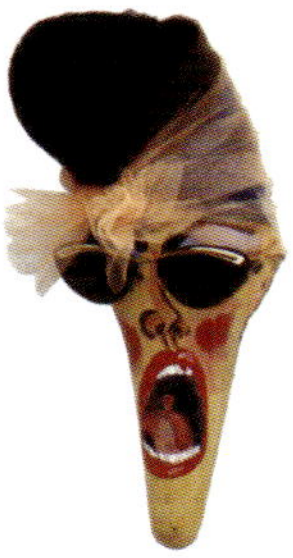

Wall Mask 1, 1984
Found objects and acrylic,
30 × 15 × 10 cm

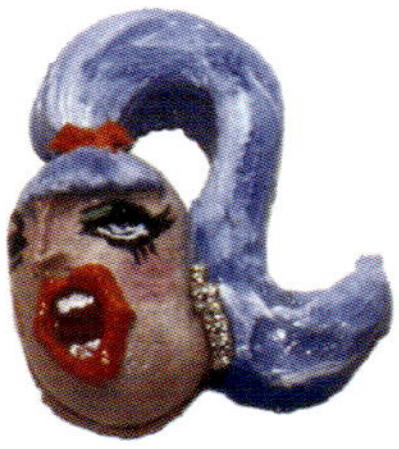

Wall Mask 2, 1984
Plaster and acrylic,
20 × 20 × 10 cm

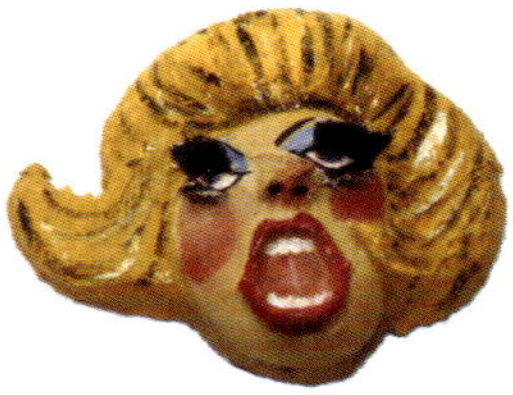

Wall Mask 3, 1984
Plaster and acrylic,
20 × 24 × 10 cm

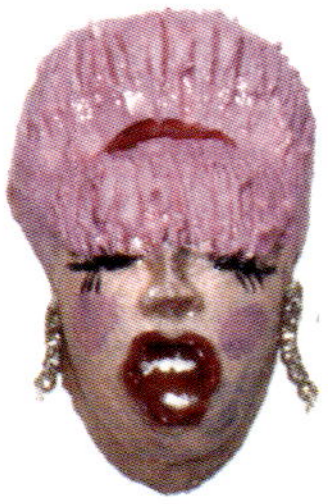

Wall Mask 4, 1984
Plaster and acrylic,
20 × 18 × 10 cm

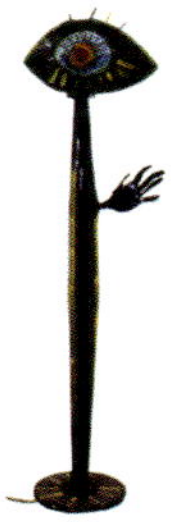

Eye on a Stick Floor Lamp, 1984
Mixed media, 152 × 30 × 20 cm

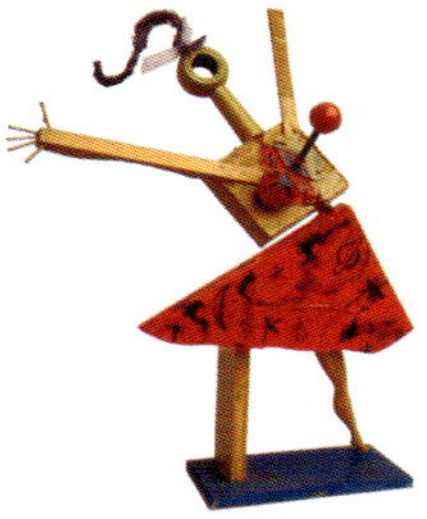

Jean Dancing, 1986
Found objects,
30 × 25 × 15 cm

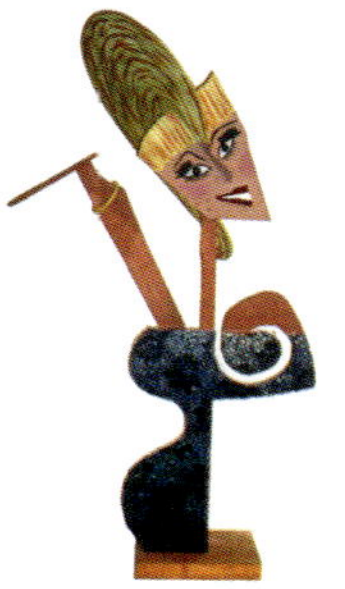

Jean in Her Bathing Costume, 1986
Found objects and acrylic,
60 × 40 × 20 cm

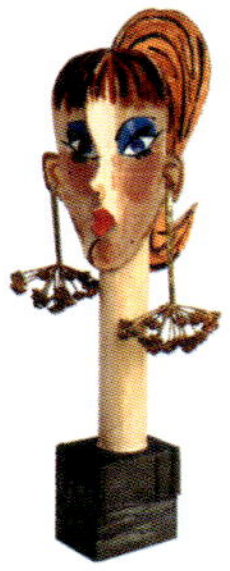

Jean's Favourite Earrings, 1986
Found objects and acrylic,
61 × 31 × 25 cm

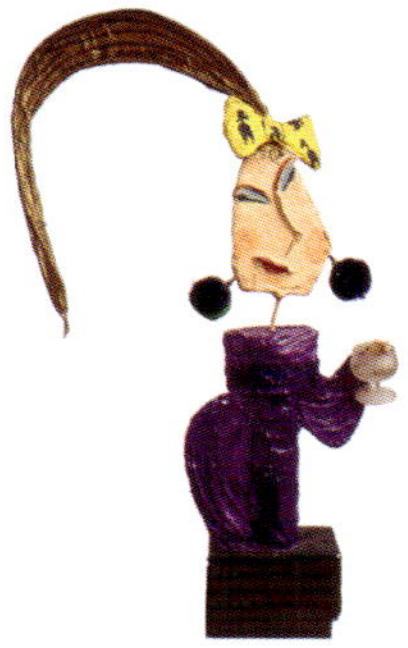

Jean's Favourite Drink, 1986
Found objects and acrylic,
91 × 30 × 20 cm

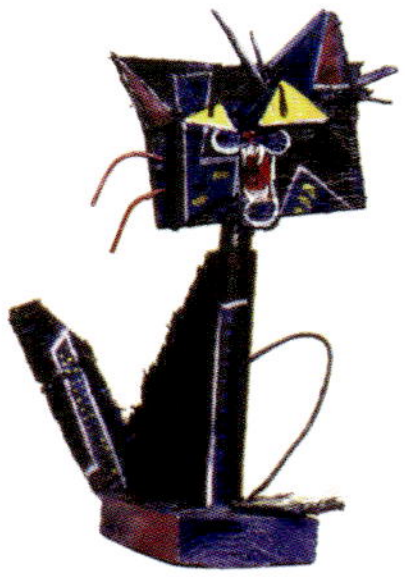

City Cat, 1987
Mixed media,
30 × 25 × 20 cm

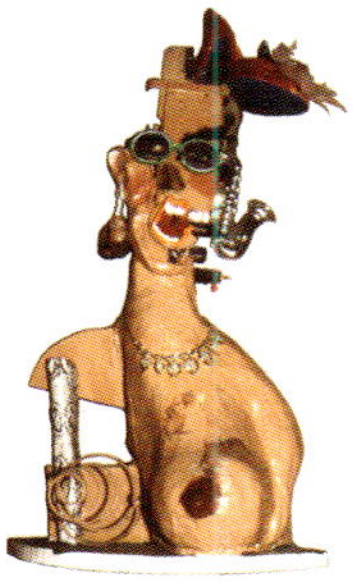

Fashion Victim, 1987
Mixed media,
91 x 46 x 30 cm

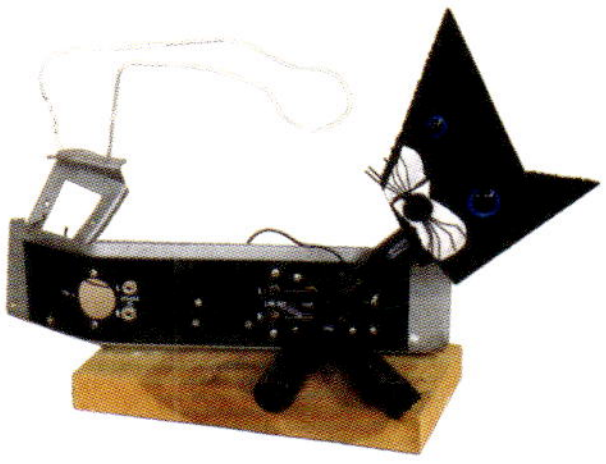

Cataphonic, 1987
Found objects anc acrylic,
30 x 61 x 25 cm

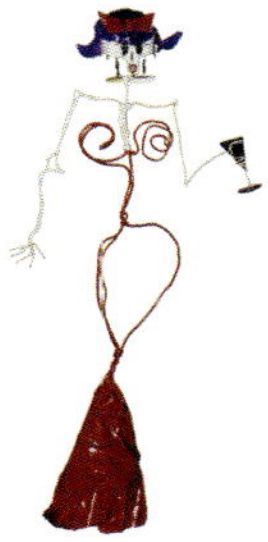

Dead Glamorous, 1987
Found objects and paper mache
61 x 30 x 20 cm

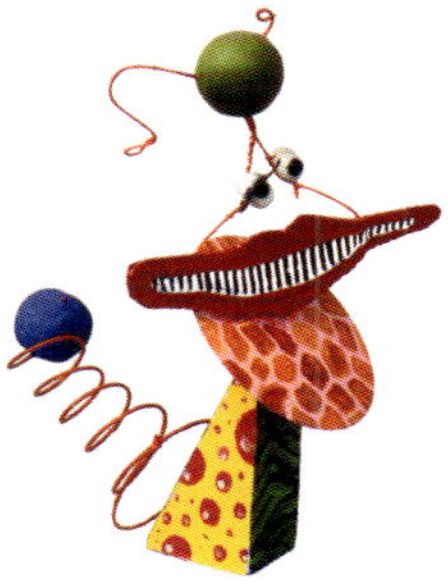

Cyber Poodle 1, 1988
Found objects,
25 x 20 x 15 cm

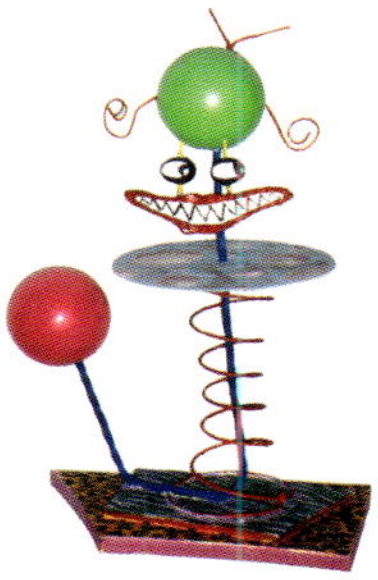

Cyber Poodle 2, 1988
Found objects,
25 x 20 x 15 cm

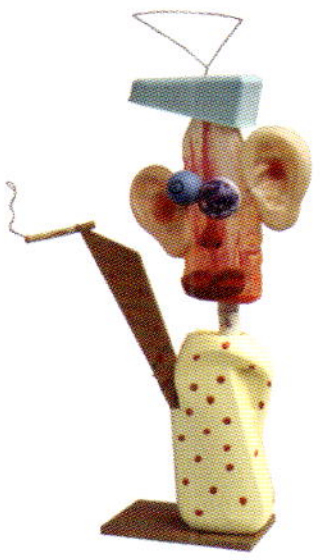

Smokey Joe, 1988
Found objects,
50 x 25 x 25 cm

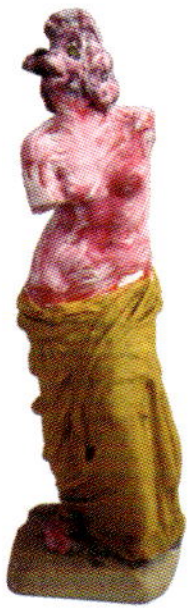

Venus de Poodle, 1988
Plaster,
25 x 10 x 10 cm

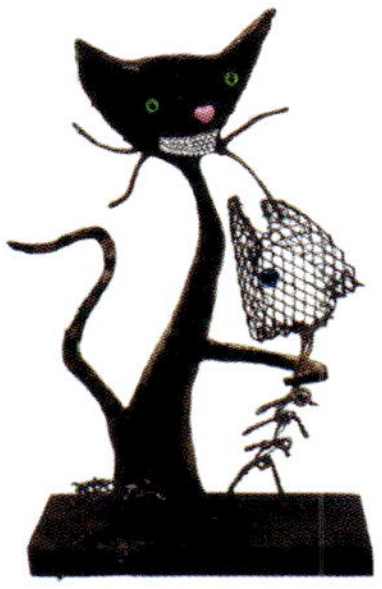

Cat with Fish, 1989
Mixed media,
40 x 25 x 15 cm

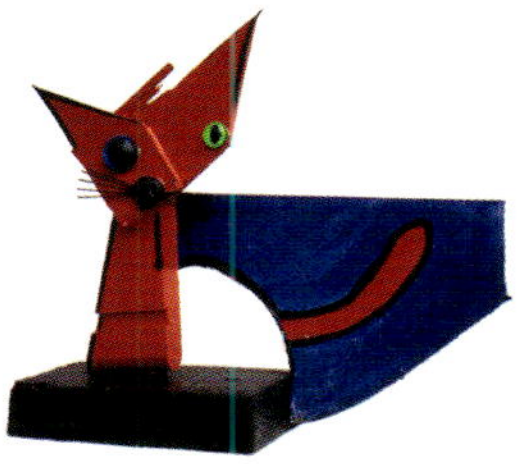

Cat, 1989
Found objects,
20 x 24 x 18 cm

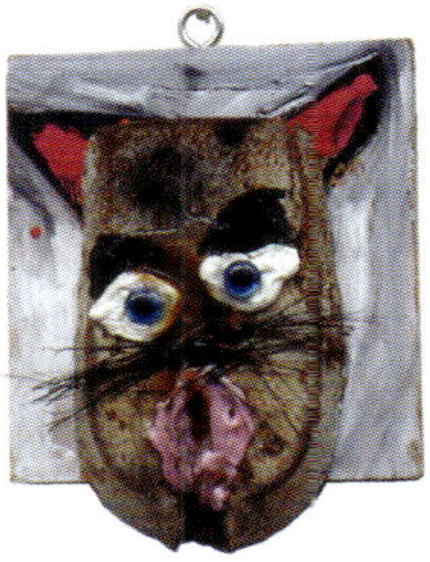

Fuck Face, 1989
Mixed media,
20 x 20 x 8 cm

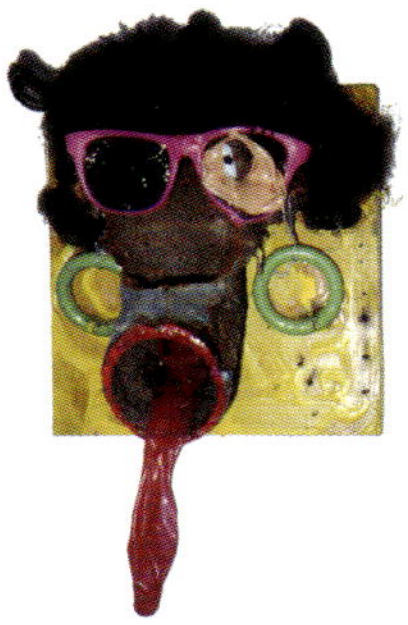

Gargirl, 1989
Found objects,
20 x 20 cm

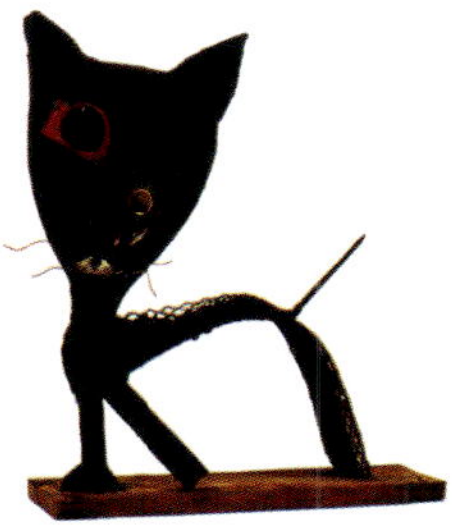

Stray Cat Strut, 1989
Mixed media,
25 x 25 x 15 cm

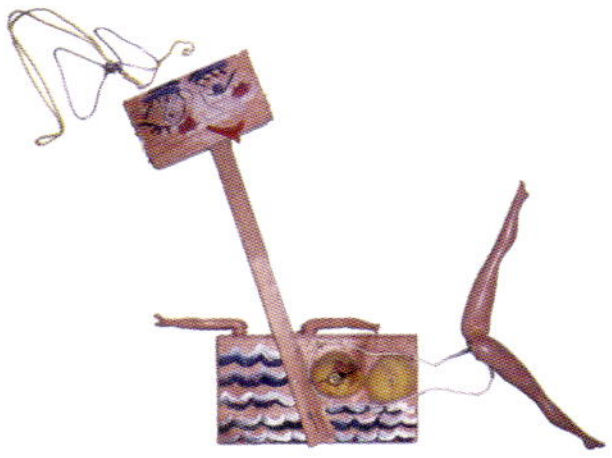

Swimmer, 1989
Found objects and acrylic,
30 × 30 × 20 cm

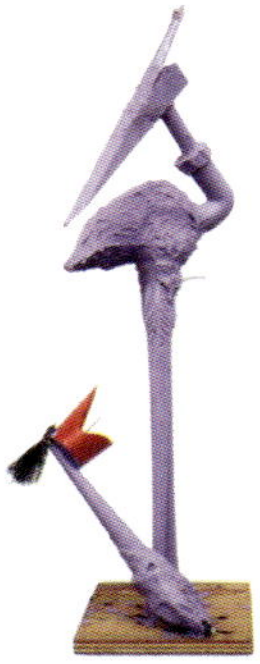

Heron and Young, 1990
Mixed media,
60 × 20 × 20 cm

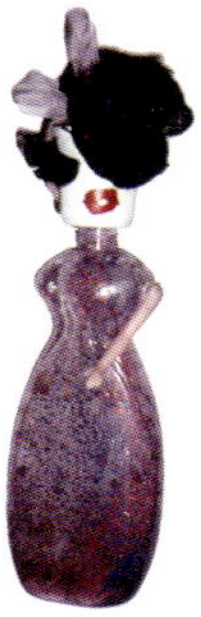

Pinkietessa, 1992
Found objects and acrylic,
25 × 15 × 15 cm

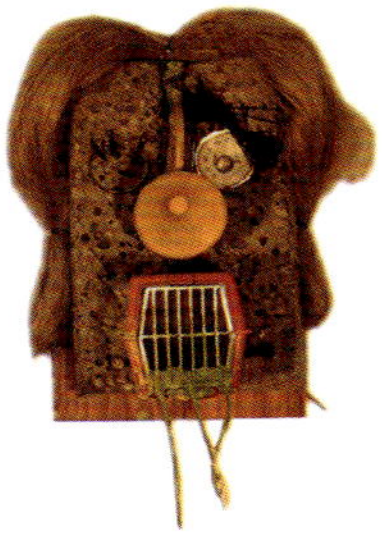

Cat Flu, 1992
Found objects,
20 × 13 × 10 cm

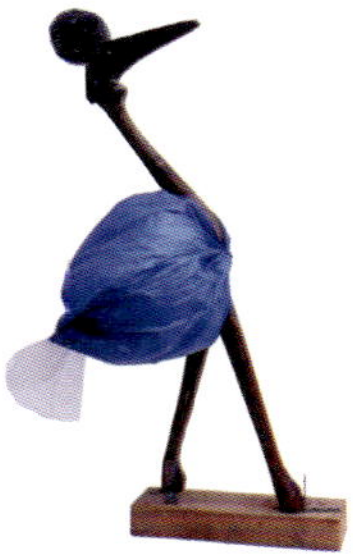

Rubbish Heron, 1992
Mixed media,
38 × 30 × 25 cm

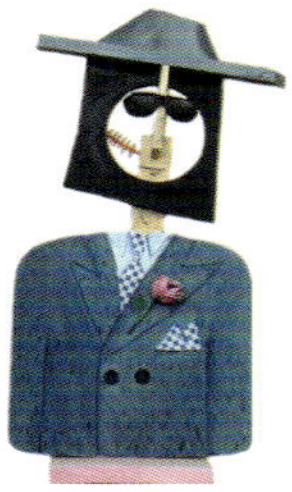

Ska Face, 1994
Found objects and acrylic,
60 × 46 × 12 cm

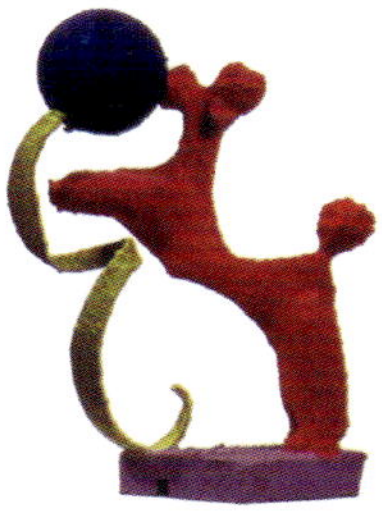

Circus Poodle, 1995
Found objects,
30 × 20 × 18 cm

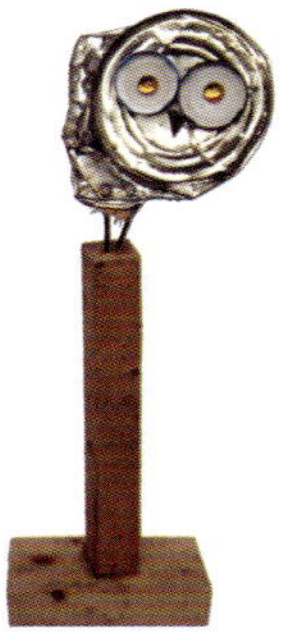

Owl, 1995
Found objects,
46 × 20 × 20 cm

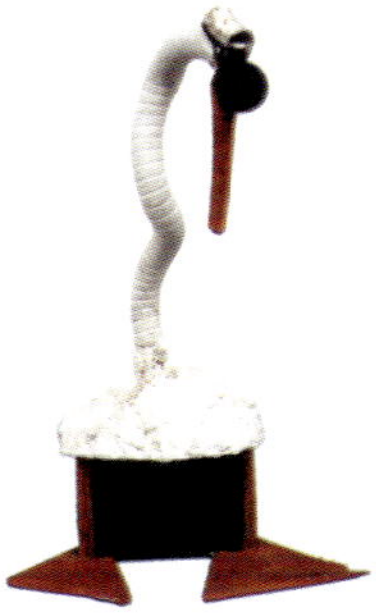

Swan, 1996
Found objects,
50 × 30 × 28 cm

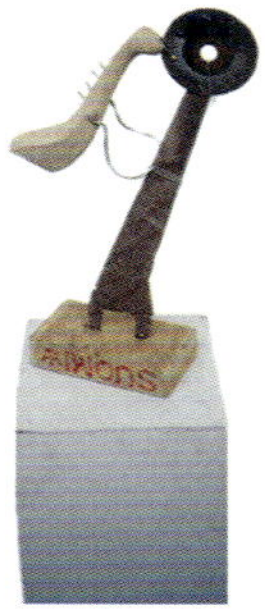

Saxophonist, 1996
Found objects,
36 × 20 × 20 cm

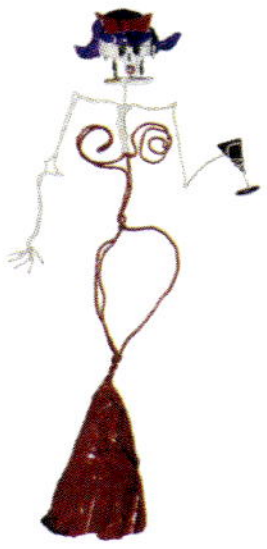

Dead Glamorous, 1997
Found objects and paper mache,
61 × 30 × 20 cm

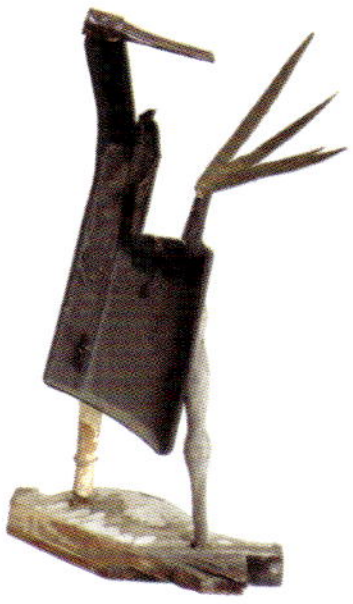

Preening Stork, 1997
Mixed media,
60 × 30 × 20 cm

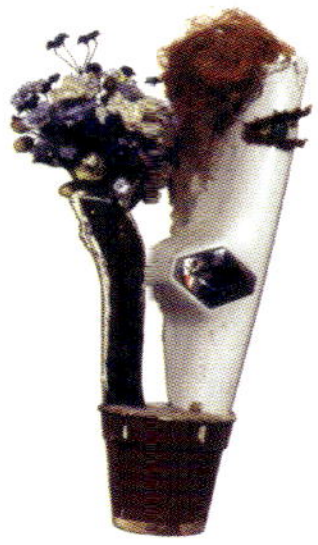

Say It With Flowers, 1997
Found objects,
30 × 15 × 15 cm

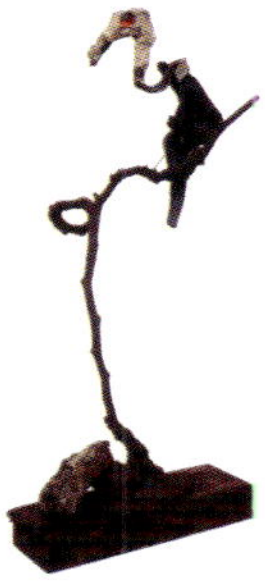

Vulture, 1997
Mixed media,
30 × 20 × 20 cm

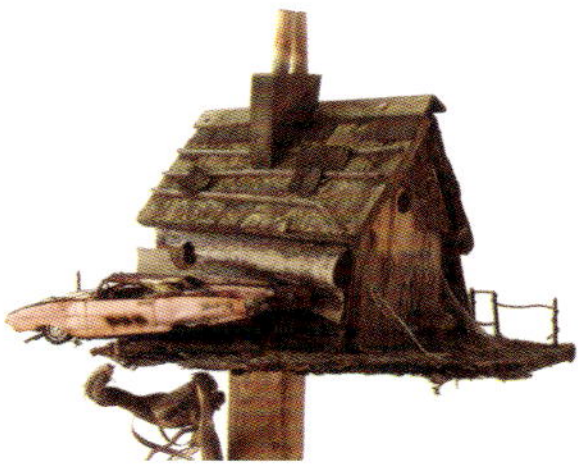

Derelict Birdhouse, 2001
Found objects,
54 × 183 × 48 cm

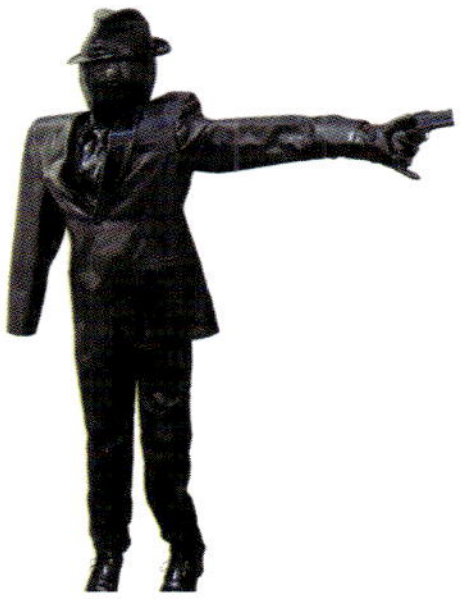

Black Scarecrow, 2004
Found objects and black tar,
190 × 140 × 40 cm

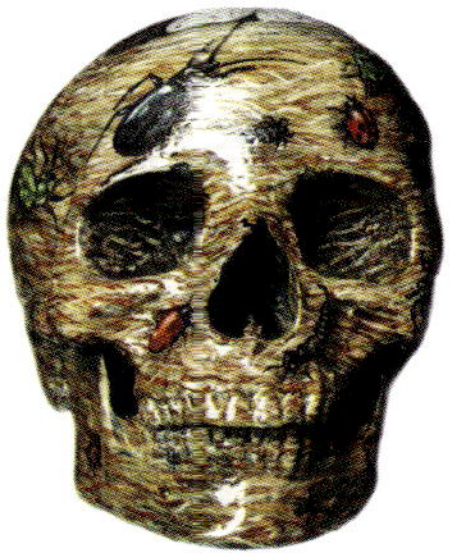

Life After Death, 2005
Oil on plastic skull,
26 × 20 × 25 cm

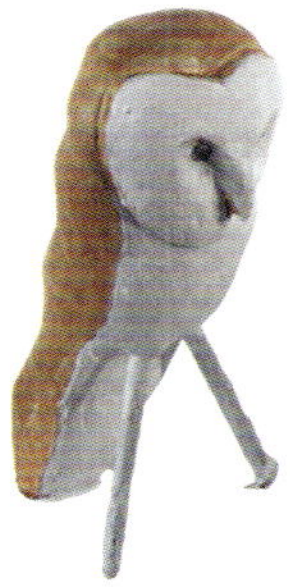

White Owl, 2008
Oil and nails on clay,
4 × 7 × 6 cm

Other Paintings, 1979–2008

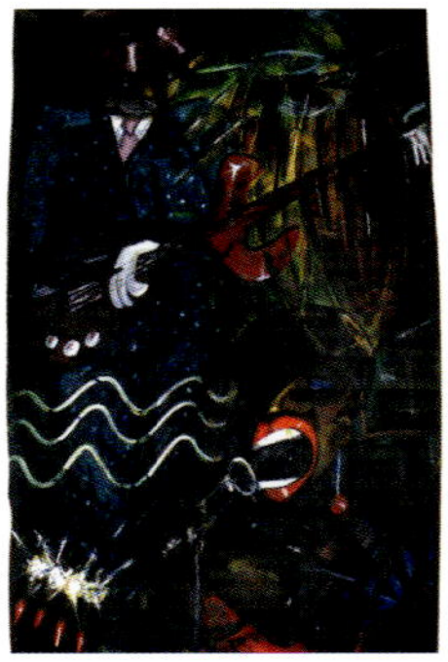

Bluebeat, 1979
Acrylic on paper, 150 x 80 cm

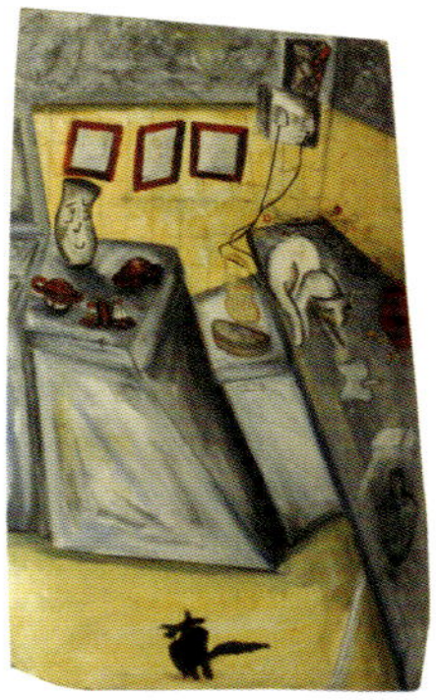

Kitchen at Foxley House, 1979
Acrylic on canvas, 90 x 60 cm

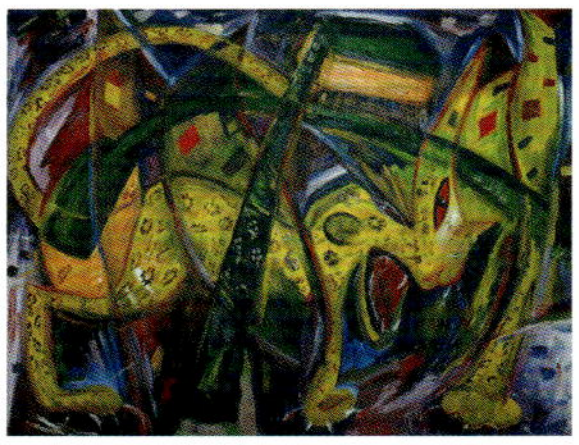

Leopard in the City, 1979
Acrylic on canvas, 91 x 122 cm

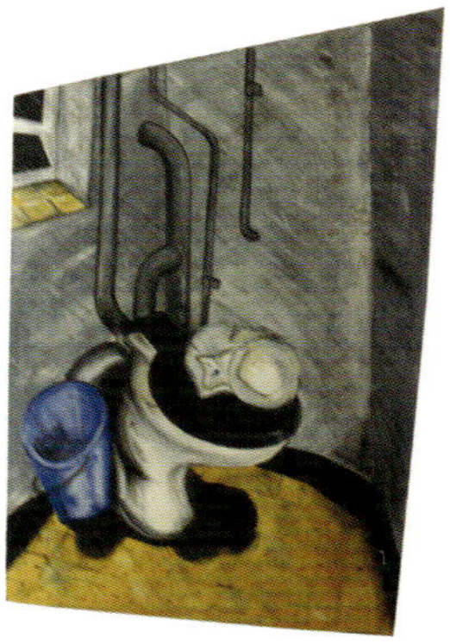

Toilet at Foxley House, 1979
Acrylic on canvas, 90 x 60 cm

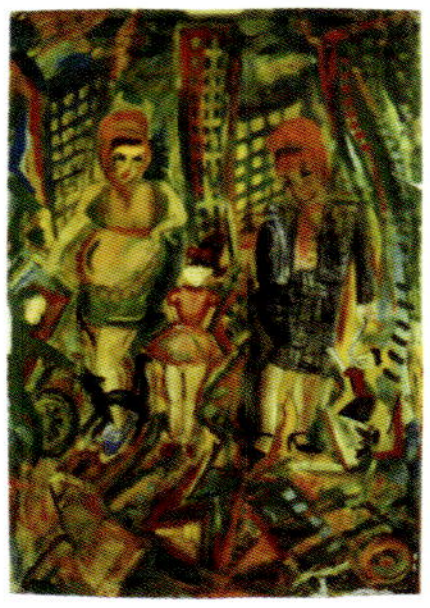

Street Argument, 1979
Acrylic on paper, 33 x 15 cm

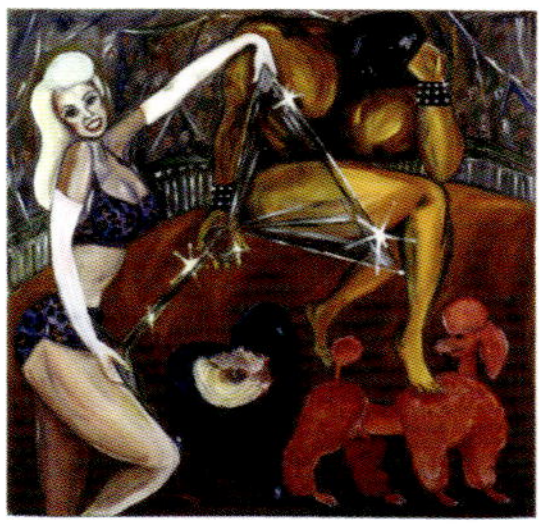

Fairground Attractions, 1980
Acrylic on canvas, 152 x 152 cm

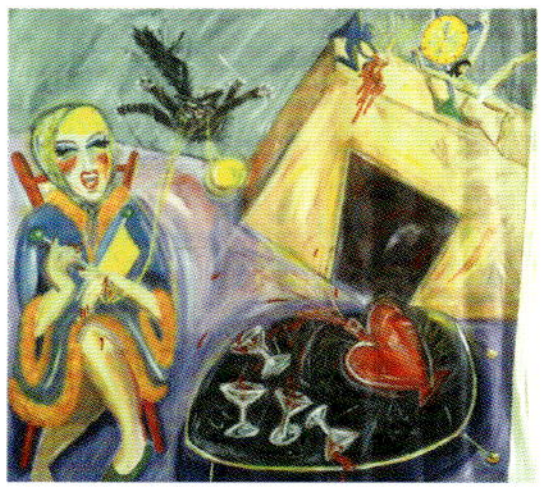

Religious Cocktails and the Stigmata, 1980
Acrylic on canvas, 150 x 155 cm

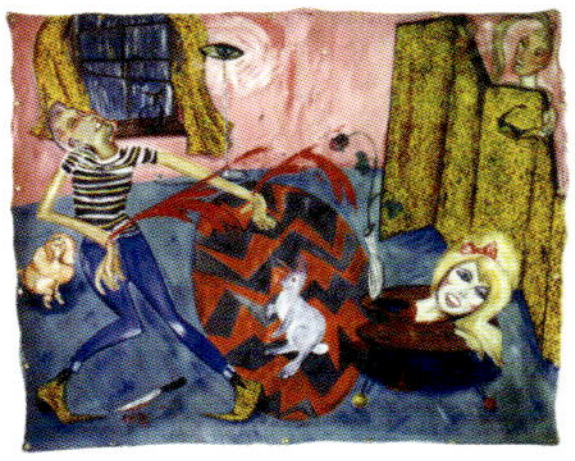

I Commit Suicide, 1980
Acrylic on canvas, 150 x 150 cm

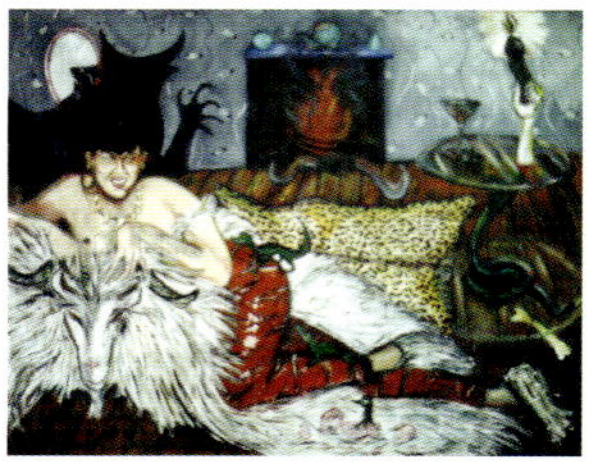

Devil Woman, 1980
Acrylic on canvas, 122 x 183 cm

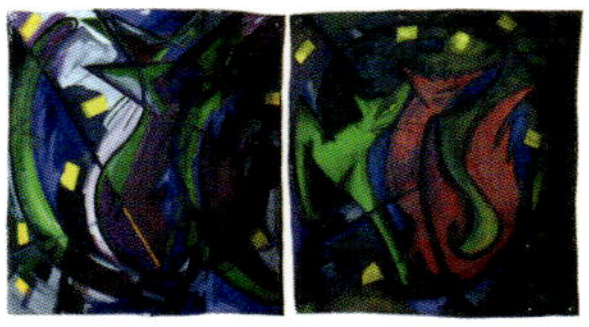

Cats in Love, 1980
Acrylic on canvas, 40 x 80 cm

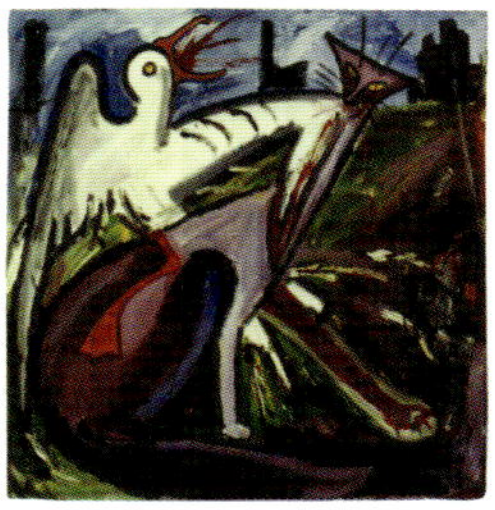

Tyrone's Dream, 1980
Acrylic on canvas, 70 x 70 cm

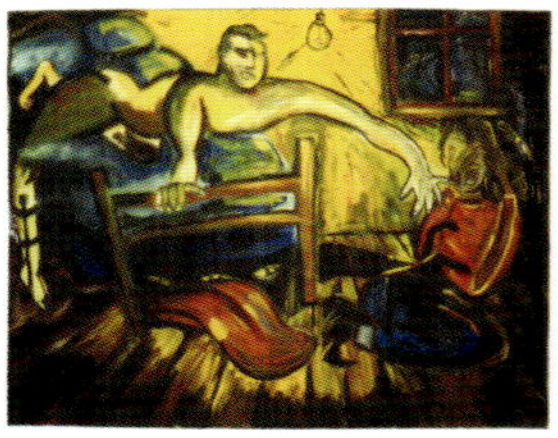

Sick Bed, 1980
Acrylic on canvas, 152 x 183 cm

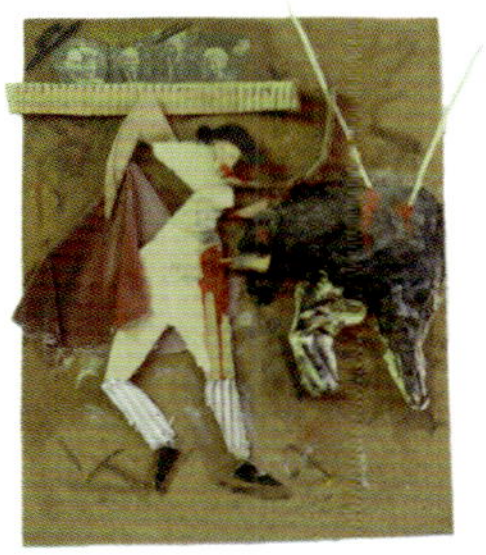

Bull Fighter, 1981
Acrylic and paper mache on wood, 50 x 40 cm

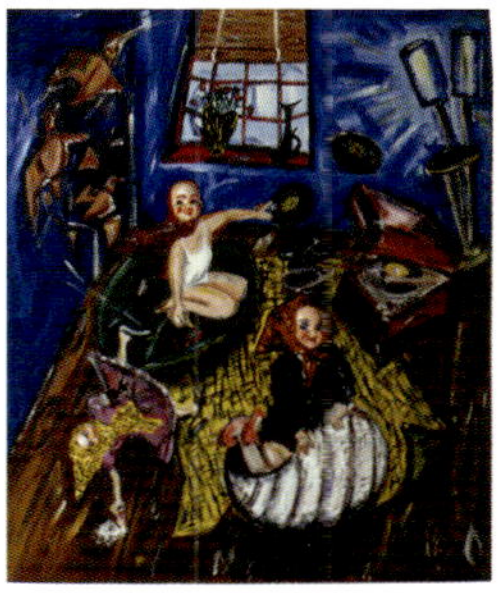

Dead Mother, 1981
Acrylic on wood with doll heads, 152 x 152 cm

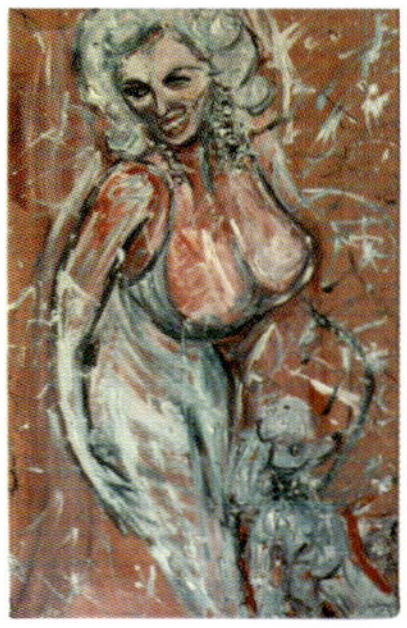

Flash Bulbs, 1982
Acrylic on canvas, 150 x 80 cm

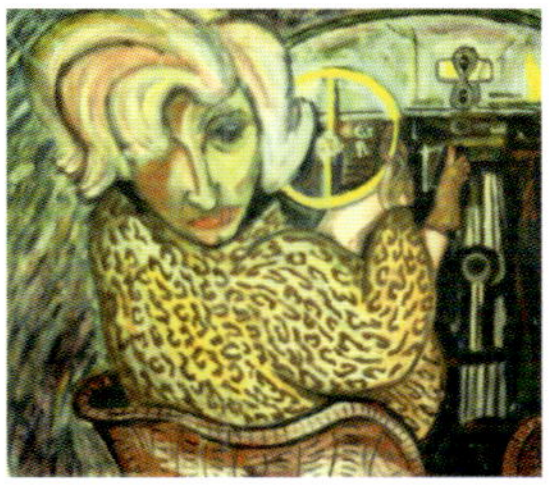

Julia, 1983
Acrylic on canvas, 41 x 63 cm

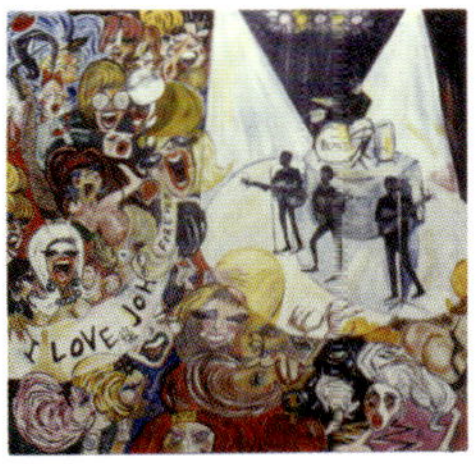

Hysterical Women, 1984
Ink and pva on canvas, 75 x 75 cm

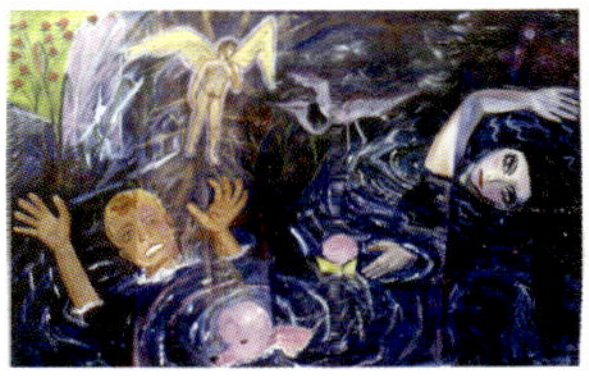

Midnight Swim, 1984
Acrylic on canvas, 61x 122 cm

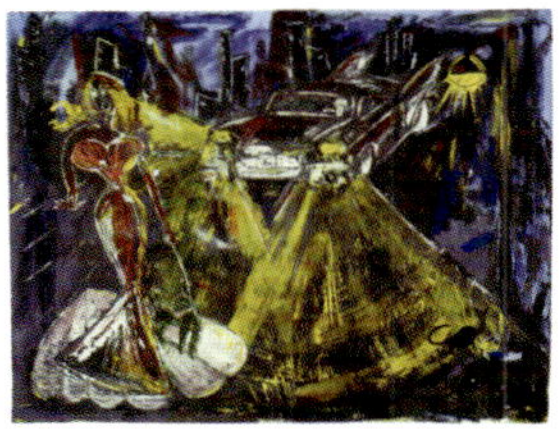

Birth of Venus, 1985
Plaster and ink on wood, 61 x 91 cm

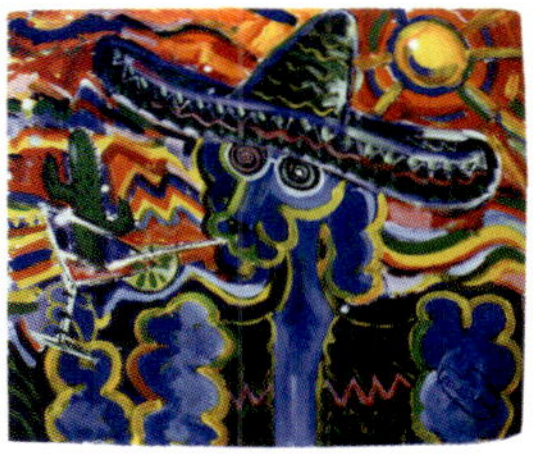

Tequila Sunrise, 1986
Acrylic on canvas, 61 x 77 cm

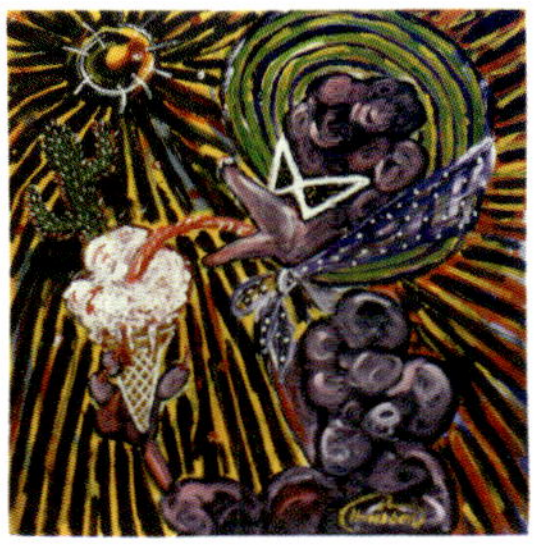

Tequila Ice Cream, 1986
Acrylic on canvas, 76 x 76 cm

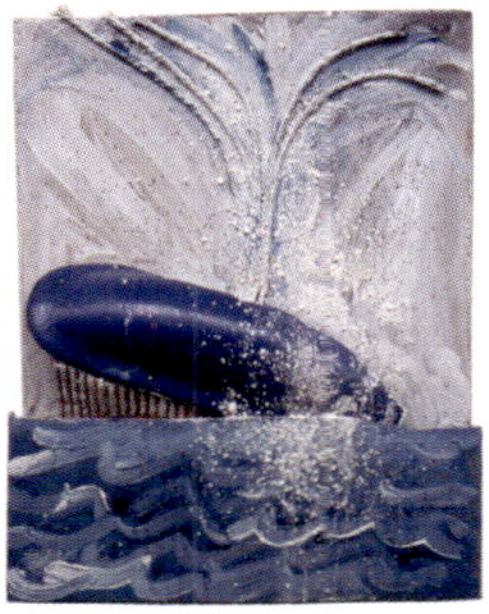

Thar She Blows, 1987
Found objects and acrylic on wood, 30 x 20 x 7 cm

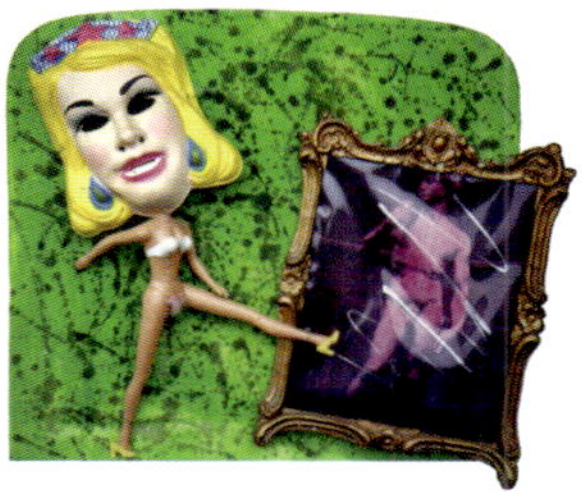

Wonder Woman Through the Looking Glass, 1987
Found objects and acrylic on wood, 28 x 30 cm

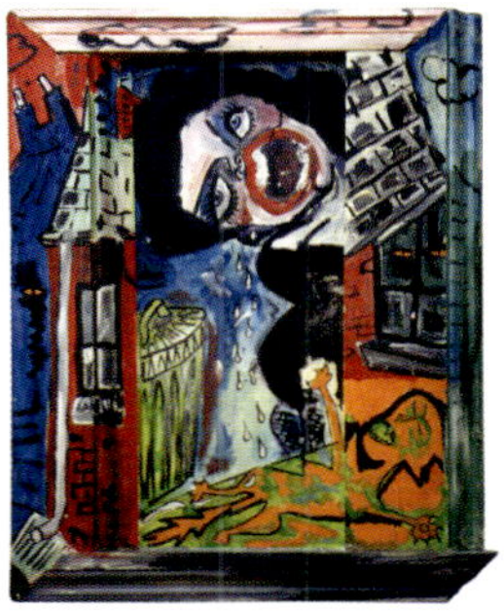

The Council Murdered Her Cats, 1989
Acrylic on wood, 70 x 60 cm

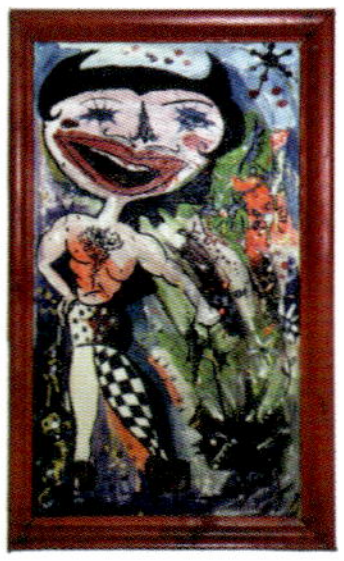

Pet Sparrow, 1989
Acrylic on wood, 60 x 25 cm

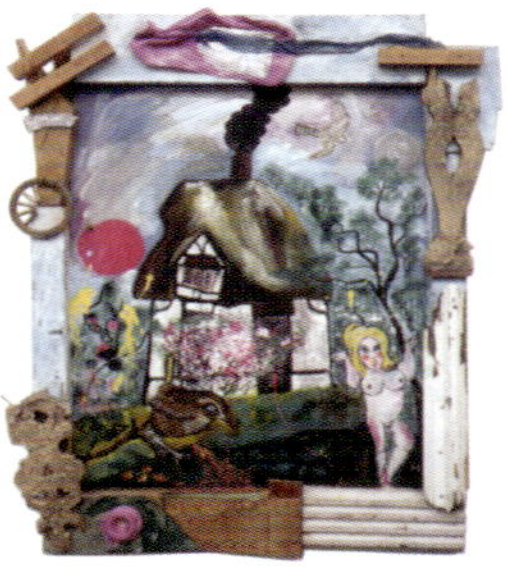

Pretty Little Cottage, 1989
Found objects and acrylic on wood, 50 x 46 cm

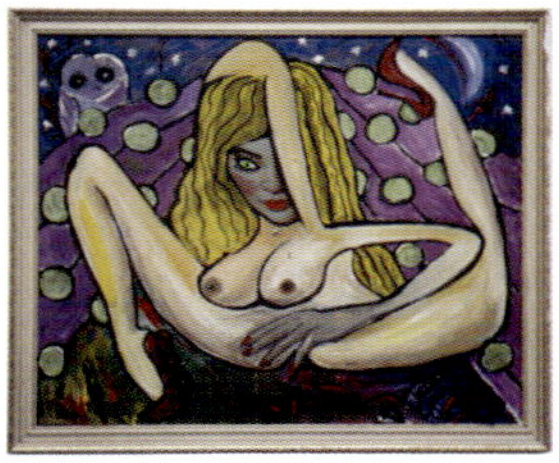

Bewitched, 1991
Acrylic over Tretchikoff print, 59 x 70 cm

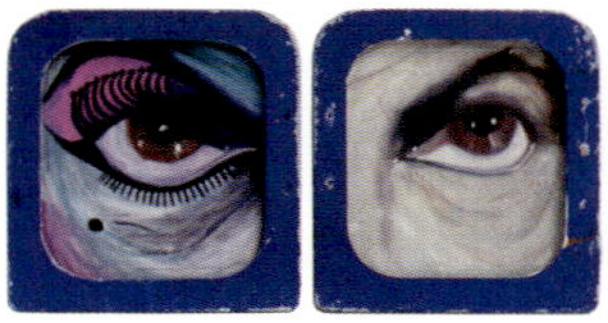

Vincent's Eyes, 1991
Acrylic on canvas, 37.5 x 34.5 cm

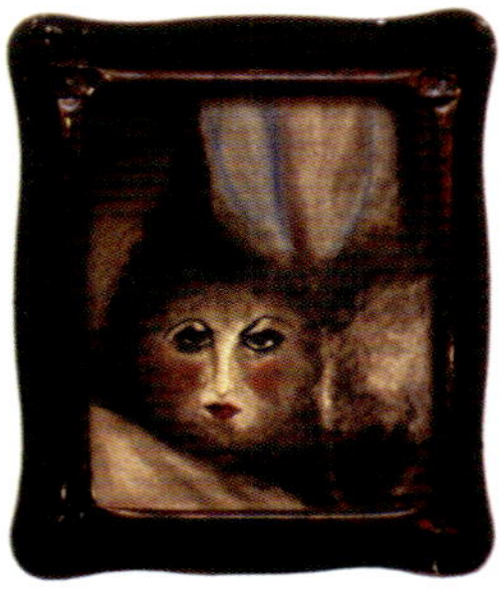

Safer Sex, 1992
Oil on wood, 46 x 30 cm

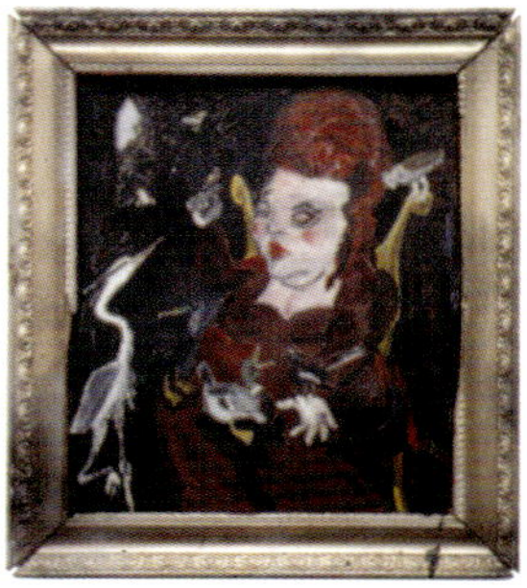

Countess Groan, 1995
Oil on wood, 53 x 46 cm

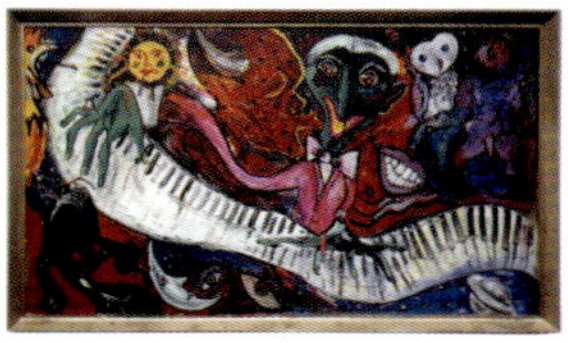

Conservatoire in Hell, 1995
Acrylic on wood, 28 x 40 cm

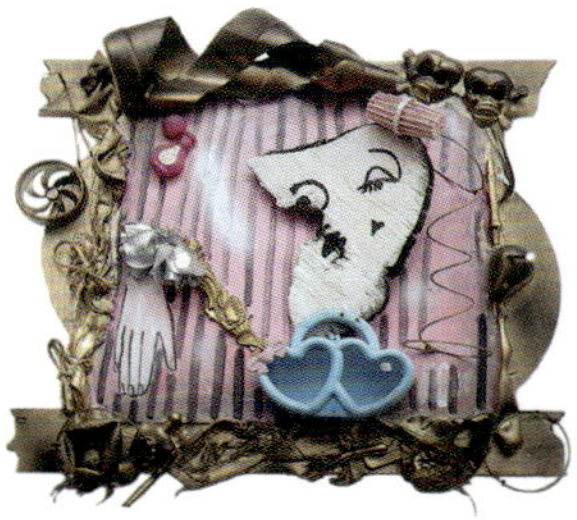

Fop At His Toilette, 1996
Found objects and acrylic on wood, 37 x 37 cm

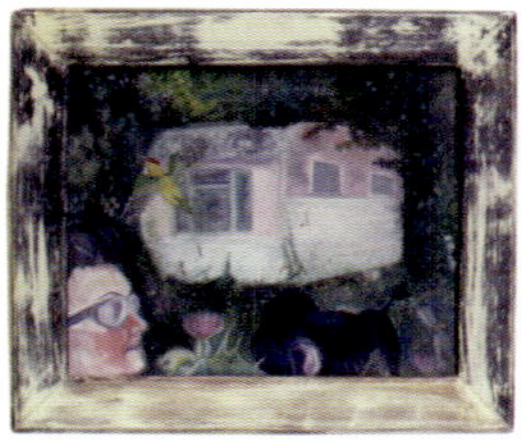

Lola and Jez at the Caravan, 1997
Oil on wood, 60 x 76 cm

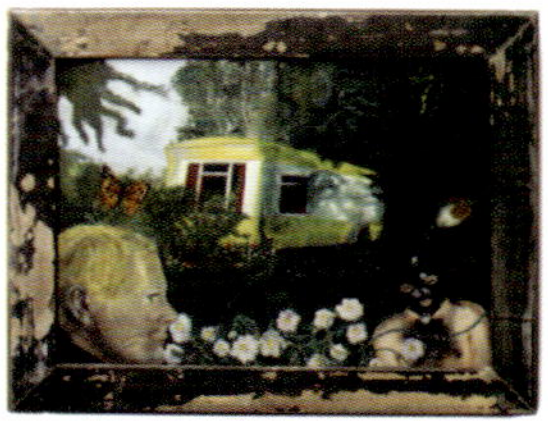

Dark Side of Gazza, 1998
Oil and collage on wood, 46 x 60 cm

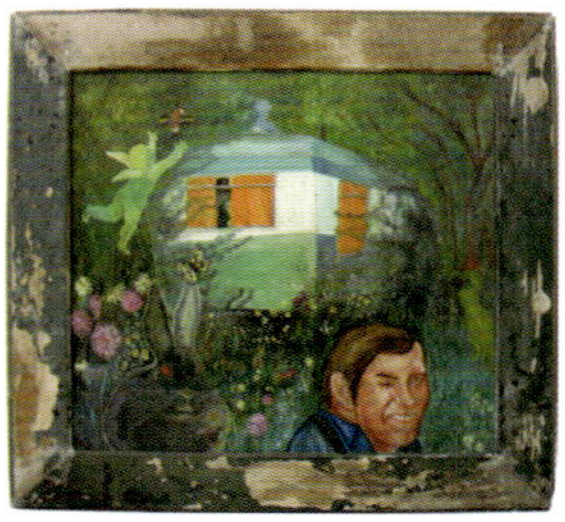

The Enchanted Caravan, 1998
Oil on wood, 60 x 60 cm

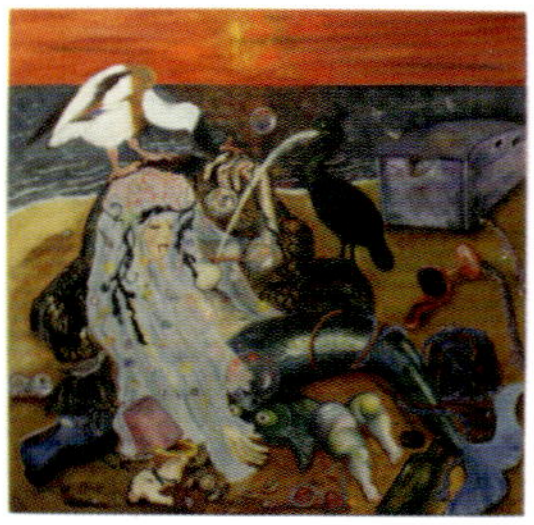

Flotsam and Jetsam, 1998
Oil on canvas, 182 x 182 cm

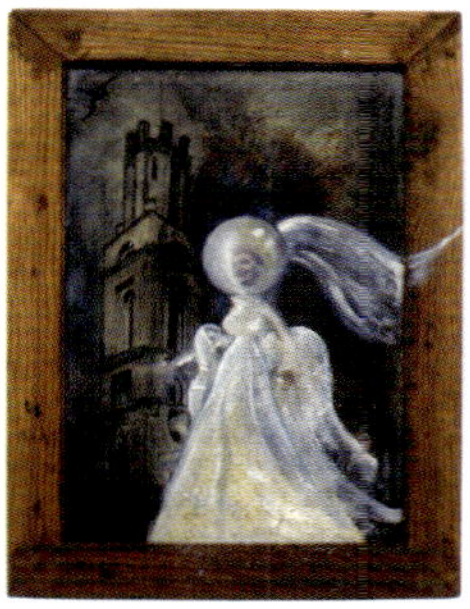

Gazza's Big Day, 1998
Oil and collage on wood,
30 x 25 cm

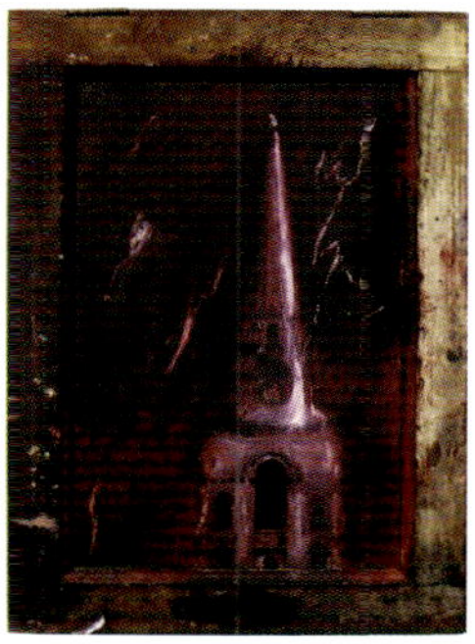

Hawksmoor Red Storm, 1998
Oil on wood, 43 x 30 cm

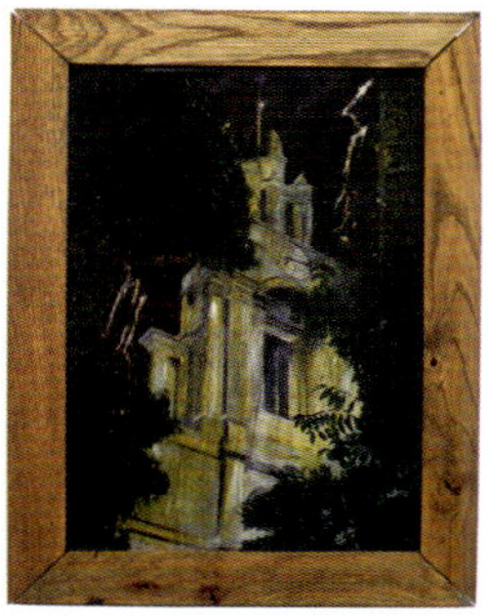

Hawksmoor in a Storm, 1998
Oil on wood, 39 x 29 cm

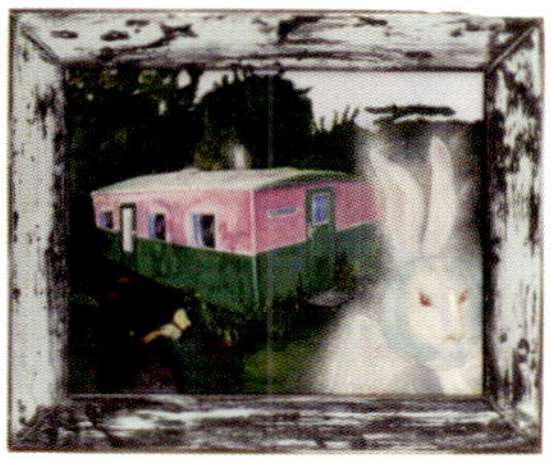

Light and Dark Angel, 1998
Oil on wood, 46 x 60 cm

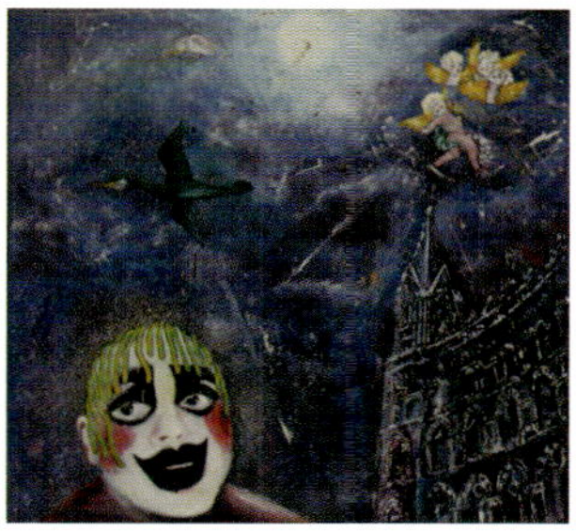

Holidays in the Sky, 1998
Oil on wood, 80 x 83 cm

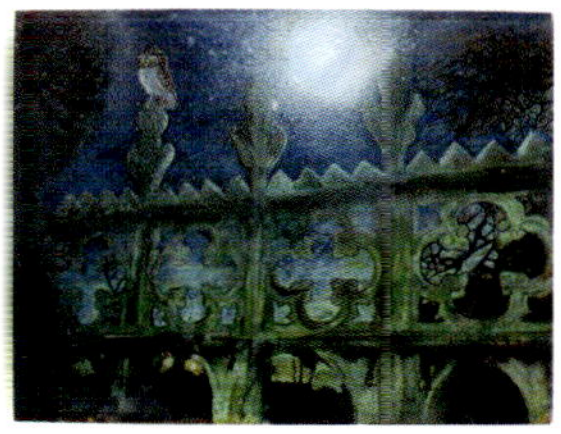

Little Owl on Cemetery Gate, 1999
Oil on wood, 32 x 40 cm

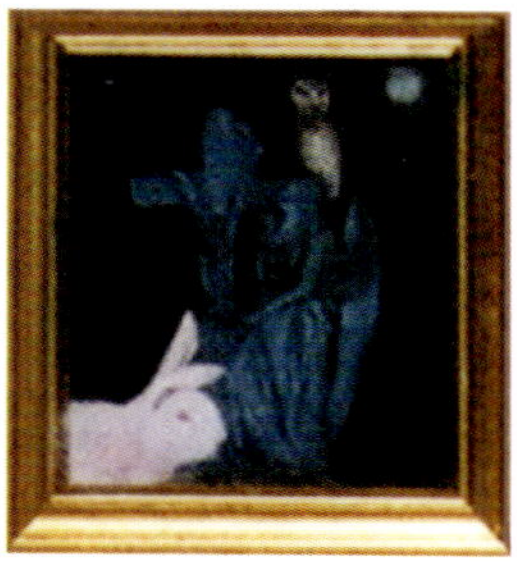

Angel and a Rabbit, 1999
Oil on wood, 39 x 29 cm

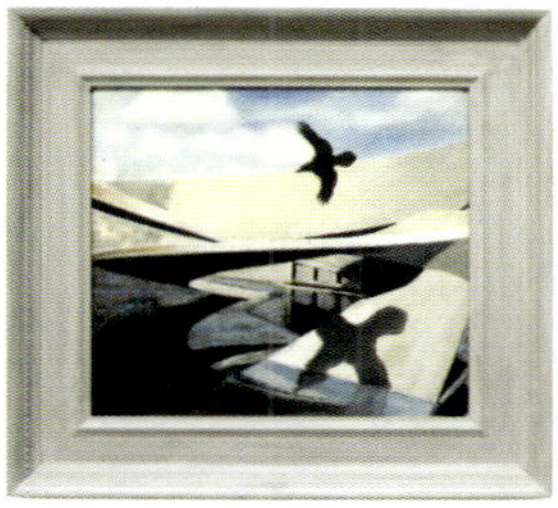

One Flew Over the Penguin
Pool, 1999
Oil on wood, 34 x 40 cm

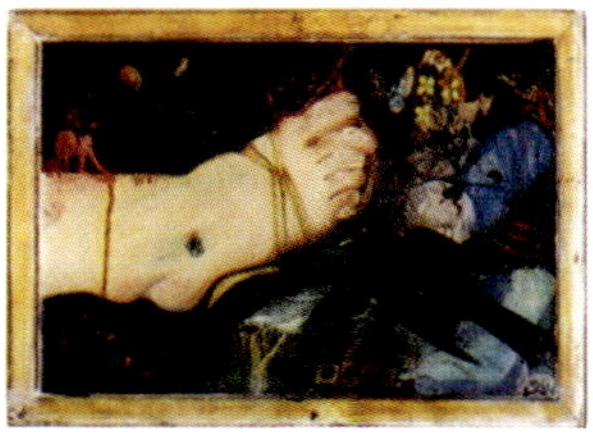

Welcome to the 21st Century, 1999
Oil on wood, 25 x 35 cm

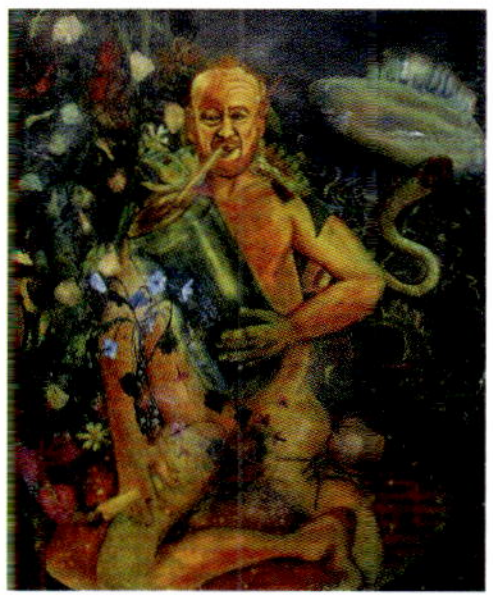

Twisted Gnome, 1999
Oil on canvas, 100 x 82 cm

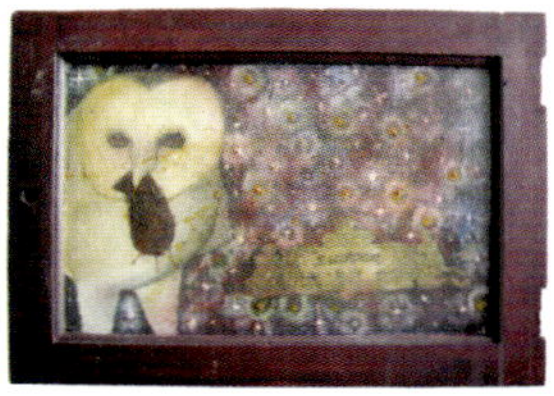

Ballroom Owl, 2000
Oil on wood, x 36 x 55 cm

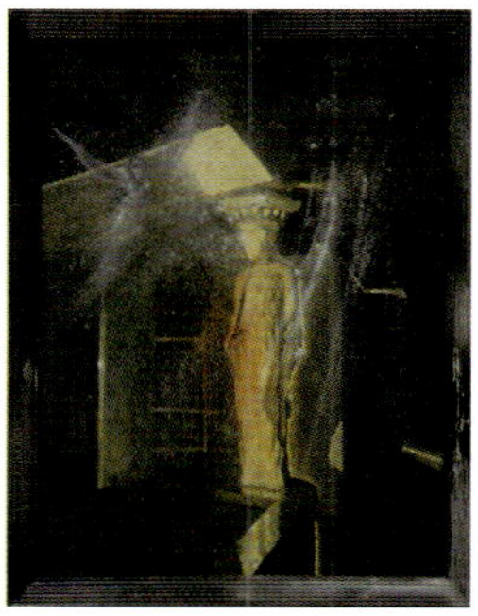

Classic Entrance, 2000
Oil on wood, 44 x 34 cm

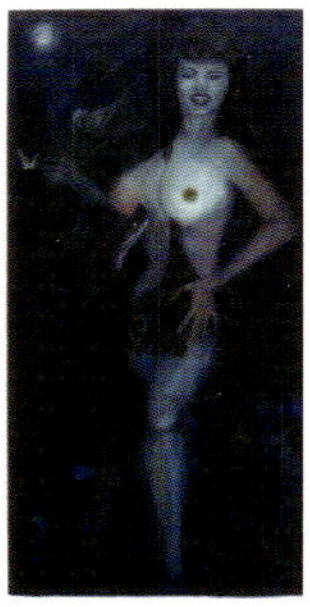

Diana Hunts But Never Kills, 2000
Oil on canvas, 140 × 80 cm

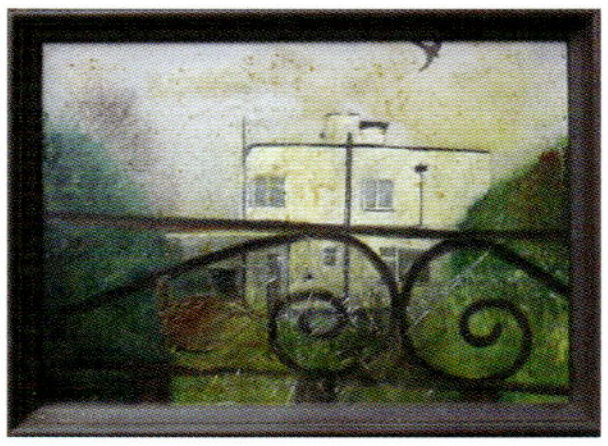

Wren on Gate, 2000
Oil on wood, 30 × 43 cm

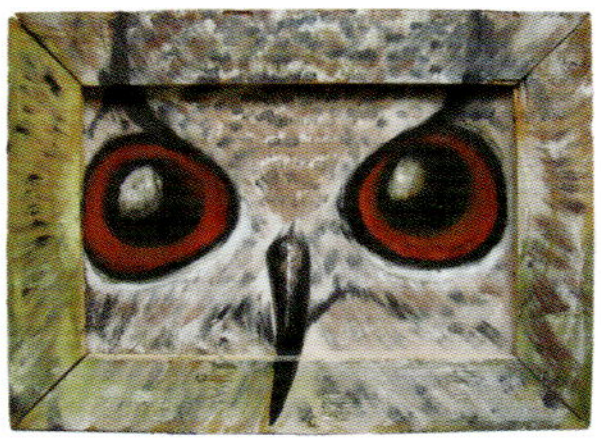

Owl's Eyes, 2001
Oil on wood, 41 × 54 cm

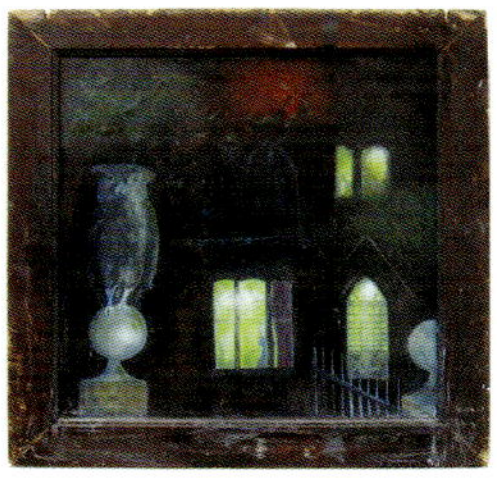

Home Alone, 2001
Oil on wood, 60 × 60 cm

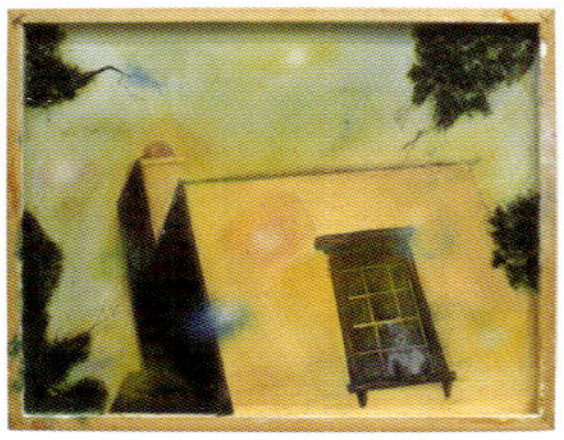

Home Alone Two, 2001
Oil on wood, 41 × 51 cm

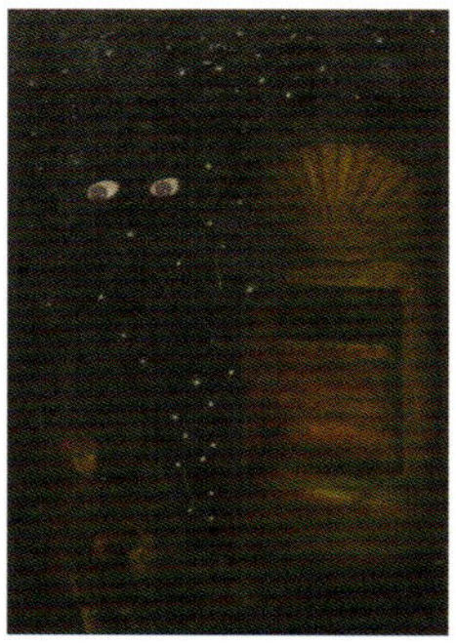

Little Red Riding Hood, 2001
Oil on wood, 58 × 46 cm

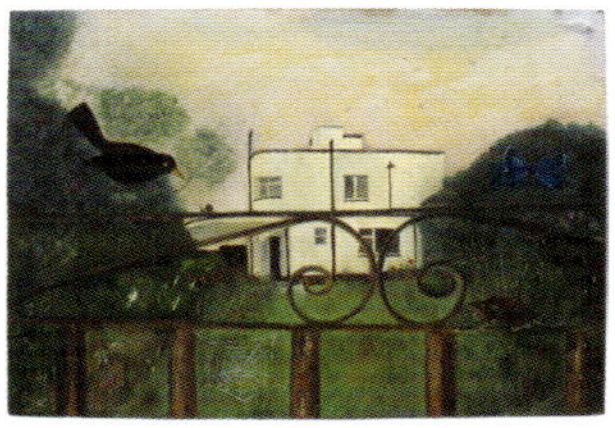

House in Essex II, 2002
Oil on wood, 30 × 43 cm

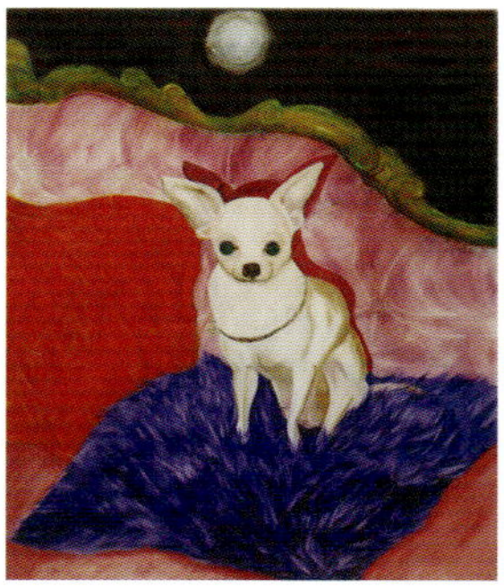

Velvet Goldmine, 2002
Oil on canvas, 91 × 76 cm

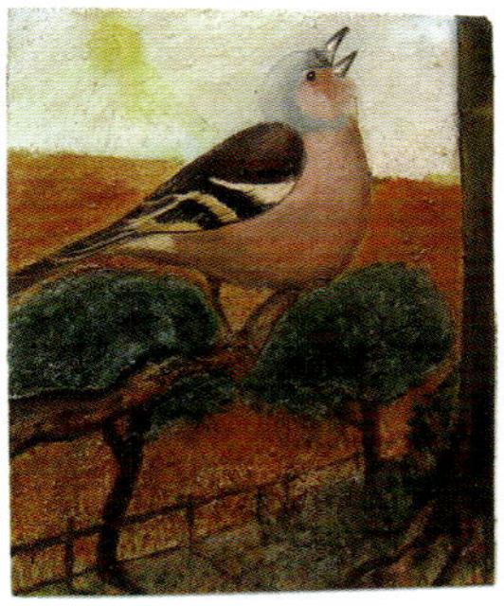

Bowled Over, 2003
Oil on wood, 15 × 13 cm

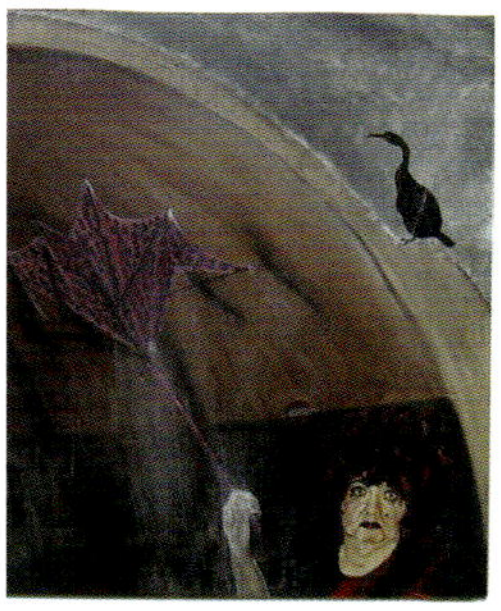

Fancy a Shag Luv?, 2003
Oil on wood, 46 × 35.5 cm

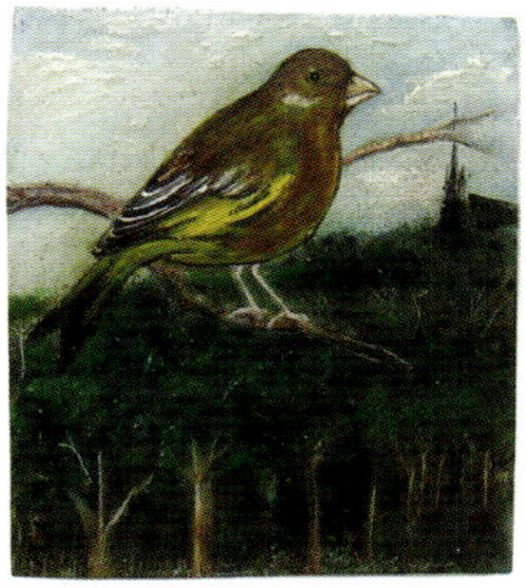

Greenfinch, 2003
Oil on wood, 15 × 15 cm

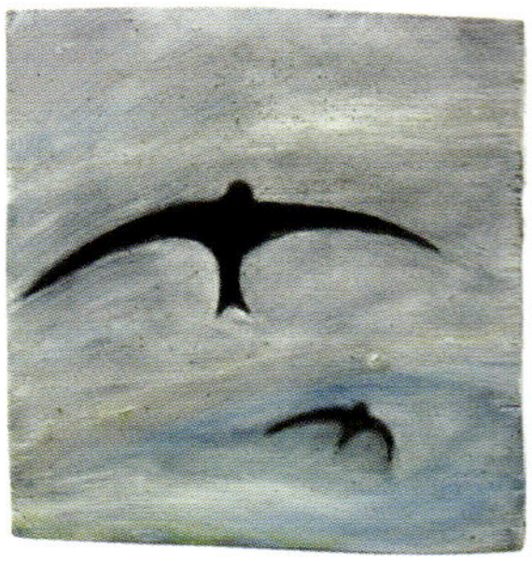

Hidden Screams, 2003
Oil on wood, 18 × 15 cm

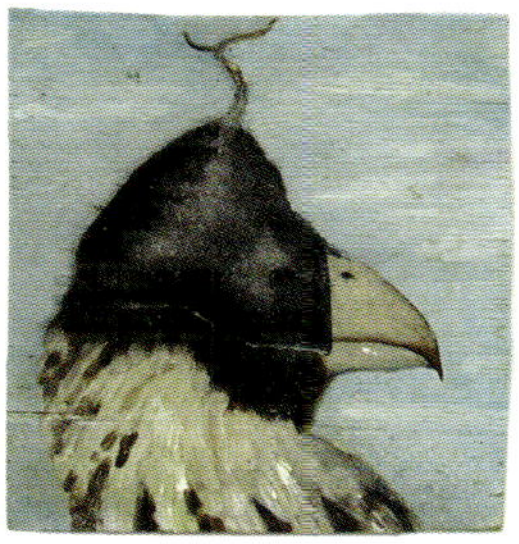

Hoodwinked, 2003
Oil on wood, 15 × 15 cm

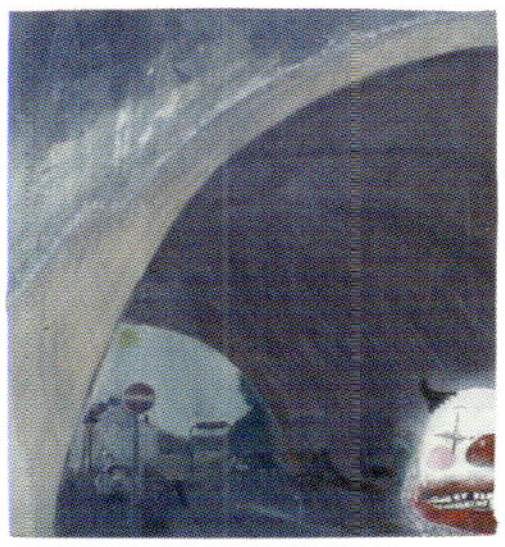

No Entry, 2003
Oil on wood, 45 × 35.5 cm

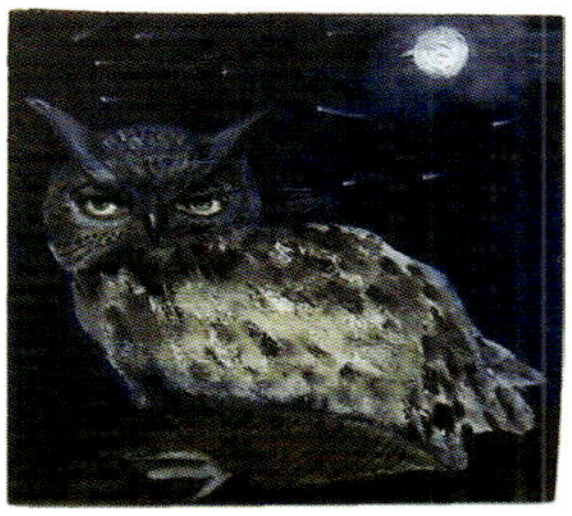

Nightwatch, 2003
Oil and collage on wood, 19 × 22 cm

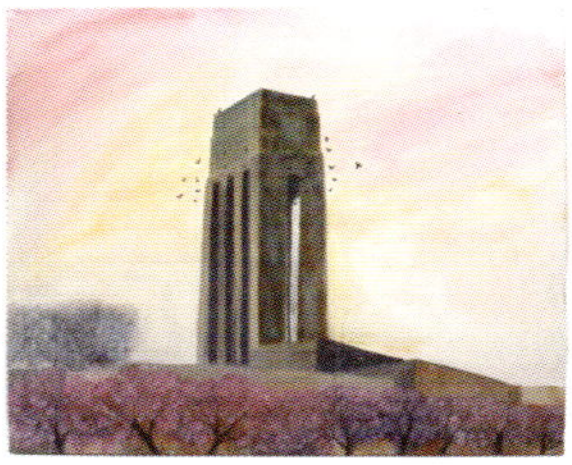

Pigeon Tower, 2003
Oil on wood, 30 × 46 cm

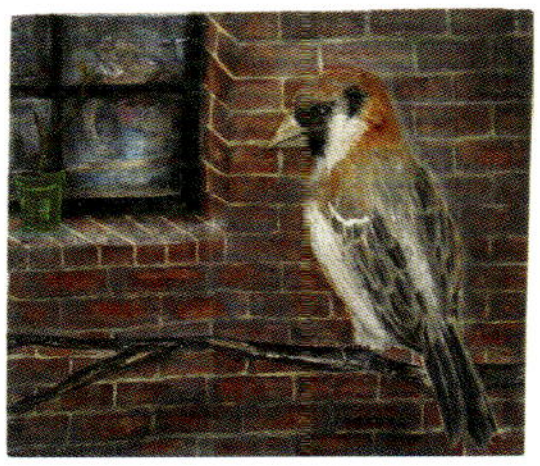

Single Room Furnished, 2003
Oil on wood, 18 × 21 cm

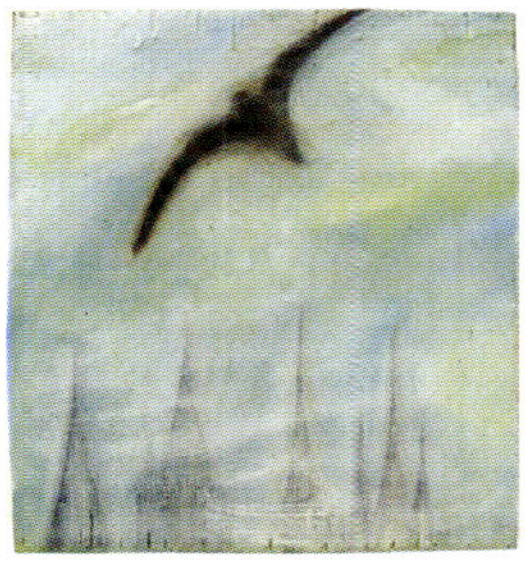

Swift and Spires, 2004
Oil on wood, 15 × 15 cm

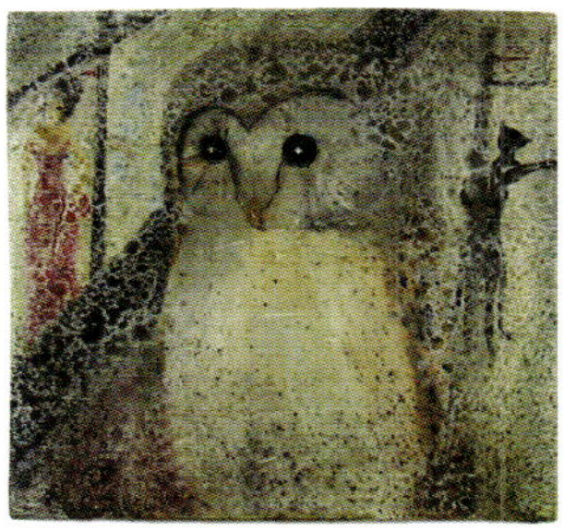

Window Shopping, 2004
Oil on wood, 15 × 15 cm

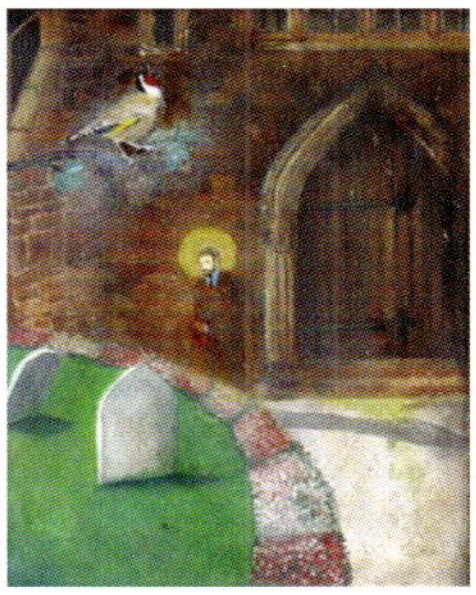

Jesus in a Suit, 2004
Oil on wood, 48.5 × 38 cm

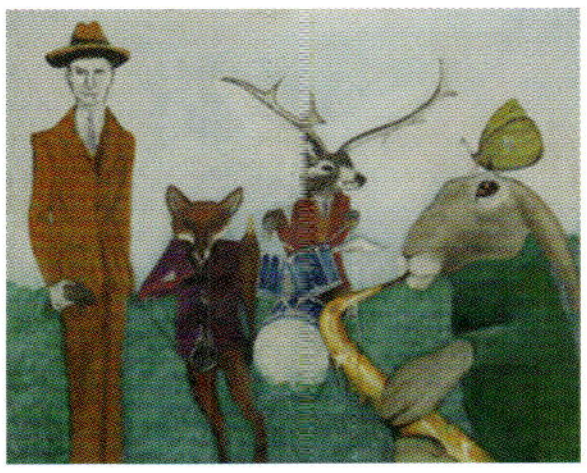

Hunted Melody, 2005
Oil on wood, 37 × 45.5 cm

Night Sight, 2005
Oil on glass, 27 × 22 cm

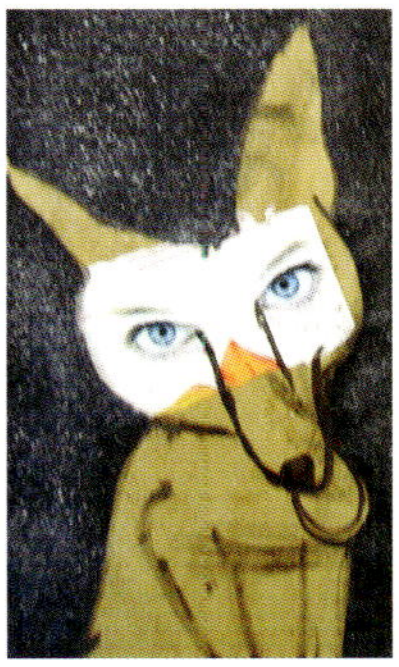

Blue Eyed Fox, 2005
Oil and collage on wood, 28 × 20 cm

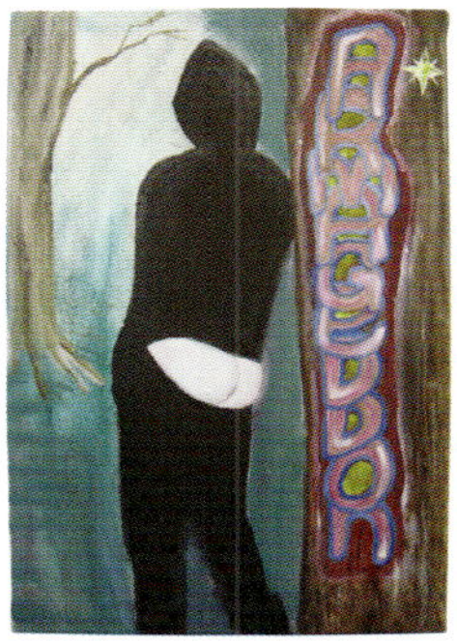

Armageddon, 2005
Oil on canvas, 46 × 34 cm

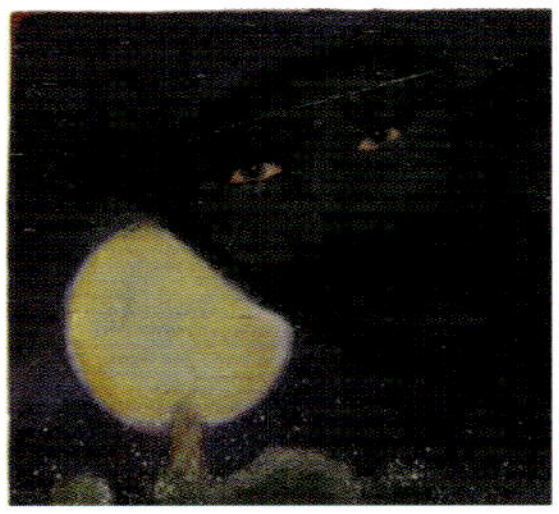

Night Patrol, 2005
Oil and collage on wood, 18 x 19 cm

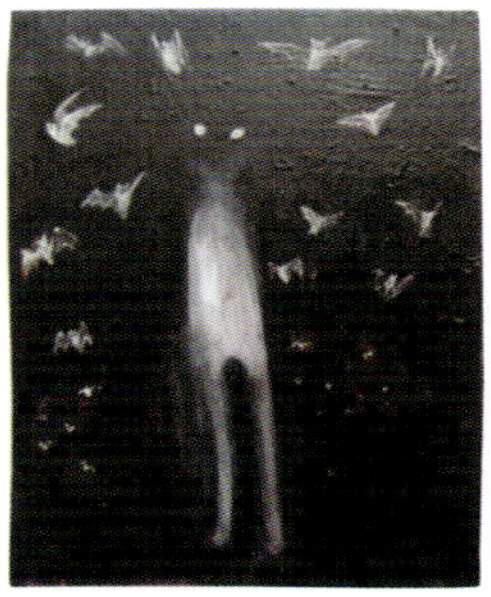

Cat with White Bats, 2005
Oil on wood, 21 x 17 cm

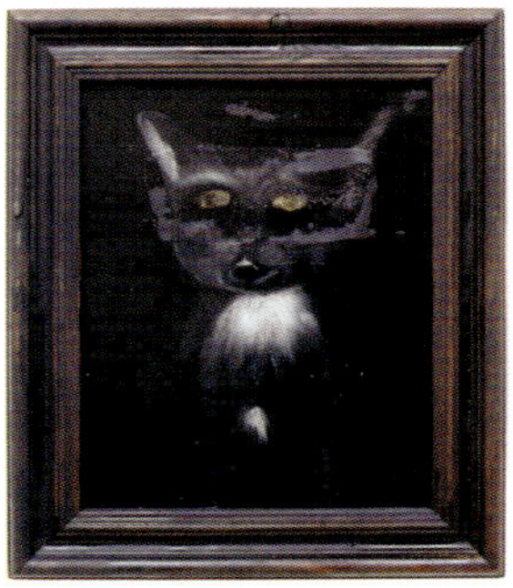

Family Resemblance, 2005
Oil and collage on wood, 26 x 20 cm

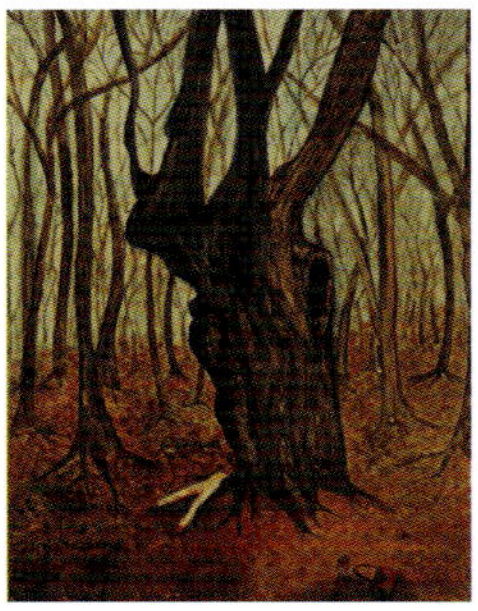

Autumn Leaves, 2006
Oil on wood, 46 x 34 cm

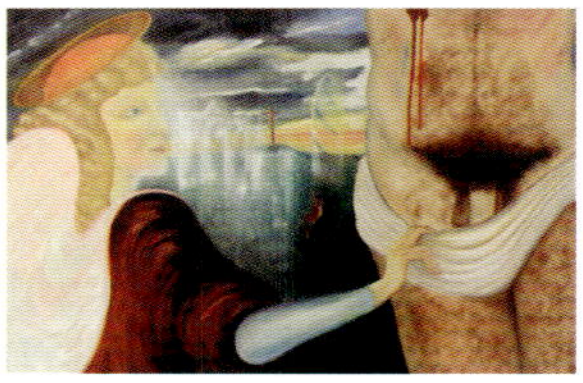

I Am a Curious Angel, 2007
Oil on canvas, 62 x 93 cm

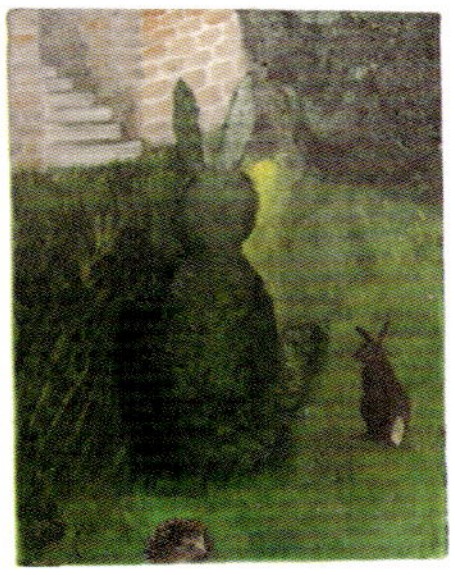

In the Garden, 2008
Oil on canvas, 20 x 16 cm

NOTES

Introduction

1. Adrian Searle, 'David Harrison', *The Guardian*, 8 April 2005, http://www.guardian.co.uk/culture/2005/apr/08/2.

Green and Pleasant Land

1. Adrian Searle, 'David Harrison', *The Guardian*, 8 April 2005, http://www.guardian.co.uk/culture/2005/apr/08/2.

2. In interview with the author, July 2008.

3. Mark Shepard, 'Pathetic Fallacies & Category Mistakes: making sense and non-sense of the (near-future) Sentient City', *Sentient City*, http://www.sentientcity.net/blog/?p=3.

4. John Russell, *Francis Bacon* (London: Thames & Hudson, 1971), 55

5. In interview with the author, July 2008.

6. R.C. Baker, 'Stan Van Der Beek at Guild & Greyshkul; Diana Al-Hadid's 'Reverse Collider'; Josef Koudelka at Pace MacGill', *The Village Voice*, 30 September 2008, http://www.villagevoice.com/2008-10-01/art/stan-vanderbeek-at-guild-greyshkul-diana-al-hadid-s-reverse-collider-josef-koudelka-at-pace-macgill/.

7. In interview with the author, July 2008.

8. See *Absorption and Theatricality: Painting and Beholder in the Age of Diderot* (Berkeley: University of California Press, 1980) for his development of the idea of theatricality.

9. Linda Walsh, 'Romantic Painting', http://www.open2.net/historyandthearts/arts/romanticpainting_p.html.

10. Ibid.

11. 'The only choice: "Safety first" won't win us a fourth term, we need a radical New Labour agenda for the future', Progressonline, 1 February 2008, http://www.progressonline.org.uk/Magazine/article.asp?a=2396.

12. In interview with the author, 2004.

Timeless City

1. The fulfilment of this prophecy is implied in the *Book of Revelation* (21:23, 22:5), where it said that there will be no more sun or moon, since god's splendour will give light.

2. Sigmund Freud, *The Uncanny* (London: Penguin, 2003), 124, 147.

3. In interview with the author, July 2008.

4. Ibid.

5. Jonathan Swift, *Travels into Several Remote Nations of the World Known as Gulliver's Travels* (London: Longman, 1972), 199–269.

6. One such painting by Magritte is *The Dominion of Light* (1949), which depicts a dimly-lit evening street with a daytime sky overhead.

7. Johann J. Winckelmann, *Reflections on the Imitation of Greek Works in Painting and Sculpture* (La Salle, IL: Open Court, 1987).

8. Joris-Karl Huysmans, *Against Nature* (London: Penguin, 1974), 86.

Bad Fairies

1. In interview with the author, July 2008.

2. The term derives from the phrase in *Ecclesiastes* (1:2) in the *Old Testament*: 'Vanitas vanitatum ... et omnia vanitas,' usually translated as 'Vanity of vanities ... all is vanity.'

3. In interview with the author, July 2008.

4. William Gilpin, *Three Essays: on Picturesque Beauty; on Picturesque Travel; and on Sketching Landscape; to which is added a Poem, on Landscape Painting* (London: printed for R. Blamire, 1794).

5. Knight's *An Analytical Inquiry into the Principals of Taste* (London: printed by Luke Hansard, 1805) is his principal contribution to the field.

Existence

1. In interview with the author, April 2009.

2. Ibid.

3. John Donne, from *The Exstasie* in *The Complete English Poems* (London: Everyman's Library, 1991), 100.

4. C. Baudelaire, from *Moesta et Errabunda* in *The Flowers of Evil* (London: Routledge and Kegan Paul, 1955), 80.

5. C. Baudelaire, from *To the Reader* in *The Flowers of Evil*, 4.

6. Lois Boe Hyslop, *Baudelaire: Man of His Time* (New Haven: Yale University Press, 1980), 69.

7. Lewis Carroll, *Through the Looking Glass* (Maidenhead: Purnell Books, 1977), 56.

8. C. Baudelaire, from *Evening Harmony* in *The Flowers of Evil*, 60.

9. Lewis Carroll, *Alice's Adventures in Wonderland* (London: Macmillan, 1991), 64.

10. C. Baudelaire, from *Love and the Skull* in *The Flowers of Evil*, 164.

An Interview with Peter Doig

1. John Cowper Powys, from *De Egyptu* in *Wolf's-bane Rhymes* (London: Village Press, 1975), 43.

ACKNOWLEDGEMENTS

There are a great many people I would like to thank. But firstly, I would like to thank the spirit of nature for allowing me to exist and grow in its beautiful and complex garden, and all the fascinating and magical creatures that have influenced my life and dreams. I would like to thank my friends, and my parents, brothers and sister, who have maintained a stability throughout my life. A big thanks to Keith Pointing for his design, and to the publisher Philip Wilson and his wonderful team – Slobodan, Matt and David – who have done such a great job and have been a joy to work with; a big thanks to the hard working staff at Victoria Miro Gallery who have contributed to this book; a warm and grateful thanks to Alistair Robinson, Lucinda Lambton and Peter Doig for their contributions; a special thanks to Deborah Phillips for all her hard work, time and patience, to Justin Phillips for his technical know-how, and to Dan Salmon for keeping my archive and website www.poodle666.com alive; and above all, thank you to Victoria Miro for her belief and faith in my work.

David Harrison

PHOTOGRAPHIC CREDITS

John Jones
Justin Phillips
Dan Salmon

Stephen Brayne
Emmie and Charlie, 2007
God, 2007
Green and Pleasant Land (Stonehenge), 2006
Green and Pleasant Land (The Ascent), 2006
Green and Pleasant Land (The Wall), 2006
Swan Song, 2006
Moon and Dangly, 2004
Saddam Haresain, 2004

Christopher Burke
Daniel Reich Gallery Installation Images, 2008
Moonbird, 2008
The Calling of Friends, 2007
Green and Pleasant Land (Burn the Witch, She's Not Like Us), 2007
Green and Pleasant Land (Final Sunset), 2007
Green and Pleasant Land (Teenage Kicks), 2007
Once Upon A Time, 2007
Pan Has Risen, 2007
Persephone Tempts Cerberus, 2007
Spectre Lady at Home, 2007
Spectre Lady, 2007
Stars in Their Eyes, 2007
Egg Houses: A Natural Development, 2006
Green and Pleasant Land (In the Park), 2006
Green and Pleasant Land (Stonehenge the Ascent), 2006
Green and Pleasant Land (Woodland Walk), 2006
Moondrop, 2006
And Your Bird Can Sing, 2005
Chance Meeting, 2005
Honey I'm Home, 2005
St Peter, 2005
The Crucifixion, 2004
Disappearing Worlds, 2004
Timeless City, 2004
Cycles of the Moon, 2000
The Master That Never Returned, 1999

Stephen White
Blue Hare Nest, 2009
Midnight Butterfly, 2009
Night Flight, 2009
Pink Haremaphrodite, 2009
Blue Haremaphrodite, 2008
Cadaverina and the Apparition, 2008
Changeling, 2008
Dead Glamorous, 2008
Green and Pleasant Land (An English Country Stream), 2008
Hallucinajicky, 2008
Hare Nest Day, 2008
Hare Nest Night, 2008
Hare Nest 2, 2008
Hare Witch Project, 2008
Hareditary, 2008
Red Jacket, 2008
Shalimar Noir, 2008
She's Not a Girl Who Misses Much, 2008
Up the Garden Path, 2007
Masks, 2006
City Gent, 2005
Magic Moments, 2005
Velvet Goldmine, 2002
The Meek Shall Inherit the Earth, 2001
On Some Faraway Hill, 2001
Daphne Chaste, 2000
Lords and Ladies, 2000
King's X Boogie Woogie, 1995

BIOGRAPHY

1954 Born in England
1954– Lives and works in London

EDUCATION

1980–83 BA Hons Fine Art, St Martin's School of Art, London
1979–80 Foundation Course, St Martin's School of Art, London

SOLO EXHIBITIONS

2009 *Existence*, Victoria Miro Gallery, London
2008 *Green and Pleasant Land*, Daniel Reich Gallery, New York
2005 Victoria Miro Gallery, London
2000 *Sickbed*, Cubitt Gallery, London
2000 *Dance Macabre*, curated by Peter Doig, London
1998 *Escape into Reality*, Dash Gallery, London
1997 *Hanging Gardens*, Cubitt Gallery, London
1989 *David Harrison New Works*, The Space, London
1986 *David Harrison One-man Show*, Cowboys and Poodles Gallery, San Francisco

GROUP EXHIBITIONS

2009 *Leather Lane Biennale*, Omni Colour & K2 Screen, London
2009 *1984*, The Kowalsky Gallery, London
2007 *Each for Oneself and God Against All*, Galeria OMR, Mexico City
2006 *Defining the Contemporary*, Whitechapel Gallery, London
2006 *John Moores 24*, Walker Art Gallery, Liverpool
2005 *Showroom Dummies: Bone Idle*, The Charing X Gallery, London
2005 *Cubitt Auction*, Cubitt Gallery, London
2005 *Art Aid Auction*, Charity Show, Art Aid, London
2005 *Thinking the Unthinkable or Against Nature*, Northern Gallery for Contemporary Art, Sunderland
2005 *London Now: Are We In Love Yet?*, Arts Centre St Petersburg, Florida
2004 *Rare Birds*, Store Gallery, London
2004 *East End Academy*, Whitechapel Art Gallery, London
2004 *Concert in the Egg*, The Ship, London
2004 *Collage*, Bloomberg Space, London
2004 *Dead Bird Show*, Whitechapel Project Space, London
2003 *Prospects Drawing Show*, Loading Bay Gallery, Old Truman Brewery, London
2003 *Bad New Things*, Whitechapel Project Space, London
2002 *Prospects Drawing Show*, Essor Gallery Project Space, Prospects Gallery, London
2001 *Christmas Painting Show*, Vilma Gold Gallery, London
2001 *Works on Paper from Acconci to Zittel*, Victoria Miro Gallery, London
2000 *Art & Business Exhibition*, curated by Sacha Craddock, Butler's Wharf, London
1998 *Bird Rapide*, Cubitt Gallery, London
1995 *Group Exhibition*, Slaughterhouse Gallery, London
1987 *Pitch Art Experience*, The Kentish Town House, London
1985 *Art You Can Fit in a Shoebox*, Air Gallery, London
1984 *Hunting Group Exhibition*, Hunting Group Competition Show, London
1984 *Hysterical Women*, The Derelict Café, London

BIBLIOGRAPHY

2009 Rochelle Steiner, feature article, *World of Interiors*, September
2009 Rachel Potts, 'In The Studio: David Harrison', *Garageland 8: Nostalgia*, June
2009 Eugen Bolshakov, *Contemporaty Fantasy*, The Agency of Cultural Information, http://www.TIF.by, April
2008 Yuki Minami, *Fugitive Tales "Poetic"*, Mute, No.1, Tokyo, Japan
2008 Roberta Smith, 'Green and Pleasant Land', *The New York Times*, 10 October
2008 R.C. Baker, 'Green and Pleasant Land', *The Village Voice*, 1–7 October
2008 Michael Killeen, 'Dancing Gargoyles Cause Mayhem; Glued Ants Pile Up: Chelsea Art', Bloomberg, 30 September
2007 Felicity Roma Bowers, Helen Elwes and Micalef (eds.), *William Blake Birthday Book* (Bow of Burning Gold Publishing), Limited Edition, November
2006 'Space to Think: Visionaries & Dreamers', *The Space*, Issue No. 2, Winter/Autumn
2005 Fisun Güner, 'Gothic Worlds Collide', *The Metro*, 29 March
2005 Adrian Searle, 'David Harrison', *The Guardian*, 8 April, http://www.guardian.co.uk/culture/2005/apr/08/2
2005 *Time Out*, 13–20 April
2005 Gabriel Coxhead, 'A Perfect Climate for Painting to Triumph', *Financial Times*, 13 May
2005 Dean Rhys Morgan, 'Doggy Style', *Attitude*, April
2003 Lucinda Lambton, *Sublime Suburbia*, Clementine Television, ITV Television, May
2003 Lesley Gillian & Dave Young (eds.), *Kitsch Deluxe* (London: Mitchell Beazley)
2000 Angelika Taschen & Jane Edwards (eds.), *London Interiors* (Germany: Taschen)
1999 David Harrison, 'A London View', *Granta 65: London: The Lives of the City*, February
1998 *The Art of Recycling*, Working with Contemporary Art Series, BBC Two Television, London, May
1997 Des Res, *Profile of 19 Foxley House*, ITV Television, London, May
1996 Lucinda Lambton, 'A Shrine to Hoover', *Lucinda Lambton's A to Z of Britian* (London: HarperCollins); see also the programme of the same name, BBC Two Television, London, August
1996 Lucinda Lambton, 'Why Does a Bird Fly?', *World of Interiors*, June
1990 Linda Lucardi, *Talking to Dead Pets*, Channel 4 Television, London, May
1989 *Profile of My Life, Flat and Work*, Through the Keyhole, BBC One Television, London, July
1983 *Profile of My Life and Home*, Good Afternoon, ITV Television, London, September

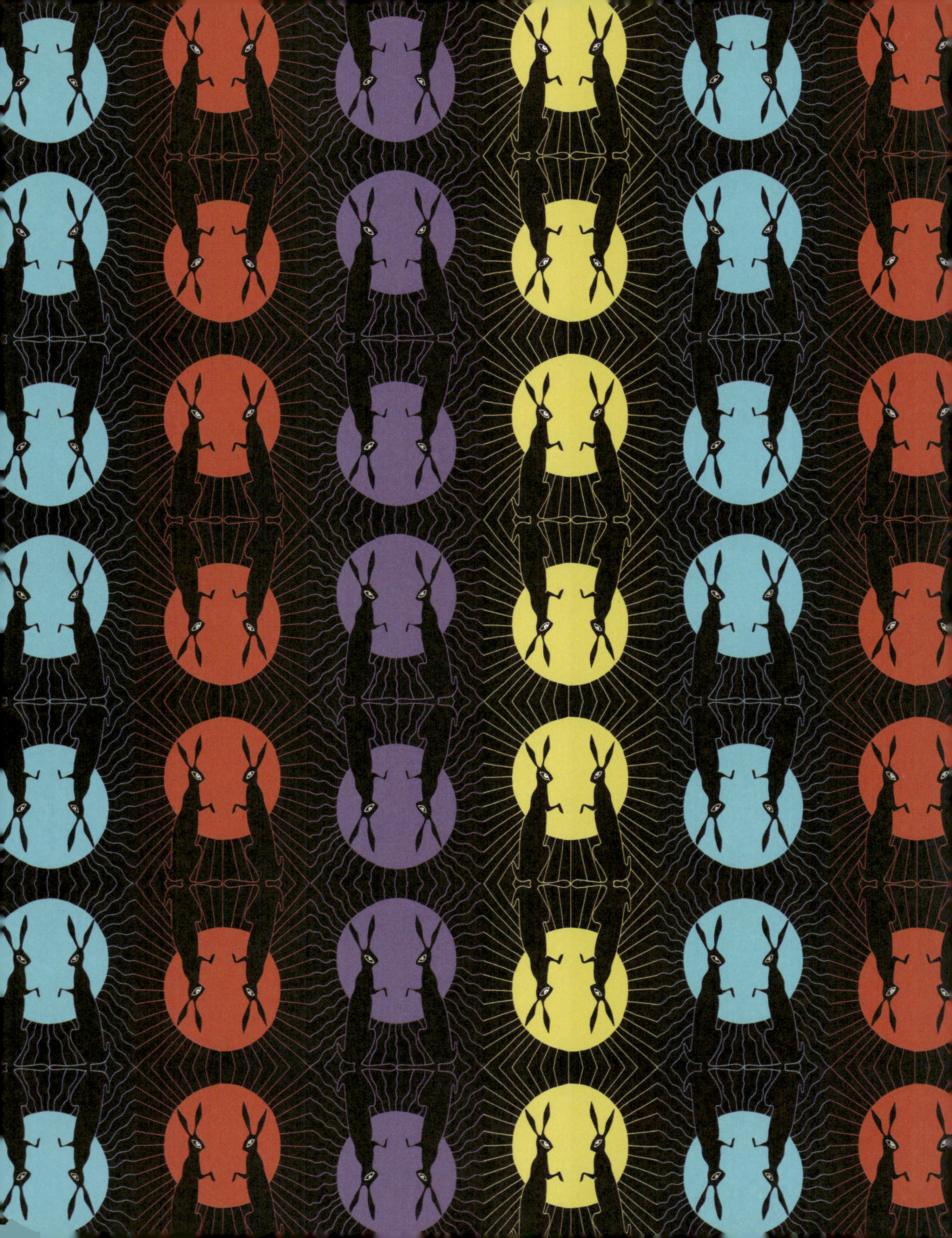